THE TAXATION OF
CORPORATE INCOME IN CANADA

By J. RICHARDS PETRIE

THE TAXATION OF CORPORATE INCOME IN CANADA

Sponsored by the Canadian Tax Foundation

UNIVERSITY OF TORONTO PRESS ~ 1952

Printed in Canada
Reprinted in 2018
London: Geoffrey Cumberlege
Oxford University Press
ISBN 978-1-4875-8057-5 (paper)

IN MEMORY

OF

MY FATHER

WHO TRIED TO EDUCATE ME

FOREWORD

TAXATION of corporate income now accounts for more than a quarter of Canada's federal tax revenue, and in other countries today the corporate entity is being taxed even more heavily. The conventional view that the corporation income tax is a direct tax in the same sense as the personal income tax has received legal sanction from its operation under the same statute and is congenial to public opinion in view of the high yield and low political liability. On the other hand, there is increasing awareness that an incorporated business is essentially a device for productive employment of savings, having no real tax-paying capacity apart from that of the owners, customers, or employees. This more realistic view discloses underlying questions of equity and economic effects extending to the processes of capital formation, investment, and the price system on which the vitality of a free economy depends. Although all of these questions cannot be answered with finality it is necessary to demonstrate and examine them in order to prevent the deception of easy appearances in this matter.

Dr. Petrie investigates these questions as they have appeared in Canada since the end of the Second World War, approaching them as an economist. The object of his study is to analyse consequences rather than to describe methods. The fact that major amendments of the tax law occurred while his study was in progress complicated his task but confirmed its purpose, and if the reader detects some unavoidable discrepancies between the current state of the law and the author's observations it is not necessarily the former that will prove the more durable.

This study was commissioned by the Canadian Tax Foundation in the spring of 1949 as an outside research project and was completed after Dr. Petrie had joined the Foundation's staff as Director of Research. While it therefore stands as a mark of his valued work in that capacity, it is published as a presentation of his own views in accordance with the Foundation's regular policy and original understanding with the author that he was free to express them.

MONTEATH DOUGLAS
Executive Director
Canadian Tax Foundation

Toronto
June 3, 1952

PREFACE

THIS STUDY was begun in May 1949, and was originally completed in December of that year. Meanwhile, the Minister of Finance forecast in his 1949 budget speech important new corporation tax legislation respecting depreciation and the undistributed earnings of private companies. But delay in the enactment of the legislation precluded any save passing comment at that time. The new legislation is very far reaching, and it answers several of the criticisms of the corporation tax contained in my original manuscript. I considered it desirable, therefore, to rewrite a considerable portion of it, and this was possible after I joined the Foundation's staff in 1950. Furthermore, the heavy defence programme growing out of the Korean war and the threat to our future security will certainly result in levels of taxation unprecedented in our history save in the period of World War II. This crisis has forced a fundamental change in my basic philosophy of fiscal policy; the text has been changed accordingly, and an additional chapter has been added, presenting my views on defence financing.

I have long held that taxation should be designed primarily for raising revenue, and I developed that theme at some length in the introduction to my original manuscript. The main arguments are still there. But I am now convinced that the present crisis necessitates fiscal and monetary policy designed to curb the increasing tempo of inflation. It is the only alternative to the imposition of over-all direct controls over prices and wages, which in my opinion would neither be effective in the long run, nor be acceptable to the Canadian people save in a period of total war.

This is not to be construed as an abandonment of my traditional position. Rather it is a temporary retreat from it, caused by no lack of faith in *laissez-faire*, but by what I believe to be the need to fight fire with fire. Never before have we been in a position of adding billions of dollars of unproductive and inflationary expenditures in a full-employment peacetime economy. Inflation is as great a threat to our security as external aggression, and that fact must be faced now.

Because we are confronted with the most crushing taxation in our peacetime history, it becomes all the more necessary to remove the inequities that still exist in the Income Tax Act, and to give careful study to the impact of taxation on the incentive to produce efficiently and on the formation of new capital required to further our need to expand production. While fiscal policy aimed at curbing inflation appears now to be an inescapable element of national policy, its objective will be frustrated if it defeats the basic objective of increasing production to the maximum in order to maintain our position as a free nation. This is the underlying theme of the following pages.

I am greatly indebted to Monteath Douglas, Executive Director of the Canadian Tax Foundation, for his assistance and sympathetic encouragement during the years when this study was in preparation. I acknowledge with gratitude the meticulous editorial work of Miss Helen Foster, who checked the entire manuscript and all the citations. I also acknowledge the assistance received from all my other colleagues on the Foundation's staff, whose constant good nature made the task infinitely lighter. I am grateful to K. LeM. Carter, Harvey Perry, Stuart Thom, Philip Vineberg, and John Willis, who read various sections of the manuscript and whose criticism has both improved the presentation and deleted errors. Finally, I acknowledge with thanks the statistical material prepared for me by Robert Beattie of the Bank of Canada, and Mark Sprott of the Department of National Revenue.

I accept, of course, full responsibility for any errors which may still be found in the text, and for all the views expressed in the following pages. A year ago I wrote that all my conclusions should be regarded as tentative. They should now be considered all the more so in the light of developments over the past few months. It would be a brave or a foolish man indeed who would now pronounce a final and definitive view on tax policy.

J. R. P.

Toronto
November 30, 1951

ACKNOWLEDGMENTS

GRATEFUL ACKNOWLEDGMENT is made to the following publishers and journals for permission to quote from copyright material: *The Accountant,* vol. 122 (April 1950), Editorial. American Accounting Association, *The Accounting Review* (December 1935), "Depreciation and the Financing of Replacements," by Perry Mason. *The American Economic Review* (March 1920), "Immediate Future of the Excess Profits Tax," by T. S. Adams; (March 1942), "The Incidence of the General Income Tax," by E. E. Oakes; (March 1945), "The Corporate Income Tax and the Price Level," by Richard Goode; (March 1946), "The Incidence of the Corporation Income Tax: A Rejoinder," by Richard Goode; (December 1946), "Incidence or Effects of the Corporation Income Tax," by C. Ward Macy. The Blakiston Company, *The Shifting and Incidence of Taxation* (1942), by Otto von Mering. The Bobbs-Merrill Company Inc. (copyright 1947), *Taxation for Prosperity* by R. E. Paul. The Brookings Institution, *Depreciation Policy and Postwar Expansion* (1946), by Lewis H. Kimmel; *Postwar Tax Policy and Business Expansion* (1943), by Lewis H. Kimmel. *Canadian Bankers' Association Journal,* vol. 7 (July 1900), "The Taxation of Corporations in Ontario," by James Mavor. Canadian Bar Association, *Definition of the Term Income,* address at Washington, D.C., September 20, 1950, by R. deW. MacKay, Q.C.; *Resolution presented to the Canadian Bar Association,* September 18, 1950, by J. M. Coyne. *Canadian Chartered Accountant,* vol. 52 (April 1948), "The Rise and Fall of LIFO," by E. B. Wilcox; vol. 54 (February 1949), "Changes in Income Tax Law," by J. G. Glassco; vol. 55 (July 1949), "Historic Costs—The Lesser Evil," by George Moller; vol. 55 (October 1949), "Some Aspects of Income Taxation in Canada," by Charles Gavsie; vol. 56 (June 1950), "Diminishing Balance Depreciation under the Income Tax Act," by A. W. Gilmour. *Canadian Chartered Accountant Tax Review* (March 1949), Editorial. The Carswell Company Ltd., *The Law Relating to Income Tax in Canada* (1947), by H. A. W. Plaxton, C.C.H. (Canadian) Ltd., *Private Companies, Special Tax on Undistributed Income* (1950), by K. LeM. Carter and J. L. Stewart. Columbia University, *Proceedings of the Academy of Political Science,* vol. XI (May 1924), "Income Taxes and the Price Level," by E. R. A. Seligman. Columbia University Press, *The Impact of the Undistributed Profits Tax, 1936-1937* (1948), by George E. Lent; *Shifting and Incidence of Taxation* (1921), by E. R. A. Seligman. Committee for Economic Development, *A Postwar Federal Tax Plan for High Employment,* 1944. Committee on Postwar Tax Policy, *A Tax Program for a Solvent America,* 1947. Dominion Association of Chartered Accountants, *Brief to Senate Committee,* April 1946. Dun & Bradstreet Inc., *A Study of the Theory of Corporate Net Profits* (1949), by Roy A. Foulke. *Economist* (June 12, 1948); (May 20, 1950). *Harvard Business Review,* vol. 26 (September 1948), "The Reality of Inventory Profits," by Charles A. Bliss; (November 1948), "Concepts of Income," by George D. Bailey. Harvard University, Graduate School of Business Administration, *Effect of Federal Taxes on Growing Enterprises* (1945), by J. Keith Butters and John Lintner. *Law and Contemporary Problems,* "The Question of Taxing Capital Gains: The Case for Taxation," by Arthur H. Kent (Duke University School of Law, Durham, North Carolina; copyright 1940 by Duke University Press). *Law Quarterly Review,* No. 49. Macmillan & Co., London, *Principles of Economics* (1916), by Alfred Marshall. The Macmillan Company, New York, *Accounting* (1924), by W. A. Paton; *Encyclopaedia of the Social Sciences*, vol. 4 (1931), "Cost," by Jacob Viner; *Financial Accounting* (1946), by George O. May. McGraw-Hill Book Company Inc., *Applied Business Finance* (1941), by Edmond E. Lincoln; *Corporation Finance* (1947), by H. E. Hoagland; *Postwar Taxation and Economic Progress* (1946), by Harold M. Groves; *Production, Jobs and Taxes* (1944), by Harold M. Groves. Mr. Beverley Matthews, Q.C., *Address* to the Board of Trade of the City of Toronto, October 2, 1950. National Association of Cost Accountants, *Bulletin*, vol. 25, No. 24 (August 15, 1944). National City Bank of New York, *Monthly Letter* (November 1947; January 1949). National Planning Association, *Fiscal and Monetary Policy* (1944), by Beardsley Ruml and H. C. Sonne. National Tax Association, *Bulletin*, vol. 29, No. 8 (May 1944), "The Corporation Net Income Tax and the Cost-Price Structure," by C. Ward Macy; vol. 30, No. 3 (December 1944), "The Taxation of Business," by A. G. Buehler; vol. 31, No. 7 (April 1946), "Corporation Income Tax and Production," by Oscar F. Litterer; No. 9 (June 1946), "Some Aspects of Corporate Taxation," by Roy Blough. National Tax Association, *Proceedings* (1936), "Shall We Tax Corporations or Business?" by M. H. Hunter; (1944), "Fiscal Policy and Taxation," by Beardsley Ruml; (1947), "Alternative Approaches to the Integration of Corporate and Individual Income Taxes," by Richard Goode; (1947), "The Fiscal Significance of the Corporation Income Tax," by Louis Shere; (1947), "The Place of the Corporate Income Tax in the Tax System," by Louis Schreiber; (1947), "Some Economic Aspects of the Present Corporate Income Tax," by R. S. Ford; (1947), "Would the Complete Integration of the Corporate and Personal Income Taxes Injure Small Business?" by J. Keith Butters. *National Tax Journal* (March 1948), "Incidence of the Corporation Income Tax: Capital Structure and Turnover Rates," by Carl Shoup; (June 1949), "Federal Corporate Income Tax," by Louis Shere. Ronald Press Company, *Agenda for Progressive Taxation* (1947), by William Vickrey. *Taxes—The Tax Magazine*, vol. 25 (February 1947), "Declining Balance Depreciation," by Gerhard J. Mayer; vol. 27 (October 1949), "The Old and New Depreciation Problem," by J. H. Landman. Tax Institute, Inc., *How Should Corporations be Taxed?* (1947), articles by Richard Goode, Roy G. Blakey, Matthew Woll, Howard R. Bowen, S. H. Ruttenberg, Norris Darrell, W. L. Hearne, H. C. Sonne, J. Keith Butters. Tax Policy League, *How Shall Business be Taxed?* (1937), articles by Mabel L. Walker, Roy Blough, Harold M. Groves, A. G. Buehler, Carl Shoup. Twentieth Century Fund, *Financing Defense* (1951), by A. G. Hart and E. C. Brown. United States Treasury Department, *Postwar Corporation Tax Structure* (1946), by Richard Goode. *University of Chicago Law Review* (December 1946), "Federal Tax Reform," by Henry G. Simons.

CONTENTS

Foreword vii
Preface ix
Acknowledgments xi

I. Introduction and Major Conclusions 3
Scope of the Study 3
The Canadian Tax System 7
Objectives of the Tax System 14
Major Conclusions 23
1. Rationale of the Corporation Tax 23
2. Incidence of the Tax 23
3. Economic Effects of the Tax 24
4. Business Losses 26
5. Valuation of Assets 27
6. Approach to the Problem of Double Taxation: Integration of Corporation and Personal Income Taxes 27
7. The Problem of Small Business 30
8. Final Conclusion 31

I. Background and Evolution of the Corporation Tax 32
Introduction 32
Income versus Capital 33
The Changing Concept of the Corporation Tax 50
1. Background 50
2. Tax Avoidance—The Problem of Undistributed Profits 53
3. The 1950 Legislation 64
4. The 1951 Legislation 71
5. Tax-Paid Undistributed Earnings versus Tax-Paid Dividends 75
Special Corporations 77
1. Co-operatives 77
2. Exempt Corporations 82

3. Non-Resident-Owned Investment Corporations 87
Ministerial Discretion 88
Conclusions 95
Note on Consolidated Returns 95

III. The Rationale of the Corporation Income Tax 98
Special Benefits Received 99
Ability to Pay 102
Social Control 105
1. Control of Monopoly Profit 107
2. Concentration of Economic Power 109
3. Over-Complication of the Corporate Financial Structure 109
Economic Considerations 111
1. Economic Control and Fiscal Policy 111
2. Fiscal Yield 116
Conclusions 120
1. Special Benefits Received 120
2. Ability to Pay 120
3. Social Control 121
4. Economic Considerations 122

IV. The Incidence of the Corporation Income Tax 123
Scope of Analysis and Definition of Terms 123
Incidence 125
1. Traditional Theory of Incidence 126
2. Cost of Production Theory 135
3. The Diffusion Theory 141
Summary 143

V. Economic Effects of the Tax 144
Double Taxation and Regressivity 144
Effects on Saving and Investment 148
1. Individual Saving and Investment 148
2. Corporate Saving and Investment 150
3. Conclusions 164
Effects on Prices 166
Effect on Methods of Corporate Financing 168
Effect on the Form of Business Organization 171
Effects on Small Business and New Enterprises 173
1. Definition of Small Business 173
2. Effects of the Tax 174

Summary and Conclusions 181
1. Saving and Investment 181
2. Prices and Wages 181
3. Corporate Financing 183
4. Form of Business Organization 183
5. Small and Expanding Enterprise 183

VI. The Problem of Business Losses 185
The Problem 185
1. Equity Considerations 188
2. Economic Considerations 188
Approach to the Problem 190
1. Longer Accounting Period 190
2. Averaging Devices 190
3. Carry-over of Business Losses 200

VII. The Problem of the Valuation of Assets 208
The Problem 209
Concepts of Income 213
1. The Accounting Concept 214
2. The Tax Concept 214
3. The Economic Concept 217
4. Conclusions 218
Elements of the Problem 218
1. Inventory Valuation 218
2. Valuation of Fixed Assets 232
Conclusions 259

VIII. The Integration of Corporation and Personal Income Taxes 261
Total or Partial Integration? 263
1. Total versus Partial Integration? 264
2. Criteria of an Acceptable Plan for Integration 267
3. Special Problems 269
Alternative Approaches to Integration 284
1. Repeal of the Corporate Income Tax 284
2. Exemption of Dividends from Personal Income Tax 285
3. The Partnership Approach 285
4. The Dividends-Paid Credit Approach 290
5. The Withholding Tax Approach 294
6. The Dividends-Received Credit Approach 299

Summary and Conclusions 303
1. Approaches to Integration 303
2. The Problem of Small Business 305
3. General Conclusions 308

IX. Defence Financing and the Corporation Tax 309
Introduction 309
Indicated Policy 311
Government Policy: The 1951 Budget 315
1. Tax Policy 316
2. Deferred Depreciation 318
Fiscal Control and the Corporation Tax 327
Conclusions 332
Appendix: Notes on "Invested Capital" 334
Bibliography 343
Index 375

TABLES

I.	Total Current Revenue Collected from the Public in Canada by Federal, Provincial, and Municipal Governments, 1937, 1941, 1944, 1946, 1948	10
II.	Summary of Rates and Exemptions for Federal Corporation Income Tax, 1917-1952	34
III.	Relationship between Corporation Income Tax and Total Income Tax, Total Federal Tax Revenue and Total Revenue, 1919-1952	114
IV.	Federal Tax Receipts in Canada, Fiscal Years 1944-5 to 1951-2	115
V.	Relationship between Corporation Taxes, Personal Income Taxes, and Total Tax Revenues in Canada, the United Kingdom, and the United States, 1942-1947	118
VI.	Relationship between Corporate and Personal Saving in Canada, 1938-1948	153
VII.	Corporate Profits before and after Taxes, and Undistributed Profits in Canada, 1938-1950	160
VIII.	Forecast Private and Public Investment in Canada, 1951	326

THE TAXATION OF CORPORATE INCOME IN CANADA

CHAPTER ONE

INTRODUCTION AND MAJOR CONCLUSIONS

SCOPE OF THE STUDY

THIS STUDY is an attempt to answer the following questions: Are there any really significant problems connected with the present method of taxing corporate income and dividends in Canada? If so, what are they? What are the economic effects of this method under the present rate structure? Is the tax affecting production adversely? Has it affected the pattern or volume of saving and investment? Has it had any effect on the way in which the financing of corporations is conducted? Has it affected costs and prices? Has it discriminated between different classes of corporations? What are its effects on small business? What is the incidence of the tax? Is there a serious double taxation resulting from the taxation of corporate income and the subsequent taxation of dividends paid to the shareholders? If so, then what should be done to remedy the situation? Is the recently announced government policy of reduction of the rate on the first $10,000 of corporate income and the granting of dividend credits to shareholders a step in the right direction, or is there a better approach?

Were one to secure tenable answers to all these questions, undoubtedly the millennium would have been reached. But such, unhappily, is not the case. The conclusions drawn in this study are the result of a careful scrutiny of the very considerable volume of literature on the subject,[1] and discussions with many members of the accounting and legal professions, members of the federal civil service, and a large number of business men. Above

[1]A selected bibliography is presented at the end of the volume.

all, these conclusions are the result of the writer's peculiar conception of taxation in the modern state.

The necessity of compromising between what is desirable and what is practicable, from an administrative and political viewpoint, has been kept in mind as much as possible. If one were to discourse on purely theoretical grounds, a set of conclusions would be drawn which would differ substantially from those that are presented here. But a purely theoretical approach is unlikely to have much practical usefulness in the foreseeable future. An attempt has been made to arrive at one or more proposals that might be made to fit the situation as it exists in Canada today. As indicated in the Preface, however, all conclusions must be regarded as tentative. The complexities encountered in attempting to answer the questions enumerated above should serve as a warning against any doctrinaire or dogmatic approach.

Considerable concern over tax equity will be noted in the following pages. It is readily conceded that a blind adherence to the principles of equity results in the pursuit of a will-o'-the-wisp and complete frustration. But some idea of rough justice should be pre-eminent in the intellectual pursuit of a tax system which purports to raise the necessary revenue with the minimum social sacrifice.

With this in mind, it may be stated that the problems connected with the taxation of corporate income, or indeed, those connected with any form of taxation, should not be divorced from the problems inherent in the tax system as a whole. Having decided upon the imposition of a particular tax, we should consider its function in the tax system in the light of its own probable effects along with those of the other components of the over-all system on such things as employment, the standard of living, saving, investment, production, consumption, and business initiative.

While certain disadvantages may be inherent in a given tax, conceivably these may be moderated to some extent by other component parts of the tax system. It would be difficult to demonstrate this effect, but there seems to be good presumptive evidence for it. One can say with certainty only that all taxation is confiscatory by nature because it involves the seizure of private property for public use without direct compensation to the taxpayer. Benefits are received from government, of course, but it has been a very long time indeed since any attempt has been made to relate an individual's tax burden to the benefits he receives.

The prevailing philosophy of taxation today results in the greatest direct benefits being received, relatively, by those who pay the least taxes. This principle is known as taxation in accordance with ability to pay, as opposed to the earlier doctrine of taxation in accordance with benefits received. The ability theory is almost universally accepted without question. But it should not be forgotten that it is of comparatively recent vintage, emerging with the evolution of welfare economics, and not without violent opposition. It was once a revolutionary doctrine, based upon moral and ethical considerations, involving a humanitarian philosophy as exemplified in the principle, "the greatest happiness of the greatest number."

But ability to pay is not a quantity susceptible of measurement, or susceptible even to unequivocal definition. As stated by Professor William Vickrey, "ability to pay and the equivalent terms, 'faculty' and 'capacity to pay,' have served as catch phrases, identified by various writers through verbal legerdemain with their own pet concrete measure to the exclusion of other possible means. Ability to pay thus often becomes a tautological smoke screen behind which the writer conceals his own prejudices."[2]

Out of the ability doctrine arose the concept of the graduated personal income tax and, to a lesser extent, the death duties as they have existed in recent times. It is significant, however, that no attempt has been made, outside the books of theorists, to construct an entire tax system based on the ability to pay. At our present stage of development such a programme would be impractical for political reasons and because of the impossibility of finding a suitable yardstick with which to measure taxpaying ability. Income is probably the best conceivable single measure. But the inherent difficulties of computing it for tax purposes make it a yardstick on which we cannot read the scale. It is far from

[2]*Agenda for Progressive Taxation*, pp. 3, 4.

certain, therefore, that if a tax system based upon income taxation alone could be developed, the inequities contained within it would be appreciably less than those contained in a revenue system using several different and well-integrated tax bases. While such a proposal lends itself readily to sober reflection and leisurely contemplation, it is too far divorced from practicality to merit further discussion at this time.

Nevertheless, the ability doctrine has coloured the thinking of practically all serious students of taxation, and the legislative trend has reflected the underlying theory. The conclusions drawn in this study are definitely conditioned by a conscious adherence to this principle.

During the evolution of the ability doctrine there was little change in the traditional doctrine that taxation should be for revenue purposes only, that is, for meeting the running expenses of government. Certain sumptuary taxes have long been used, of course, and the idea of using taxation to control monopoly is not new. Yet, for all practical purposes, the fundamental doctrine of taxation solely for revenue purposes prevailed over a very long period.

An inescapable result of implementing tax policy based on the ability doctrine is the reduction of the degree of economic inequality among individuals. This occurs, whether or not by legislative design. As the ability doctrine has evolved, and become the subject of careful study, elaboration, and refinement, there has developed a school of thought which advocates using the taxing power deliberately to eradicate, or at least to reduce to an ill-defined minimum, economic inequalities among individuals.

Another development in the philosophy of taxation has taken place over the last two decades. A profound and revolutionary shift has occurred in the thinking of many students of taxation and fiscal policy. This was a period of grave depression, followed by war and an unprecedented level of economic activity. The new economic philosophy, conceived by theorists and implemented by governments in Canada[3] and elsewhere, involves the idea that taxation is a key tool of fiscal policy and should be used as such

[3]Canada's current fiscal policy of imposing very heavy commodity taxes to discourage consumption, and the policy of deferring depreciation to curb new investment, are indicative of the trend.

to attain and maintain a high level of employment and price level stability. It is a basic part of the doctrine that the attainment of these goals is dependent not only on the amount of taxes levied within the economy, but also by the way in which they are imposed.

Whether or not one is in agreement with such doctrine, it follows that it implies a serious appraisal of all taxes in the light of a tax system which is to be used for other than purely revenue-raising purposes. A socio-economic-fiscal tax system must be designed as such, and if future tax policy in Canada is to be geared deliberately to promoting a welfare state and stabilizing the national economy, the existing tax system requires extensive overhauling. Furthermore, constitutional amendments seem unavoidable if the process is to be made really effective.

Even if the tax system is to be used for no purpose other than raising the revenue necessary to finance government expenditures, the taxes imposed will nevertheless have important bearing on the economy. Regardless of whether taxes are designed consciously to affect employment, production, and prices, they do it anyway. It is surely of fundamental importance that the revenue requirements be raised in such a way as to have the least adverse effect upon production and therefore on employment. The old adage of not killing the goose that lays the golden eggs is still as sound as it ever was.

The Canadian Tax System

The Canadian tax system, composed as it is of a multitude of federal, provincial, and municipal taxes of every conceivable species and sub-species, grew without much conscious direction prior to the war, and is still in large part devoid of any rational integration. It is a result of the ever increasing scramble for revenue by all the tax-levying bodies in the nation.

Revenue requirements, coloured by political considerations, have produced in Canada a tax system designed to yield the necessary revenue with the fewest political repercussions. Periodically one finds lip service paid to the principles of tax equity. The result is a conglomeration of taxes, ranging from the anachronism of the personal property and poll taxes, through an intricate maze of consumption taxes, to the steeply graduated tax on personal income.

Until 1940 little regard was given to an equitable distribution of the tax burden, and as far as legislation is concerned, only a token recognition of the problem was to be found. The 1949 and 1950 federal budgets recognized the hardships imposed on small corporations, and some relief was given to them. But when the over-all tax system is considered, one is safe in concluding that the chips have been allowed to fall where they would. This should not be surprising, when it is remembered that there are thousands of tax-levying bodies in the nation, each striving to meet its own revenue requirements without heed to the others.

Furthermore, no analysis seems to have been made of the economic effects of taxation at its present level. There is abundant evidence, however, although scattered and uncorrelated, that in some tax fields the saturation point has been approximated, or even passed. If the over-all impact of a revenue system which is supposed to raise the means with which to provide the maximum public welfare kills initiative and discourages or impairs investment, then it destroys any possibility of achieving its end.

What definite pattern there is to the Canadian taxing system is conditioned by the British North America Act (Sections 91 and 92). The division of taxing power between the federal government, on the one hand, and the provincial governments and their political subdivisions on the other, is based partly upon the distinction between direct and indirect taxation.[4] No attempt to define direct and indirect taxation is found in the statute. Eighty years of judicial interpretation of this curious constitutional provision have converted what must have been a perfectly clear concept to the framers of the legislation into an amorphous delineation circumscribed only by the natural limitations to the ingenuity of succeeding generations of provincial legislators.

[4]There is no constitutional limitation to the federal taxing power. Section 92 limits the provinces to "direct taxation within the province in order to the raising of a revenue for provincial purposes." The provincial legislature has been held to be supreme within the limits of Section 92, and, under the plenary powers granted it, has authority to delegate taxing power to any of its municipalities. It follows, therefore, that any municipal tax must fall within the constitutional limitations to the provincial taxing power.

Virtually any tax will now be declared "direct" by the judiciary, if the legislation is drawn to describe it so.

At the outbreak of World War II the Canadian tax system was a hodge-podge of overlapping taxes levied by the federal, provincial, and municipal governments. Income and sales taxes were imposed at all three levels. Death duties, composed of a combination of estate taxes and succession duties, levied by all nine provinces and the Yukon Territory, resulted in serious multiple taxation. Reciprocal arrangements among the provinces had far more form than substance. The taxes levied on corporations by the federal, provincial, and municipal governments resulted in tax pyramiding and flagrant inequity. The only saving feature of the pre-war structure was that the burden was relatively low, even in the aggregate.

Such a system, however, could not have persisted with the rates of taxation necessitated by war. In many cases the vertical overlapping of federal, provincial, and municipal taxes, as well as the horizontal overlapping of provincial taxes, would have been ruinous. Accordingly, by temporary wartime agreement between the federal and the provincial governments, all personal income taxes and corporation taxes were centralized in the hands of the federal government. This step removed immediately one of the worst features of the pre-war system, multiple taxation of corporations. Furthermore, it resulted in uniform tax treatment of corporations throughout the nation.

At the conclusion of the war the agreements expired. The federal government sought to have them renewed and enlarged on a voluntary basis, with succession duties included. All the provinces save Quebec and Ontario have entered into new agreements with the federal authority, so that a considerable amount of improvement over the pre-war situation still exists. But with the two largest provinces outside the fold, the situation is far from satisfactory. These agreements expire on March 31, 1952, and it is of fundamental importance that all ten provinces enter into new tax agreements with the federal government in order to facilitate the defence taxation programme.

The pattern of the Canadian revenue system before World War II, and the transition that has taken place since, are shown

TABLE I

TOTAL CURRENT REVENUE COLLECTED FROM THE PUBLIC IN CANADA BY FEDERAL, PROVINCIAL, AND MUNICIPAL GOVERNMENTS 1937, 1941, 1944, 1946, 1948[a]

(millions of dollars)

Type of revenue	1937		1941		1944		1946		1948[b]	
	Am't	%	Am't	%	Am't	%	Am't	%	Am't	%
Personal income tax	54.8	5.5	310.3	15.1	673.4	21.1	670.7	18.4	762.8	20.7
Corporation taxes	102.1	10.3	374.0	18.2	625.9	19.6	691.0	18.9	646.3	17.5
Succession duties	36.7	3.7	34.4	1.7	40.7	1.3	57.7	1.6	54.7	1.5
Real estate taxes	241.5	24.3	256.2	12.5	274.8	8.6	284.9	7.8	341.3	9.3
Taxes on consumption[c]	381.8	38.4	765.5	37.3	844.8	26.5	1120.0	30.7	1238.5	33.6
Licences, permits, and fees[d]	44.2	4.4	52.0	2.5	54.8	1.7	67.8	1.9	83.7	2.3
Other revenue	132.9	13.4	261.9	12.7	675.9	21.2	758.0	20.7	556.8	15.1
Total current revenue[e]	994.0	100.0	2,054.3	100.0	3,190.3	100.0	3,650.1	100.0	3,684.1	100.0

[a]Compiled from data provided by the Research Department of the Bank of Canada.
[b]Estimated.
[c]Includes import duties and taxes, liquor revenue (including profits on sales by government stores), tobacco taxes, gasoline taxes, sales taxes, and amusement taxes.
[d]Includes motor vehicle licences.
[e]Excludes amounts received from other governments.

in Table I. It will be noted that in 1937 taxes on consumption yielded more revenue by far than any other form of taxation, and real estate taxes were the revenue source second in importance. Together, these two forms of taxation provided about 63 per cent of Canada's total current government revenue. Personal income taxation was relatively unimportant, yielding little more than licences, permits, and fees. Corporation taxes yielded only 10.3 per cent of the total revenue. Together, the personal income tax, corporation taxes, and succession duties accounted for only 19.5 per cent of the revenue collected from the public in 1937. Thus, the revenue system was substantially regressive, and did not reflect much adherence to the theory of taxing in accordance with ability to pay.

During the war, when revenue requirements reached unprecedented levels, considerably more reliance was placed upon the personal income tax and corporation tax than at any other time in Canada's history. In 1941 these two taxes together accounted for 33.3 per cent of the total revenue, and by 1944 they accounted for 40.7 per cent of it. While taxes on consumption rose very sharply, too, they declined in relative importance, although they still remained the most important revenue source. It is significant that during this period succession duties, real estate taxes, licences, permits, and fees remained almost stable, and therefore became much less important, relatively, in the over-all revenue picture. Thus, during the war years the Canadian revenue system became less regressive than at any time since Confederation. In 1944, 42 per cent of the total revenue collected from the public was derived from the personal income tax, the corporation tax, and succession duties, the three taxes generally conceded to be the most equitable and reflecting, in some considerable measure, taxpaying ability.

This wartime trend was changed to some extent during the immediate post-war period. Receipts from consumption taxes have continued to rise, and reached a peak in 1948. Revenue from the personal income tax was somewhat less in 1946 than in 1944, but despite reductions in rate and increased exemptions it had reached a new peak by 1948, and is still rising. This rise, of course, is a reflection of the post-war boom in employment and income. The corporation tax also yielded considerably more in 1948 than it did in 1944, for similar reasons. But the relative yield of the personal and corporate income taxes was less in both 1946 and 1948 than it was in 1944, principally because of the sharp increase in the yield, absolute and relative, of taxes on consumption. Thus, the post-war revenue system places considerably more reliance on consumption taxes, both absolutely and relatively, than did the wartime revenue system at its peak. But it has not returned to the pre-war pattern, and it is not conceivable that it will. Estimated current revenue receipts of all governments in 1948 were 270 per cent greater than in 1937. Yet corporation taxes were 533 per cent greater and personal income taxes were 1,292 per cent greater.

Over-all governmental requirements are increasing very substantially. Even before the Korean war, the social security programme, to which all political parties are committed, indicated an increase in government outlay of more than $200 million, on a basis of $40 per month for all persons 70 years of age. The unprecedented peacetime defence expenditures, estimated at $1,700 million in 1951, are an indication of the shape of things to come, taxwise.

The pattern of the revenue system is likely to be determined in large part by what political leaders think the public will stand, and in part by considerations of counter-inflationary fiscal policy. There are two separate upper limits to any tax. First, there is the economic saturation point, which is the point where the tax breaks down because of its economic effects. This point is not often reached because of another taxable limit lower down on the scale, which may be called the political upper limit. When this point is reached taxpayer reaction is such that, short of a critical national emergency, such as war, political leaders dare not go beyond it.

While no scale of tax rates can be constructed with these two upper limits indicated, they certainly exist. But they are flexible, and only experience can indicate even roughly where they lie on the scale. For example, before World War II few observers would have forecast anything but collapse of the private enterprise system under the rates of taxation that were reached during the war and prevail today.[5] During the war the political tax limit was unimportant because of the grave emergency that existed. It is doubtful if the economic limit was even approached, because the national economy was subject to controls over virtually every phase of economic activity. The impact of the tax programme on private investment was offset by supplementary public investment.

How long such a programme could have been continued is an imponderable question. By the war's end stresses and strains within the economy were increasingly apparent. While the wartime programme could have gone on indefinitely under war con-

[5]It is interesting to note Mr. Winston Churchill's reference in the 1902 budget debate to a tax of 1*s.* 3*d.* in the pound as "the extreme limit of practical peace-time taxation." See Philip Guedalla, *Mr. Churchill*, p. 100.

ditions, the longer it was perpetuated the greater would have been the difficulty in returning to a private enterprise system free of controls.

With the war's end, the political upper limit to personal income taxation became apparent. There was a general demand for rate reductions and exemption increases, and the federal government met both demands, at least in part. That the income tax was approaching the higher economic limit, at least in some brackets, was seen in the loss of incentive, the squandering of funds on expense accounts, the growth of absenteeism, the general dissatisfaction among taxpayers.

Under normal peacetime conditions it does not appear that the Canadian revenue system could be made much more progressive through greater reliance upon the progressive personal income tax. It seems likely that, regardless of future revenue requirements, the over-all pattern as it existed in 1948 will remain fairly constant. This is borne out by the character of the federal tax changes since the outbreak of war in Korea. In the 1951 budget both the personal and the corporation income tax rates were increased by 20 per cent, while the general sales tax was increased by 25 per cent. Of course if another world war takes place, it is almost certain that the present revenue structure would be completely distorted because of the need of complete mobilization of all resources. Under such circumstances an excess profits tax, a capital gains tax, and perhaps even a capital levy could be expected.

It is difficult to say whether the post-war revenue system is definitely more equitable than the pre-war system. All that one can be certain about is that the former relies more heavily on taxation of income, both personal and corporate, than did the latter. Theoretically, this points towards the conclusion that the post-war system is more equitable. But caution should be exercised in drawing conclusions. It is virtually impossible to measure with any degree of accuracy the economic effects of raising revenue in any particular manner. All that is known is that the collection of an estimated $3,684.1 million from the Canadian people in 1948, in the way that it was collected, has had profound effects on the Canadian economy. It has effected a very substantial redistribution of income. It has affected, as will be argued later in this study, the form of business enterprise; it has affected the capital market, corporation policy, dividend payments, and practically every phase of economic activity. Whether, in the final analysis, the ramifications of the existing tax system are "better" or "worse" than before the war will depend upon whether the general long-run welfare of Canadians as a people has been enhanced.

It is tempting to try for conclusions now. But the race has not been run yet, and judgment should be reserved. If, in the pursuit of the alleged blessings of a welfare state, we should destroy initiative, if enterprise should wither, if there should be increasing concentration of economic power and the decline of small enterprise, if production should be curtailed or economic expansion discouraged, accompanied by unemployment and a lower standard of living, then equity, according to this writer's definition, will have disappeared beyond lost horizons. It is fundamental that care be exercised lest the means used to achieve the end do not make its achievement impossible.

A case in point is the universal old age pension programme introduced in Parliament on October 25, 1951. The bill provides for the payment of $40 per month to all Canadians who are seventy years of age and older, irrespective of their means. The *additional* net cost to the federal government will next year be $225 million, making the total cost of pensions for the seventy-year-olds (including the present cost of some $100 million) about $325 million. As time passes this cost will rise steadily because of the increasing number of aged persons. By 1971 the annual charge is expected to reach $500 million.

Under present conditions of heavy defence expenditures and continuing inflation, the implementation of such a programme appears to be an improvident, short-sighted, and irresponsible allocation of priority in the expenditure of public funds. The inflationary effect of this outlay seems likely to offset considerably the assistance that is intended for the old and needy.

Objectives of the Tax System

Before reaching any conclusions regarding the taxation of corporations the writer's views on the objectives of fiscal policy should be indicated. The conclusions originally reached in this study in 1949 were admittedly based upon definite views which the writer has long held, views which condition the whole argument regarding corporation taxes.

For present purposes it is necessary only to outline a basic conception of the normal objectives of the tax system. These objectives are as follows, in order of importance:

1. The raising of the necessary revenue with which to meet the expenses of government.

2. The fostering of production through

(*a*) the maintenance of a balanced relationship between saving and investment;

(*b*) the conservation of national resources;

(*c*) the preservation and development of incentive to produce on the part of both labour and management.

3. The spreading of the tax burden in the most equitable manner possible, consistent with the above objectives.

These are the writer's basic views on tax policy, and they are indicated to assist an understanding of why certain conclusions are reached. No attempt will be made to formulate a tax programme for Canada consistent with these principles. Not only would that involve an unforgivably lengthy volume, but it is outside the terms of reference of this study.

Comment on the first of these objectives is hardly necessary. The primary objective of any revenue system is to raise revenue. Furthermore, the revenue system must be flexible enough to meet readily the fluctuating revenue requirements of the modern state in an unsettled world.

The three elements contained in the second objective seem fundamental to a sound revenue system. In the first place, the maintenance of a balance between saving and investment at a high level is necessary if a healthy and expanding economy is to be maintained. While it would be difficult, if not impossible, to define accurately what constitutes the proper balance between these factors in a dynamic and ever changing economy, it seems obvious that consumption and production should be kept in some rough equilibrium. Furthermore, saving should be sufficient to provide the investment necessary for replacement of worn-out and obsolete equipment, for the expansion of existing industry, and the creation of new enterprise.

It follows that the maintenance of an adequate consumers' market is of basic importance. A tax system which raises the greater part of its revenue from the lowest levels of income will have the effect of undermining the consumers' market and imperilling the stability of the economy, particularly if the total revenues collected from the public are large relative to national income.

Similarly, a tax system which discourages saving or investment, or both, is likely to be most detrimental to economic stability. From the available evidence it seems that taxation is likely to have much more effect upon investment than upon saving. People tend to save regardless of taxation,[6] and regardless of the interest rate, because of a desire for future security or future consumption, or simply because of ingrained habit. On the other hand, both the volume and the pattern of investment seem sensitive to tax policy. The amount of risk or venture capital available at a given point in time surely depends on the expectations investors hold of a future return commensurate to the risk involved. Judging from experience there appears to be little doubt that excessive taxation will cause a dearth of investment funds. It follows, then, that the tax system should be so devised as to minimize its effect on the consumers' market and on the amount of funds made available for investment.

The second aspect of the problem of gearing the tax system to production involves the conservation of national resources. Such resources include people, as well as materials, and a nation's human resources are its principal asset. The tax system should avoid any impairment of the health, efficiency, and morale of the people through taxes that result in lowered living standards. At the same time the tax system should avoid encouraging the wasteful exploitation of material resources such as timber lands and mines. For example, an annual levy on the capital value of such

[6]This is not to say that heavy taxation does not affect saving. There can be no personal saving when the tax burden is so great as to leave no surplus after necessary living expenses have been paid. Taxation can, and will, of course, affect saving. This is a point which will be developed more fully in a later chapter.

assets may well cause carrying charges so heavy as to result in uneconomic exploitation without regard for the future.

As important as any effect of taxation is its impact on the incentive to produce. Production incentive rests in both labour and management, and both can be, and have been in Canada, affected adversely by taxation. During the war, and particularly in the immediate post-war period, there were instances in which the high rates of personal income tax reduced labour's incentive to work. Workers in more than a few trades and industries determined the minimum take-home pay they wanted, say for a week, and when that figure had been reached, they stopped work for the rest of the week. The resulting absenteeism was reflected in a decline in per capita output and a rise in unit cost. At the same time the ability to consume is weakened, and the consumers' market thereby impaired.

As for management, taxes which reduce seriously the rewards for initiative, enterprise, and risk-taking are likely to affect the economy adversely. In the first place, existing business establishments may lose incentive for efficient operation because they feel that too large a share of any further increments of net income will be taken by the tax-gatherers. This attitude was not uncommon during the period of excess profits taxation, and was reflected in an unhealthy nonchalance towards expenses chargeable against income for tax purposes. In the second place, high taxation of corporate and personal incomes is likely to have an adverse effect on the willingness of investors to undertake new risks. If this is true, there will be a diminution in the number of new enterprises. The creation of a new enterprise has a definite element of uncertainty, if not actual hazard, attached to it. Should the tax structure be such as to leave too little of the rewards of success to the enterpriser, and to take no notice whatever of losses, it appears certain, on *a priori* grounds, that many an enterprise will remain unborn.

Turning to the third of the objectives, tax equity, we come to an intangible concept. Tax equity, or fairness, will have a meaning for one person which is very different from its meaning for another. The range of meaning spreads probably from the notion that equity means equalization of wealth and income for all persons, to that of total tax neutrality. Individual views will necessarily be contingent upon the whole complicated mass of individual prejudices, biases, and moral background that help to form personal opinion.

In the outline of the author's views on tax objectives, that of tax equity was placed third on the list, and made subordinate to the first two—raising the revenue, and fostering production. It does not follow from this, however, that maximum production is the only objective of economic life. What does follow is that there is inevitable conflict between the desire for equity and the concern for maintaining a high level of economic activity on the part of private enterprise. The resolution of this conflict should be possible through compromise rather than a discarding of one of the conflicting objectives. Indeed, compromise seems to be the only answer to the problem, for taxation designed exclusively to foster production would ultimately react, in a free and democratic society, in a wave of mass revulsion. Conversely, taxation designed exclusively to promote tax equity in its most literal form would almost certainly cause the collapse of the private enterprise system.

It is a widely held view that taxation should be used deliberately to redistribute wealth and income. This is the familiar line of thought regarding tax equity and social justice. The standard argument on strictly economic grounds holds that if the nation's income flows into the hands of too few people, the resulting amount of saving will be greater than can be absorbed, thus leading to unbalance between saving and consumption, and perpetual economic disequilibrium. Therefore the tax system should be designed to distribute income "more fairly." "Fairly" is, of course, a relative term, and one finds no concrete proposals for the fair distribution of income and wealth for the obvious reason that any such proposals could be demolished too easily as having none but a purely arbitrary foundation. Few would advocate flat equality. But many writers discuss in general terms the desirability of breaking up "large" holdings of wealth through heavy death duties, and preventing future accumulations through heavy personal income taxation in the upper brackets.

Such a direct attempt to achieve specific tax equity does not fit into the approach to fiscal problems employed by this writer. All taxation redistributes wealth and income, of course, and the degree to which such distribution takes place depends not only upon the pattern of the revenue system, but upon the pattern of government expenditures as well, and the bargaining position of the groups affected by taxation. It should not be forgotten that the public welfare and social security programme of the modern welfare state goes a long way towards achieving social justice. It is maintained here that the redistribution of wealth and income should be incidental to taxation rather than a fundamental objective to be written into the revenue-raising programme, lest both the golden eggs and the goose be destroyed. In the Canadian tax system, which is hardly designed consciously to break up family fortunes, we have had the all-too-familiar results of the impact of succession duties and income taxes on many economic enterprises, particularly family and private corporations. Any virtue attached to a "fair" redistribution of wealth and income is more than offset when taxation forces the liquidation of productive business enterprises. In the end no one profits, and the national economy is the poorer.

The tax system should recognize the basic principle of equity that persons in like circumstances should receive like treatment. It should go further, by taxing in accordance with ability to pay. But it should not go to the point where the tax burden impedes production through the impairment of incentive, saving, and investment. As far as possible, taxation should be imposed upon economic surpluses rather than upon costs and prices. But it should not be allowed to impinge upon economic surpluses to the point of eating up the reserves necessary for replacement of existing assets and the creation of additional ones. This argument has much bearing on the conclusions that will be drawn later.

It seems unlikely that the high level of revenue requirements in the post-war economy can be met chiefly by taxation in accordance with ability to pay without affecting production very seriously and disrupting the economy. The government has recognized this, if the pattern of the federal tax system is any indication of its fiscal views.

It will be noted that in the above outline of objectives of the tax system no mention was made of taxation as an instrument of fiscal policy to control the economy. So widely held is this idea among theorists that not to hold it probably amounts to economic heresy. But this writer is not prepared to accept such a use of the taxing power as a general principle. A modification of it is not only acceptable but necessary under certain conditions, however, which will be explained presently.

To the logical theorist the use of taxation to offset the forces that cause inflation and deflation seems unassailable. On paper the plan looks sound, just as manipulation of the rediscount rate and open market operations by a central bank seem to be remedies for undesirable economic fluctuations. It is argued[7] that when inflationary pressures are heavy, taxes should be imposed at rates sufficiently high to remove or curb the pressure. Conversely, when deflation threatens, the tax system should be designed to encourage the investment of savings, and to leave purchasing power in the hands of consumers so that the market can be strengthened through the additional demand thus created. This is the theme, stripped of its many variations and refinements. It necessarily involves sharp fluctuation in tax rates in accordance with the economic planners' view of the economic situation at a given moment and their forecast of conditions in the future.

Herein lie the objections to the principle. In the first place, sharply fluctuating tax rates are undesirable from the point of view of business planning. This point need not be laboured, since it is obvious that a sudden and drastic rise in tax rates could have most serious effects upon the operations of any business where production planning and price policy had been determined, and the programme for a given period was well along the way to completion. Conversely, a sudden and drastic fall in tax rates, designed to counteract deflationary forces, would certainly result in undeserved windfall gains. While it might be possible to offset these by special tax provisions, they would complicate an already over-complicated tax system.

Tax policy designed to curb demand, if really effective, affects not only producers, but distributors as well. It would add to the problems of production planning because of the added difficulty

[7]See, for example, R. E. Paul, *Taxation for Prosperity*, pp. 412 ff.

in forecasting markets in a situation where the government might decree at any moment a change in the given market. Similar problems would emerge for wholesalers and retailers, who could never be certain about their inventory requirements. The hazards of private enterprise are already great enough without adding a gratuitous Damocles' sword in the form of unpredictable tax rate changes for purposes of controlling the price level. It seems far better in a private enterprise system to maintain the greatest possible stability of tax rates consistent with revenue requirements.

The second criticism of the use of taxation for economic control purposes is that the problems to be solved contain so many variables, many of them uncontrollable (particularly the human variable), that confusion may result rather than a solution. There is no doubt that tax policy can be so designed as to discourage and even prevent the purchase and consumption, and therefore the production, of goods. All that is required is a sufficiently high rate of taxation. The notion of sumptuary taxes is not new. Similarly, if in the economic planners' judgment the volume of private saving and investment is too high, that, too, can be remedied through taxation designed to reduce it. But so complex are the interrelated forces at work in the economy that the ultimate effects of such policy cannot be foretold accurately. We have, of course, the experience of fiscal policy in World War II as an indication of what can happen. Heavy taxation, coupled with compulsory saving and direct controls, did hold the inflationary forces well under control, and few observers would quarrel with the need for such policy under the circumstances. Under ordinary conditions, however, it appears that taxation is too blunt an instrument of fiscal policy to control a private enterprise economy. The difficulty of accurate timing, the difficulty of maintaining a fine balance when the point of that balance is shifting constantly as economic conditions change, and the impossibility of determining in advance the end results of a given measure, all suggest that such a policy should be avoided as a general principle.[8]

Nevertheless, as suggested earlier, there may be occasions when taxation should be used for other than revenue purposes, as

[8]Professor Harold M. Groves has stated the case succinctly in these words: "An economy run by its tax system would indeed be the tail wagging the dog." *Postwar Taxation and Economic Progress*, p. 14.

it was during World War II. During that period, when it was an essential part of national policy to hold the production of a wide range of consumers' goods to a minimum, the curbing of purchasing power as a supplement to direct commodity and wage controls aided materially in the control of inflation. This, of course, was an abnormal period, when the volume of production could not keep pace with demand because of machine tool, manpower, and material shortages.

We are again faced with a repetition of the crisis which represents a continuation of the struggle for survival. In peacetime guns are used for shooting game. In war they are used for legalized murder. In the same sense taxation must be adapted, and all concepts of normal tax objectives must be revised accordingly.

The indicated defence programme of $5,000 million over the next three years is to be superimposed upon an economy already operating at the level of full employment. This is certain to exert forces on the national economy which have little in common with our experience in World War II or with our post-war experience up to now. Our prospective defence programme is so great that it will aggravate seriously the inflationary forces that are already manifest so strongly. Accordingly, whether or not direct controls are imposed, tax policy now has to be used deliberately as a measure of economic control, repulsive as it is to this writer, and despite the practical and theoretical shortcomings of this instrument of control. Comments on the place of the corporation tax in this scheme of things are presented in the concluding chapter of the study, which was written long after the main text had been completed. This is not to say, however, that the long-run tax objectives outlined earlier are to be ignored. They still stand. The departure from them outlined in chapter IX represents only the willingness of the writer to adapt himself to the exigencies of what he hopes to be a temporary crisis.

In conclusion, it may be stated that the problem of devising a revenue system falls into two parts. First, the over-all policy must have some definite pattern of objectives. Second, the intricate details of each component part should be worked out with the view of placing all the parts into a workable whole. Unfortunately, we have had the cart before the horse for a very long time in Canada. Until 1940 the only objective was that of raising revenue. Now comes the twofold task of integrating the components and devising a tax system as an instrument of economic control.

With this introduction as a backdrop, we now turn to the one corner of the over-all problem with which this study is concerned—the place of the corporate tax in the Canadian tax system. The approach used is an examination of the rationale of the tax, its fiscal importance, its incidence, its economic effects, of the problem of measuring corporate profits, of the various proposals for integrating the tax with the personal income tax, and finally, of its role as a tax for purposes of economic control.

Major Conclusions

1. *Rationale of the Corporation Tax*

The best argument in favour of the corporate income tax is its heavy yield. The tax produced an estimated $810 million in the fiscal year ending March 31, 1951. This was 26.1 per cent of the total national revenue in that year.

Even though the tax has many defects and strong theoretical arguments have been made against it, it still remains one of the better taxes because corporate income represents an economic surplus. It is argued that taxes should be placed, as much as possible, on economic surplus rather than on costs. The extent to which this can be done without serious economic effects is uncertain. However, the net economic effect of raising a fairly substantial portion of the revenue from this tax is no more serious than would be the effect of abolishing the tax and substituting others for it. In view of the importance of the tax in the federal revenue system, it is not considered practical or desirable to abolish it.

2. *Incidence of the Tax*

Incidence is used in its narrow sense as a short-run concept, in contrast to the economic effects of the tax, which are long-run. The economic analysis of short-run incidence appears to be convincing in its general conclusions that the corporate income tax is not passed to the consumer in the form of higher prices, and that it has no short-run significance as far as wages are concerned.

As a general proposition, the tax falls on the shareholders of the corporation. This conclusion holds under conditions of competition, monopolistic competition, and monopoly. It is apparent, however, that there are exceptions to the rule. At a given time there may be many. But it appears unlikely that under normal conditions these exceptions are widespread enough to invalidate the general conclusion that the short-run incidence of the tax rests on the owners of corporate enterprise.

3. *Economic Effects of the Tax*

The economic effects of the existing method of taxing corporate income and dividends make themselves felt in the long run. They are difficult to trace, and impossible to measure precisely. But in some cases, the pattern seems reasonably clear.

(*a*) Double Taxation

Since short-run incidence of the tax appears to be on the shareholders, the taxation of both corporate income and dividends constitutes double taxation. From the viewpoint of equity, however, this double taxation does not seem to be as serious as it might appear at first glance. The element of regressivity is probably minimized by the fact that most dividends are received by individuals for whom the personal income tax rate is at least as high as the prevailing rate on corporate income. But the double taxation of this income at the existing high rates has serious effects on investment, corporate financing, and small business.

(*b*) Effects on Saving and Investment

One of the most important economic effects of the present tax is its impact on saving and investment. If individual saving is not actually impaired, at least its pattern is changed, and this change affects the pattern of investment. Individuals in the higher income brackets, who receive most of the dividends that are declared, have their saving potential reduced by heavy taxes on corporate income and personal income.

The long-run effects of the tax on corporate saving seem fairly clear. Certainly the heavy taxation of corporate profits reduces the total available for dividends and re-investment. But corporations may increase their saving at the expense of dividends paid out. During the early post-war years the volume of corporate saving (undistributed profits) increased very sharply. The total corporate saving in Canada was 132 per cent greater in 1948 than in 1944, and the percentage of net profits retained after taxes, was 61.9 per cent in 1948, compared with 54 per cent in 1944.

Up through 1950 the volume of savings has remained high. While there was a decline in savings in 1949, a substantial part of that decline was recovered in 1950, but the volume is still considerably below the all-time peak reached in 1944. The pattern of savings has been changed drastically, with a much larger proportion being done by corporations than during World War II. In the peak war year of 1944 the ratio of corporation to personal saving was 19.8, while in 1950 it was 94.2.

The pattern of investment by individuals appears to have gone through a marked change away from investment in corporate securities in the direction of government bonds and life insurance. While taxation has not been wholly responsible for this shift, it probably has had an important bearing on it. The net result of the shift has been a diminution in the domestic supply of risk capital for corporate financing. This in turn has affected the method of financing corporate enterprise.

(*c*) Effects on Corporate Financing

The tax discrimination against dividends results in making debt financing more attractive than equity financing. But debt financing imposes a rigidity on the corporate structure which can have serious if not fatal results during depression. That there is no marked trend in the direction of bond financing in Canada is probably a result of the fear of excessive fixed charges. Rather, the trend is strongly in the direction of internal financing through the retention of earnings, which may well have the cumulative effect of discouraging the purchase of equity securities still further.

(*d*) Effects on Prices and Wages

While the tax on corporate income and dividends does not appear to have any direct effect on the general price and wage levels, it may, through long-run diffusion, affect both. Its ultimate effect on prices and wages depends upon its effect on the relationship between consumption and investment. If private investment is discouraged to the extent that it is out of balance with consumption, serious economic disequilibrium will probably result, affecting prices, employment, and wages.

(*e*) Effects on the Form of Business Organization

It is concluded that the effect of the tax on the form of business organization has no serious implications for the Canadian economy. Most large businesses have to use the corporate form, regardless of tax discriminations. Most of the small concerns which are not incorporated have no need to incorporate, and it is very doubtful if they would, even if there were no tax discrimination.

(*f*) Effects on Small and Expanding Enterprise

Generally speaking, the effect of the tax has been greater on small than on large corporations in terms of their creation and of their expansion once they have been put on an operational footing. This accentuates the trend towards concentration of productive capacity in the hands of a relatively small number of large corporations, thereby reducing competition, creating an unhealthy price rigidity under conditions of near monopoly, and resulting in public reaction against the private enterprise system. Here is the most serious indictment of the present system of taxing corporate profits.

High corporate taxes restrict the creation of new enterprises because of their impact on the prospective return from venture capital. It appears to be increasingly difficult to secure risk capital for new ventures. The tax restricts the growth of small corporations by reducing the attractiveness of risky expansions to management; by making difficult the acquisition of outside capital on satisfactory terms; and by curtailing the amount of capital available from retained earnings. Retained earnings are of critical importance to the expansion of small companies. The method of taxing corporate income should, therefore, be revised so as to have the minimum effect on the earnings of small and growing enterprises.

4. *Business Losses*

The loss carry-over device is the best approach to the problem of business losses. The carry-forward of losses is preferable to the carry-back, which should be used over a very short period. The period of the loss carry-forward should be sufficient to allow depression losses to be offset against boom profits. The Canadian legislation is constructive and probably meets the problem of most corporations. But there is a good case for the extension of the loss carry-forward over an indefinite period, if all profit and loss contingencies are to be given consideration.

5. *Valuation of Assets*

The most desirable approach to this problem is to allow any accounting practices that are suitable to an industry or a given type of business operation, provided that the taxpayer is compelled to use his system consistently. The Canadian legislation is generally constructive in its treatment of the valuation of assets, but it would be better if it had made the diminishing balance method of depreciation optional rather than mandatory.

6. *Approach to the Problem of Double Taxation: Integration of Corporation and Personal Income Taxes*

The existing system of taxing corporate income and dividends is inequitable in that it does not touch the problem of undistributed corporate profits, and thus perpetuates the discrimination between incorporated and unincorporated businesses. Furthermore, it has adverse effects on investment in equity shares, making it difficult for any save the large and well-established companies to secure new capital to meet expansion requirements.

The heart of the problem appears to be undistributed corporate earnings. Integration of the corporate and personal income taxes seems to be necessary, therefore, on both equity and economic grounds. The minimum requirements of an acceptable plan of integration are: (1) the equitable taxation of dividend income of shareholders in all groups; (2) the prevention of undue avoidance of taxes or postponement of personal income taxation by shareholders through the retention of corporate earnings; (3) the least possible adverse effect on investment and incentive; and (4) administrative feasibility and simplicity, with due regard for revenue requirements.

(*a*) Approaches to Integration

(i) Repeal of the corporate tax

The simplest approach is the outright repeal of the tax on corporate income. This is not considered feasible for three reasons: (1) the immediate revenue loss would be intolerable; (2) it would require the use of a capital gains tax to meet the problem of undistributed corporate earnings, and a capital gains tax involves so many administrative problems that its adoption is not recommended in Canada; and (3) the tax on corporate profits, if integrated properly with the individual income tax, is considered by the writer to be a sound tax.

(ii) Exemption of dividends from personal income taxation

This exemption would not result in a relatively serious revenue loss. In 1947 the total dividends declared for tax purposes by individuals in Canada amounted to $111.8 million. But such an exemption would result in serious inequities in the graduated personal income tax based upon the ability doctrine. For this reason, the proposal is discarded.

(iii) The partnership approach

The partnership approach, which would tax all corporate earnings in the hands of the shareholders, whether or not distributed, would equalize completely taxes on undistributed profits and other forms of income. This approach is, logically, the line of uncompromising insistence on equity at all costs, but it has no recommendation beyond the realm of pure theory. It is ruled out as a complete solution on practical grounds by the character of the modern corporation and the varied patterns of financial structure and share ownership which would confront it with insoluble difficulties. As a partial solution it is unsatisfactory because of the serious complications involved in drawing a line between corporations which are to be treated as partnerships and those which are to be taxed as corporations.

(iv) The withholding approach

The withholding approach, as used in the United Kingdom, provides an equitable method of eliminating the existing differences in the taxation of distributed corporate earnings and other forms of personal income. But, if very substantial refunds are to be avoided, the lowest personal income tax rate should approximate the corporate rate. This is not the case in Canada, nor is it likely to be, so that the problem of refunds represents a practical objection to the plan.

(v) The dividends-received credit approach

The dividends-received credit plan, whether based on a complete or a partial credit allowance (as now in force in Canada), does not conform to the theoretical requirements of an acceptable plan of integration. It is not an equitable method of taxing undistributed profits, and it discriminates against low income shareholders. On grounds of equity, this plan is not as desirable as the withholding approach or the dividends-paid credit approach, and it cannot be used to eliminate completely the double taxation of corporate income without serious distortion of equity in the personal income tax structure. On the other hand, it may be a practical approach to meet the peculiar situation in Canada where such a large part of corporate dividends is paid to non-resident shareholders.

(vi) The dividends-paid credit approach

Under this plan, dividend payments are deductible from corporate income, just as is bond interest, before net taxable income is determined. The plan appears to conform to the four minimum criteria of an acceptable approach to integration outlined above. First, it provides equitable taxation of dividend income to shareholders in all groups. Second, it meets, at least in part, the problem of undistributed corporate earnings, since the corporate tax is paid only on earnings that are not paid out as dividends. Third, it would assist materially in minimizing the adverse effects on investment that follow from the present system. And fourth, there are no special administrative problems attached to the plan, as there are in the withholding approach.

The only difficulty with this plan is that its full use would result in a serious revenue loss. In 1948 total corporate profits before taxes were reported to be $2,174 million. Of this amount, $540 million was distributed as dividends. Had this amount been deductible for tax purposes, the revenue loss would have been $162 million at the 30 per cent corporate rate then in force. But if dividends were deductible from corporate income, it is likely that a much larger part of corporate income would be distributed, resulting in a much greater reduction in the yield of the corporate tax.

Part of the loss in the corporate tax yield would be recovered under the personal income tax on extra dividends paid because of their deduction from corporate income. But a large part of the dividends paid by Canadian corporations goes to the United States. The withholding tax on such dividends is at present 15 per cent. Thus a very considerable loss is incurred, when it is remembered that most of this dividend income would have been taxed in excess of 50 per cent had it been paid to resident shareholders. It is not considered feasible to raise the withholding tax to offset such a loss, because of the possible adverse effects on future American investment in Canada.[10]

7. *The Problem of Small Business*

Regardless of what approach to integration is used, the problem of the small and growing business still remains a special case which merits consideration.

The problem involves the formulation of policy which is designed on the one hand to prevent the use of the corporate form for the purpose of avoiding taxes through the retention of earnings, and on the other hand, to encourage small enterprise which must rely for the most part upon the retention of earnings to finance expansion. The task of distinguishing between proper and improper accumulation of earnings represents one of the imponderables attached to the formulation of equitable tax policy. Whatever is done, only rough justice can be achieved, and in this case it is difficult to advocate strict neutrality in tax policy when incentive taxation appears to be indicated.

The Canadian government has recognized the problem, and the tax rate is now 15 per cent on the first $10,000 of corporate income and 38 per cent on income in excess of $10,000. While corporate income is not, *per se*, a good criterion of taxpaying ability, and graduation of rate is therefore difficult to justify on theoretical grounds, nevertheless this relatively low rate on low corporate income has effected considerable relief to small com-

[10]I still consider the dividends-paid credit to be the best approach to a solution of the problem of double taxation, despite the fact of heavy dividend payments to non-resident shareholders. If a complete dividends-paid credit results in too serious a revenue loss, then a partial credit could be applied, just as a partial dividend credit is now applied at the shareholder level.

panies. One feature of the legislation which should be changed is the limitation of the low rate to one of a group of "related" companies, related as now defined in the statute. Surely blood relationship of shareholders by itself should not impose a tax penalty. Relationship should be determined by business relations between one company and another.

8. *Final Conclusion*

An attempt has been made to indicate the defects of the existing method of taxing corporate income and dividends in Canada. Some of the economic effects appear to be serious, and substantial inequity exists within the present framework. But there is no one solution to all the problems connected with this aspect of taxation. The situation requires a bold new approach, and in theory the writer leans towards the dividends-paid credit plan as at least a partial solution to the problem of integration. In view of the increase in the corporation tax rate that appears necessary to help finance the heavy defence programme, serious consideration should be given now to a better method of alleviating the problem of taxing corporate income and the dividends received by corporate shareholders. The existing situation calls for careful reconsideration—more careful than ever before—of the economic consequences of the tax treatment of corporate income in the hands of the company and its shareholders.

It is the writer's view that the corporation tax is not a good instrument of fiscal control. Heavy taxation of corporations to curb inflation may produce an inflationary rather than a stabilizing result, may impair incentives and efficiency. Such refinements as deferred depreciation and other gratuitous departures from accepted accounting practice have no place in the corporate tax structure.

CHAPTER TWO

BACKGROUND AND EVOLUTION OF THE CORPORATION TAX

INTRODUCTION

THE CANADIAN GOVERNMENT first introduced an income tax in 1917[1] to raise revenue with which to help meet the cost of World War I. The legislation provided for a tax on both personal and corporate income under the Income War Tax Act. Despite its emergency nature the tax has never been abandoned by the federal authority. Rather, it has long since become an integral and key part of the federal tax system. It will be seen in chapter III how important a revenue source the corporate tax has been in the last decade, and it is most unlikely that it will become any less important in the future.

This Act, after drastic amendments in 1926 and subsequent years, provided the basis of the federal income tax until 1948, when it was repealed and replaced with the Income Tax Act. The new statute has not altered the original law in any of its basic principles. The redrafting of the law was done, according to the Minister of Finance in his 1947 budget speech, "in an effort to improve its arrangement, to make it clearer and simpler, and to remove ambiguities and anomalies."[2] Whether this objective has been achieved is a matter of opinion, but the new legislation is generally considered to be constructive.

A full discussion of the development of the corporation tax in

[1]This was not, however, the first income tax in Canada. The Province of British Columbia had been levying such a tax since 1876, and Prince Edward Island entered the field in 1894.

[2]*House of Commons Debates*, April 29, 1947, p. 2625.

Canada would involve a separate study.[3] The discussion in this chapter will be confined to a general statement on the meaning of income, the development of the concept of the corporate tax and the problem of undistributed profits, the tax treatment of special corporations, and the problem of "ministerial discretion." Special problems arising out of the taxation of corporate income, such as the measurement of net profit and the double taxation of corporate income, will be discussed in later chapters.

INCOME VERSUS CAPITAL

The Income War Tax Act was perhaps modelled on the American income tax legislation, but it has been interpreted according to British jurisprudence. Like the British act, it has never included capital gains in taxable income. Without exploring the extremely complicated question of what comprises income, a brief indication of the principles applied in Canada and the problem arising out of income tax practice should serve as a background for later discussion.

The Canadian law has always confined itself to general principles, enumerating where possible, and applying them to specific individual cases, as appropriate. The original legislation enacted in 1917 contained a positive definition of income,[4] which re-

[3]For a detailed treatment of the Income War Tax Act, see H. A. W. Plaxton, *The Law Relating to Income Tax and Excess Profits Tax of the Dominion of Canada.* Current and historical material may be found in detail in *Canadian Tax Reporter,* vol. I, and *Canada Tax Manual.*

[4]"Sec. 3 (1). For the purposes of this Act, 'income' means the annual net profit or gain or gratuity, whether ascertained and capable of computation as being wages, salary, or other fixed amount, or unascertained as being fees or emoluments, or as being profits from a trade or commercial or financial or other business or calling, directly or indirectly received by a person from any office or employment, or from any profession or calling, or from any trade, manufacture or business, as the case may be; and shall include the interest, dividends or profits directly or indirectly received from money at interest upon any security or without security, or from stocks, or from any other investment, and, whether such gains or profits are divided or distributed or not, and also the annual profit or gain from any other source; including the income from but not the value of property acquired by gift, bequest, devise or descent; and including the income from but not the proceeds of life insurance policies paid upon the death of the person insured, or payments made or credited to the insured on life insurance endowment or annuity contracts upon the maturity of the term mentioned in the contract or upon the surrender of the contract." The above phrase—"and also the annual net profit or gain from any source;"—might have been used as a basis for taxing capital gains. In 1927 the semicolon was dropped, and the phrase was emptied of significance.

TABLE II

SUMMARY OF RATES AND EXEMPTIONS FOR FEDERAL CORPORATION INCOME TAX, 1917–1952

Taxation year	*Rate of tax*	*Amount of income exempt*
	%	$
1917	4	3,000
1918	6	3,000
1919–24	10 —when taxable income was more than $2,000 but less than $5,000 10.5 —when taxable income exceeded $5,000 (In 1920 (effective 1919) the rate was 10% but there was a provision added whereby the tax was increased by 5% on taxable income over $5,000.)	2,000
1925	10 (In 1926 (effective 1925) the increased rate on taxable income in excess of $5,000 was repealed.)	2,000
1926	8.1 (In 1927 (effective 1926) the rate was 9% but the tax was reduced by 10% giving an actual rate of of 8.1%.)	2,000
1927–29	8 (Enacted in 1928, effective 1927)	2,000
1930	10 (Enacted in 1931, effective 1930)	2,000
1931	11 —when taxable income was more than $2,000 but less than $5,000 11.55—when taxable income exceeded $5,000 (In 1932 (effective 1931) the rate was 11% but there was a provision added whereby the tax was increased by 5% on taxable income over $5,000.)	2,000
1932–33	12½ 13½ —on consolidated returns } (Enacted 1933)	nil
1934	13½ 15 —on consolidated returns } (Enacted 1935)	nil
1935–39	15 17 —on consolidated returns } (Enacted 1936)	nil
1940–46	18 20 —on consolidated returns } (Enacted 1939)	nil
1947–48	30 32 —on consolidated returns	nil
1949–50	10[a] —on the first $10,000 33 —on amount in excess of $10,000 —an additional 2% on consolidated returns	nil
1950	15 —on first $10,000 38 —on amount in excess of $10,000 —an additional 2% on consolidated returns	nil
1951	15 —on first $10,000 45.6 —on amount in excess of $10,000 —an additional 2% on consolidated returns	nil
1952[b]		

[a]It is to be noted that the special rate on the first $10,000 applies only to one of a group of related companies.

[b]Enacted October 1951 (effective January 1, 1952) 2% was added to the corporate income tax rate as a charge for old age security. In 1951 (effective January 1, 1952) the right to file consolidated return was repealed.

mained virtually unchanged until the repeal of the Income War Tax Act in 1948. The new Act does not attempt to define precisely either income or capital. What definition there is appears in very general terms. Section 2 states that "The taxable income of a taxpayer for a taxation year is his income for the year minus the deductions permitted by Division C." Section 3 provides that "The income of a taxpayer for a taxation year for the purposes of this Part is his income for the year from all sources inside or outside Canada and, without restricting the generality of the foregoing, includes income for the year from all (*a*) businesses, (*b*) property, and (*c*) offices and employments." Section 4 states that "income for a taxation year from a business or property is the profit therefrom for the year." Sections 6 to 8 and 73 enumerate what shall be included in income, and Section 10 states what shall not be included. Beyond this there is no detailed method of determining business profit set out in the statute. Implicit reliance is placed upon accounting practice, save where there is a specific limitation provided in the Act, and upon the judicial interpretation of the meaning of the terms "income," "profit," and "capital."

There are certain indications in the Act that the word "income" is not intended to include capital gains. For example, Section 7 deals with payments which are partly of an income nature and partly of a capital nature, and includes in taxable income only that part which is of an income nature. Section 6(*j*) differentiates between amounts received that were dependent upon the use or production from property, whether or not they were "instalments of the sale price" and "instalments of the sale price not dependent upon use or production." Reference is made in Section 11 (1)(*i*) to the "capital element" of an annuity as being a proper deduction in computing the income of a taxpayer. Section 12 (1)(*b*) provides that in the computation of income no deductions shall be made in respect of "an outlay, loss or replacement of capital, a payment on account of capital or an allowance in respect of depreciation, obsolescence or depletion except as expressly permitted by this Part." These sections indicate that the intention behind the legislation is to exclude capital gains from the concept of taxable income.

As suggested above, one must turn to the courts and the

decided cases to discover the difference between income and capital gains. But even there, as Plaxton points out, "No infallible criterion emerges from the cases, since each of them turns upon its own facts; but the decisions are useful as illustrations and as affording indications of the kind of considerations which may relevantly be borne in mind in approaching the problem of discriminating between an income disbursement and a capital disbursement."[5]

There is a large body of English case law on the distinction between capital and income, and the Canadian Supreme Court has generally followed the principles laid down by the British courts. The Supreme Court has said that the definition of income in the Income War Tax Act does not restrict the meaning of the word in its ordinary and natural sense, and it has consistently pronounced that the word "income" does not include capital gains.

The distinction between a capital gain and income turns on whether the gain is in the form of a profit made as a result of a business venture or carrying on a trade, or whether it is an accretion to capital. For example, in *Anderson Logging Company* v. *The King*, Duff J. said:

> In dealing with the major question it may be assumed, as it was assumed on the argument, that the distinction between the accretions to capital, such as the capital profit realized upon the sale of a capital investment, and the profit derived from the labour, or capital, or both combined, in carrying on or carrying out a venture or a business for profit, is a distinction both admissible and proper. . . .[6]

In *Merritt Realty Co.* v. *Brown*, the same judge observed:

> The principle of law governing this appeal is not in dispute or doubt. In *California Copper Syndicate* v. *Harris* ((1904) 5 Tax Cases 159) it was laid down that the test to be applied is whether the sum in dispute was "a gain made in an operation of business in carrying out a scheme for profit-making." That test was adopted by the Judicial Committee in *Commissioner of Taxes* v. *Melbourne Trust, Limited* ([1914] A.C. 1010), which decision was followed in this court in *Anderson Logging Company* v. *The King* ([1925] Can. S.C.R. 49), the decision of this court being subsequently affirmed by the Judicial

[5] *The Law Relating to Income Tax in Canada*, p. 30.
[6] [1925] S.C.R. 45, 47.

Committee of the Privy Council ([1926] A.C. 140). The test was reaffirmed by the Houses of Lords in *Ducker* v. *Rees* ([1928] A.C. 127 at 140).[7]

It is no easy task, however, to define what constitutes carrying on a trade. The Income Tax Act, Section 127 (1)(*e*) states that " 'business' includes a profession, calling, trade, manufacture or undertaking of any kind whatsoever and includes an adventure or concern in the nature of trade but does not include an office or employment." This is an adaptation of Section 237 of the British Income Tax Act, and it does not carry us far. It has been said that "it is not possible to lay down definite lines to mark out what is a business or a trade, or adventure, and to define the distinctive characteristics of each. It is the facts that establish the nature of the enterprise, so that the carrying-on of a trade is a compound fact, not a matter of law."[8]

A number of the British cases turn on the phrase "adventure in the nature of trade," which is found in the rules under Case VI in the British Act. This was not a feature of the old Canadian Income War Tax Act, but its absence did not interfere with the application of British jurisprudence to Canadian cases.

One of the most frequent points of litigation has been over the question whether single or casual transactions constitute trading. In view of the British judicial decisions it is difficult to lay down a general principle.

In *Erichsen* v. *Last* it was held that "when a person habitually does a thing which is capable of producing a profit for the purpose of producing a profit and enters into a contract habitually, he is carrying on a trade or business."[9] This judgment introduces the notion of habitual action as well as profit motivation as elements of carrying on trade. But later cases indicated that a single and isolated venture might be considered as carrying on a trade,

[7][1932] S.C.R. 187, 188.

[8]"Trade or Business," *Taxation*, March 4, 1950, p. 497. But see Simon, who says, "Whether or not a trade is being carried on is a mixed question of fact on the one hand and of law on the other. It is for the Appeal Commissioners to consider whether there is a trade or the exercise of a trade by considering a number of business facts (*Wilcock* v. *Pinto & Co.*, [1925] 1 K.B. 30). But a question of law is also involved, inasmuch as failure by the Appeal Commissioners to appreciate the nature of the facts submitted in relation to a trade may render their decision invalid in law (*Bomford* v. *Osborne*, [1942] A.C. 14)." *Simon's Income Tax*, II, 19.

[9](1881) 4 T.C. 422, 427.

and that motive had no necessary relationship to the matter.

The leading case regarding income tax liability on the profits derived from a single transaction is *Martin* v. *Lowry.*[10] A machinery merchant who had never had any connection with the linen trade purchased surplus linen from the government and sold it at a profit. The House of Lords held that the fact that there was only one purchase did not prevent the transaction from being a trade. In *Rutledge* v. *Commissioners of Inland Revenue*[11] the profit from the purchase and sale of a large quantity of toilet paper was held to be taxable on the ground that in the case of a purchase made for no purpose except that of resale at a profit, the transaction is in the nature of trade, even though it may be wholly insufficient to constitute a trade by itself. In *Beynon* v. *Ogg*[12] it was held that a company carrying on business as coal merchants was liable for tax on the profits made from a single speculative purchase of wagons for sale to its customers. The mere fact that this was an isolated transaction did not exclude it from the company's business transactions.

In *Pickford* v. *Quirke,* where the taxpayer had been interested in buying and selling cotton mills on several occasions, and while each transaction considered separately was a capital one, it was held that taken collectively they were carried out in the course of business, and therefore taxable. Rowlatt J. said:

> Now of course it is very well known that one transaction of buying and selling a thing does not make a man a trader, but if it is repeated and becomes systematic, then he becomes a trader and the profits of the transaction, not taxable so long as they remain isolated, become taxable as items in a trade as a whole, setting losses against profits, of course, and combining them all into one trade.[13]

Quite obviously a purchase and resale of property may be either a trading transaction or a transposition of capital. It was stated by Rowlatt J. in *Pearn* v. *Miller*:

> If it is desired to tax the difference between what a man has bought goods for, or property for, and sold them for, you can only tax

[10][1926] 1 K.B. 550 (C.A.); (1927) 11 T.C. 297; [1927] A.C. 312.
[11](1929) 14 T.C. 490.
[12](1918) 7 T.C. 125.
[13](1927-1928) 13 T.C. 251, 263.

it in my judgment, if you can say that what he did was a trade or adventure or concern in the nature of trade. I think you cannot get under Case VI a tax out of appreciation of property; you have to get it under Case I. There is no halfway house between a transaction which is a trading transaction and one which is a sale of a capital asset.[14]

But the dividing line is difficult to perceive. For example, in *Gloucester Railway Carriage and Wagon Co. Ltd.* v. *Commissioners of Inland Revenue*[15] the litigation arose over the nature of a transaction made by a company which carried on the manufacture of wagons for the purpose of selling them or letting them out on hire. It sold the wagons that had been hired out, and contended that this was a sale of assets, and that the isolated transaction resulted in a capital profit. But the House of Lords decided that in fact the transaction was part of the company's business of making a profit out of wagons, and that the profit derived from the isolated transaction was taxable.

In *Jones* v. *Leeming*,[16] however, the situation was reversed. The taxpayer, along with other persons, acquired two rubber estates with a view of selling them to a public company to be formed for the purpose. The General Commissioners decided that the property had been acquired with the sole object of turning it over at a profit, and that the taxpayer at no time had any intention of holding it as an investment. It was held that the assessment should be discharged, and this decision was affirmed by the House of Lords. Similarly, in *Pearn* v. *Miller*[17] it was held that the profit resulting from the purchase and sale of a number of properties by a builder's foreman on his own account was not taxable under Case VI.

It is apparent in these decisions that whether or not a transaction is in the nature of a trade depends upon the circumstances peculiar to each case. There may be the carrying on of a trade even though there was no intention of making a profit. In the *Incorporated Council of Law Reporting Case* it was held that "it is not essential to the carrying on of trade that the people carry-

[14]*Simon's Income Tax*, II, 23.
[15][1925] A.C. 469.
[16][1930] A.C. 415.
[17](1927) 11 T.C. 610.

ing it on should make a profit, nor is it even necessary to the carrying on of trade that the people carrying it on should desire or wish to make a profit."[18] And in *Commissioners of Inland Revenue* v. *Stonehaven Recreation Ground Trustees*[19] it was held that the question of what constitutes carrying on a trade is not simply dependent upon motives, or even upon the general objects of an operation. It depends rather on what is actually done, and on the practical effect of what is done.

It is the border-line cases that cause the difficulty, and the British court decisions have been made, of course, with reference to the British income tax law which clearly specifies sources of income.[20] There are rules contained in each of the schedules and cases providing how the profits are to be computed, and if a profit or gain cannot be brought within any of the provisions of the various schedules, then it is not income within the purview of the Act. The Canadian Income Tax Act, on the other hand, does not attempt to classify the source of income, except specifically to include certain types of transactions within the purview of the word "income," even though they are "capital" in their nature, and to exclude certain transactions which are "income" by their nature.

It has been indicated above that the Canadian courts have followed the British decisions when the matter of capital *versus* income came up under the Income War Tax Act. What the interpretation of the new Act will be is still a matter of conjecture.

[18](1888) 3 T.C. 105, 113.

[19](1929) 15 T.C. 419, 425.

[20]The tax under Schedule D is charged by paragraph 2 of Schedule D in six cases, as follows:

Case I – Tax in respect of any trade not contained in any other Schedule.

Case II – Tax in respect of any profession . . . or vocation not contained in any other Schedule.

Case III – Tax in respect of profits of an uncertain value and in respect of other income described in the rules applicable to this Case.

Case IV – Tax in respect of income arising from Securities out of the United Kingdom, except such income as is charged under Schedule C.

Case V – Tax in respect of income arising from possessions out of the United Kingdom.

Case VI – Tax in respect of any annual profits or gains not falling under any of the foregoing Cases and not charged by virtue of any other Schedule.

It has ignored the old definition of income, and as pointed out by R. deWolfe MacKay, K.C., "The main problem . . . is whether or not the Canadian Courts are likely to interpret the word 'income' as used in its undefined context in the new Act in its broadest sense in the manner in which the American Courts have done, rather than in the manner in which the English Courts have done. . . ."[21]

The position of capital gains is thus obscure under the existing legislation, and during the past year there has been considerable agitation to have the Income Tax Act amended specifically to exclude them from tax. A recent Canadian Exchequer Court decision in *McDonough* v. *Minister of National Revenue*[22] has caused no little anxiety on the part of many taxpayers regarding the taxation of capital gains, and the decision in *Brown* v. *Minister of National Revenue*,[23] decided by the Income Tax Appeal Board in February 1950, has added to the anxiety. Both decisions were arrived at by applying the well-known test laid down in *California Copper Syndicate* v. *Harris*, when Clerk L. J. stated:

> It is quite a well settled principle in dealing with questions of assessment of Income Tax, that where the owner of an ordinary investment chooses to realize it, and obtains a greater price for it than he originally acquired it at, the enhanced price is not profit . . . assessable to Income Tax. But it is equally well established that enhanced values obtained from realisation or conversion of securities may be so assessable, where what is done is not merely a realisation or change of investment, but an act done in what is truly the carrying on, or carrying out, of a business. . . .
>
> What is the line which separates the two classes of cases may be difficult to define, and each case must be considered according to its facts; the question to be determined being—Is the sum of gain that has been made a mere enhancement of value by realising a security, or is it a gain made in an operation of business in carrying out a scheme for profit-making?[24]

In the *McDonough Case* the taxpayer conceived the idea of amalgamating a number of mining properties under one new

[21]"Definition of the Term 'Income,'" Address to the Taxation Section of the Canadian Bar Association, Washington, D.C., Sept. 20, 1950.

[22][1949] C.T.C. 213.

[23](1950) 1 Tax A.B.C. 461.

[24](1904) 5 T.C. 159, 165-6.

company. Arrangements for acquisition of the properties were made and the new company was incorporated, but not until the appellant had found a purchaser for an initial block of shares which he had contracted to take up from the new company. By successive option agreements the appellant took up further blocks of shares, in each case having previously completed arrangements for their resale at a profit. At no time did he advance any funds of his own, and no stock of the new company was taken up for which a resale had not already been arranged. The appellant's active interest in the promotion and direction of the project extended from April to December of 1939, when he entered the air force. During that period he had no other occupation, and the promotion of this project occupied his entire time and attention.

Tax was claimed by the Minister of National Revenue on the profit made from this transaction, and the Exchequer Court held that the profits received by the appellant were of a revenue nature as being profits or gain derived from a trade or business. It was stated by Cameron J.:

> It seemed to the Court that the appellant organized himself with the help of a friend into carrying out a scheme for profit-making. . . . If a man engaged in a transaction with the express purpose of profit-making he was carrying on a transaction in the nature of a business. "Business" might be defined as anything which occupied the time and attention of a man for profit; the money of the appellant's friend and the attention of the appellant had been directed to making a profit by selling the options.[25]

The *McDonough Case* followed a long line of decisions, and was consistent with established jurisprudence. Why, then, did it cause such a reaction? For one thing, viewed uncritically, it seemed to run counter to the notion that the profit from an isolated transaction constituted a tax-free capital gain. But this by itself is a mistaken assumption, as seen in many of the British decisions. McDonough was in the mining business, and quite properly the venture in question was considered a trading transaction. Perhaps more important was the feeling in the mining industry that the decision cast some doubt on the ruling made by the Department of National Revenue in 1941 that the profits made

[25][1949] C.T.C. 213, 228.

by a prospector and his backers on the sale of a mine constituted non-taxable capital gains. But the status of prospectors' gains was clarified in 1950 when Section 73B was added to the Act specifically exempting them from tax.

The *Brown Case* involved transactions made by an employee of a packing company in charge of receiving and shipping eggs. In 1946 in addition to his regular duties he made forty-five purchases and thirty-three sales of frozen eggs on a wholesale basis for his own account, from which he realized a net profit of over $4,000. He also received some $1,200 in commissions on sales made for a broker. The Tax Appeal Board decided that Brown had engaged in the business of dealing in eggs, and that the profits derived from such a business were taxable income.[26] The significance of this decision is that it is a short step from the taxation of the profit made from the speculative ventures in egg trading to the taxation of gains made in casual stock-market speculation or, indeed, in any type of speculation. Subsequent decisions of the Board have given rise to a fear that a new pattern of income tax law interpretation is being evolved.

A case in point is *Central Assets Ltd.* v. *Minister of National Revenue.*[27] The company was incorporated in 1926 by two men who had extensive land holdings in Saskatchewan, most of which were under agreement for sale. These two shareholders sold to their company the agreements for the sale of land which they held for an amount which was payable over a period of years. The company acquired no new assets, but from time to time purchasers under agreements originally assigned to it defaulted. The land reverted to the company and was resold. The government contended that profit on the sale of such property was taxable income, but the company argued that it was purely a realization company, and that any excess in the amounts received from over the amounts paid for such property should be treated as a non-

[26](1950) 1 Tax A.B.C. 461, 468. The question which arises in this case arose in *Morrison* v. *Minister of National Revenue,* [1928] Ex. C.R. 75; *Anna Hinchey Martin* v. *Minister of National Revenue,* [1948] C.T.C. 189; *The Economic Trust Co. of the City of Winnipeg* v. *Minister of National Revenue,* [1946] C.T.C. 142. The facts are not exactly the same as in the *Brown Case,* but they were considered sufficiently similar for the application of the principles set forth therein to the *Brown Case.*

[27](1950) 2 Tax A.B.C. 323.

taxable appreciation of capital. The Board held that the profits were taxable. It was stated in the judgment:

. . . the whole object of this company, from its incorporation, was to deal in these parcels of land and sell them as advantageously as possible. I find as a fact, therefore, that it was the business of this company to dispose of these parcels of property, at a profit if possible, and that that was their business. Under these circumstances, any profit realized by the appellant on the sale of the properties in question was income in its hands from its business, and was liable for income tax under the provisions of the act.[28]

No reference was made in this judgment to the two British cases dealing with land realization companies that seem to have some relevance to the questions that were before the Board. Some observers felt that this decision was a departure from precedent.[29]

In *Badame* v. *Minister of National Revenue*[30] the Board ruled that in this case the gain from betting on horse races was taxable income. The appellant raised and raced horses, trained them, and took his horses from one track to another. In addition he made a practice of betting on his own horses as well as on horses owned and raced by others. As a result of this judgment the appellant became taxable on betting winnings of $8,435.44 and $4,907.86 in 1947 and 1948, respectively. The decision in this case appears to have turned on the fact that the appellant was in the business of raising, training, and racing horses. In *Walker* v. *Minister of National Revenue*,[31] where a farmer won substantial sums from betting on horse races, the winnings were held not to be taxable income.

In *Cragg* v. *Minister of National Revenue*,[32] the appellant, an employee of a life insurance company, purchased eleven houses and sold nine at a net profit of over $61,000. He appealed his assessment for 1946 with respect to some $7,500 representing profit on the sale of properties. It was held that because he purchased them with the intention of selling them in the hope of

[28] *Ibid.*, at p. 331.

[29] See, for example, Stuart Thom, "About Your Taxes," *Financial Post*, Nov. 4, 1950.

[30] (1951) 3 Tax A.B.C. 226.

[31] (1950) 2 Tax A.B.C. 159. This decision followed *Graham* v. *Green*, [1925] 2 K.B. 37; see *Gordon's Digest*, p. 89.

[32] (1950) 3 Tax A.B.C. 203.

realizing a profit, he had therefore been carrying on a business, and the profit was taxable income.

In another case, *Campbell* v. *Minister of National Revenue,*[33] a retired police officer had entered into a number of profitable real estate transactions which culminated, in the relevant years, in the building and selling of two large apartment houses. He stated that the houses or apartments were built or purchased to give his family a home, but that in each case the home proved unsuitable. It was held that the profit realized on the sale of these properties was taxable income.

These decisions appear to indicate that the test of taxability is the presence of an intention to make a profit. If motivation is to be the test of the distinction between a capital gain and income, a capital gain is likely to be a rare occurrence. Indeed the sale of a company's assets may result in taxable income.[34]

The question is whether these decisions go beyond the intent of the statute. In his budget speech of March 29, 1950, the Minister of Finance reiterated the government policy with respect to the taxation of capital gains:

> Perhaps I might also take this opportunity, in view of recent public interest in the question, to assure the house that it is not the policy of the government to tax capital gains. Under any income tax law there is always a very difficult problem in drawing a line between gains which are profits from carrying on a trade or business and those which are not. To my knowledge no tax legislation has ever been passed in any country that has removed all doubts on this score. In England, where our basis of income tax had its origin, the matter has been settled almost entirely by the courts, taking into account the facts in each individual case. Much as I would like to introduce greater certainty, I do not believe that it can be done satisfactorily by legislation. We now have a readily available income tax appeal board that has been set up to determine questions of this sort.[35]

[33] (1951) 3 Tax A.B.C. 315.

[34] See, for example, *Cabus Creek Logging Company Ltd.* v. *Minister of National Revenue,* (1951) 3 Tax A.B.C. 305. The company made a profit from the sale of all merchantable standing timber on a property covered by a timber licence held by the appellant. The appellant claimed that its main object was logging, that it had purchased the timber licence in question for that purpose, but finding that it would be uneconomical to log it had sold the timber, and considered the proceeds to be capital. It was held that the profit was taxable income.

[35] *House of Commons Debates,* March 28, 1950, p. 1217.

In view of the recent Canadian decisions it is apparent that the law and the common understanding of the public with regard to what constitutes a capital gain are a long way apart. The courts appear gradually to be extending the concept of "business transaction" to include casual speculative profits which a few years ago would probably have been held exempt from tax as capital gains.

There is currently a considerable volume of Canadian opinion in favour of amending the Act by defining capital and income in order to clarify the situation.[36] But as the Minister of Finance pointed out in his budget speech in March 1950, it is extremely doubtful that definition of income pointed at eliminating capital gains could really result in a solution to the problem. Stuart Thom has recently made an excellent comment on the proposal, as follows:

> "What the Income Tax needs is a definition of income which will make it impossible to collect a tax on capital gains," the President of the Board of Trade, Toronto, was reported to have said a few days ago, and almost in the same breath: "I do not want to suggest the language that should be used because it is the responsibility of the Department of Justice and its officers to find the proper language to prevent the application of a capital gains tax not intended."
>
> Before shifting the responsibility in this way, it is worth pausing a moment to consider that the legal lights in the Department of Justice and their brethren in the Department of National Revenue, skilled as they are in drafting tax legislation, have over the years devoted more of their time and talents to sharpening the tax axe than to dulling it.
>
> Businessmen, fearful of what may be in store for them and looking for shelter by way of legislation, might be well advised to undertake for themselves the drafting of protective clauses they think necessary. It would at least start out in the right direction.

[36]For example, Mr. Beverley Matthews, K.C., in an address to the Toronto Board of Trade on October 2, 1950, made the following statement: "What is the remedy? I say that the only remedy is by legislation. That there are difficulties in achieving accuracy and certainty in a definition of 'income' for tax purposes is fully accepted. But it is not impossible. . . . Experience would undoubtedly show weaknesses in the first attempt and probably further weaknesses in subsequent attempts. Let us accept that absolute perfection would never be achieved. Surely, however, it is possible to come close enough to the ideal. With the most modest confidence Parliament should feel assured of improving the present situation. And in any event, the position could hardly be worse than it is at the present time."

This does not imply, however, and the spokesmen for business do not suggest that the Minister of Finance and those advising him have their tongue in their cheek when they disclaim any intention to tax capital gains. The villain in the piece appears to be some twist which the courts have given to the Act.

To be fair to Ottawa, it should be noted that the new Act makes a real effort, despite what some of its critics may say, to avoid overstepping the invisible line dividing taxable from non-taxable gain. The effort is of a negative variety and consists of using words like "income" and "profits" without defining them in anything but the most general terms.

Section 3 says that income includes income from businesses and property. Section 4 says that income from a business or property is the profit therefrom. Business and property are defined with some care, but the words that count are left wide open—which is to say that in the final analysis words like "profit" or "benefit" will have the meaning which a court will give them.

The decision of a court, where it is not controlled by a prior decision on identical or very similar facts, is governed by general principles laid down in earlier decisions. The most critical opponent of capital gains taxation can have little fault to find with the principles which the courts profess to follow. They are couched in language which appears to be the model of clarity and definiteness. The trouble starts when those principles are applied to particular cases, particularly those on the borderline which lead to hard decisions.

Presumably the principles which should govern the distinction between taxable profits and nontaxable capital gains could be hammered out and lodged in the Act. It would be a harrowing undertaking, as anyone who has worked with tax legislation is well aware, and assumes that the great multitude of taxpayers are all of one mind about a number of vital matters.

Actually this is a quite unwarranted assumption. Many interests other than those of business claim a part in drafting tax legislation and if the principles presently followed by the courts are set aside in the course of searching for something better, the result is more likely to be chaos than agreement.

But if the task were at last accomplished, what would be gained? The principles stated in the Act would still have to be applied to particular cases and the courts would continue to perform the function they perform today, but within the rigid terms of the statute. If the principles were stated with any degree of generality, the uncertainty which is assailed as vicious and iniquitous in the present set-up would remain. If the policy were to state principles with respect to particular situations, the results might be deplorable from the businessman's point of view.

The belief that our legislators would choose to legislate certain categories of profits out of the tax act at the cost, say, of raising the personal rates or lowering the personal exemptions, is touching but unrealistic. The tendency could quite easily be the other way, not because of any open antagonism to the theory of exempting capital gains, but because those gains offer a ready source of much needed revenue.

On several occasions, Parliament has amended the act to declare that certain receipts were taxable after a court decision had said they were not. There have been very few amendments going the other way. Only one comes readily to mind, namely, the mining promotion exemption contained in section 73B passed last spring. The unfortunate feature of section 73B is that the specific exemption of profits of a certain character arising from a mining promotion may lead by irresistible implication to the taxation of similar profits where the promotion is in another field of business activity and which are presently regarded as not taxable. Tax legislation directed to particular matters can be a two-edged and erratic weapon.

Canada is not generally regarded as a socialist country, but a more sympathetic understanding of the practices and rewards of capitalism and free enterprise can be expected from the courts than from Parliament. It may be difficult even impossible in close cases to forecast the decision in any given case, but that is the price of enjoying the protection which the courts have always been ready to afford against the demands of the state.

Moreover, it is misleading and inaccurate to say that the courts under the present statutes interpret taxable income very differently from its commonly understood business meaning. In the first place the new Income Tax Act has not received judicial attention in any reported decision. There may be, in some of its sections, opportunities for the Government to claim tax on gains now regarded as exempt. At the best, these possibilities are matters of opinion only. Such claims have not yet been made by the Tax Department and if and when made, they will have to pass the scrutiny of the courts.

As regards recent decisions of the Tax Board and the Exchequer Court under the Income War Tax Act, some of which have been severely criticized, they all are faithfully grounded on well established principles derived from the law of England. Whether these principles have been wrongly understood or applied is another question. If the principles themselves are satisfactory, and no one has yet come forward with improved versions, hasty recourse to Parliament is not a recommended cure.[37]

The basic problem is not whether an attempt should be made to amend the Income Tax Act so as to make a clear distinction between income and capital receipts. Rather, it is the question whether capital gains should be taxed. Strict adherence to the theory of taxation in accordance with ability to pay leaves no logical grounds for excluding capital gains from the concept of taxable income. At this point the problem becomes one of deciding whether capital gains should be treated as ordinary income or made subject to a special tax.

Capital gains are usually casual and irregular, and in the absence of some averaging device there would often be a severe tax penalty on such income if subject to normal tax under a graduated rate structure. Moreover, if capital gains are to be taxed, losses on capital account should be deductible. If capital gains are treated as ordinary income, capital losses should be deductible from all income. Perhaps this procedure is justified on theoretical grounds as being in accordance with the ability doctrine. But it appears more desirable to confine deductions on account of capital losses to receipts from capital gains.

On balance if capital gains are to be taxed it seems that they should be subject to a special tax, as in the United States. It is quite possible that there will be a popular demand in Canada for such a tax. The typical taxpayer receives his total income in the form of either salary or wages and of course pays full tax on such income. Continuing conditions of inflation with increasing tax-free capital gains accruing to a minority of Canadian taxpayers may result in such obvious tax inequity that such windfall income will have to be taxed. This may become an important policy question in the immediate future.

Certainly a capital gains tax would add considerably to the national revenue. But against this is the fact that it would necessitate drastic changes in the Act and would result in complete

[37] *Financial Post*, Nov. 8, 1950.

negation of all the case law on which the present procedure is based. Far from providing a solution to the problem of distinguishing between capital and income is concerned, a capital gains tax would leave the situation unchanged. It would still be necessary to decide what constitutes a capital gain for tax purposes. On balance it appears that the imposition of a capital gains tax at this time is undesirable, and that it is also undesirable to attempt a revision of the statute to define capital and income.

The Changing Concept of the Corporation Tax

1. *Background*

It would be an interesting diversion to explore the philosophical background of the corporation tax. All that can be done here, however, is to indicate the changing concept of the tax in Parliament, and the complications that have developed from it. The rationale of the tax is discussed in chapter III.

In the early days of taxing corporate profits in Canada the corporation apparently was not considered to be a taxable entity, separate from its shareholders. In British Columbia, where an income tax was first imposed in 1876, all dividend income was excluded from the personal income tax base. It was only in the 1930's that this practice was modified, when dividends were subjected to a graduated surtax. Prince Edward Island also excluded dividend income from the personal tax. The Canadian Income War Tax Act, as it was enacted in 1917, applied the same rate (4 per cent) to corporate income as was applied to personal income (save for the graduated rate of the personal supertax starting at $6,000), and corporate income was subject to the same basic exemption of $3,000 as was personal income in the case of married persons. Corporate dividends were considered to be income, being specifically included in the definition of income, Section 3 (1). But it was provided in Section 3 (1)(*d*) that "for the purpose of the normal tax, the income embraced in a personal return shall be credited with the amount received as dividends upon the stock or from the net earnings of any company or other person which is taxable upon its income under this Act."

Thus, through the exemption of dividends from normal personal tax, there was complete integration of the corporate and normal personal taxes, and to this extent the problem of the double taxation of corporate income did not exist. Surtax rates still applied, however, to dividends in the hands of individuals. The underlying philosophy of the taxation of corporate income was not that of treating the corporation as a separate taxable entity, as distinct from the shareholder. Rather, the corporate tax was aimed at a point in the income stream, i.e., the corporate net profit, and was considered a tax on the shareholders. For this reason, the shareholder was not required to pay tax on his share of corporate profit when it finally reached him in the form of dividends. This was a simple and straightforward concept, and there were relatively few problems as long as it was followed. For example, under complete integration of the two taxes there is no problem connected with using the corporate form as a tax avoidance device, and had Parliament clung to the original concept immeasurable grief from a legislative and administrative standpoint would have been avoided.

James Mavor, an outstanding Canadian economist of his time, saw the danger that the corporation might be singled out as a taxpayer in its own right, and taxed as though separate from its shareholders. Writing in 1900, he said:

> In the popular mind while some corporations are associated with certain prominent personalities who may or may not really own any considerable part of the stock, corporations are in general supposed to possess an entity apart from the persons who compose them, and that taxes paid by them are therefore not taken from the pockets of individuals, but are taken from an abstraction whose character is open to suspicion. This illusion is similar in kind to that which is prevalent about the taxation of land, the idea in both cases being that a tax may be paid by a thing and not by a person.[38]

Mavor's fears have, of course, been realized fully. But there is ample evidence that great pains were taken at the outset to avoid double taxation. From 1917 to 1925 the basic concept of the corporation tax appears to have remained unchanged. The corporation tax rate was changed[39] in 1918 and again in 1919.

[38]"The Taxation of Corporations in Ontario," *Journal of the Canadian Bankers' Association*, July 1900, pp. 336-7.

[39]The corporate tax rates from 1917 to 1951, as well as basic exemptions, are given in Table II.

These new rates no longer corresponded with the personal rates, and this may mark the point where corporate income began to be considered a thing apart.

In 1926 the whole structure of individual tax rates was overhauled. The old normal rate and the graduated rates for supertax were replaced with a single graduated rate structure. At the same time, the exemption of corporate dividends from personal tax was abolished, so that for 1925 and subsequent years such dividends became taxable in the hands of the shareholders. From that time forward the Canadian legislation was based upon the principle of taxing corporate income, first in the hands of the company as such, and again upon distribution to the shareholders in the form of dividends, actual or constructive. As will be seen presently, this precipitated a new problem with respect to undistributed profits, resulting in endless complications.

An official rationalization of this policy was made in the debates of the House of Commons in May and June, 1926. The Minister of Customs and Excise, speaking for the Minister of Finance, said that the change had been made in response to general requests from taxpayers that earned income be taxed at a lower rate than unearned income. He indicated that the government had been unable to discover a satisfactory method of achieving this result, but felt that it was a step in the right direction to tax dividends as heavily as earned income. The ability to pay doctrine was invoked as an argument for this policy, and it was contended that a person receiving $10,000 dividend income should pay tax on it just as a person pays on $10,000 of earned income.

After the change of government that resulted from the general election in 1930, an attempt was made to provide relief from double taxation. Mr. R. B. Bennett, who was then Minister of Finance as well as Prime Minister, made several tax proposals in his first budget speech in June 1931. Among these was a resolution which would have exempted dividends from personal income taxation up to one-half the taxpayer's income, but not in an amount exceeding $10,000. His explanation of the proposal was as follows: "In addition it is proposed that dividends from Canadian corporations, up to $10,000, shall be exempt from taxation, to the extent of one-half the income of the taxpayer. In other words, if a man has an income of $20,000 per annum, of which $10,000 is derived as dividends from Canadian corporations, he will not pay a second tax on his dividends, because it has already been paid through the tax paid by the company. That was the law at one time and still is the law in most countries."[40] This resolution, along with others, caused an outbreak of strong opposition, and the debate was very acrimonious; it was charged, among other things, that the tax proposals were designed to favour the Prime Minister personally, and his friends. In the end the proposed dividend exemption was discarded, along with most of the other proposed income tax changes. It was many years indeed before any further official attention was paid, publicly, at least, to the problem of double taxation.

2. *Tax Avoidance—The Problem of Undistributed Profits*

The change in principle resulted in serious problems for the administration which in turn later raised serious problems for the taxpayer. Most of these problems hinged on the need to prevent the use of the corporate form for tax avoidance purposes, especially as personal income tax rates rose.

The original statute took cognizance of the possibility of avoiding surtax on personal income through failure to distribute earnings. Section 3 (4) provided that for purposes of supertax only, an individual was required to return and pay tax on his share of undistributed profits of a corporation, just as though they had in fact been distributed to him, "unless the Minister is of the opinion that the accumulation of such undivided and undistributed gains and profits is not made for the purpose of evading the tax, and is not in excess of what is reasonably required for the purposes of the business."[41]

This section was repealed in 1919, and the substituted section, while expressing somewhat the same idea in a negative way, demonstrates a changing attitude towards corporate income, indicating that more and more the corporation was being considered as a separate entity, distinct from its shareholders. The new Section 3 (4) provided that the income of a corporation should

[40]*House of Commons Debates*, June 1, 1931, p. 2174.

[41]This is the introduction of the doctrine of Ministerial Discretion, which will be discussed later.

not be considered income of the shareholders unless distribution was withheld for purposes of tax avoidance. This is in contrast with the original provision, which considered as income to the shareholder his proportionate share of a company's earnings unless distribution were withheld for some good reason.

It was not until 1924 that thought was given to the position of undistributed corporate income on the winding up or discontinuance of a company. In that year the English Court of Appeal held that accumulated corporate income, distributed during the liquidation of a company, was not the payment of a dividend, but simply the distribution of the company's capital. Any profit to the shareholders was deemed a capital gain, and not subject to tax.[42] In the same year the Canadian tax law was amended to counter this decision by adding Section 3 (9) as follows: "On the winding-up, discontinuance or reorganization of the business of any incorporated company, the distribution in any form of the property of the company shall be deemed to be the payment of a dividend to the extent that the Company has on hand undistributed income."

It soon became apparent that there were loopholes through which corporations could escape the provisions of this section. With the abolition of the exemption of dividends from the normal personal tax in 1926, it became even more important to plug these loopholes. This was the beginning of a long battle of wits between the administration and the taxpayers which was never entirely successful from the former's viewpoint, and resulted in a considerable complication of the tax law.

Since dividends were now taxable in the hands of shareholders, resulting in double taxation, intercorporate dividends raised the problem of triple taxation. In 1926 the law was amended by adding Section 3 (12) to exempt dividends paid by one corporation to another. But this added still further avenues of escape from personal tax which required attention. For example, a person owning a company with a considerable amount of undistributed earnings could create a new company and sell his shares to it at a price calculated to include the entire undistributed income of the first company. The first company could then de-

[42]*Inland Revenue Commissioners* v. *Burrell*, [1924] 2 K.B. 52.

clare a dividend equal to its entire undistributed income. This division would be free of tax to the second company, which could then use the dividend in part payment of the shares of the first company bought from the owner. Thus the owner could escape tax on the undistributed earnings of the first company.

A road block against this was set up in 1926 by Section 4 (11):

> Where a person or persons owning shares of a corporation transfers such shares or a portion thereof to a second corporation acting as his or their agent, trustee or attorney or promoted at his or their instance or controlled by him or them, which second corporation subsequently receives a dividend from the first mentioned corporation and applies the income thus received, in whole or in part, directly or indirectly
> (*a*) in payment of the shares purchased by the second corporation from such person or persons: or,
> (*b*) in the discharge of any liability incurred to such person or persons by reason of and in connection with the purchase of such shares: or,
> (*c*) in the discharge of a loan obtained by the second corporation for the purpose of paying for such shares,
> then such person or persons shall be taxable in respect of such dividend as if he or they had received it in the year that the first mentioned corporation declared the dividend.

In 1924 a provision had been enacted, Section 3 (9), to ensure that undistributed earnings could not be distributed tax free as "property" of a corporation on winding up or reorganization. It was necessary in 1926 to go further and prevent, in Section 4 (12), avoidance of personal tax by the transfer of an income surplus to capital account by the issue of new shares. Further restriction was provided in the same year by Section 4 (9) to prevent, among other things, the distribution of a capital surplus without first distributing, or at least paying tax on, accumulated income. This section applied only to reduction and redemption, and it was not until 1943 that it was amended to include conversion of shares.

Another change was made in 1926 by adding Section 4 (10):

> Where a corporation, having undistributed income on hand, redeems its shares at a premium paid out of such income, the premium shall be deemed to be a dividend and to be income received by the shareholder.

This section was amended in 1934 to provide that the premium should be a taxable dividend, whether or not the company had undistributed income on hand, and whether or not the premium was paid out of such income.

Under this section the case *National Trust* v. *Minister of National Revenue*[43] arose. Sir Lyman Melvin Jones held 2,900 of the 7 per cent preferred shares of the Massey-Harris Co. Ltd. After the shares had been issued, supplementary letters patent gave the company the right to redeem the preference shares at 110 or, at the shareholder's option, exchange them for 5 per cent preference shares. Sir Lyman's shares were redeemed at 110. The premium was assessed as income. The assessment was contested on the ground that the company had transferred undistributed income to "surplus account," and that the company's funds were therefore not undistributed income on hand. The Court held that the transfer of undistributed income to "surplus account" did not change the character of the undistributed income on hand, and the premium was held to be taxable.

The same question came before the Court in 1939 in *Executors of Massey* v. *Minister of National Revenue*,[44] affirmed on appeal to the Supreme Court. It concerned a redemption of the same class of Massey-Harris shares prior to the 1934 amendment noted above. It was argued that the shares were redeemed out of the proceeds of the sale of new shares, a fact borne out by the bank records of the company. The undistributed income had been invested in physical plant. It was held by the Court (Davis J. dissenting) that the source of the actual money used for redemption made no difference, and the premium was held to be taxable.

In 1926 another measure was incorporated into the law to prevent the funds of a company from being distributed to and used by a shareholder virtually as his own without payment of tax. The new amendment, Section 4 (8), provided that any loan or advance by a corporation to a shareholder shall be deemed a dividend. This provision did not apply to loans or advances made

[43][1935] Ex. C.R. 167. [44][1939] Ex. C.R. 41 and [1940] S.C.R. 91.

by a corporation in the ordinary course of its business, where the lending of money is part of such business.

The prohibitions on the various ways of distributing undivided profits, either directly or through capitalization, resulted in a serious problem where large accumulations had been built up over the years. In 1930, Section 19 (1) was amended to make the distribution of such earnings on winding up, discontinuance, or reorganization taxable only to the extent to which the company "has on hand undistributed income earned in the taxation period 1930 and subsequent periods." In effect, this meant that any corporation could now make a tax-free distribution of all retained profits earned prior to 1930. This right continued until 1934, when the section was restored to its original form, and, effective July 3 of that year, full tax had to be paid on the distribution, actual or constructive, of all undivided profits from 1917 on. Thus the problem of large accumulations remained unsolved, and the law has since been amended on two different occasions to provide relief. These amendments will be discussed presently.

In 1936 a new prohibition was added to the law in Section 19 (2) to prevent shareholders of a company about to be wound up from incorporating a new company and selling their shareholdings to it. By this device a tax-free distribution might be made by the first company to the second, and the second company, having no undistributed income on hand, could on liquidation effect a tax-free distribution to the shareholders. The new section provided that the distribution from the first to the second company is a taxable dividend, and, being income, is taxable again in the hands of the shareholders of the second company upon distribution. The triple tax feature of this section could be avoided in legitimate cases of dissolution of subsidiaries by having the subsidiary declare a dividend of all surplus income before winding up.

The final steps in the series of amendments designed to prevent tax-free distribution of the undivided profits of companies came with the adoption and subsequent amendments of Sections 32A and 32B.

Section 32A, enacted in 1938, was designed to reinforce all the other prohibitions discussed above, and to provide a means by which the government could prevent any conceivable tax avoidance on the distribution of corporate earnings. Accordingly, subsection (1) provided that where the Treasury Board is of the opinion that the main purpose for which any transaction was effected was the avoidance or reduction of tax liability, the Board may make such adjustment of tax liability as it sees fit.

Subsection (2) set out one set of circumstances where the Treasury Board is entitled to find that the main purpose of a transaction was to avoid taxation. It was sufficiently wide to cover almost any sale of shares of a corporation with undivided profits on hand. It was worded, in part, as follows:

> . . . if upon examination of any transaction or transactions made directly or through the medium of third parties, or by the creation of new or intermediary companies, it appears to the Treasury Board that any payment or benefit in cash or otherwise, received by any person subsequent to the year 1939 as a result of such transaction or transactions has been received directly or indirectly from a company having undistributed income on hand, then the Treasury Board may find that the main purpose of such transaction or transactions was to reduce or avoid taxation, and it shall thereupon be deemed for the purposes of this Act that such person, whether he received any such payment or benefit in the form of capital or otherwise, has received income subject to tax in such year or years since 1939 and in such amount or amounts the Treasury Board may determine, and tax shall be assessed and levied upon such person and shall be payable as in this Act provided.

Subsection (3) was apparently designed to cover a case missed by Sections 14 and 19 (2). In the absence of a provision to the contrary, the shareholders of Company A, which has an undistributed surplus, could sell shares to Company B at a price based upon capital plus surplus. Company B might then have a dividend declared by Company A out of undistributed income, and thereby recover the part of the purchase price represented by the surplus of Company A. Accordingly, it was provided in subsection (3) that:

> . . . if substantially all the shares of a company having undistributed income on hand have been purchased since the coming into force of this

Act, by any other company or companies, the Treasury Board may find that the main purpose of the sale by the vendor was to reduce or avoid the tax which would have been paid by the shareholders of such company having undistributed income on hand on the distribution to them of the said undistributed income, and in such case . . . the dividends paid or deemed to be paid by the company having undistributed income on hand and received or deemed to be received by any such other company or companies shall upon being so received or deemed to be received be taxed against such company or companies and the tax shall be assessed, levied and paid as in this Act provided.

Section 14 would not have covered this situation, for it applied only in specific cases where the dividend was used by Company B in payment of the shares or in the discharge of liability incurred in paying for the shares. Section 19 (2) covers only "winding up, discontinuance or reorganization."

It was further provided in subsection (4) that in any appeal from an assessment made as a result of a Treasury Board finding under Section 32A, the Exchequer Court of Canada shall have jurisdiction to determine whether the main purpose of a transaction was one of tax avoidance.

The vesting of this extraordinary power in the Treasury Board was carried forward in the new Income Tax Act (effective 1949) in Section 126. Such provisions represent a sharp break from the time-honoured doctrine that a taxing statute must be strictly construed and that only Parliament can impose a tax, and even then requires the clearest of words to do so. The basic principle was reaffirmed by the House of Lords in a recent case, as follows:

It may be well to repeat two propositions which are well established in the application of the law relating to Income Tax. First, the name given to a transaction by the parties concerned does not necessarily decide the nature of the transaction. To call a payment a loan if it is really an annuity does not assist the taxpayer, any more than to call an item a capital payment would prevent it from being regarded as an income payment if that is its true nature. The question always is what is the real character of the payment, not what the parties call it.

Secondly, a transaction which, on its true construction, is of a kind that would escape tax, is not taxable on the ground that the same result could be brought about by a transaction in another form which would attract tax. As the Master of the Rolls said in the present case (page

16 *ante*): "In dealing with Income Tax questions it frequently happens that there are two methods at least of achieving a particular financial result. If one of those methods is adopted tax will be payable. If the other method is adopted, tax will not be payable. . . . The net result from the financial point of view is precisely the same in each case, but one method of achieving it attracts tax and the other method does not. There have been cases in the past where what has been called the substance of the transaction has been thought to enable the Court to construe a document in such a way as to attract tax. That particular doctrine of substance as distinct from form was, I hope, finally exploded by the decision of the House of Lords in the case of *Duke of Westminster* v. *Commissioners of Inland Revenue,* 19 T.C. 490.[45]

It has been stated editorially in *Canada Tax Service* that:

Directions of Treasury Board under section 126 . . . are virtually an extension of the legislative arm of Parliament in making taxable something which might not otherwise be assessable under other sections of the Act. It will be almost impossible for any taxpayer to determine in advance whether or not a transaction may be referred to the Treasury Board by the administration, or if so referred, will be considered by the Treasury Board to have had as one of its main purposes, the reduction or avoidance of income or excess profits taxes.

It would appear that a taxpayer if he were to follow the evident intention behind these sections must always so arrange his affairs as to pay the maximum amount of tax. This is contrary to accepted judicial thinking and to the underlying philosophy of most taxing legislation. It has been said that a tax is not to be imposed without clear words establishing the purpose and that if the Crown cannot tax within the explicit letter of the law, the taxpayer is not taxable regardless of whether he be within its spirit. *Re Micklethwait,* 6 T.C. 538.[46]

While the desire on the part of the tax administration to prevent tax evasion and avoidance is thoroughly understandable, the extension of power now contained in the tax law seems quite unwarranted in the minds of many people. In recommending the repeal of Sections 125 and 126, the Taxation Section of the Canadian Bar Association and the Legislation Committee of the Dominion Association of Chartered Accountants stated, in part:

[45]*Commissioners of Inland Revenue* v. *Wesleyan & General Assurance Society,* (1948) 30 T.C. 11, 25.

[46]*Canada Tax Service B,* p. 125-11.

We believe that in a true democracy such as Canada citizens should be free to do whatever is permitted by law, and that the freedom should not be hedged in and rendered dubious by the retention of shadowy and undefined powers by the Crown. Our ancestors struggled for centuries to limit and define the powers of the Crown, and to make them subject to the law, particularly in regard to taxation. If the law itself is now to be used as a means of restoring that arbitrary power, the struggle will have been won in vain, but the forces which won it centuries ago are still present in the character of the Canadian people and will operate with increasing vigour until the situation is restored.[47]

While there is obviously powerful and well-informed opposition to this provision of the Canadian law, it must be remembered that social and tax thinking have moved a long way from the ultra-conservative approach of the House of Lords. In the United States, for example, it is accepted judicial practice to give effect to intention and substance when interpreting a statute.

Stripped of its emotional content, the argument against the vesting in the Treasury Board of such powers as are granted in Section 126 appears sound in principle. In terms of tax equity, however, it may be asked whether it is proper that one taxpayer, able to secure outstanding legal advice and so arrange his affairs as to avoid his fair share of the tax burden, should escape through a legal loophole, while another pays the full amount on a similar income?

In a free society, and under our parliamentary system, there should be room for reliance upon government not to abuse this type of power, but to use it only in cases of flagrant tax avoidance. And, of course, the taxpayer is not without the protection of the courts. Section 126 (4) provides that the Exchequer Court has exclusive original jurisdiction in all actions in respect of claims for failure to pay tax imposed pursuant to Section 126.

Section 32B was added to the old Act in 1938 to prevent a corporation from distributing assets to its shareholders at a price below market. For example, it would be relatively easy for some companies to distribute inventory to their shareholders at a price

[47]*Recommendations on the Income Tax Act, submitted to the Minister of Finance*, by the Taxation Section of the Canadian Bar Association and the Legislation Committee of the Dominion Association of Chartered Accountants, March 13, 1950, p. 11.

below market in the amount of their undistributed profits. Section 32B provided as follows:

Where on winding up or otherwise a company distributes any assets to its shareholders without sale or at a sale price substantially below the fair market price, which assets if sold at the market price would create income of the corporation within the meaning of this Act, the Minister shall have power to determine the fair market price of such assets and the company shall be deemed to have sold such assets at the price so determined and thereby to have received income subject to tax and the distributable portion received by a shareholder or member shall be deemed to be a dividend.

The sections just outlined apparently blocked any plan to distribute the property of a corporation to its shareholders free of personal income tax. The method of calculating the amount of undistributed income on hand was described by the Royal Commission on the Taxation of Annuities and Family Corporations as follows (pp. 59-60):

Mr. T. W. Bullock, C.P.A., Assistant Deputy Minister (Assessing) of the Taxation Division of the Department of National Revenue gave evidence as to the method followed by the Division in calculating the amount of "undistributed income on hand" for the purpose of taxation under section 19 and related sections of the Act. From his evidence it appears that the assessed income of the corporation for all years from 1917 to the date of distribution is totalled. To this is added exempt income (dividends from other corporations or tax-free bond interest). From this total is deducted operating losses, sustained during these years, capital losses to the extent that they exceed capital profits which have not been distributed; dividends paid during the period, Income, Business and Excess Profits Tax paid during the period, and expenses which have been incurred but not allowed for income tax purposes. The remainder is the "undistributed income on hand." It is apparent therefore that income earned prior to the commencement of the fiscal year of the corporation ending in 1917—income earned before the effective date of the original Income Tax Act—is not brought into charge on a distribution under Section 19 nor is any capital surplus on hand.

This provision applies, however, only to a distribution on winding up, discontinuance, or reorganization. It is well established that apart from such cases, and apart from a distribution of capital as a step in an authorized capital reduction, any payment made by a company to its shareholders, whether a distribution of what is capital in the hands of the company, a distribution of income accumulated prior to 1917, or a distribution of income earned after 1917, is considered a dividend and is taxable income in the hands of the shareholders.[48]

The problem of accumulations of undistributed profits still remained serious in the case of closely held private companies. Companies which had not taken advantage of the special legislation in force between 1930 and 1934 to distribute pre-1930 earnings in many cases had large amounts of undistributed surplus built up over two or three decades. In 1944 the Ives Commission was appointed to investigate the problem and make recommendations.

The nature and gravity of the problem was summarized by the Commission as follows:

> The problem with which we have to deal relates to the combined effect of income taxes and succession duties arising on the death of any of the principal shareholders of closely-held corporations with accumulated surpluses. In many instances the principal asset of the deceased is represented by his equity in the company and, in order to pay succession duties, it is found necessary to distribute a substantial part, if not all, of the accumulated surplus as a dividend. The impact of the income taxes at the prevailing rates on such a distribution is extremely serious and when combined with Federal and Provincial Succession Duties may result in the confiscation of almost the entire estate.
>
> Many of these companies are owned by one individual or by a few individuals or by a family. Often they have begun with a small amount of capital, but by turning back into the undertaking most of the profits they have earned they have gradually accumulated large undistributed surpluses. In many cases a substantial part of the surplus is represented by fixed assets or current resources needed for the conduct of the business, so that a large distribution would place a severe strain on the finances of the company, even without the impact of personal income tax on the shareholder. The current levels of income tax create for many companies an impossible situation.[49]

The Commission made two recommendations regarding this problem. The first, applicable to surplus accumulated prior to

[48]Cf. *McConkey* v. *Minister of National Revenue,* [1937] Ex. C.R. 209.
[49]*Report,* p. 61.

1940, was that private companies (as defined in the Dominion Companies Act) be given the right, within a specified period, to pay a special tax on such surplus at rates varying between 15 and 33 per cent, depending upon the amounts attributable to each shareholder. Any surplus on which such tax was paid would be considered as tax-paid and distributable free of further tax, or, alternatively, could be capitalized. It will be noted that a price is attached to this distribution, whereas the relief granted to pre-1930 surplus was tax-free.

The second recommendation, concerned with surpluses accumulated in 1940 and subsequent years, was an attempt to provide a continuing solution of the problem. It was recommended that "on the reorganization of a private company which involves a change in beneficial ownership, or on the winding up or discontinuance of business of any such company, the undistributed income which is deemed to be the payment of a dividend under the present law be reduced by an amount equal to 20 per cent of the income after tax earned in the 1940 and subsequent taxation years."[50]

The first of these recommendations was adopted in 1945 under Part XVIII, Section 94. A private company was defined to be one with no more than 75 shareholders, exclusive of employees, and it was provided that such companies might elect at any time up to December 31, 1947, to pay a special tax on undistributed surplus on hand at the end of the 1939 fiscal year. The rate of tax ranged from 15 to 33 per cent. Upon payment of the special tax, such surplus would be free of further tax. Thus, for a second time, tax relief was accorded to past accruals of undivided profits. But the government did not adopt the second recommendation, and it was inevitable that there would at some later day be a recurrence of the old problem.

3. *The 1950 Legislation*

In his budget speech of March 22, 1949, the Minister of Finance indicated that the problem had again become acute, and stated: "So severe is the application of our present law in such cases that many such businesses [private companies] have been driven into a great variety of extremely complicated and cumber-

[50]*Ibid.*, p. 76.

some devices to secure legal avoidance of the excessive tax burden to which they are now potentially liable. As a result we are losing revenue to which we think the public treasury has a justifiable claim.[51]

He forecast legislation to meet the situation, and a year later in his budget speech of March 28, 1950, he said: "If the proposed legislation did no more than take care of past surpluses, a new problem with respect to the future would immediately start developing. I think it desirable, therefore, that the present legislation should provide a comprehensive solution to the problem as a whole rather than merely deal in ad hoc fashion with the past.[52]

The new legislation contained in the amended Sections 73, 73A, 95A, and 27 went farther than any previous legislation towards meeting the problem, because it provided for both past and future surpluses.

Private companies were given the right to elect (*a*) to pay a tax of 15 per cent on undistributed earnings on hand at the end of the 1949 taxation year, and (*b*) to pay a tax of 15 per cent on amounts not exceeding the total dividends paid in completed taxation years subsequent to 1949. No election may be made under (*b*) in the case of a company eligible to elect under (*a*) unless it has so elected under (*a*). Once the special tax has been paid on any undistributed earnings, those earnings may be capitalized and treated as capital on subsequent distribution. There is no time limitation on this privilege, such as was contained in the 1945 law, and payment of the tax need not be followed by an immediate act of capitalization from the standpoint of company law. It can be deferred indefinitely, and it may be made in the manner that appears most suitable to existing conditions.

The procedure was confined to private companies, as stated above. These fell into two classes, companies with no more than 75 shareholders, exclusive of employees, and companies controlled by other companies, if control was acquired after May 10, 1950. Such controlled companies could have any number of shareholders.

[51]*House of Commons Debates*, March 22, 1949, p. 1800.
[52]*Ibid.*, March 28, 1950, p. 1218.

Under the 1945 law the normal rule was that earnings on which the special tax had been paid could be distributed to the shareholders as a tax-free dividend, on the theory that the company had paid the shareholder's tax for him. But the new law provides in principle for tax-paid capitalization as distinct from tax-paid distribution, and does not alter the basic rule that all dividends to individuals are taxable without distinction. Consequently, a distribution of tax-paid earnings under the new law must take the form of a distribution or reduction of capital if further taxation in the hands of shareholders is to be avoided. It was precisely the various transactions of this character that the legal road blocks noted above were intended to frustrate. All these preventive provisions continue in effect. The distinctive relief offered under the new law is that they no longer apply to surplus that has been segregated on a tax-paid basis. The result is, therefore, that a private company may now capitalize its earnings and effect a reduction or distribution of capital without exposing its shareholders to further tax penalty, to the extent that its undistributed income has borne the extra 15 per cent tax.

There were good and sufficient reasons for deciding upon this policy compared with the procedure followed under the 1945 law, which was designed simply to release undistributed earnings accumulated prior to 1940. The graduated rate structure provided in the 1945 law represented an attempt to have the corporation pay about the same tax on these earnings as would have been paid had they been distributed evenly during the decade prior to the war. Clearly any attempt to follow that procedure now, in view of the very high rates of tax during the war, would make the plan completely unattractive and would not touch the underlying problem. The new plan is forward-looking, and introduces a continuing remedy, applying it to existing accumulations as its point of departure.

It is likely that many private companies will elect to pay the 15 per cent tax on pre-1950 undistributed earnings, and then declare a stock dividend in redeemable shares, either common or preferred. If funds are available, redemption can take place at once, putting cash in the shareholders' hands. Even if funds are not available for redemption of preference shares, the affairs of a closely held company are placed in a more manageable position for the future.

Considerable discussion has been devoted to the timing of an election by a company to take advantage of the new law. Companies which neglected to take advantage of the 1945 law are now in a better position than they would have been, because the new law is much more liberal. But it does not look now as though any more favourable treatment can be expected in the foreseeable future.

There are, however, two sides to the question that confronts all private companies having any considerable balance of undistributed profits. On the one hand, they can pay the special tax and arrange a distribution to the shareholders. In many cases this procedure will be deemed desirable, and represents the final opening of a door which has long been padlocked. On the other hand, there are many cases where the profits have been ploughed back into the business and there is no desire on the shareholders' part to liquidate them now. If they are profitably invested, why disturb them and pay an unnecessary tax? In such cases election to come under the new law might be deferred until after the death of a principal shareholder. But this could result in higher death duties in that the 15 per cent tax would not reduce the shareholder's equity at the date of death. Moreover, such a delay entails a gamble that the new law will not changed.

The choice of time at which to elect to pay tax on pre-1950 undistributed profits is affected, of course, by any decision regarding post-1949 income, because the former election must be made before subsequent earnings can be so treated. Since the treatment of earnings for future years is liberal, compared with the possible alternatives for the shareholder, it may appear desirable in many cases to elect to pay the special tax each year, and that, of course, presupposes election with respect to pre-1950 earnings.

A company which has elected to distribute pre-1950 surplus and earns $100,000 in the 1950 taxation year for a principal shareholder, may, after payment of the corporation tax, pay $50,000 to him as a cash dividend, pay 15 per cent on the remaining $50,000, and distribute this remainder as a tax-free stock dividend in the form of redeemable preference shares. Assuming that the shareholder has no other income, is married, and has no deduction save the basic $2,000 allowed a married man, election to distribute half and capitalize half the earnings would result in an over-all tax of $24,964 ($17,464 on his cash dividends and $7,500 on the amount transferred to capital). Thus he would receive $75,036 in cash and securities out of the $100,000 earned for him, after corporation tax had been paid.[53] Had he taken the whole amount earned as a cash dividend, his personal tax would have been $45,564, leaving him only $54,436 after all taxes.[54] Provided a shareholder wants to clear his position each year, the new law allows him to

[53]The computation is as follows:

(1) Personal tax on $50,000 cash dividends, after deducting basic $2,000 exemption		$20,560
(2) 4% tax on $50,000 investment income after deducting $2,400 allowance		1,904
	Total	$22,464
(3) 10% tax credit on $50,000 of dividends		5,000
	Net total	$17,464
(4) Special tax of 15% on $50,000 of profits transferred to capital account		7,500
	Total tax	$24,964
Portion of original $100,000 now available to shareholder after all taxes,	$75,036	

NOTE: The above computation was made before the 20 per cent surcharge was applied to the personal income tax in 1951.

[54]Computed as follows (1950 rates):

(1) Personal tax on $100,000 cash dividends, after deducting basic $2,000 exemption		$51,660
(2) 4% tax on $100,000 investment income, after deducting $2,400 allowance		3,904
	Total	$55,564
(3) 10% tax credit on $100,000 of dividends		10,000
	Net tax	$45,564
Portion of the original $100,000 now available	$54,436	

save substantially on his tax bill—$20,600 in the example used above.

If a company decides upon annual election to use the new law, the shareholders are consolidating their position as they go along, and they are also taking out insurance against a revision of the government's policy at some future time. The premium on this insurance is the special 15 per cent tax, the loss of the 10 per cent dividend credit, and the lost return that the company could have made on the capital paid out.

It is not necessary, however, to make a distribution after paying the special tax, and this is perhaps the best feature of the plan. Because of this, a company may put its shareholders on a tax-free basis with respect to undistributed earnings without disturbing its operating position.

The 1950 limitation of the plan to private companies, defined by statute to be those having no more than 75 shareholders, exclusive of employees, probably worked a hardship in borderline cases. It is impossible to determine a satisfactory dividing line between private and public companies. Most of the large public companies would probably not elect to pay a tax of 15 per cent to distribute undivided profits because of the tax and because they do not want them distributed in many cases. It was argued that there was no reason, therefore, to confine the legislation to a class of company determined by an arbitrary number of shareholders.[55]

The inclusion of corporations controlled[56] by other corporations within the meaning of a private company, regardless of the number of shareholders, made it possible for even the largest of

[55]J. M. Coyne, in a paper presented at the Canadian Bar Association's meeting in Washington, D.C., September 18, 1950, proposed the following resolution: "RESOLVED that the Taxation Section of the Canadian Bar Association welcomes the enactment of Part IA of the Income Tax Act as introducing a constructive and equitable method of dealing with accumulated corporate surpluses, but is of the opinion that the arbitrary limitation of the provisions of Part IA to private companies as defined therein is not justified and that these provisions should be made applicable to all companies without distinction."

[56]Control must be acquired after May 10, 1950, and it is provided in Section 27 (1B) that one corporation is controlled by another corporation if the latter owns more than 50 per cent of the former's issued share capital, having full voting rights under all circumstances.

public companies to take advantage of the 15 per cent tax. All that was necessary was to form a new company which would hold more than 50 per cent of the old company's share capital. But this is neither desirable nor practical in most cases, and moreover there are difficulties presently attached to the operation of the new legislation in the case of related companies.

In the case of a private company which controls another private company, the tax-paid undistributed income of the controlled company loses its identity when capitalized and transferred to the parent company. It is excluded from the income of the parent company by Section 73(4). Apparently it must be considered as a special item in the capital surplus account, and it cannot be made available to the shareholders of the parent company without subjecting them to tax on any of the parent company's undistributed income on hand at the time of distribution. This has the effect of freezing the tax-paid undistributed income of a subsidiary company in the hands of the parent company. The situation has been described as follows:

Where a private company has subsidiary companies which are also private companies, problems may arise as to the best procedure to be adopted for the distribution of undistributed income on hand of the subsidiary companies, whether or not they are controlled corporations which are subject to the provisions of section 27 (1A) to (IF) inclusive.

If, for example, a subsidiary company which is a private company had undistributed income on hand at the end of the 1949 taxation year, the question may arise as to how its undistributed income may be paid over to the parent private company and in turn distributed to the shareholders of the parent company, without attracting more tax than is necessary. In most circumstances it would appear desirable that the subsidiary should elect under section 95A (1) to pay the 15% tax and then distribute its undistributed income to the parent company by one of the procedures contemplated in section 73. If this were done the dividend deemed to be received by the parent company under section 73 would not be added to its undistributed income on hand under section 73A (1)(a). The parent private company may then elect to pay the 15% tax on any undistributed income which it has on hand in respect of which it is entitled to elect under section 95A (1) or (2). It could then make a distribution to its shareholders of the amount received from the subsidiary together with its own undistributed income on hand, by carrying out one of the procedures contemplated in section 73 which are listed above. Such a distribution would be entirely or partially free of tax in the hands of the shareholders of the parent company. It will be noted, however, that upon such a distribution these shareholders would be subject to tax on any undistributed income on hand of the parent company on which the 15% tax had not been paid.

If, however, the subsidiary, instead of carrying out the above procedure, should pay an ordinary dividend to the parent company, such dividend would become part of the undistributed income on hand of the parent company and, of course, would not have been accumulated by it prior to the 1950 taxation year. The parent company would therefore not be entitled to make an election with respect to such undistributed income under section 95 (A)(1), but only under section 95A (2) after it had paid to its shareholders dividends equal to the amount in respect of which it made the election. Since these dividends would be taxable in the hands of individual shareholders at the regular individual rates, it will be seen that in many cases higher aggregate taxes would result from this procedure than from that outlined in the preceding paragraph.[57]

The logical solution to this problem appears to be to preserve the identity of tax-paid undistributed income as it passes from one corporation to another.

4. *The 1951 Legislation*

Bill 296 to amend the Income Tax Act, passed on June 19, 1951, contained two major amendments. The first opened the right to elect to pay the 15 per cent tax under Part IA to public as well as private corporations. The second denied a subsidiary controlled corporation (defined by Section 127 (1) (*ao*) to be a corporation of which more than 50 per cent of the issued share capital belongs to the corporation to which it is subsidiary) the right to elect the 15 per cent tax on undistributed income under Section 95A (2) with respect to earnings subsequent to the 1949 taxation year.

With reference to the amendment that now opens the legislation on undistributed income to public as well as private companies, the argument against such an extension is that the legis-

[57]K. LeM. Carter and J. L. Stewart, *Private Companies, Special Tax on Undistributed Income*, pp. 12-13.

lation regarding private companies is designed primarily to provide relief from the disabilities affecting shareholders of closely held companies which do not apply in the case of owners of marketable shares of public companies. Furthermore, the form of the legislation is not well suited to a rule affecting corporate enterprise generally, and that its extension to all companies gives rise to confused expectations in the minds of shareholders, resulting in needless problems for management. Finally, the typical public company will remain outside the operation of this legislation in any event.

On the other hand, the extension of this legislation to public as well as private companies now removes the arbitrary dividing line between a public and a private company contained in the 1950 legislation, thereby eliminating the difficulty of border-line cases. There is now no need to resort to the holding company device in order to create the status of a "controlled corporation" within the meaning of Section 95A (3) of the 1950 legislation. The new amendment is good in that it removes the need for unnecessary complication of the corporate structure to secure a tax advantage.

The other important amendment in 1951 was the denial of the right of subsidiary controlled corporations to elect to pay the 15 per cent tax on undistributed income under Section 95A (2) with respect to earnings subsequent to the 1949 taxation year. This measure was taken to block the obvious loophole of a corporation acquiring another corporation with substantial undistributed income by borrowing the money for the acquisition of shares and then retiring the loan by means of a tax-paid distribution of such undistributed income. But, as the Canadian Tax Foundation said in its submission on Bill 296 on May 29, 1951, "we suspect that the weight of the plug may prove to be out of proportion to the size of the loophole."[58]

This provision results in at least two serious hardships.[59] (1) Minority shareholders of subsidiary companies are now denied

[58]See *Memorandum Submitted to the Minister of Finance* by a Committee of the Canadian Tax Foundation, May 29, 1951, p. 6.

[59]See my paper "Memorandum on Part IA on the Income Tax Act Respecting Tax-Paid Undistributed Income," Canadian Tax Foundation, *Tax Bulletin,* Nov.-Dec., 1951, p. 153.

the future continuing benefit of the Part IA legislation which was its distinctive improvement over Part XVIII of the Income War Tax Act. This hardship is especially unfortunate in the case of subsidiary companies under "bare control." (2) There is a resulting paralysis of the mechanism previously provided under Section 27 (1A), in conjunction with Part IA, whereby "designate surplus" of a controlled corporation could by degrees be rendered tax-paid by election and payment of tax under Section 95A (2) concurrently with payment of dividends out of current earnings. While the provisions of Section 27 originally conveyed the intention that a "designated surplus" should be cleared in this way, it would now appear to be frozen, and this consequence will be more serious with the passing of each taxation year after 1949. Under the 1951 legislation, that part of the undistributed income of a subsidiary controlled corporation earned subsequent to 1949 and prior to the commencement of the fiscal year in which control was acquired is taxable under Section 27 (1A) in the hands of the parent company upon distribution. Referring to the amendment in the debate on the income tax bill as a "loophole provision," the Minister of Finance said: "I will be prepared to pursue alternative measures. I have not been able to find anything yet; so that at this time I think that this is a provision which must be inserted in the Act."[60]

No provision was included in the 1951 legislation to rectify the problem, mentioned earlier, of the loss of identity in the hands of a parent company of a subsidiary company's tax-paid undistributed income transferred to it in whole or in part.

The Canadian Tax Foundation made a recommendation to the tax authorities on December 21, 1950, for an amendment which would preserve the identity of tax-paid undistributed income as it passes from one corporation to another. This recommendation was as follows:

[60]*House of Commons Debates,* June 18, 1951, p. 4234. It is to be noted that there is now another loophole in the legislation. As the law now stands the definition of a "subsidiary controlled corporation" in Section 127 (1)(*ao*) is different from the definition of "controlled corporation" in Section 27 (1B). A corporation which is a controlled corporation under Section 27 (1B) can qualify to make an election under Section 95A (2) by having some of its shares transferred from the parent company to another person with whom the parent company does not deal at arm's length.

Repeal subsection (4) of Section 73 and substitute therefor the following:

> "(4) Where a dividend is under this section deemed to have been received by an individual in a taxation year, the amount thereof to be included in computing the individual's income for the year is the amount of the dividend minus the individual's portion of the payer corporation's tax-paid undistributed income as of the time the dividend is deemed to have been received.
>
> "(4A) Where a dividend is under this section deemed to have been received by a corporation from another corporation having tax-paid undistributed income, there shall be added to the tax-paid undistributed income of the receiving corporation the lesser of the amount of the dividend or the receiving corporation's portion of the payer corporation's tax-paid undistributed income as of the time the dividend is deemed to have been received."

Insert in Section 73A (1)(*b*) immediately after the words "Income War Tax Act" in the first paragraph thereof, the following words:

> "... plus amounts added to the corporation's tax-paid undistributed income by reason of subsection (4A) of Section 73."

Amend Section 73A (1)(*b*) by inserting a new clause (ii) reading as follows and renumbering the present clause (ii) as (iii):

> "(ii) all amounts deemed to have been received as dividends from the corporation by other corporations before that time and added to the tax-paid undistributed incomes of such other corporations by virtue of subsection (4A) of Section 73 of this Act, and . . . ."

Repeal paragraph (*e*) of subsection (1A) of Section 27 and substitute therefor the following:

> "(e) the amount of the designated surplus upon which tax had been paid by the payer corporation under Part IA before the dividend was paid and the amount of the designated surplus that had been added before that time to the tax-paid undistributed income of the payer corporation by virtue of subsection (4A) of Section 73 of subsection (6) of section 73A and . . . ."

The foregoing amendments are suggested with the intention that they would apply as from the original effective date of the relative legislation.

No action has been taken on these recommendations, although the principle appears to be sound and within the announced intention of the legislation. The enactment of these provisions or something like them would put an end to the anomaly that arose in the original legislation.

5. *Tax-Paid Undistributed Earnings versus Tax-Paid Dividends*

It has been argued on various occasions that the Part IA legislation should not have been complicated by the requirement of capitalizing tax-paid undistributed income but rather should have followed the Part XVIII provisions of the Income War Tax Act, under which a cash dividend could be paid free of tax to the shareholders of a private company. Such a proposal was made by Stanley E. Edwards in a paper read to the Canadian Bar Association's meeting in Toronto, September 11, 1951.[61] His recommendation[62] was as follows:

(*a*) that a corporation, upon paying a dividend not in excess of its tax-paid undistributed income, may file with the Income Tax Department a form designating the dividend as a "tax-paid" dividend;

(*b*) that a corporation's tax-paid undistributed income shall be reduced by the amount of all tax-paid dividends paid by the corporation;

(*c*) that any portion of a tax-paid dividend which is received by an individual shareholder shall not be included in his income, and consequently no income tax shall be deducted therefrom by the corporation;

(*d*) that any portion of a tax-paid dividend which is received by a corporate shareholder shall be included in its income (subject to a deduction under Section 27 (1), and shall be included in its tax-paid undistributed income.

(*e*) that paragraph (i) of Section 95A (2) be amended by inserting in the first line after the words "dividends" the words "other than tax-paid dividends."

This proposal has the immediate merit of simplicity. It is in line with the provisions of Part XVIII, Section 95, of the Income War Tax Act, and it cuts through all of the complications arising out of the existing formula of transferring tax-paid undistributed income to capital account.

In considering any formula to meet the problem of undistributed income, it should be remembered that throughout the

[61]"Problems of Company Law Arising under the Undistributed Income Provisions of Income Tax Act."

[62]As subsequently amended in a later memorandum to me.

years attention has been centred on private companies as distinct from public companies, and that the objective has been one of placing the undistributed earnings of a closely held company in a tax-paid position so as to ease the tax penalty on shareholders upon winding-up or under other circumstances when an actual or notional distribution takes place. This attitude has been maintained consistently by the tax authorities. During the debate on Bill 296 last June the Minister of Finance reiterated his earlier views as follows: "The purpose of the section [95A] was to facilitate capitalization of an earned surplus. It was not necessarily or primarily intended to facilitate the distribution of the capitalized surplus if it had been capitalized. I know that in fact in law it has not been too difficult to effect that distribution, but the primary purpose was not to facilitate an easy distribution; it was to facilitate an easy capitalization without attracting too high a tax."[63] Perhaps the tax-paid dividend proposal has merit in the case of private or closely held companies. But its extension to public companies appears to be an unwarranted tax concession to the shareholders of such companies.[64]

In conclusion, the problem of undistributed income is trying, complicated, and quite insoluble from a perfectionist viewpoint. The attempt to rectify it has resulted in an extraordinarily complicated addition to the Canadian income tax legislation, which has benefited not only the companies whose shareholders needed relief, but their accounting and legal advisers as well. Final judgment on the legislation must be reserved until broader experience under it has been acquired.[65]

[63]*House of Commons Debates*, June 18, 1951, pp. 4235-6.

[64]In effect public companies can now achieve the same result by going through the required capitalization procedure. But it is less likely that public companies would elect under Part IA, as now constituted, than under the straightforward procedure of a tax-paid dividend. I cannot help objecting to such an unnecessary tax concession to the holders of listed shares of public corporations.

[65]I have deliberately refrained from discussing several other technical difficulties here, such as the definition of "undistributed income on hand," computation on the basis of a notional winding up of "shareholder's portion" under Section 73A (1)(*c*) and of "receiving corporation's portion" under Section 27 (1F), and adjustment respecting subsequent reduction or impairment of "1949 surplus" in case of postponed elections under Part IA. A discussion of these points may be found in the Canadian Tax Foundation's *Memorandum Submitted to the Minister of Finance*, May 29, 1951, and in my "Memorandum on Part IA on the Income Tax Act."

Special Corporations

Special tax treatment provided under the Act for certain classes of corporations merit some discussion.

1. *Co-operatives*

The Income War Tax Act was amended in 1930 by adding paragraph (*p*) to Section 4. This amendment exempted from income tax co-operative companies and associations. The exemption also applied to companies and associations owned or controlled by co-operative companies and organized for the purpose of financing their operations. There was a considerable expansion of co-operative activity during the war when other business organizations were bearing a crushing tax burden. As a result of public demand for an inquiry into the exemption of co-operatives, a Royal Commission was appointed in 1944 to investigate the matter.

The first recommendation of the Commission was that Section 4 (*p*) of the Income War Tax Act be repealed because "As a result of the ambiguities of language and the difficulty of administering the section, and because we are of the opinion there is no general class or group of co-operative associations in Canada today whose income should be declared not to be liable to taxation, we are of the opinion that the section in its present form cannot survive the attacks made upon it."[66]

It was further recommended that co-operatives be placed on the same basis for income tax purposes as other forms of business enterprise. The Commission recognized that co-operatives differ from other forms of business enterprise in that they are, to some extent, obligated to make return to the members in proportion to their patronage, and that these returns resemble in part an ordinary price rebate or discount. While the character of these so-called patronage dividends is complex and ambiguous, the Commission recommended that such of these payments as are made readily available to the members or customers of co-operatives should be considered as income of the recipients and not income of the co-operative. To avoid discrimination, it recommended that similar treatment be applied to patronage dividends distributed

[66]*Report of the Royal Commission on Co-operatives*, p. 40.

by ordinary companies, partnerships, or individual proprietorships.[67]

It was also recommended that newly formed co-operative associations be exempt from income tax for the first three fiscal periods following the commencement of operations.

The Government adopted these recommendations, but introduced a modification with respect to the deduction of patronage dividends. In his 1946 budget speech the Minister of Finance said:

> After careful consideration, the government has, therefore, come to the conclusion that it should accept the Commission's recommendations that patronage dividends and similar payments be treated as a deduction from income subject to one relatively minor limitation designed to avoid at least some of the discriminatory effects I have mentioned. The limitation is this: that no company or association shall be able to go so far in its distribution of tax-free patronage dividends as to reduce its taxable income below a reasonable return on capital, employed in the business. This reasonable return will be defined as three per cent on the capital employed, including borrowed capital, less the interest paid by the company or association on borrowed capital that is allowed as an expense in the computation of the taxpayer's income. The principle underlying this rule is that amounts set aside out of taxable income to be distributed in proportion to patronage by a co-operative or company which does not pay at least three per cent on the capital employed in its business contain earnings which arise from the employment of capital and ought not to escape tax entirely.[68]

Section 66 (1) of the Income Tax Act provides for exemption from tax in the case of a co-operative corporation during the first three taxation years after it commences business. The exemption is confined to co-operatives incorporated under provincial legislation respecting the establishment of co-operative corporations for the purpose of marketing (including processing incident to or connected therewith) natural products belonging to or acquired from its members or customers, of purchasing supplies, equipment, or household necessities for or to be sold to its members or customers, or of performing services to its members or customers.

[67] *Ibid.*, pp. 44-5.
[68] *House of Commons Debates*, June 27, 1946, p. 2921.

The further limitations on the exemption contained in the Act are (1) that the prospect of payments being made to members or customers in proportion to their patronage must be contained in the statute under which the co-operative was incorporated, its charter, articles of association or by-laws, or its contracts with its members and customers; (2) that no member has more than one vote in the conduct of the corporation's affairs; (3) that at least 90 per cent of its members are individuals, and at least 90 per cent of the shares are held by individuals; (4) that the rate of interest on capital subscribed by its members or the dividend rate on shares does not exceed 5 per cent per annum; (5) that the volume of business transacted with non-member customers does not exceed 20 per cent of the total business done; and (6) that the business of the co-operative must be a new enterprise and not a continuation of a previous business in which "a substantial number of its members had a substantial interest."[69]

The reason for this three-year exemption is indicated in the *Report of the Royal Commission on Co-operatives,* which states:

> It has been pointed out to us on numerous occasions that co-operative associations are difficult to organize and that their rate of mortality is high, especially in their earlier years. They are not in a position to attract capital for investment purposes, except in small amounts. Moreover, they are apt to find it difficult to finance the employment of the necessary managerial personnel. In addition, there is a pronounced tendency to organize cooperatives in times of economic stress. We are, therefore, of the opinion that in the public interest, co-operative associations, upon consent of the Minister, should be exempt entirely from income tax during the first few years of their operation.[70]

This argument could be applied quite as well in the case of many other small business units in their first years, because they, too, often experience great difficulty in obtaining capital, and their mortality rate is high. It is difficult to rationalize a tax policy which discriminates between different types of business operations.

[69]This last limitation has particular significance in that it bars newly created federations of established co-operatives from the three-year exemption.

[70]P. 43. The Commission recommended total exemption for credit unions, farm insurance companies (co-operative or private), telephone, electric utility, medical, and hospital co-operatives.

Section 68 (1) provides that any taxpayer may deduct, in computing income for a taxation year, the aggregate of all patronage dividends and similar payments to his customers. It is to be noted that this deduction is not restricted to co-operatives, and follows the recommendation of the Royal Commission. Section 68 (3) contains a limitation of such deductions in the stipulation that patronage dividends may not reduce the income of a co-operative to an amount less than 3 per cent of the capital employed in the business at the beginning of the year, after deducting interest on borrowed capital (excepting money borrowed from a chartered bank or a credit union). In effect, any corporation, whether a co-operative or not, that pays its shareholders 3 per cent on the capital employed in the business, and then distributes the remainder of its income as patronage dividends, has no taxable income in that year.

The rationale of this procedure is the assumption that the principle of co-operative trading is operation at cost. Where this principle is applied, it usually involves the return to customers of surplus in excess of cost, a procedure which is generally authorized by by-law and is an obligation of the association. Patronage dividends, therefore, appear to be a price adjustment comparable to a trade discount, and not income of the business, regardless of whether operated co-operatively or otherwise.

Patronage dividends are included as income of the recipient in the year of payment. If a certificate of indebtedness is taken in lieu of payment, the value of the certificate is included as income of the recipient. But patronage dividends paid on the purchase of goods for consumption of a non-business nature are not considered taxable income in the hands of the recipient. This applies generally to the dividends paid by the consumer co-operatives for the obvious reason that the consumer taxpayer would not ordinarily be able to deduct the cost of consumption expenses from his income.

The whole field of taxing co-operatives is highly controversial, and in Canada there have been sporadic clashes of opinion on the matter. The co-operative movement in Canada has made great progress in recent years. It is reported that in 1949 there were 2,637 co-operative associations of all kinds, with a membership of

1,219,712, and doing business to the amount of $1,001, 437,990.[71]

The finding and recommendations of the Royal Commission are not based upon any clear principles. One observer has said: "What meagre theoretical argument is provided is questionable, and inconsistent. As a study of political expediency, however, of a Commission picking its way among conflicting forces in our economy, this Report has much interest. It is incomprehensible without some appreciation of the pressures that operated upon the Commission."[72] The Canadian legislation, based as it is upon the recommendations of the Commission, is likewise in essence a compromise. It is now substantially similar to the tax treatment of co-operatives in the United Kingdom, which has been well established since 1933.

In 1920 a Royal Commission on the Income Tax recommended in a majority report that a co-operative society in the United Kingdom "should be treated exactly as a limited liability company trading in similar circumstances and under similar conditions,"[73] and that "any part of the net proceeds which is not actually returned to members as 'dividend' or 'discount' is a profit which should be charged to Income Tax."[74] This recommendation was not adopted at that time. In 1932 a Parliamentary Committee (the Raeburn Committee) was appointed to open the matter again, and it recommended in 1933, along the lines of the earlier Commission, that co-operatives should be taxable, that dividend patronage be treated as an expense, and that the existing statutory exemption be repealed.[75] Its recommendations were accepted and introduced as Sections 31 and 32 of the Finance Act, 1933. These sections apparently have caused little trouble, and the situation seems to have been stabilized in the United Kingdom, after long and bitter controversy.

The Canadian legislation, while it seems to be a political compromise, appears to achieve some measure of rough justice be-

[71] J. E. O'Meara, *Co-operation in Canada, 1949*, p. 1.

[72] H. C. Pentland, "The Royal Commission on Co-operatives," *Commerce Journal*, March 1947, p. 60.

[73] *Report*, p. 121.

[74] *Ibid.*, p. 120.

[75] *Report of the Committee Appointed to Enquire into the Present Position of Co-operative Societies in Relation to Income Tax*, Cmd. 4260, p. 9.

tween co-operative and other types of business enterprise. In the main it appears to be a reasonable approach to the problem of taxing co-operatives.

2. *Exempt Corporations*

The following types of corporation are exempt from the corporation income tax.

(*a*) Crown and Municipal Corporations

Section 57 (1)(*c*) and (*d*) provides that no tax is payable by any municipal government body or by any corporation, 90 per cent of the shares of which are owned by the Crown or a municipality. This provision includes public utility companies, manufacturing and other companies, and a wholly owned subsidiary company of such a Crown or municipal corporation.

This exemption is in line with Section 125 of the British North America Act, 1867, providing that "No lands or Property belonging to Canada or any Province shall be liable to Taxation," but it represents a deviation from the income tax law of the United Kingdom, which deems income received from a business or trade to be taxable income whoever receives it.

(*b*) Charitable Organizations

The Income War Tax Act extended tax exemption under Section 4 (*e*) to religious, charitable, and educational institutions. The new Act was amended in 1950, Section 57 (1)(*ea*), to provide exemption in the case of "a charitable organization, whether or not incorporated, all the resources of which were devoted to charitable activities carried on by the organization itself and no part of the income of which was payable to, or was otherwise available for the personal benefit of, any proprietor, member or shareholder, thereof."

Since religious and educational institutions are charities in the eyes of the law, they automatically fall within the meaning of the new law. It is significant that all the "good works" of a charitable organization must be conducted directly by the organization. That is, no part of the income of a charitable organization may be given to another organization for distribution. The interpretation of what constitutes a charitable organization is dependent upon case law, and it excludes charitable trusts,[76] which are provided for in a special subsection, as follows.

(*c*) Charitable Trusts

Charitable trusts are exempted from tax by Section 57 (1)(*ec*) if they meet the following conditions: (1) All the property of the trust must be held "absolutely in trust exclusively for charitable purposes"; (2) the trust may not, after June 1, 1950, have acquired control of any corporation; (3) the trust may not carry on any business during the period in which exemption is claimed;[77] (4) the trust must have incurred no indebtedness after June 1, 1950, other than obligations arising in respect of salaries, rents, and other current operating expenses; and (5) the trust must have made gifts amounting to not less than 90 per cent of its income during the period for which exemption is claimed.

Special provision is made in Section 57 (3)(*b*) that all gifts received by a trust, other than gifts specifically earmarked as capital for the purpose of earning income, shall be included in income. Accordingly, at least 90 per cent of such income must be donated for charitable purposes if the trust is to qualify for tax exemption.

(*d*) Labour Organizations, Fraternal, and Benevolent Societies

Section 57 (1)(*f*) exempts all labour unions, lodges, fraternal organizations, and benevolent societies.

(*e*) Agricultural Organizations, Boards of Trade, and Chambers of Commerce

Section 57 (1)(*e*) provides for the exemption of such organizations if no part of their income is available for the personal benefit of any proprietor, member, or shareholders. An agricultural association is one concerned with any phase of the advancement of agriculture, including the raising of livestock and husbandry.[78]

(*f*) Non-Profit Corporations

Section 57 (1)(*g*) extends tax exemption to social clubs,

[76]Cf. *Peter Birtwistle Trust* v. *Minister of National Revenue*, [1939] S.C.R. 125.

[77]This restriction of not doing business applies to charitable trusts but not to the charitable organizations described above.

[78]Cf. *Rex.* v. *Davenport*, [1928] 2 D.L.R. 852; *Brooks* v. *Moore*, (1907) 13 B.C.R. 91; and *Rex* v. *Manitoba Grain Co. Ltd.*, [1922] 66 D.L.R. 406.

service clubs, lodges, fishing clubs, and community organizations. Obviously there are border-line cases in this category. The deciding factors in determining whether or not such an organization is exempt are (1) that it is strictly a non-profitmaking organization, and (2) that no part of the income accrues to the benefit of a shareholder or member either as a dividend or as an increase in the value of any interest or share he might have in the organization.[79]

(*g*) Mutual Insurance Corporations

Section 57 (1)(*h*) provides for the exemption of mutual insurance companies that receive their premiums wholly from the insurance of churches, schools, or other charitable organizations.

(*h*) Credit Unions

Section 57 (1)(*i*) provides for the exemption of credit unions. In order to qualify for exemption the association must (1) be restricted to carrying on business in one province, (2) derive its revenue primarily from loans made to members residing within that province, or from federal or provincial bonds, (3) have as members corporations or associations organized as credit unions which derive their revenue primarily from loans made to members or from government securities and are organized under provincial legislation, or organized for charitable purposes, or corporations or associations whose shareholders derive no benefit from the income.

(*i*) Housing Corporations

Section 57 (1)(*j*) exempts the limited dividend housing corporations as defined in the National Housing Act, 1944.

(*j*) Personal Corporations

Personal corporations, which may be described loosely as family investment holding companies, are exempt under Sections

[79]The leading Canadian case on this point is *Moose Jaw Flying Club Ltd.* v. *Minister of National Revenue*, [1949] C.T.C. 279. The appellant had been granted exemption on the grounds that the company's articles specifically prohibited the payment of dividends. There was a voluntary winding-up of the company in 1942, at which time assets were distributed to the shareholders in the amount of $51 per $10 share. The income of the company was held to be taxable because its accumulated income eventually benefited the shareholders. This decision was, of course, based upon Section 4 (*h*) of the old Act. It is not certain whether the reasons for this decision would apply to a similar case under Section 57 (1)(*g*).

57 (1)(*k*) and 61 (2). It is an essential feature of a personal corporation that it does not carry on active financial, commercial, or industrial business. It is also essential that the persons controlling the company be resident in Canada.

There appear to be two reasons for the exemption of the income of personal corporations from the corporation tax: (1) to prevent avoidance of tax through the accumulation of undistributed profits, and (2) to allow families to take advantage of the corporate form to hold their securities without paying the penalty of double taxation. In effect the personal corporation is accorded the same treatment as a partnership. The corporate form is ignored for tax purposes.[80] All income of the corporation is deemed to have been distributed to the shareholders in each taxation year, and is taxable to them under the personal income tax. It is immaterial that the income may not have been distributed.

(*k*) Investment Companies

In order to qualify for the exemption of investment companies provided in Section 62, a company must meet the following requirements throughout the whole of the taxation year: (1) at least 80 per cent of its property must be in cash and securities; (2) not less than 95 per cent of its income must be derived from such investments; (3) not more than 10 per cent of its property may be the securities of any one corporation or debtor, say the Crown or a Canadian municipality; (4) it must have at least 50 shareholders, none of whom may hold more than 25 per cent of all the shares; (5) not less than 85 per cent of its taxable income must be distributed to the shareholders before the end of the year; and (6) no election shall have been made within 90 days of the beginning of the year to pay the corporation tax.

The theory behind exempting investment corporations of this type is similar to that by which personal corporations are exempted. If 95 per cent of such a company's income is derived from investments, the company is merely a pipeline through which investment income flows to its shareholders. Under the

[80]In *Black* v. *Minister of National Revenue*, [1932] Ex. C.R. 8, the court stated that the position of the shareholders of a personal corporation is the same "as if there never had been any transfer of securities to the corporation by the shareholders, and as if the personal corporation had never existed." Maclean J., at p. 13.

Income War Tax Act the exemption was denied to investment companies with outstanding funded debt, but this restriction has been removed in the new Act.

Provision is made for an investment company, within 90 days of the commencement of the taxation year, to elect to forego the exemption privilege and pay the normal corporation tax. Such an election would allow the shareholders to apply the 10 per cent dividend credit to their personal tax, a procedure denied to them if the corporation claims exemption.

(*l*) Foreign Business Corporations

Section 64 (1) provides that no tax is payable by a foreign business corporation on its income. The following conditions must be met if it is to be exempt: (1) it must not be a personal corporation; (2) it must have filed a return in prescribed form and paid a fee of $100 within 120 days from the end of the year; and (3) its business operations must be of an industrial, mining, commercial, public utility, or public service nature, and carried on entirely outside Canada, except for management, or it must be a wholly owned subsidiary of a corporation whose business operations are as just defined, or its business must be of an investment or financial nature, conducted entirely outside Canada and its property (except bank deposits and shares of other foreign business corporations) must be located outside Canada.

The exemption of foreign business corporations is designed to provide freedom from tax for companies which are substantially non-resident, but which, from a strictly legal point of view, are resident and would therefore be taxable. Control and management may be vested in a Canadian head office, but if all the corporation's business is transacted abroad, there is no tax liability in Canada.

(*m*) Superannuation Trusts

Section 57 (1)(*o*) provides that no tax is payable by a trust or corporation established or incorporated solely in connection with an approved superannuation fund or plan. This is an extension of Section 4(*z*) of the old Act to include corporations.

(*n*) Trusts under Profit Sharing Plans

Section 57 (1)(*p*) provides exemption in the case of a trust under an employees' profit sharing plan to the extent provided by Section 71A. This is new legislation. Enacted in 1950, it had no counterpart in the old Act.

The essential features of an employees' profit sharing plan, as set out in Section 71A (1), are: (1) there must be profit sharing by employer and employees; (2) the payments made by an employer must be made to a trustee in trust for the employees' benefit; (3) it is permissible but not necessary that the employees also contribute to the trust; and (4) there must be a complete annual allocation by the trustee to the participating employees of all amounts received and of all profits from the trust property.

If these conditions are met, the trust is not taxable on its income; the employer's contributions are treated as a deductible expense (but an employee may not deduct any of his contributions to the trust); the employee is taxable on amounts allocated to him from the trust, whether made absolutely or contingently by the trustee. But the employee is not taxable on the amounts paid to him out of the trust, except such amounts as were not included in his income for that or a previous year, and were not attributable to contributions made by him to the trust.

3. *Non-Resident-Owned Investment Corporations*

Special treatment is accorded to non-resident-owned investment companies, generally referred to as "N.-R.-O." companies. In order to qualify for such treatment, the company must fulfil the following requirements throughout the whole of the taxation year: (1) at least 95 per cent of the value of its shares and 100 per cent of the value of its funded debt must be beneficially owned by non-residents, owned by trustees for the benefit of non-residents, or owned by one or more other corporations, regardless of where incorporated, which are in turn owned by non-residents or by trustees for such persons; and (2) the income of an "N.-R.-O." company must be derived from the ownership of or trading in securities, from lending money, from rents, annuities, or royalties, or from estates and trusts.

This type of company was originally created to attract foreign investment to Canada. It is usually owned entirely by non-residents, and, as seen above, its operations are excluded from the usual commercial, manufacturing, or merchandising activities of an ordinary corporation. They are taxed at a special rate of 15 per cent which corresponds to the 15 per cent withholding tax on interest and dividend payments made to non-residents.

Ministerial Discretion

Before its repeal the Income War Tax Act contained approximately one hundred sections or subsections wherein the Minister of National Revenue was empowered to exercise discretion. In addition to the discretionary powers granted to the Minister, important powers of a discretionary nature were vested in the Treasury Board under Section 32A.

These discretionary powers covered a wide variety of subjects, ranging from purely administrative matters to matters which affected the quantum of taxation, where there was almost a delegation of the power to tax. The discretionary powers have been grouped in five main divisions as follows:

A. Administrative and punitive powers
B. Powers which make the minister the judge of reasonableness or equity
C. Powers which constitute the minister the judge of the facts
D. Powers to grant or refuse exemptions and allowances
E. Power to approve a pension fund or plan.[81]

Mr. C. Fraser Elliott, K.C., when Deputy Minister of National Revenue for Taxation, made the following grouping of the discretionary powers:

1. Allowance of Reserves
    (*a*) Depletion
    (*b*) Depreciation
    (*c*) Bad debts
    (*d*) Inventory reserves (E.P.T.)
2. Limitation of Expenses
    1. Expenses
    2. Salaries
    3. In capital expenditure allowance
    4. Interest.

[81]Senate of Canada, *Proceedings of the Special Committee on Taxation,* no. 4, April 3, 1946, p. 79.

3. Determination of true nature of transactions where lessening of tax may be involved with reference to companies and individuals.
   1. Inter company purchases and sales.
   2. Value of shareholders' property transferred to company.
   3. Unreasonable payment to non resident companies.
   4. Transactions between husband and wife and parent and child.
4. Determination of nature of income
   1. Interest portion
   2. Tax free living allowance.
5. Determining nature and effect of certain legal documents (mortgage and international agreements).
6. Approval of Pension Schemes.
7. Minor Administrative Discretions.
   1. Extending time for making return.
   2. Require production of letters and documents involved in assessment.
   3. Require keeping of books.
   4. Demand payment of taxes for a person suspected of leaving Canada.
8. Regulations to carry Act into effect.
9. Waiving penalties.
   1. Failure to file return.
10. Determination of Standard Profits.
    (*a*) Commencement of business.
    (*b*) Nature of business.
11. Adjust Standard Profits.
    1. Basis of partial fiscal period.
    2. Alteration of capital.
12. Direct a reference to Board of Referees in case of new or substantially different business.[82]

Widespread dissatisfaction with some of the discretionary powers prevailed among the accounting and legal professions, particularly under circumstances where there was no appeal from a ruling made by the Department of National Revenue.

It has been said that "A Judicial tribunal looks for some law to guide it; an administrative tribunal, within its province, is a law unto itself" and that "A person aggrieved by . . . [an administrative] tribunal's decision cannot complain to a court of

[82]*Ibid.*, no. 3, Nov. 20, 1945, pp. 80-1.

law of administrative dealings with substantive matters, because he cannot show that he is wronged; he has been denied what he asked for but he had no legal right to it; he is disappointed but not injured."[83]

In some cases the discretion appears to have been final. For example, Section 6 (3) of the Income War Tax Act provided that the "decision of the Minister on any question arising under this sub-section shall be final and conclusive." Similar provision was also made in other sections dealing with discretionary powers.

The judicial opinion on this type of "final" discretion is interesting. In the *Pioneer Laundry Case,* Davis J. commented:

> The *Income War Tax Act* gives a right of appeal from the Minister's decisions and while there is no statutory limitation upon the appellate jurisdiction, normally the Court would not interfere with the exercise of a discretion by the Minister except on grounds of law.[84]

In a later case, *Nicholson Ltd.* v. *Minister of National Revenue,* the comments of Thorson J. are pointed:

> The purpose of granting a right of appeal from an assessment is to ensure to the taxpayer that it shall be a correct one. It is not to be assumed that Parliament in granting such right meant that the Court should apply a different standard for adjudicating as to the correctness of the assessment under appeal from that laid down for its correct levy by the Minister in the discharge of his functions. The Court must apply the law and section 6 (2) is binding upon it. The Court may not, therefore, substitute its own opinion as to the correct amount of expense to be disallowed for the amount determined by the Minister in his discretion under section 6 (2). The amount so determined is not open to review by the Court. *The right of appeal to the Court conferred by the Act does not carry with it any right of appeal from the Minister's determination in his discretion under section 6 (2).*[85]

An editorial comment on this case stated:

> This judgment contains one of the most important and far-reaching decisions ever handed down by a Canadian Court in the realm of income tax law. It is far-reaching because in the *Income War Tax Act* there are more than one hundred instances in which Ministerial or

[83]D. M. Gordon, "Administrative Tribunals and the Courts," 49 *Law Quarterly Review,* quoted in "Ministerial and Administrative Discretion," *Dominion of Canada Taxation Service,* March 15, 1947, p. 6008.

[84][1939] S.C.R. 1, 8. [85][1945] C.T.C. 263, 276. Italics mine.

administrative discretion may be exercised. *The Excess Profits Tax Act, 1940,* also contains its share of such provisions, while the *Customs Act* and other portions of Canadian fiscal legislation abound in such examples of a potent bureaucracy. Upon many occasions the Courts of Canada and the United Kingdom have enunciated sound and well-defined principles and safeguards with which to measure and circumscribe the improper exercise of such discretion. This judgment, however, is of the greatest importance because it pushes back the frontier of juridical thought in a direction never before attempted in Canada. . . . In the present decision Thorson, J. has not only set out his conclusions with clarity of expression . . . but in so doing he has perforce clarified a number of lesser points which have for years been the subject of muddled thinking. The principal among these misconceptions is the belief that an appeal is provided from the Minister's discretion under the *Income War Tax Act.*[86]

On October 24, 1945, the Senate decided to appoint a Special Committee to examine the provisions and workings of the Income War Tax Act and the Excess Profits Tax Act, and to formulate recommendations for the improvement, clarification, and simplification of the methods of assessment and collection of taxes thereunder. A number of hearings were held, and the Committee stated in its Final Report: "There is dissatisfaction with the appeal procedure as now found in the Income War Tax Act and with the lack of facilities afforded taxpayers to have cases decided rapidly and objectively. Co-existing with this feeling is the more technical and less widely held objection to the use of ministerial or administrative discretion and to the absolute authority of the administration in many matters of substantive importance."[87]

The tenor of the criticisms on the above points is exemplified in the submission to the Senate Committee by the Dominion Association of Chartered Accountants. This body maintained that the contemporary law was open to the following criticisms:

(a) The liability of taxpayers in many cases cannot be ascertained with certainty when the tax is due to be paid.

(b) Where prospective transactions may result in taxation, the amount of which depends on the exercise of discretion, ap-

[86]*Ibid.*, p. 264.

[87]Senate of Canada, *Proceedings of the Special Committee on Taxation,* no. 12, May 28, 1946, p. 378.

plication for a ruling must be made before the tax can be ascertained. This involves expense and delay and in some cases the taxpayer is unable to obtain a ruling on the point at issue.

(c) In the absence of any public knowledge of the principles which govern the exercise of discretion there may be inconsistency and involuntary discrimination in the application of the tax to the taxpayer.

(d) The deputy minister is required to accept an unfair degree of responsibility and is entrusted with more power and authority than should be entrusted to a single individual.[88]

This submission recommended, among other things, that the entire Act be rewritten, that the "number and the range of discretionary powers . . . should be materially reduced and that those that may be continued should, as far as possible, be clarified by publication of regulations, interpretations and rulings."[89] In the case of appeal procedure, it was recommended that there be a board of review, independent of the tax administration, and from which there would be recourse to the Exchequer Court of Canada. Similar recommendations were made by the Taxation Section of the Canadian Bar Association[90] and by the Canadian Chamber of Commerce.[91]

The Special Committee of the Senate recommended in its Final Report that "the following principles be adhered to as conditions precedent to any solution that may be reached in this phase of the problem"—(1) that a Board of Tax Appeals be

[88]*Ibid.*, no. 4, April 3, 1946, p. 79.

[89]*Ibid.*, p. 91.

[90]It was recommended that all "unnecessary" discretions be eliminated, and that an "absolutely independent Board of Tax Commissioners should be appointed." *Ibid*, no. 5, April 9, 1946, p. 114.

[91]See its brief to the Senate Committee, in which it was pointed out that "not only is the Minister given power to make regulations, but, in addition, many sections of the Act give him a broad power to exercise discretion in making tax assessments. In some sections there is an obvious intention to preclude appeals from the Minister's decision, this intention being expressed in phrases which refer to the Minister's decision as 'final and conclusive.' We submit that no Minister of the Crown should, in fairness to himself and in equity, be asked to exercise such wide discretionary power without a right of appeal to the judiciary or some special body created for the purpose of assuming it, and that tax legislation should be so drafted as to minimize the necessity for the delegation of discretionary power and with greater regard for the fundamental principles of democratic government." *Ibid.*, no. 7, April 30, 1946, p. 227.

created, which "should be entirely divorced from and independent of the control of that Department of Government which is charged with the levying and collecting of taxes"; and (2) "that the administering officials of the Department which levies and collects the taxes be not accorded any authority relating to the exercise of administrative or ministerial discretion, the levying of assessments, or the imposition of penalties which is not subject to the immediate, effective and conclusive jurisdiction of an independent tribunal.[92]

In 1948 the Income War Tax Act was amended to provide for an Income Tax Appeal Board, to be appointed by the Governor-in-Council, consisting of a chairman and not less than two or more than four other members. The Board did not come into being, however, until after the new Act became operative for the 1949 taxation year.

The Board has the full jurisdiction of a court, and may hear and decide all questions of fact and law arising under an income tax assessment. In the case of Section 126, however, which gives broad discretionary powers to the Treasury Board, the jurisdiction of the Appeal Board is limited to the determination of whether the discretion was properly exercised in accordance with sound principles of law.[93]

When the new Act was finally drafted, most of the discretionary powers contained in the old Act had disappeared. In explaining the new Act, while still in bill form, to the Banking and Commerce Committee, the Minister of Finance said:

> An attempt has been made to improve the arrangement of the law, to remove ambiguities, and to generalize certain provisions which in the old law dealt with specific situations. Over the past thirty years various provisions have been inserted to take care of particular situations. These special provisions intermingled with the main body of the law have tended to confuse the main pattern of the legislation. One of the changes in arrangement which I think will add to the clarity of the law is the plan of setting up special sections for special cases following

[92]*Ibid.*, no. 12, May 28, 1946, pp. 382-3.

[93]In *Anger* v. *Minister of National Revenue,* (1949) 1 Tax A.B.C. 163, 169, the Chairman of the Board remarked that "whenever Parliament gives to the Minister a discretionary power, it imposes upon him a corollary duty to exercise it and to exercise it according to proper legal principles."

the main body of the law. Special groups only are interested in these particular provisions—such as for instance taxation of trustees—and it is unnecessary that they should, shall I say, clutter up the main body of the law. The definition section, which is quite long, has been transferred to the final part of the Act rather than having it precede the main body of the law. This, I think, is an improvement.

One of the most general complaints of the present Income War Tax Act is against the extent of ministerial discretion. Bill 338 has retained very few of these cases where the minister is to exercise discretionary power. It is possible that we have gone too far in this direction. There are some situations where ministerial discretion is the only fair way to have certain questions settled. It is a device which avoids the rigidity of a written statute, and it is a means whereby real cases of hardship may be avoided. Frequently the law cannot anticipate all the situations which may arise, and in the absence of ministerial discretion there is no alternative to enforcing the letter of the law.

In connection with the elimination of ministerial discretion, the committee is aware that the Income Tax Appeal Board will concurrently be functioning. This will be an easily accessible court where the costs to the taxpayer for his day in court will not be more than $15.[94]

One of the most warmly welcomed steps taken by the government was the repeal of Section 9 in 1950. This was the section that gave the Minister power to deem a dividend paid to the shareholders in such amount as he considered a company's undistributed earnings to be in excess of what was reasonably required for the business. The repeal of this section was connected with the new provisions for capitalizing earned surplus on the payment of the special 15 per cent tax.

The most persistent criticism of this section was not so much against the actual effect of the additional taxation imposed, as against the principle by which the judgment of company management was summarily superseded by that of tax officials. Now, under the new treatment of undistributed income, there is no logical place for such powers.

Only experience under the new Act will indicate whether the movement away from ministerial discretion is conducive to greater tax equity. There is much to be said for the discretionary

[94]House of Commons Standing Committee on Banking and Commerce, *Minutes of Proceedings and Evidence,* no. 13, June 15, 1948, p. 550.

power used in an enlightened and impartial way, as opposed to the rigidity of a tightly drawn statute. By its use, consideration can be given to conditions peculiar to a particular case. But where the procedure is spelled out in the law and the regulations, and no discretion allowed, such special consideration cannot be given by the tax administration. The courts can only decide what the law means and whether it has been applied properly.

CONCLUSIONS

Two important trends are apparent in the thirty-four years of taxing corporate income in Canada. The first involves the concept of the corporate form as a separate taxable entity. During the first eight years of the tax, dividends were free of normal tax in the shareholders' hands. But in 1925 they became fully taxable; then arose the contentious problem of double taxation and then began the long series of amendments to prevent tax avoidance. Finally, in 1949, provision was made for a 10 per cent dividend credit, with an implied promise of more to come later. This is a distinct reversal of policy which had been firm for more than two decades. Whether the pendulum will swing completely back to its starting point must be a matter for conjecture. But the fact that it has swung part way is significant, and there are no logical grounds now for stopping short of a complete return to the view that the corporation is not a person distinct from its shareholders.

The second trend is the movement away from ministerial discretion in the direction of a more precise statute and regulations. The current agitation for a definition of income in the Act is evidence that many people want even more detailed legislation than now exists. How far this trend will develop is another matter for conjecture. It shows a decided influence of American practice. Possibly experience under the existing legislation will indicate that there is wisdom in proceeding slowly and with caution.

NOTE ON CONSOLIDATED RETURNS

The right to file a consolidated return for an allied group of corporations dates from the 1932 taxation year. For some curious reason there has always been an extra tax charged for exercising this right. The rate was 1½ per cent from 1932 to 1934, and 2 per cent thereafter. In his 1951 budget speech, the Minister of Finance stated: "The right of corporations to file consolidated returns will be withdrawn in respect of taxation years ending after December 31, 1950."[95] Later, during the budget debate, this provision was amended to become effective during the taxation year 1952.[96]

A number of corporate taxpayers have filed returns on a consolidated basis, despite the 2 per cent tax penalty. Presumably in certain corporate operations it has been advantageous to file a consolidated return. From an accounting and economic viewpoint, the only accurate measurement of an operation conducted by allied companies is a consolidated statement.

The withdrawal of the right to file a consolidated return was not covered by a budget resolution, and no reason for the withdrawal was given in the budget speech. During the debate on the income tax bill the Minister of Finance stated concerning its withdrawal: "The principal reason of course is that, now we have introduced into the Act the principle of carrying losses forward and backward, this has ceased to have the practical significance it used to have."[97]

It is also understood that the repeal of this right was premised upon the anticipated difficulties of the application of a consolidation to the ill-fated relief provision with reference to capital employed.[98]

As far as the first argument is concerned, perhaps there is some truth in the allegation that the introduction of provisions for the carry-over of losses has offset the advantage of consolidated returns as far as a comparison of aggregate revenue yields is concerned.[99] But there are certain advantages in consolidation of a more technical nature, for instance where consolidation permits the separate incorporation of a certain part of a business for

[95]*House of Commons Debates*, April 10, 1951, p. 1811.

[96]*Ibid.*, June 18, 1951, p. 4232.

[97]*Ibid.*

[98]See chapter IX, pp. 317–18.

[99]I still have reservations about this, however, in the case of an affiliated company whose nature does not allow it to show a profit over an indefinite period of time, such as an exploration and development company.

reasons of provincial law. Furthermore, there are arrangements already set up by taxpayers on a consolidated basis that cannot easily be broken down into constituent interests. For example, there is the case of a group pension plan approved and operating through the single agency of an association of allied companies; probably similar situations will be encountered.[100]

Apparently the repeal of Section 75, in which a consolidated return was allowed, was dictated not by any calculation of alternative revenue yields, but rather as a matter of administrative convenience. If this inference is correct, surely the convenience and established practice of taxpayers should have received at least equal consideration with the convenience of the tax authorities.[101]

[100]See the Canadian Tax Foundation's *Memorandum Submitted to the Minister of Finance,* May 29, 1951, p. 5.

[101]It is my conviction that where a tax measure balances between administrative convenience as opposed to the convenience of the taxpayer, the latter should have the decisive weight. After all, it is the taxpayer who pays all of the government's bills.

CHAPTER THREE

THE RATIONALE OF THE CORPORATION INCOME TAX

EVEN A CASUAL examination of the literature concerning the taxation of business, and particularly the taxation of corporation income in the hands of corporations, reveals a great area of disagreement among students of taxation everywhere. There is no agreement on such a fundamental point as whether there is any theoretical ground for taxing corporations. Neither is there agreement as to the economic effects of the tax, its incidence, or its effects on business policy and organization.

Opinion ranges from the emphatic view that the tax is vicious in all its aspects, and should be abandoned,[1] to the other extreme that the tax ranks with the personal income tax and the death duties as the best forms of taxation yet devised.[2] Probably most students of the problem find themselves in the middle ground between these two extremes, admitting part of the argument expounded at both flanks, and seeking ways in which to fit the tax into the tax system with the least possible inequity and adverse economic effects.[3]

[1]Mr. Beardsley Ruml is a leading exponent of this school of thought. See his "Fiscal Policy and Taxation," *Proceedings of the National Tax Association,* 1944, pp. 168 ff. See also Beardsley Ruml and H. C. Sonne, *Fiscal and Monetary Policy,* pp. 9 ff. Professor Henry C. Simons, one of the ablest tax students of his time, was one of the most unequivocal opponents of the tax. Typical of his statements is this: "There should be no taxation of business as such and certainly no such taxes confined to incorporated business." "Federal Tax Reform," *University of Chicago Law Review,* Dec. 1946, p. 56.

[2]See Paul Studenski, "Toward a Theory of Business Taxation," *Journal of Political Economy,* Oct. 1940, 621-54. In this article Professor Studenski lists and explains some eight theoretical justifications for the taxation of business, in all of which he finds some validity.

[3]Professor Harold M. Groves is representative of this group and has written extensively on the matter. See his "Equity and Expediency in Business Taxation,"

The arguments for and against the corporation tax fall into four broad groups[4] based upon (1) the benefits conferred on corporations by the state; (2) ability to pay; (3) the need for social control; and (4) economic considerations.

Special Benefits Received

The traditional equity argument in favour of imposing a special levy on the corporate form of business enterprise is based upon the idea of exacting payment for special privilege conferred upon it by the state. The roots of the argument lie in the differentiation that is made between corporations, as legal persons, and their shareholders. The corporation receives and enjoys special privileges and benefits of a legal and economic nature, such as limited liability, perpetual life, easy transfer of ownership, and greater access to the capital market than is open to any other form of business enterprise. In some cases corporations such as public utilities and common carriers are given exclusive and monopolistic rights in their franchises. While the normal control over such enterprises is exercised through rate regulation by a public body, it is argued that such special privileges should properly be grounds for special taxation.

While it can hardly be denied that the corporate form of enterprise does receive benefits from the state, the partnership and the proprietorship, which are simple, flexible, easily organized and dissolved, and free from many of the restrictions imposed upon corporations, also receive benefits. Furthermore, incorporation is open to any business on relatively easy terms (save for taxation), and some observers conclude, therefore, that an ordinary corporate charter probably has little distinct economic value. Certainly the high rates of taxation on corporate income and excess profits applicable during and since the war cannot be justified in terms of this benefit theory. Yet the advantages derived from the

---

How Shall Business be Taxed? pp. 34-44; "Postwar Federal Taxation," *Proceedings of the National Tax Association*, 1944, pp. 199-206; *Postwar Taxation and Economic Progress*, chaps. II-VI; "Revision of the Corporation Income Tax," *Proceedings of the National Tax Association*, 1947, pp. 97-104.

[4]Mr. Richard B. Goode classifies them as equity and economic arguments. For a summary of these arguments, see his *Postwar Corporation Tax Structure*, pp. 6-14.

corporate form of business organization probably are great enough to merit special taxation. Even Mr. Ruml concedes this, in suggesting "a small franchise tax of 5% on corporation income, which represents the value of doing business in the corporate form."[5] The difficulty attached to measuring this benefit is apparent, and Mr. Ruml's 5 per cent is completely arbitrary, as any such attempt must be.

Such advantages as accrue to business concerns should be reflected in their net income, which is assumed to be the measure of these benefits. This yardstick of benefit ignores the rate of return on the investment, and is therefore likely to be quite unfair in the case of any two corporations. As Professor A. G. Buehler has pointed out, "It is not known how to measure the benefits [received by business] from government and it is not demonstrable that those benefits flow in any certain ratio to income."[6]

Perhaps one of the chief advantages to be gained from incorporating a business under the existing tax structure is the possibility of using the corporate form as a tax avoidance device, or at least as a device for postponing taxation of personal income. It is here that the case for discriminatory tax treatment of corporations has real weight.

While it is impossible to determine the extent to which the corporate form has been assumed in Canada as a result of tax considerations, it is nevertheless certain that many corporations in this country do owe their existence to this cause. The practice has not been without its hazards, however, in the case of private corporations. Where there was a substantial accrual of undistributed earnings at the time of a principal shareholder's death, the combined impact of death duties and personal income taxes on his share of the undistributed earnings often resulted in an extremely heavy burden. This situation has now been alleviated under Section 95A, enacted in 1950.[7]

Normally the retention of profits in a corporation for tax avoidance purposes has resulted only in a postponement of personal income tax on such earnings, pending the day of actual distri-

[5]"Fiscal Policy and Taxation," p. 169.

[6]"The Taxation of Business," *Bulletin of the National Tax Association*, Dec. 1944, p. 87.

[7]See chap. II.

bution through winding up or in some other manner. But complete avoidance could be achieved if the corporation were sold for an amount reflecting the value of its physical assets and the accrued and undistributed earned surplus, after taking liabilities into account. Under the pre-1950 law, however, this was not likely to be easy if prospective purchasers were tax-wise and understood the full implications of the situation.

The existence of undistributed profits gives strength to the argument for taxing corporate income. Under a general tax on net income some tax is paid annually, even though it may be considerably less than would have been paid under the personal income tax had the income been distributed. This is rather a cart-before-the-horse argument for a general corporation tax, however. The real case is for a special tax on undistributed corporate earnings in order to prevent tax avoidance.

If there were no general corporation tax and no special tax on undistributed earnings, the result would be exemption of corporate savings from taxation. If corporate savings were exempt, other savings should be exempt in the interest of equity. But, as Richard Goode has pointed out, the "exemption of savings would transform the income tax into a spendings tax, which would be a drastic remedy for any existing 'double taxation' or relative overtaxation of distributed corporate profits."[8]

Another equity argument sometimes used in favour of taxing corporation income is based upon the economic distinction that is said to exist between corporations and their shareholders. It is asserted that in many instances management and ownership are completely divorced in the corporate form of enterprise, or so much so that the corporation can be regarded as a going concern, separate and distinct from its shareholders. This is true, in some cases, where the shareholders have little, if any, control over the policies of their companies. But it is probably not typical. Most business enterprises, whether incorporated or not, are relatively small,[9] and in these there is hardly likely to be such a dichotomy

[8]"The Postwar Corporation Tax Structure," *How Should Corporations be Taxed?* p. 51.

[9]In the 1946 taxation year 13,654 (59 per cent) of the 23,166 active taxable corporations reporting a profit in Canada reported income under $10,000. They accounted for only 3.2 per cent of the $1,387,302 million of aggregate taxable

between ownership and management. If tax policy were to be formulated in terms of this argument, surely there should be a clear differentiation made between corporations in which management and ownership are divorced, and those in which they are not. The inherent administrative problems attached to a plan of this type are so great as not to recommend it. Mr. Goode makes the following comment that is worth consideration: "The fact that some realistic distinction can be drawn does not in itself, however, argue for separate taxation of corporations and their stockholders, unless one takes it for granted that all economic entities should be taxed. The argument seems to be more in the nature of a rebuttal of the charge of double taxation than an independent support for the corporate income tax."[10]

From this cursory examination of the principal arguments for taxing corporations on a benefit theory, it appears that they are on somewhat less than firm ground. Taxation in accordance with benefits received is an outmoded concept and should not be invoked, save in very special instances, where there is some reasonable measure of the benefits received. Special assessments on real estate can be defended on the benefit theory, because there is some hope of measuring the benefit received through street paving or other local improvements that are reflected in the capital value of real property. But, in general, an equitable system of taxation should be rationalized on the ability to pay doctrine.

Ability to Pay

If it can be demonstrated that corporations have ability to pay taxes, a strong case can be made for taxing them. But here, again, one finds marked difference of opinion.[11] It is argued by some tax

income reported. See *Taxation Statistics,* 1948, Table E, p. 44. This situation is closely paralleled in the United States. In 1944, of the 289,000 corporation returns reporting net income, 64 per cent reported net income under $10,000 and they accounted for only a little more than 2 per cent of the $27 billion aggregate net income reported. See Louis Shere, "The Fiscal Significance of the Corporation Income Tax," *Proceedings of the National Tax Association,* 1947, p. 6.

[10] *Postwar Corporation Tax Structure,* p. 12.

[11] Reporting on discussions held during a conference on business taxes, sponsored by the Tax Policy League, Mabel L. Walker said: "It became evident that not only was there lacking a consensus among economists concerning whether business taxes should be based on the benefits received or the ability to pay principle, but there was also no general agreement as to what constituted tax-

students that a corporation as such cannot bear a tax because it has no taxpaying ability. Mr. Louis Schreiber states: "The business corporation may be a separate entity in the eyes of the law; it may have special attributes not found in other forms of doing business; but the fact remains that it is essentially only a form in which individuals, either singly or in groups both large and small, engage in activities intended to produce a profit for those individuals."[12] This argument ignores the fact that in some corporations, at least, where management and ownership are divorced, there is a tendency to formulate policy for the good of the corporation itself, rather than for the shareholders, who often receive only a small fraction of the net earnings.

Professor M. H. Hunter states: "Ability to pay is a subjective concept and has to do with personal feelings, sacrifices, utility, etc., none of which can have any application to a corporation, a business as such, or any other inanimate thing."[13] Professor Studenski, on the other hand, deems fallacious the argument that

---

paying ability on the part of a corporation, and whether indeed a corporation could be said to possess such 'ability' at all, in the generally accepted sense of that term." *How Shall Business Be Taxed?* p. vi.

[12]"The Place of the Corporate Income Tax in the Tax System," *Proceedings of the National Tax Association,* 1947, pp. 107-8.

[13]"Shall We Tax Corporations or Business," *Proceedings of the National Tax Association,* 1936, p. 239. He uses an illustration to "show that the concept of ability to pay cannot be applied to a corporation. Here are two corporations, one with a net income of $100,000 and the other with a net income of $25,000. If income represents ability, then the one has four times the ability of the other, or, if we accept the theory of progressive rates, more than four times the ability. But here we are not dealing with individuals with subjective reactions. When we begin to consider the interest of such individuals in the matter, the picture may change completely. For example, let us assume 100 shareholders of equal amount in the corporation with $100,000 income and but 5 shareholders in the other. In the first case, then, each *individual* owner has a claim to but $1,000 of the income of the corporation while in the other case each owner has claim to $5,000. Instead, then, of the larger income representing a larger ability to pay, it in fact represents a smaller one when the effect upon the individuals concerned is taken into consideration." He concludes: "Obviously, then, the taxation of corporations or of any other businesses cannot be supported on their ability to pay taxes; such can only apply when a natural person is involved."

This argument is based upon the tacit assumption that there is no possibility of shifting the tax to the consumer or to the wage earner but that it must be borne by the shareholder. This is another area in which there is considerable disagreement, as will be indicated in a later section of this study. Furthermore, it ignores the problem of monopoly gains where there is a real economic surplus over and above the normal return on the shareholders' investment, including a reasonable loading for risk.

the corporation tax is merely an attempt to collect taxes indirectly from corporation shareholders. He states that the idea that ability to pay is confined to individuals is "founded . . . upon the false association of business enterprises with the owners thereof."[14] He argues that "the strictly personal or individual concept of ability to pay must be supplemented by an impersonal or group concept of it."[15]

The whole discussion of the ability concept tends to become somewhat metaphysical, and it is apparent that different writers mean different things when they use the term. There is obvious need for clarification of terminology.[16]

Ability to pay is, for most observers, a personal idea, and accordingly it is used in connection with natural persons. An exception is made by some, however, in the case of monopoly profits, which are considered to be an indication of corporate tax-paying ability, and the doctrine is invoked to justify an excess profits tax. But ability to pay should be ruled out completely as a justification for any tax on business. The distinction between a corporation and its shareholders is legal fiction only, and the sooner it is forgotten, for tax purposes, the easier it will be to devise a rational tax system. Taxes imposed on corporations are

[14]"Toward a Theory of Business Taxation," p. 633.

[15]*Ibid.*, p. 634. It is interesting to note the position taken by the United States Treasury. At the hearings before the Senate Committee on Finance on the Revenue Bill of 1935, R. H. Jackson, Assistant General Counsel of the Treasury, said that ". . . from the Treasury's viewpoint (facts showing increasing concentration in large-scale corporations) point to a source of revenue to be drawn upon in accordance with ability to pay. The ability to pay is, in our view, based in large part upon advantages which large corporations have over smaller ones, so that increased levies upon the former would not only be based upon the theory of ability to pay, but would be based upon benefits received." United States Senate, Committee on Finance, *Hearings on H.R. 8974*, 74th Cong., 1st Sess., p. 217. Cited by Roy Blough, "Flat versus Graduated Rates for Business Net Income Taxes," *How Shall Business Be Taxed?* p. 78.

[16]William Vickrey makes these pointed remarks: "Many modern writers have shied away from notions of utility and sacrifice, but the net result has been to complete the confusion. Some have taken refuge in the phrase 'ability to pay,' but unless ability to pay is in some way identified with 'utility,' it turns out to be another obfuscation. More often than not, ability to pay turns out to mean just about what the user wants it to mean; so that as a tool for determining the progressiveness of a graduation it is useless. Indeed one finds serious discussion of the ability to pay of corporations as such; at such a point one suspects that the concept of ability to pay has degenerated to a notion very close to 'inability to squawk,' or at least inability to vote." *Agenda for Progressive Taxation*, pp. 374-5.

not borne by them, as such. They are borne by the shareholders through decreased dividends, by consumers through increased prices, by labour through decreased wages, or by all these groups.[17]

The fallacy of considering that corporate income indicates ability to pay taxes has resulted in widespread use of rate progression for corporation income tax purposes.[18] Assuming that the tax is borne in most cases by the shareholders,[19] its inherent regressivity is magnified under rate progression. There are likely to be more small income shareholders of large corporations than of small, because of the greater market for the shares of the former. But a progressive income tax on corporate income imposes the heaviest rate on the large income, ignoring the circumstances of the shareholders, and taxing some of them at a rate which would never be tolerated under the personal income tax.

It has already been noted that corporate income by itself is meaningless as a measure of taxpaying ability. It is not the size of the income that has meaning, but the relationship it bears to the investment. It is not realistic, therefore, to impose a tax on net corporate income at progressive rates. If there is any case at all for rate progression in corporation taxes, it must be based upon rate graduation according to the percentage return on capital, not according to the absolute size of the income. This in itself leads to so many complications that the proposal should be avoided.

Social Control

A more pertinent argument for imposing taxes on corporations is one of social expediency, the need for some degree of control over business institutions and activities alleged to be anti-social. Among the objectives sought through taxation is the control of monopoly, of concentration of wealth and economic power, and

[17]See Lewis H. Kimmel, *Postwar Tax Policy and Business Expansion*, p. 9.

[18]Professor Mabel Newcomer reported in 1937 that in twenty-two countries levying the tax, eleven used progressive rates. "European Taxation of Business," *How Shall Business be Taxed?* p. 69. Roy Blough has written an excellent paper, "Flat versus Graduated Rates for Business Net Income Taxes," *ibid.*, pp. 74-85. Federal corporate rate progression in the federal corporation tax was introduced for the first time in Canada in the 1949 budget.

[19]The incidence of the tax is discussed in chapter IV.

the prevention of over-complication of the financial structure of corporations.[20]

In addition to the customary difference of opinion, the literature on taxation for purposes of social control indicates a considerable amount of confused thought, not only regarding objectives, but regarding the means of achieving them. For example, one finds tax proposals based upon the assumption that big business is undesirable, and that the tax system should be used to discourage or eliminate it. Such a line of thought ignores the fact that in some industries large size is inevitable because of the vast amount of capital required, and that size, *per se,* should not be considered as anti-social.[21] The steel industry is a case in point. Furthermore, there is no necessary relationship between the size of an enterprise and the rate of return on the investment. In the United States medium-sized business units, with assets ranging from $500,000 to $10,000,000 tend to earn higher percentages, before taxes, than either the very large or the very small corporations.[22]

The large-scale operation, with its mass production techniques, has made a notable contribution to the satisfaction of human wants. It need hardly be pointed out that in the United States, where mass production has reached its greatest development, the people have the highest living standard in the world. Admittedly the development of the super-corporation with its assembly line production methods has caused many social and economic problems. But their solution does not lie in scrapping the mass production system. Any tax system designed to accomplish this end is itself anti-social.

[20]See Harold M. Groves, ("Equity and Expediency in Business Taxation," *How Shall Business be Taxed?* pp. 43-4), who discusses the problem under these headings. The objective of controlling the economy through taxation will be discussed under the heading of economic considerations.

[21]There is, however, a serious problem when monopoly or imperfect competition results from the sheer size of a company large enough to dominate an industry and its market through price leadership and the various other techniques developed in such cases. This point will be discussed presently.

[22]In 1942 corporations with assets of $100 million and over earned an average 13.8 per cent before taxes, compared with 26.7 per cent for corporations with assets between $1 million and $5 million, and 19.5 per cent for corporations with less than $50,000 in assets. See Henry E. Hoagland, *Corporation Finance,* p. 546.

1. *Control of Monopoly Profit*

The existence of monopoly profit, resulting from prices higher than would prevail under competitive conditions, is used as an argument for the taxation of corporations.

Professor Groves states: "The recapture of monopoly profits may be justified on the ground of special benefit or privilege, on the ground of ability to pay, and on the ground of social expediency."[23] He argues that there is a strong case for the use of an excess profits tax to meet the problem of monopoly profits, and while conceding that "its basis of administration is so capricious as to deprive it of much virtue," he concludes that it "contains so much that is theoretically sound and sensible that it seems that we should not drop it from the tax system without further attempts to find for it a workable system of administration."[24] Lewis H. Kimmel takes the opposite view. He writes:

> An excess profits tax for control purposes cannot be justified. If, for example, certain corporations earn extremely high profits by reason of monopoly or near-monopoly positions and if these profits are regarded as a discordant element in the economy, an excess profits tax is not the proper solution. Actually, it would not be a solution at all. Acceptance of this approach would be tantamount to a willingness to perpetuate the degree of monopoly prevailing—or even have it increase—on the ground that the financial rewards would accrue to the government rather than to the owners.[25]

Groves's case might be defended on the theoretical ground of what he calls "social expediency," but not on the benefit or ability grounds. The ideal of social justice dictates that monopoly profits be prevented, or, if this is not possible, that they should be kept out of the hands of the monopolists who have exploited the consuming public. But Kimmel seems to be on sound ground when he argues that taxation cannot prevent monopoly, and may even perpetuate it. If monopoly profit results in exploitation of consumers, as it surely must, the consumer is not relieved of his exploitation simply because the state prevents the monopolist

[23]"Equity and Expediency in Business Taxation," *How Shall Business be Taxed?* p. 39. [24]*Ibid.*, p. 40.

[25]*Postwar Tax Policy and Business Taxation*, p. 9. Groves concedes this point. "Equity and Expediency in Business Taxation," *How Shall Business be Taxed?* p. 40.

from keeping that part of his net earnings deemed to be derived from his monopolistic position. Nor is he likely to benefit by any price reduction resulting from the taxation of excess profits. Judging from available evidence, the tendency under the wartime taxation of excess profits at a rate of 100 per cent was in the direction of building up deductible charges against such profits rather than in that of reducing them through price cuts.

The difficulties attached to any attempt to administer rationally an excess profits tax to control monopoly profits would be tremendous. For example, how are monopoly profits to be distinguished from greater than average profits secured through efficient management with no extra cost accruing to the customer?[26] To tax away such an earned increment of income on the ground that it is excessive (and therefore anti-social) is to penalize and destroy initiative and the incentive to be efficient. This is the worst feature of excess profits taxation on the straight-line basis.[27] Furthermore, the excess profits tax is considered to rank first among the taxes having repressive effects on business and investment incentives.[28]

The problem of anti-social profits will remain a challenge in a private enterprise economy. Indeed, it may be increased, in view of the current trend in the direction of an increasing decline of competition in many branches of industry. The problem of

[26]Groves meets this point by arguing: "Even superior management, where it results in a high rate of return for the corporation, may, however, indicate some ability to pay if corporations may ever be said to have this attribute" (*ibid.*). This invocation of the ability theory is not acceptable to me; I maintain that the theory cannot be applied satisfactorily to corporations.

[27]Professor A. G. Buehler argues: "Excess profits taxes are open to the further criticism that they have a tendency to rest more heavily on the successful small corporations than on the large, because the smaller successful corporations usually enjoy higher rates of profit than the larger, and also because the earnings of the smaller corporations tend to fluctuate more than the earnings of the larger. As a result of the latter tendency, a small corporation with a series of deficits or with relatively low profits over a period of years may pay a high tax rate in its years of prosperity, while a large corporation with relatively stable earnings, but with a higher average rate of return on its investment, may escape from the excess profits tax either largely or entirely." "Critique of Present Methods of Business Taxation in the United States," *How Shall Business Be Taxed?* p. 54.

[28]United States Senate, *Document 69*, 78th Cong., 1st Sess., p. 382; cited by Kimmel, *Postwar Tax Policy and Business Taxation*, p. 10. The following ranking of repressive taxes was suggested: (1) excess profits tax; (2) corporate net income tax; (3) personal net income tax; and (4) estate and gift taxes.

control through other than tax measures must always be extremely difficult, but the use of taxation to effect such control is even more so, in view of the serious inequities resulting from the imposition of an excess profits tax.

2. *Concentration of Economic Power*

One of the problems arising out of the tendency for corporations to grow larger and fewer in many industries through combination is the resulting concentration of economic power. This is a matter which is the cause of serious concern to many people. But to use it as a basis for justifying the corporation tax is unsound in principle, as well as illogical.

A steeply progressive corporation income tax rate might well achieve the objective of breaking up the very large business unit and preventing the creation of new ones. But the tax then is based, not upon the fact of incorporation, but upon the size of the enterprise. As already indicated, size by itself should not be the subject of economic criticism. It is only the possible ill effects that the size of a corporation can have on the price structure and upon labour relations, among other things, that can be considered anti-social.

The taxation of corporate income should not be considered a cure for this problem of concentration of economic power. The inequities that must inevitably attach themselves to a tax programme designed to prevent such concentration should rule it out completely.[29] The personal income tax and death duties, based upon a proper conception of the ability doctrine, lend themselves far better to a solution of this problem.

3. *Over-Complication of the Corporate Financial Structure*

Professor Groves has suggested another non-fiscal objective to be achieved through the taxation of corporations, i.e., the simplification of the corporate structure. He argues that "an entangled and top-heavy financial structure is definitely anti-social. The tax system should recognize that fact." When intercorporate dividends

[29]Professor Blough comes to the conclusion that "progressive general corporation income taxation is much too crude an instrument with which to discourage socially undesirable economic power." "Flat versus Graduated Rates for Business Net Income Taxes," *How Shall Business be Taxed?* p. 84.

are exempted from taxation, and the option of filing a consolidated return is given to a corporate taxpayer, encouragement is given to the use of holding companies. The holding company may pay little or no tax. Groves approves of the American provision that 15 per cent of the amount of intercorporate dividends must be declared as taxable income by the recipient company, and believes that the privilege of filing a consolidated return should be very narrowly circumscribed.[30]

There can be little doubt that the provisions of the corporation income tax laws both in Canada and in the United States have resulted in a complication of the structure of many business enterprises. Whether such a complicated corporate structure, when it results in tax avoidance, is anti-social is a nice ethical question. There would be divided opinion on that point. But when an excessive complication of business structure results in the pyramiding of securities through the holding company device, the long-run economic effects can be very serious, and certainly anti-social. The impact of the last depression on some business organizations with an unduly complicated structure was much more severe than it would otherwise have been, wiping out security values completely, and ruining investors. The Insull Empire is a case in point.

Obviously the tax system should not force business concerns into unnecessarily complicated organization. But just how the tax system should be made to prevent over-complication is not easy to determine. While the taxation of intercorporate dividends would have the effect of discouraging the use of holding companies, an indiscriminate application of it would react against this device when it is legitimate and has no anti-social results. The existing problem of double taxation of corporate income would be elevated to one of multiple taxation. As long as the tax on corporate income is retained in anything like its present form, it will have bearing on the structure of business enterprise. Perhaps the most that can be hoped for is legislation which will minimize the need for elaborate corporate structures designed to meet the impact of the tax.

[30]"Equity and Expediency in Business Taxation," *How Shall Business be Taxed?* p. 40.

The objectives of control for social purposes examined above do not appear in themselves to provide a sound basis for the taxation of corporations. It seems that any attempt to control monopoly profits, the concentration of economic power, and the structure of the corporate form of enterprise through the taxation of corporations is quite likely to result in as much new inequity as might be removed through such a programme.

Economic Considerations

There are two chief economic arguments advanced in favour of taxing corporate income. The first of these involves the use of the tax system as a key instrument of fiscal policy, designed to to control the economy, to keep it in equilibrium at a high level of production, employment, and national income. The second economic argument is based upon the fiscal yield of the tax.

1. *Economic Control and Fiscal Policy*

As pointed out in the introduction to this study, there has been widespread acceptance in recent years of the doctrine that fiscal policy should be designed for purposes of controlling the economy. This marks a radical shift in basic thinking about taxation away from the traditional philosophy of taxation for revenue purposes only. As a result, one finds strong support for certain taxes which, on other grounds, would be discarded as unacceptable, or at least would be assigned a minor role in the tax system.

Interesting as it would be to explore the intricate web of Keynesian economics and unravel its implications for a national tax policy, such an exercise is beyond the scope of this study. Undoubtedly some of the theories of the Keynesians have validity, but, as Professor Roy G. Blakey remarks, "others seem mostly products of the great depression and their proponents may, in the light of history, appear as the apologists of those who wished to try unorthodox experiments to solve problems they did not know how to meet."[31] All that will be attempted here is a comment on the central problems attached to the implementation of fiscal policy for economic control.

[31]"Evaluation of Postwar Tax Proposals Made by Various Groups and Individuals," *How Shall Corporations be Taxed?* p. 17.

The objectives of taxation acceptable to the writer have been outlined in the introductory pages of this study.[32] They are, in order of importance, (1) the raising of revenue; (2) the fostering of production; and (3) the spreading of the tax burden as equitably as possible, consistent with the achievement of (1) and (2).

This approach falls far short of the objectives proposed by the more ardent Keynesians, whose approach centres about the savings-investment-consumption relationship, which they think should be kept in balance by means of the tax structure. Could this be done, it is argued, the problem of the business cycle could be kept within manageable bounds.

It is widely believed that too much of the national income is saved in relation to what is spent, although there is no irrefutable evidence that over-saving is an important and persistent problem, even in a wealthy country like the United States.[33] The proposed remedies lie in the taxation of undistributed corporate earnings (to discourage saving), or in other methods of removing the tax differential against distributed earnings.

The difficulties attached to such a programme are very great indeed. In the first place, how is it to be decided if and when saving becomes excessive? Even if that problem could be settled on some satisfactory basis, the tax measures designed to accomplish the proper balance between saving and spending would create grave problems in themselves. American experience with a tax on undistributed earnings indicates the magnitude of the difficulties attached to it.

Furthermore, in the time lag between recognition of a situation of disequilibrium and the effective implementation of tax measures designed to cure it, the situation might be so changed that the corrective measures would be inadequate or worse. Not only does it take time to enact tax measures (unless, of course, the authority of parliament is to be subjugated to rule by order-in-council), but it also takes time for their collection, upon which the economic effects of the control are predicated.

The consumption-saving argument is used to support the corporation tax on the ground that it reduces consumption less and saving more than would any alternative tax which could

[32]*Supra*, p. 15.

[33]See Groves, *Postwar Taxation and Economic Progress*, p. 364.

feasibly be made to replace it. This conclusion is based on the assumption that the tax is borne by the shareholders and not shifted to consumers, an assumption on which there is a good deal of difference of opinion.[34]

Two distinct aspects of the tax are involved in this argument. To the extent that the tax reduces the amount of net income retained by corporations, it falls entirely upon current saving, and has no effect upon consumption. This is considered a desirable end by those who believe that excessive saving is an undesirable feature of the private enterprise economy. Furthermore, it is a widely advocated principle that taxation be levied on surpluses rather than on costs and consumption. The writer subscribes to this as a theoretical principle.

The impact of the tax on individual recipients of dividends, on the other hand, reduces both saving and consumption in so far as it reduces personal income. But since dividends are heavily concentrated in the hands of individuals in the relatively high income brackets, individuals who habitually save a considerable portion of their incomes, it appears likely that the tax affects consumption much less than it does saving.

It is concluded that short of a national emergency such as war, the revenue system should not be used as an instrument of economic control. Taxation is a blunt and discriminatory means of fostering any desired economic condition. Elsewhere in this study the writer has accepted the need for using taxation deliberately to check inflation under current conditions. But it is clearly indicated that the choice is a choice of evils. In any event, the corporation tax should not be included in the taxes levied for controlling the economy. Untold and lasting economic damage could be done by manipulating the corporation tax rate structure to control investment. This tax should be used purely for revenue purposes.

Compared with the tax on corporate income, sales taxes, excises and other taxes on consumption, and pay roll taxes are probably much more regressive, and therefore have a considerably greater effect upon consumption, thus reducing the demand for consumer goods. This is deemed to be deleterious to the maintenance of a high level of production, employment, and income.

[34]See the discussion of incidence, chapter IV.

TABLE III

Relationship between Corporation Income Tax and Total Income Tax, Total Federal Tax Revenue, and Total Revenue 1919–1952

(1) *Year ended Mar. 31*	(2) *Corporation income tax*[a]	(3) *Total income tax collections*[a]	(4) *Ratio (2) to (3)*	(5) *Total federal tax revenue*	(6) *Ratio (2) to (5)*	(7) *Total revenue*	(8) *Ratio (2) to (7)*
	$000,000	$000,000	%	$000,000	%	$000,000	%
1919	34.4[b]	42.3	81.3	233.7[e]	14.7	312.9[e]	11.0
1920	51.2	64.4	79.5	293.6	17.4	349.7	14.6
1921	54.7	87.2	62.8	368.8	14.8	436.3	12.5
1922	61.7	101.5	60.8	320.0	19.3	382.3	16.1
1923	41.0	72.7	56.4	335.5	12.2	403.1	10.2
1924	33.3	58.9	56.5	341.7	9.7	406.6	8.2
1925	33.8	58.9	57.4	293.9	11.5	351.5	9.6
1926	32.9	56.7	55.7	327.6	10.0	382.9	8.6
1927	30.0	48.1	62.4	346.6	8.7	400.5	7.5
1928	34.3	57.5	59.7	364.7	9.4	429.6	8.0
1929	35.1	59.9	58.6	395.9	8.9	460.2	7.6
1930	42.0	69.2	60.7	378.6	11.1	453.0	9.3
1931	44.4	71.1	62.4	296.3	15.0	357.7	12.4
1932	36.5	61.3	59.5	275.1	13.3	334.5	10.9
1933	36.1	62.2	58.0	254.3	14.2	311.7	11.6
1934	27.4	61.4	44.6	271.9	10.1	324.7	8.4
1935	35.8	66.8	53.6	304.4	11.8	362.0	9.9
1936	42.5	82.7	51.4	317.3	13.4	372.6	11.4
1937	58.0	102.4	56.6	386.6	15.0	454.2	12.8
1938	69.8	120.4	58.0	448.7	15.6	516.7	13.5
1939	85.2	142.0	60.0	435.7	19.6	502.2	17.0
1940	77.9	134.4	57.9	467.7	16.6	562.1	13.9
1941	155.4	272.1	57.1	778.2	20.0	872.2	17.8
1942	317.5[c]	645.5	49.2	1,360.9[f]	23.3	1,483.5[f]	21.4
1943	791.2	1,364.7	58.0	2,136.7	37.0	2,240.3	35.3
1944	758.7	1,620.5	46.8	2,591.8	29.3	2,765.0	27.4
1945	718.0	1,538.6	46.7	2,374.1	30.2	2,687.3	26.7
1946	683.5	1,432.0	47.7	2,274.9[g]	30.0	3,013.2[g]	22.7
1947	659.8[d]	1,412.1	46.7	2,457.9	26.8	3,007.9	21.9
1948	578.0	1,286.9	44.9	2,452.1	23.6	2,871.7	20.1
1949	530.7	1,342.8	39.5	2,436.1	21.8	2,771.4	19.1
1950[h]	601.4	1,270.9	47.3	2,323.2	25.9	2,580.1	23.3
1951	810.0	1,524.0	53.1	2,780.9	29.1	3,105.3	26.1
1952[i]	976.0	1,906.0	51.2	3,438.0	28.6	3,730.0	26.2

[a]Compiled from *Taxation Statistics*, 1949, Tables A, C, and D, pp. 15, 18, and 19.

[b]Data from 1919 to 1930 include excess profits tax. It is impossible to break down these figures to differentiate between excess profits tax on incorporated and on unincorporated business, so that the collection figures for corporations are somewhat exaggerated. The error is not, however, very large. The greatest yield from the World War I excess profits tax was $44.1 million, in 1920. In the year of the greatest yield from the World War II tax (1946) the ratio of tax on unincorporated to incorporated businesses was slightly over 5 per cent. Thus, the data on the yield of corporation taxes from 1919 to 1930 are probably not exaggerated by more than 5 per cent.

[c]The data on yield from 1941 to 1949 include excess profits taxes paid by corporations as shown in *Taxation Statistics*, 1949, Table D, p. 19.

[d]Figures for the period 1947-52 include the tax on private companies.

[e]Figures for the period 1919-41 are taken from *Canada Year Book*, 1945, Table 8, p. 929.

[f]Figures for the period 1942-5 are taken from the *Budget Speech*, 1946, pp. 46-7.

[g]Figures for the period 1946-49 are taken from the *Budget Speech*, 1950, pp. 112-13.

[h]All data for the period 1950-1 are taken from the *Budget Speech*, 1951, pp. 94-5. The 1951 figures are estimates.

[i]The 1952 figures were taken from the *Budget Speech*, 1951, p. 18. They are the forecast figures used by the Minister of Finance.

TABLE IV

FEDERAL TAX RECEIPTS IN CANADA
FISCAL YEARS 1944-5 TO 1951-2[a]

	1944–45		1945–46		1946–47		1947–48		1948–49		1949–50		1950–51 (Estimate)		1951–52 (Estimate)	
	Amount	% *Total*	*Amount*	% *Total*	*Amount*	% *Total*	*Amount*	% *Total*	*Amount*	% *Total*	*Amount*	% *Total*	*Amount*	% *Total*	*Amount*	% *Total*
	$000,000		$000,000		$000,000		$000,000		$000,000		$000,000		$000,000		$000,000	
Personal income tax[b]	820.5	34.6	748.6	32.9	752.4	30.6	708.9	28.9	812.1	33.3	669.6	28.8	714.0	25.7	930.0	27.1
Corporation income taxes[c]	718.0	30.2	683.5	30.1	659.8	26.9	578.0	23.6	530.7	21.8	601.4	25.9	810.0	29.1	976.0	28.4
Succession duties	17.3	0.7	21.4	0.9	23.6	0.9	30.8	1.3	25.6	1.0	29.9	1.3	34.0	1.2	40.0	1.2
Customs duties	115.1	4.8	128.9	5.7	237.4	9.7	293.0	12.0	222.9	9.2	225.9	9.7	298.0	10.7	315.0	9.1
Excise duties	151.9	6.5	186.7	8.2	196.0	8.0	196.8	8.0	204.7	8.4	220.6	9.5	245.0	8.8	245.0	7.1
Excise taxes[d]	543.1	22.9	496.9	21.8	579.0	23.5	640.8	26.1	636.1	26.1	571.5	24.6	675.0	24.3	927.0	27.0
Other taxes	8.2	0.3	8.9	0.4	9.7	0.4	3.8	0.1	4.0	0.2	4.4	0.2	4.9	0.2	5.0	0.1
Total revenue from taxes	2,374.1	100.0	2,274.9	100.0	2,457.9	100.0	2,452.1	100.0	2,436.1	100.0	2,323.2	100.0	2,780.9	100.0	3,438.0	100.0

[a]Source: *Budget Speech*, 1947, pp. 26-7; 1949, p. 50; 1950, p. 86; 1951, p. 60.
[b]Includes individual income tax, tax on interest and dividends, tax on rents and royalties, and excess profits taxes paid by other than corporations.
[c]Includes standard corporation tax and corporation excess profits taxes. Data for excess profits taxes paid by corporations and individuals were taken from *Taxation Statistics*, 1949, Table D, p. 19. In 1949-50 there was an excess of refunds over collections of excess profits taxes, as shown in *Taxation Statistics*, 1950, Table D, p. 19.
[d]Includes the 8 per cent sales tax, which accounts for the greater part of this item.

Thus is the economic case made for taxing corporate income. While such a tax can be defended on the grounds that it is paid largely out of potential savings, and therefore has no direct effect upon consumption, it may, if heavy, indirectly impair demand by reducing the incentive to invest, thus the availability of capital funds, the physical means of production, and eventually the level of employment, and therefore demand for goods. In the final analysis one comes back to the basic problem of maintaining a balance between consumption, saving, and investment. No tax which disturbs this relationship in a continuous and fundamental way can be deemed a good tax. As far as possible the tax system should be comprised of taxes which result in the least reduction of demand both for consumer goods and for investment goods.

2. *Fiscal Yield*

The most practical argument for taxing corporate income is the fact that such a tax can be made to yield heavily without much unfavourable political reaction. Weight is given to this argument by the fact that the ratio of the yield from the corporate income tax to total income tax collections rose from an all-time low of 39.5 per cent in 1949 to 47.3 per cent in 1950 and an estimated 53.1 per cent in 1951, without arousing public antagonism. The yield of the corporate income tax and the political favour with which the tax is viewed were undoubtedly factors in its being selected by the Minister of Finance as one of the sources of revenue to defray the cost of old age pensions.[35] The estimated yield from this tax for 1952 is $976 million, more than three times

[35]On October 25, 1951, Finance Minister Abbott stated in the House of Commons, "I have made no secret of my concern over a system of taxation under which more than half of company profits are taken away by government. The effects on incentive and efficiency can be extremely dangerous at a time when maximum output and economy in operation is so important as it is today. As in the personal income tax field, my intention is to recommend the repeal of the surcharge as such, on corporations in my next budget and I shall decide in the light of the circumstances at that time, what rate structure to recommend for the calendar year 1952." *House of Commons Debates*, Oct. 25, 1951, p. 389.

Nonetheless the Minister of Finance announced a new threefold 2 per cent tax to pay for old age pensions, including a 2 per cent levy on the taxable income of all corporations, a 2 per cent levy on the taxable income of individuals with a ceiling of $60 a year, and 2 percentage points of the present 10 per cent sales tax, to be applied to an old age security fund for the payment of pensions at seventy years of age to Canadians with twenty years' residence who wish to apply for it. *Ibid.*, p. 388.

that of 1942. The yield of the tax is shown in Table III, along with its relationship to total income tax collections, total federal tax revenue, and total revenue, from 1919 to 1952.

It will be noted that taxes collected from corporations have consistently made up a substantial proportion of the total taxes levied on income. Until 1934 corporation taxes accounted for well over half of the total income tax collections, and in only eight subsequent years were they less than half the total.

Since its inception, the tax levied on corporate income in Canada has occupied a relatively important place in the federal revenue system. Before World War II taxes from this source accounted for a significant part of the total national revenue, ranging from 7.5 per cent (1927) to 16.1 per cent (1922). But during the war, with the increase in rates and the imposition of an excess profits tax, corporation taxes became much more prominent. In 1943 the combined yield of the normal tax and excess profits tax on corporate income amounted to $791.2 million, which represented 35.3 per cent of the national revenue in that year, the highest proportion in the period under consideration. During the post-war years the tax on corporate income has occupied a much more important place in the revenue system than it did at any time before the war. In the fiscal year ending March 31, 1951, it yielded an unprecedented total of $810 million, or 26.1 per cent of the national revenue.

The relationship of corporation taxes to other major federal taxes from 1945 to 1952 is shown in Table IV. It will be noted that in 1950-1 and 1951-2 the yield from this tax ranks ahead of that from the personal income tax, which led the taxation field in the previous six of the eight years under study. Previously the yield from this source stood second, save in 1947-8 and 1948-9 when it was third, slightly below that from excise taxes. During the period 1944-5 to 1951-2 taxes on corporations yielded 47.4 per cent of the total income taxes collected by the federal government, and 27 per cent of the total federal tax revenue.

The situation in Canada is compared in Table V with that in the United Kingdom and the United States during the period 1942 to 1947. It will be seen that the ratio of corporation taxes to total income taxes in the United Kingdom has been much lower

TABLE V

RELATIONSHIP BETWEEN CORPORATION TAXES, TOTAL INCOME TAXES, AND TOTAL TAX REVENUES IN CANADA, THE UNITED KINGDOM, AND THE UNITED STATES, 1942–1947

(1) Country	(2) Year	(3) *Corporation income taxes*[a]	(4) *Total income taxes*[a]	(5) *Ratio* (3) *to*(4)	(6) *Total tax revenue*[b]	(7) *Ratio* (3) *to* (6)
		$000,000	$000,000	%	$000,000	%
Canada	1942	317.5	645.5	49.2	1,361	23.3
	1943	791.2	1,364.7	57.9	2,137	37.0
	1944	758.7	1,620.5	46.8	2,592	29.3
	1945	718.0	1,538.6	45.8	2,374	30.2
	1946	683.4	1,432.0	47.6	2,275	30.0
	1947	659.8	1,412.1	46.7	2,458	26.8
United		$000,000	$000,000	%	$000,000	%
Kingdom[c]	1942	269	1,114	24.1	1,962	13.2
	1943	378	1,460	25.9	2,483	15.2
	1944	500	1,760	28.4	2,948	16.9
	1945	510	1,900	26.8	3,135	16.2
	1946	466	1,896	24.6	3,197	14.5
	1947	357	1,589	22.4	3,010	11.8
United		$000,000	$000,000		$000,000	
States[c]	1942	5,022	8,285	60.6	12,234	41.0
	1943	9,996	16,626	60.1	21,194	47.1
	1944	15,147	33,408	45.3	38,812	39.0
	1945	16,399	35,433	46.3	42,376	38.7
	1946	12,906	31,611	40.7	39,406	32.7
	1947	9,678	29,021	33.4	37,578	25.7

[a]Compiled from *Taxation Statistics*, 1949, Tables C and D, pp. 18 and 19.
[b]Compiled from the *Budget Speech*, 1946, pp. 46-7; 1950, pp. 112-13.
[c]Compiled from statistics presented by Louis Shere, "The Fiscal Significance of the Corporation Income Tax," *Proceedings of the National Tax Association*, 1947, pp. 43, 45.

than in Canada or the United States. During the period examined it was never higher than 28.4 per cent in Britain (1944), compared with 57.9 per cent in Canada (1943), and 60.6 per cent in the United States (1942). By 1947 the corporation tax comprised a greater proportion of the total income tax collections in Canada than in either of the other countries.

The corporation tax now occupies a key place in the Canadian revenue system. It is more important here than in the United States, and much more important than in the United Kingdom. The elimination of the tax would result in a major reconstruction of the federal tax system which would hardly be practicable, even in normal times. Leaving aside revenue considerations for the moment, repeal of the corporation tax would certainly result in large-scale tax avoidance or postponement by the retention of corporate earnings. If there were to be no corporation tax in the usual sense, a tax on undistributed profits would be a necessity.

The elimination of the tax would result in a serious revenue loss which would have to be offset by increases in other taxes, although perhaps not all of this loss would have to be recovered by such increases. Collections from the personal income tax would probably increase because of the larger corporate net profits available for distribution as dividends. It is impossible to determine what effect the repeal of the corporation tax would have on dividend policy. But even if dividend payments of Canadian companies were doubled as a result of repealing the corporation tax, the increased revenue received from the personal income tax would not be much more than 10 per cent of the revenue lost from the tax on corporate profits.[36] This means a heavy increase in other taxes, of which there are three major groups, the personal income tax, succession duties, and commodity taxes.

Even if the current federal revenue requirements could have been held to their 1950-1 level, estimated by the Minister of Finance at $3,105 million, the abandonment of the corporation tax would have necessitated very sharp increases in other taxes. The corporation tax was estimated to yield more than $810 million in that year, the highest yield from the tax up to that time.

While some income tax enthusiasts, such as the late Henry C. Simons,[37] have argued that most, if not all, of the national tax revenue should be raised through personal income taxation, it would not have appeared feasible to raise anything like Canada's tax requirements from this tax. Had such a policy been in force in 1951, the personal income tax would have had to yield some $2,780 million. But even in 1944, the peak year of personal income tax collections, the total yield was only $861.8 million, and the burden was generally considered to be crushing.

The yield from death duties could conceivably be increased. But to get even a significant part of what the corporation tax

[36]In the 1947 taxation year a total of $111.8 million of dividends was returned in individual tax returns for tax purposes. If this income were taxed at an average rate of 50 per cent, after the 10 per cent dividend credit, the revenue would be less than $60 million. Doubled dividend payments obviously would result only in a minor offset of the loss from repeal of the corporation tax.

[37]See his *Personal Income Taxation.*

yields would involve a very heavy rate increase. The total succession duties collected by the federal government in 1951 amounted to only an estimated $34 million.

This leaves the taxes on consumption. In 1951 the federal government collected an estimated $132 million from liquor taxes, $116 million from tobacco, $298 million from customs duties, and $471 million from the sales tax, making a total revenue of $1,017 million. The increases in commodity taxes generally since 1950-1 have resulted in sharp public criticism of the government. Many people believe that some commodity taxes (for example, the tax on tobacco) have already exceeded the saturation point, and that the economic effects of increasing commodity taxes would be serious.

One is forced to the conclusion that in view of the present level of federal cash requirements it would be simply impossible to repeal the corporation tax. The loss of the estimated $976 million from this tax in the fiscal year 1951-2 could not be made up, for both political and economic reasons, by allocating this burden to the remaining tax sources.

This is not to say, however, that the tax should not or cannot be improved. The corporation tax is in all probability here to stay as a permanent and key element of the Canadian revenue system. The fact of its heavy yield ensures this. This study will be devoted to an examination of the present tax and its weaknesses, and a consideration of various proposals to remedy them.

Conclusions

A summary of the conclusions reached in this chapter on the rationale of taxing corporate income can readily be tabulated under the headings of the various points covered in the discussion.

1. *Special Benefits Received*

The benefit theory of taxation should be discarded as conforming neither with an acceptable concept of tax justice, nor with any possible administrative device to measure benefits received from government. While corporations do receive certain benefits, so do unincorporated business enterprises.

2. *Ability to Pay*

The ability doctrine should not be invoked to support the

taxation of corporate income, since it is a concept which should be attached to individuals only, and measured by personal income. The legal fiction that makes the corporation a legal person, with a separate legal entity from its shareholders, has resulted in much confused thinking in the field of taxation. It should be abandoned for tax purposes. Even if corporate income could be considered an indication of tax-paying ability, it in itself is no yardstick of ability unless it is related to the rate of return on invested capital.

3. *Social Control*

It is obvious that certain results of the way in which a private enterprise system operates, through frictions and the imperfect functioning of competition, should be subject to control in the public interest. But it is doubtful if the long-term public interest is best served by a policy of using the tax system as a major means of such control. So many inequities seem to be attached to such a programme that it appears likely to achieve no net social gain.

(*a*) Control of Monopoly Profit

It is probably impossible to prevent monopoly by the use of taxation. The attempt to recapture monopoly profit through taxation of excess profits involves the use of a tax that is cumbersome, arbitrary, inequitable, and that discourages incentive to efficiency. A method of control other than the fiscal seems to be a more appropriate means of meeting the problem of monopoly.

(*b*) Concentration of Economic Power

It is not conceded that there is any rational argument for using the corporation tax to prevent the concentration of economic power. Such arguments as exist are based upon the notion that large size is in itself anti-social. Large-scale production has made a very material contribution to national economic welfare, and in some industries, requiring vast capital investment, large size is inevitable. In so far as it is deemed socially desirable to control the concentration of wealth and economic power through taxation, the personal income tax and death duties should be used with rate progression designed to serve the purpose.

(*c*) Over-Complication of the Corporate Financial Structure

Much of the complicated form in which corporations now

operate is a derivative of the complicated corporation tax legislation over the past three decades. The 1950 legislation with respect to private companies, as amended in 1951, should help to eliminate the need for, or the desirability of, elaborate and intricate corporation structure designed to achieve tax advantage for the shareholders of private companies.

4. *Economic Considerations*

(*a*) Economic Control and Fiscal Policy

It is concluded that the general principle of using the tax system as a key tool of fiscal policy for purposes of controlling the economy is undesirable under normal conditions on both theoretical and practical grounds. The tax system should be designed to raise the necessary revenue, and its component parts should be integrated so as to foster production without unnecessary sacrifice of social justice. But even under conditions of grave emergency, such as we had during the war and which now exist again, there is no sound ground for using the corporation tax as an instrument of economic control. This is one tax that should be used solely for revenue purposes.

(*b*) Fiscal Yield

The best argument in favour of the taxation of corporate income is its yield. The tax provides such an important percentage of the total tax collections of the federal government that its elimination is not considered feasible for practical reasons. It is doubtful if the economic effects of the tax are any more serious for the economy than would be the effects of any other taxes substituted for it.

Furthermore, there is an equity argument in favour of the retention of the corporation tax. Its abolition would cause windfall gains to common shareholders. The adage that "an old tax is a good tax" should not be ignored in this respect. This tax must surely have become partly institutionalized and discounted in advance.

It is not to be concluded, however, that nothing can or should be done to integrate the tax into the over-all system of taxation. In 1949 and 1950 constructive legislation was enacted in Canada that goes far towards achieving this objective. Comments and further proposals will be made in a following chapter.

CHAPTER FOUR

THE INCIDENCE OF THE CORPORATION INCOME TAX

SCOPE OF ANALYSIS AND DEFINITION OF TERMS

AN UNDERSTANDING of the incidence of a tax is fundamental to an analysis of its ultimate economic effects. Its effects upon saving and investment, upon production, employment, and income, as well as its equity in the tax system, depend upon where the tax actually rests. Some working hypothesis about incidence is necessary before judgment can be passed on a given tax. In the case of the tax on corporate income, the whole argument about double taxation (one of the chief arguments used against it) stands or falls in accordance with the incidence of the tax. If the tax is shifted to the consumer in the form of higher prices, as is often argued, then it is not borne by the shareholders, and there is no double taxation.

The problem of determining tax incidence is one of the most difficult in the study of public finance, and perhaps less is known about the incidence of the corporation tax than any other.[1] Not only is the theory of its incidence complicated and often abstruse, but its conclusions at times seem at odds with reality. This vexatious situation gives rise to confusion and widespread disagreement, not only among economists, but between economists and business men. One writer states simply that "we do not know where the burden of this tax finally falls."[2]

One of the underlying reasons for the confusion is the failure of many writers to distinguish between the incidence of the

[1]See E. G. Keith, "The Corporation in the Tax System," *Proceedings of the National Tax Association*, 1946, p. 388.

[2]R. E. Paul, *Taxation for Prosperity*, p. 348.

corporation tax and its effects on the economy. One's conclusions must surely be in part dependent upon the time interval under consideration. The traditional theory of incidence is based upon a narrow definition of the term, meaning "the settling or coming to rest"[3] of the tax, distinguished from its economic effects, which may be determined only over a very long time interval, and which may be diffused widely throughout the economy.

It is obvious that the conclusions reached regarding the extent to which the tax is shifted, if at all, will depend upon the meaning that is attached to the word "incidence."[4] It is important, therefore, that the terminology used in discussing the problem be clarified.[5] Richard Goode has stated that "reasonable clarity requires that all who speak of shifting specify *what* is shifted *where* or to *whom* and by what process."[6]

[3]This was Professor E. R. A. Seligman's definition, in his *Shifting and Incidence of Taxation*, p. 2. R. S. Ford writes that "incidence is 'the settling or coming to rest' of a tax at the point of its direct money burden; this term is distinguished from impact, which denotes the person or business actually subject by law to the levy and required to make the payment to the Government." "Some Economic Aspects of the Present Corporate Income Tax," *Proceedings of the National Tax Association*, 1947, p. 55. Another contemporary writer, E. E. Oakes, states that incidence may be interpreted to mean "the relation between the impact of the tax and the prices which are most intimately associated with the point of impact." But he is critical of this approach, and suggests that incidence should "be redefined so as to include not only the repercussions of the tax itself but also the results of the expenditures which the tax finances." "The Incidence of the General Income Tax," *American Economic Review, Supplement*, March 1942, p. 77. Otto von Mering states: "The further effects, that is, those which may follow the placing of the ultimate burden of a tax on certain persons or groups, are no part of the theory of tax shifting." *The Shifting and Incidence of Taxation*, p. 3.

[4]See C. Ward Macy, who writes: "When the incidence of this tax is interpreted broadly to include its effects on the functioning of the economy, *e.g.*, on investment and business expansion, the conclusion reached with respect to shifting naturally differs from that obtained when incidence is given a much narrower connotation." "Incidence or Effects of the Corporation Income Tax," *American Economic Review*, Dec. 1946, p. 904.

[5]Macy suggests, however, that "it may be argued that it is useless hair-splitting to differentiate between incidence and effects, in view of the fact that the final effects of a tax constitute the real basis for evaluating it." *Ibid.*, p. 905. He concedes, however, that "effects can hardly be determined until incidence in the narrower sense of the term is known" (*ibid.*), and appears to accept Seligman's view that "it is only when we have ascertained the incidence that we can proceed to discuss the wider effects of a tax" (*Shifting and Incidence of Taxation*, p. 14).

[6]"The Incidence of the Corporation Income Tax: A Rejoinder," *American Economic Review*, March 1946, p. 147. This comment was made in reply to a criticism by H. R. Bowen in the same issue of the *Review*, "The Incidence of the Corporation Income Tax," pp. 146-7, and the exchange of comments indicates the difficulties inherent in the terminology. Goode concludes that "It might be still better to discard the terminology entirely."

It seems desirable to retain the use of the word incidence in its narrow sense, and to differentiate between incidence used in this way and the broader long-run effects of the tax. For the purposes of this study such a differentiation will be made, because no other procedure seems to lend itself so conveniently to the economic analysis of the effects of the tax. This is done despite recognition of the validity of Professor Groves's remark that "the boundary line between incidence and effect is at times hazy."[7] But if most of the confusion can be eliminated, the chances of arriving at some logical and tenable conclusions should be reasonably good. Accordingly, the discussion of incidence is treated separately from the discussion of the economic effects of the tax.

INCIDENCE

It is an essential feature of the above differentiation that incidence is a short-run concept, while the economic effects of the tax are long-run in their character.[8] Recognition of this will help to avoid the complication resulting from trying to consider, as part of the theory of incidence, the possible long-run effects of the tax on investment and production, and hence on prices.

The various theories of corporate income tax incidence may be placed in three groups: (1) the traditional theory of economists, which holds that the tax is not shifted in the short run, but is borne for the most part, if not entirely, by the corporation, i.e., the shareholder; (2) the cost of production theory, which holds that the tax is a cost and is shifted, at least in part, to the consumer in the form of increased prices; and (3) the diffusion theory,[9] which maintains that the tax is diffused among shareholders, consumers, and wage earners.

It appears that these theories are incompatible. But again it must be remembered that there is no uniformity of terminology,

[7]Harold M. Groves, *Financing Government*, p. 121. See also Hugh Dalton, *Principles of Public Finance*, p. 50.

[8]The writer uses this term in accordance with Viner's definition—the short run is a period "long enough to permit of variations in output through more or less intensive utilization of the relatively fixed elements of a plant but not long enough to permit of any adjustment in the scale of the plant." Jacob Viner, "Cost," *Encyclopaedia of the Social Sciences*, IV, 469.

[9]This is not actually a theory of incidence in accordance with the above definition, because of the long time interval necessary for diffusion. It is included in the grouping, however, since it is discussed so commonly under the theory of incidence.

and that the time interval factor is not constant. The traditional theory is essentially short-run, and its conclusions are convincing in the short run. The diffusion theory, on the other hand, is a long-run theory, and its conclusions, too, are convincing, *in the long run.* It is important to bear this in mind constantly. The real contradiction exists between those who hold that the tax is a cost of production and those who deny it.

1. *Traditional Theory of Incidence*

The traditional theory of incidence, as developed by the classical economists and their followers, is based upon the economic theory of price, which stresses the supply side of the price determining supply-demand relationship. It is actually an examination of the effect of the tax upon supply. If, during a given period, demand and costs remain constant, the only factor that can change price is a change in supply. The analysis concentrates upon the possibility of the tax lowering supply, the only condition, under these assumptions, that would allow price to be raised and the tax shifted to the consumer.

Price is the result of the interplay of two opposing forces—demand and supply. The demand for a commodity is determined by its utility to the buyer and by the amount of purchasing power available. The supply of a commodity is limited primarily by its cost of production. The shorter the period under consideration, the more important demand becomes in the determination of price. The longer the period, the more important cost of production becomes in price determination. Market price "oscillates around normal price which approximates very closely the cost of production."[10]

According to the static economic analysis, market price must cover the costs of the high-cost producers needed to provide the supply of a commodity demanded at a certain price. That is to say, under competitive conditions price is determined by, or is at least equal to, the cost of production of the firm operating at the margin, or the non-profit point. Since the marginal firm shows no net profit, no income tax will be paid. Therefore such a tax will

[10]Oscar F. Litterer, "Corporation Income Tax and Production," *Bulletin of the National Tax Association,* April 1946, p. 201.

have no direct effect upon the continued operation and output of the marginal firm, the costs of which determine price. Assuming no change in demand (and this assumption, at best, has only short-run validity), the lack of any change in the output of the marginal firm prevents any change in the output of supra-marginal firms. Hence the total supply remains unchanged. Since supply remains unchanged, and demand is constant, there can be no increase in market price. Thus the firms showing a net profit, and paying tax on it, are unable to raise price to recover any part of the tax. According to this analysis, the tax is one on economic surplus, and is not shifted to the consumer. This is the essence of the static analysis as applied to conditions of pure or nearly pure competition.

A similar conclusion is reached when conditions of monopoly are considered. It is argued that if a monopolist takes full advantage of his monopolistic position, his price will be set so that, cost and demand considered, his net profit will be at the highest possible point over a period of time. On the basic assumption that the income tax is not a tax on cost (and there is good foundation for this assumption), it follows that the monopoly price that will yield the maximum return will remain unchanged. If price is increased in order to shift the tax to the consumer, and there is no corresponding increase in demand, the monopolist will no longer be operating at the point of maximum return, and through his attempt to recover the tax, he has actually made his position worse. Thus it is concluded that the tax is not reflected in higher prices under conditions of monopoly, and is not shifted.

But pure competition and pure monopoly are not characteristic of modern economic conditions. Most economic activity lies within a zone of imperfect competition, or monopolistic competition. Theorists have naturally turned their attention to price determination under these conditions. The refinement in equilibrium theory brought about by the use of marginal analysis, based upon the concept of marginal revenue and marginal costs, places the treatment of pure competition, imperfect competition, and monopoly on the same footing. It results in no change in the basic conclusions reached by earlier writers regarding the relationship of income taxes to supply and price.

Under the marginal analysis the output of any firm, if it is operated under rational management, will be set at the point where marginal revenue equals marginal cost, because that is the point where net revenue will be greatest. In other words, output will be expanded as long as additional units of output result in a positive increment of net revenue, however small. To go beyond this point, even by one unit of output, means that the revenue derived from that unit does not cover the cost of producing it, and therefore a decrease in total net profit occurs. To fail to reach the equilibrium point of marginal cost and marginal revenue means that net profit is not at its maximum point. With supply so determined, it is argued that market price is a derivative of the relationship between the aggregate supply of goods produced in an industry and the aggregate demand for them.

A profits tax does not enter as a cost of production in any usual sense of the word. The tax merely prevents the firm from retaining the entire differential between its costs and its revenue—its net profit. The tax (unless it be levied at a rate of 100 per cent) should have no bearing on the desirability of expanding production so long as the cost of each additional unit (marginal cost) is less than the revenue (marginal revenue) that it brings in. A unit of output which yields net revenue before taxes will yield some net revenue after taxes. Therefore it should still be desirable, despite the tax, to equilibrate marginal cost and marginal revenue in order to secure the maximum net profit. Hence it is argued that no firm will change its output because of a corporation income tax. If this is so, then the aggregate supply of goods produced in an industry is unchanged by the tax. If demand remains constant, then market price must remain unchanged. It is concluded, therefore, that the tax on net profit is not shifted to the consumer in the form of increased price, but is borne by the shareholders of the corporation. This analysis applies equally to firms operating under conditions of competition, imperfect competition, monopolistic competition, or monopoly.

The validity of this theory of tax incidence is, of course, dependent upon the validity of the price theory upon which it is based. No attempt will be made here to deal with the many intricacies and refinements in the theory of price, but some obvious qualifications will be pointed out, and conclusions drawn as to the general validity of the argument.

In the first place, a dynamic rather than static approach to the problem of market price determination seems more in keeping with the situation as it actually exists. This approach results in at least a partial modification of the conclusions derived from the static analysis.

Marshall states that it is the representative firm rather than the marginal or superior firm that plays the dominant role in the determination of the normal supply price. He defines the representative firm to be one "which has had a fairly long life, and fair success, which is managed with normal ability, and which has normal access to the economies, external and internal, which belong to that aggregate volume of production."[11] The normal supply price of a commodity must include, in addition to operating costs, "interest and insurance on all the capital," as well as "the gross earnings of management including insurance against loss by those who undertake the risks, who engineer and superintend the working."[12] While the output of the marginal firm is a price determining factor, there is no special or exclusive relationship between price and the costs of the marginal or least efficient producer.

This view seems to be in accord with the facts of life, because there are always firms which operate at a loss, even over a considerable period of time,[13] a situation which indicates that the market price of their product is not determined by their costs of production. Such firms may have one or more valid economic reasons for operating despite their inability to recover all of their costs, such as the hope for future profits,[14] or the need to secure

[11]Alfred Marshall, *Principles of Economics*, p. 317. [12]*Ibid.*, p. 343.

[13]The National Industrial Conference Board's study, *The Shifting and Effects of the Federal Corporation Income Tax*, vol. I, indicated that in the United States from 1918 to 1925 a large part of the sales of manufacturing, coal mining, and the retail and wholesale trades occurred at the margin of little or no profit. In general, the highest rate of turnover of capital was concentrated at the no-profit margin on sales. Production was continued at the no-profit point, and in many instances it was continued at a loss in order to retain a portion of the market. Cited by Harold M. Groves, *Postwar Taxation and Economic Progress*, pp. 37-8.

[14]Litterer states: "The fact that large profits are realized by some firms in an industry is a sufficient incentive for marginal and submarginal producers to stay in the business in order to try for the profits." "Corporation Income Tax and Production," pp. 203-4.

revenue even when incurring a net loss, with which to meet fixed charges such as bond interest, property taxes, and so on.

If market price is not determined solely by the costs of the marginal producers, does this change the conclusions reached under the static analysis? Under competitive conditions the output of the marginal firms has some effect upon price, but the dominant role in price determination is played by Marshall's representative firm, since such firms produce a substantial share of the total supply. Can these firms increase price in order to recover the tax that they have paid on net income? The answer must be that, without a change in demand, price can be increased only through a reduction in supply, and this is not likely to happen in any short-run period.[15] As already pointed out, the short run, as used here, includes sufficient time to permit changes in output by altering the quantities of variable factors in relation to existing fixed factors of production. And it is maintained that this period of time has a greater practical significance for most producers than has the long run, which must be sufficient to allow complete adjustments of all production factors, both variable and fixed, to changes which may result in complete rearrangement of the

[15]See National Industrial Conference Board, *The Shifting and Effects of the Federal Corporation Income Tax,* I, where the conclusion is drawn that, since the federal income tax is levied on net income, it cannot affect the greater portion of the supply by raising costs or reducing profits, and thus cannot greatly curtail the total supply, thereby raising prices. On the other hand, Litterer argues: "An income tax may cause supra-marginal firms to reduce their production as well as cause marginal and submarginal firms to cease production." "Corporation Income Tax and Production," p. 204. This argument is based, however, on very long-run considerations, which involve ultimate economic effects of the tax rather than its incidence. He bases it upon the possible effect of the tax upon risk capital. Quite obviously the supply of goods can be decreased if the supply of capital is decreased. Seligman wrote that "the continued growth of a country's prosperity depends largely upon the readiness of the able and venturesome to start new enterprises and to take the risk of the unknown. Where the hazard is great, the profits must be correspondingly great; for in the long run in new and untried fields the profits of some are likely to be counterbalanced by the losses of others. If the government, however, demands too large a percentage of these anticipated profits, the individual may prefer not to subject himself to the risk and may decide to be content with a smaller, but a surer return." "Income Taxes and the Price Level," *Proceedings of the Academy of Political Science,* XI, 1924, 19-20, cited by Litterer, p. 204. It is contended here that such an argument has no bearing on the short-run incidence of the tax, in the sense in which it is used in this study. It belongs properly in the analysis of the long-run effects of the tax.

agents of production.[16] It is concluded that according to dynamic analysis there will be no direct increase in price in the short run as a result of a tax on corporation net income. This is necessarily a generalized conclusion, however, and there are obvious cases which are an exception to it. Further qualifications are necessary.

An important qualification concerns that part of the theory dealing with monopoly. It is assumed that the monopolist sets a price which will give him the maximum net profit. But such an assumption is not always consistent with what really happens under conditions of monopoly. Monopolists or quasi-monopolists do not always charge such a price either because of ignorance, or because of fear that the too obvious existence of monopoly profits will result in the exercise of regulatory powers by the state. It is possible that in cases where the monopolist has not charged all that the traffic will bear, he may in fact be able to increase his price to recover a tax on net income.[17] But if fear of unfavourable public reaction had prevented a monopolist from charging the full price before imposition of the tax, that fear might still operate, after the tax had been levied, to prevent him from raising his price. The fact that this situation can and probably does exist involves a necessary qualification of our theory in the case of monopolistic operations. But this by itself does not invalidate the theory.

If this situation exists under monopoly, there is at least a pre-

[16]See C. Ward Macy, "The Corporation Net Income Tax and the Cost-Price Structure," *Bulletin of the National Tax Association,* May 1944, p. 233. Macy states: "The immediate and relatively short-run consequences of a tax are far more important on pragmatic grounds than the possible long-run effects under assumed and hypothetical conditions."

[17]Richard B. Goode states: "It may happen that if the profits of such a firm [monopoly] are reduced by a tax management will be stimulated to reconsider its price policy and to raise prices toward the full monopoly level. It is almost impossible to assess the importance of this possibility. Little is known about actual price policy and the extent to which firms fail to ask all the traffic will bear. It is even harder to say how such firms are influenced by tax considerations." "The Corporate Income Tax and the Price Level," *American Economic Review,* March 1945, p. 44.

In this connection it is interesting to recall the arguments evoked at the time of hydro nationalization in Quebec. It was contended that Montreal Light Heat & Power Consolidated had to pay $8,000,000 in income taxes, as a result of which it was unable to compete with the Hydro-Electric Power Commission of Ontario in terms of comparative rates.

sumption that it will be found under conditions of imperfect competition. If full information were available about the price policy of the leading corporations in the major fields of production, undoubtedly cases would be found where companies do make price adjustments as a result of the tax on their net income. But this is likely to be the exception rather than the rule.[18] The extent to which the tax can be shifted under conditions of imperfect competition depends upon several variable factors. One of these is the elasticity of the demand for the product, which is itself dependent upon the phase of the business cycle prevailing during the period under examination. Where the demand for a commodity is relatively elastic, a small price increase will result in a relatively large shift in demand, and the possibility of tax shifting is restricted accordingly. Conversely, where demand is highly inelastic, and there exists little or no possibility of using substitute commodities, tax shifting through price increases is quite likely to occur. In a sellers' market, such as has existed since the end of the war, tax shifting undoubtedly has taken place in some fields. It appears now, in view of the magnitude of the defence programme, with all its economic implications, that we are likely to have a strong sellers' market indefinitely. It is likely, therefore, that considerable shifting of the tax will take place, perhaps on an increasing scale.

Another factor in the situation is the pattern of production units in an industry. If an industry is dominated by one large unit capable of exerting a policy of price leadership, some shifting might be expected, conditioned, of course, by the general economic situation prevailing at a given time. Again, a particular supplier may control a market through geographic location, and be able, within limits, to juggle prices to recover a part of his tax. No doubt other situations such as these exist in an economy marked by imperfections in competition. The resulting exceptions to the economic theory of tax shifting cannot be denied. But it is

[18]By means of a questionnaire to the heads of the ten thousand largest corporations in the United States, the National Industrial Conference Board found that more than three-fourths of the business executives who expressed a definite opinion on the matter did not believe that the corporate income tax resulted in higher prices. *The Shifting and Effects of the Federal Corporation Income Tax*, I, 153-4. Similar results were secured from a later survey by the same body. See *Effects of Taxes upon Corporate Policy*, p. 57.

maintained that the theory is not invalidated by them; it is only necessary to recognize them as a modification of a fundamentally sound concept of short-run tax incidence.

Another point which should be considered is the fact that the traditional theory attacks the problem of tax incidence from the supply side, assuming implicitly that demand is constant. If it is conceded that price is a derivative of the interplay of supply and demand, then any price hypothesis which ignores one of the determining factors appears open to serious criticism. But here, again, the time factor is important. Over the short-run period, with which this theory of incidence is concerned, the assumption of relative demand stability appears to be in accord with reality, even though exceptions may be numerous and seasonal variations in demand prevalent in the market for many commodities.[19] The theory seems to stand up on this point as a short-run general proposition. But it will not serve as a foundation upon which to build a tenable theory of long-run "incidence," or, to use the better expression, "economic effects" of the corporation income tax. In the long run, which is a period of time sufficient to allow change in the size of plants, none of the variables assumed constant in the short run actually remains constant. Thus a theory which attacks the problem purely from the supply side, assuming constancy of demand, employment, volume of money, investment, and saving, is quite inadequate as an analytical tool. For example, it would be meaningless to argue that if a tax on net corporate income restricts investment, then supply will be reduced and price increased. Other factors must be considered, such as the effect upon employment, income, and demand. Moreover, consideration of long-run changes in price level can hardly be divorced from the implications of the quantity theory of money. Thus, if a tax does reduce the aggregate supply of commodities, prices will rise only if the quantity and velocity of cash and bank deposits does not decrease proportionately with output. For this reason the traditional theory must be confined to short-run analysis.

[19]A change in demand, as used here, means a shift in the entire demand curve, that is, a change in the quantities of a commodity absorbed in a market at any price along the curve. This takes place, of course, in seasonal industries. But barring a major upheaval in the economic system, there is not likely to be any significant change in the shape or position of the demand curve from one "in season" period to the next.

The analysis of long-run effects requires a much broader framework, which will be developed in chapter v.

The traditional argument that a tax on corporate net profits does not affect supply and therefore does not enter price remains a convincing short-run general hypothesis, subject to the qualifications outlined above.[20] Even though it is possible under certain conditions of monopoly or imperfect competition, or under conditions of very marked disequilibrium between supply and demand (a sellers' market) to raise price and shift the tax,[21] it appears unlikely that the exceptions are extensive enough to invalidate the theory.

The obstacles to shifting are considerable, and even where it might appear feasible to raise prices for tax-shifting purposes the individual firm may fail to do so because of management's fear of losing part of the market to competitors who do not raise prices.[22] As Goode points out: "Imposition of an income tax gives the individual corporation no more control over the market than it formerly had."[23]

It is concluded that the incidence of the tax on corporate net income is likely to be on the common shareholder in the *short*

[20]One important point has not been mentioned—that of business men considering the tax as a cost and so treating it in formulating price policy generally. This will be discussed in the next section which deals with the cost of production theory.

[21]Professor Carl Shoup argues that the shifting of the kind of tax levied by the United States government "depends largely upon (1) the rate of the tax, (2) the capital structure of the corporation, and (3) the nature of the industry with respect to the normal speed of turnover of assets." "Incidence of the Corporation Income Tax: Capital Structure and Turnover Rates," *National Tax Journal*, March 1948, p. 12. This article represents a departure from the usual analysis, and the case is well made. While one can agree with the proposition that the *incentive* to shift the tax is affected by its size, it is another matter when it is argued that a sharp increase in the rate "would provide the occasion for simultaneous, if not concerted, increases in the prices of the products of each of the leading companies, and the smaller concerns would presumably follow." Too many variables of the kind discussed above have to be taken into consideration. Whether the nature of a corporation's capital structure can have any influence on its ability to shift the tax depends upon the relationship of that company to its competitors in the market in terms of cost, as well as the nature of the capital structure of the companies providing most of its competition. Similarly, the relationship between ability to shift the tax and the normal speed of turnover of assets cannot be isolated from the supply-demand variables. Professor Shoup's article is worth serious consideration, and the results of a current research programme on these points, mentioned in the article, should prove interesting.

[22]It is well established empirically that even in the case of a retail sales tax many retailers absorb the tax rather than try to pass it on. See Neil Jacoby, *Retail Sales Taxation*, chap. XI.

[23]"The Corporate Income Tax and the Price Level," p. 46.

run. This proposition should not be so construed as to negate any possibility of very different long-run effects. Indeed, the long-run effects are likely to result in considerable diffusion of the tax burden, particularly if the tax rate is high. This aspect of the problem will be discussed in chapter v.

2. *Cost of Production Theory*

The proponents of this theory argue that a tax on net corporate profits is a cost of production, that it is embodied in price, like other costs, and shifted to the consumer.[24] Few would argue that the whole amount of the tax is so treated, but the C.I.O. Department of Research and Education expresses the view that "Corporate taxes on profits are supposed to be borne by corporation owners. That supposition is almost certainly false. Corporations simply anticipate what their taxes will be and add them to the prices they charge—pass them on to consumers."[25] Some business men have argued the same case. Mr. Enders M. Vorhees, Chairman of the Finance Committee of the United States Steel Corporation, declared: "Corporate taxes are simply costs. The method of their assessment does not change this fact. Costs must be paid by the public in prices, and corporate taxes are thus in effect concealed sales taxes."[26]

[24]Not all of the persons who contend that the tax is shifted in part to consumers argue that it is a cost. Their argument is based on grounds of monopoly and imperfect competition, where producers have some scope for price manipulation, as discussed in the preceding section.

[25]*The Economic Outlook,* Jan. 1944, quoted by Goode, "The Corporate Income Tax and the Price Level," p. 41.

[26]*Ibid.,* p. 40. Similar views were expressed to the Colwyn Committee in Britain. Mr. F. B. Tredwen, representing the London Chamber of Commerce, suggested that in fixing prices a trader added to his costs a margin of profit for himself. Of course it is his profit that is subject to the direct income tax, and if he wants to get a sufficient reward for his own exertions, he must put on an addition to his price sufficient to cover the profit to the government as well as the profit to himself. Another witness, Mr. P. D. Leake, contended that "the effect of this extra tax burden must be to foster the maintenance of high prices, and so to lay upon the wage-earners an extra burden of altogether unknown extent but which may probably amount to not less than 85 per cent. of that part of the employers' Income Tax burden which is inevitably reflected in the retail prices of the commodities purchased by the wage-earners." Mr. R. S. Wright, representing the National Union of Manufacturers, took an even more extreme position. His opinion was: "The difference between direct and indirect taxation hardly exists in actual fact." He was "convinced that the burden becomes automatically distributed by a law of political economy that defies all Acts of Parliament." *Report of the Committee on National Debt and Taxation,* pp. 108-9. Others who argue that the tax

The idea that a net income tax is a cost which can be included in price like other costs involves some very considerable difficulties.[27] In the first place, the amount of tax cannot be ascertained until after the amount of profit for a fiscal period has been computed, i.e. after price policy for that period has been established. In recent years even the rate of tax has been unknown in advance. If a corporation deliberately attempts to recover the tax through price adjustment, it either must estimate in advance its volume of sales, its costs, its profit, and the tax, or adjust current price in such a way as to recover the tax paid in the last preceding year. At best such a procedure can result only in a rough approximation. Furthermore, if the entire tax is to be recovered, the price increase will have to be greater than the amount of the tax. As a company increases its selling prices (assuming no change in costs), it creates a still larger taxable profit, and therefore has to pay still more tax.[28]

It is doubtful whether any save the most exceptional firm will actually base selling price upon any deliberate effort to recover the full amount of its tax on profits. Indeed, it seems likely that relatively few firms will make any conscious effort to set prices in accordance with a preconceived notion of what net profit should be, after taxes.[29] Every business man knows that under normal

---

is a cost and is therefore included in price are Beardsley Ruml, "Fiscal Policy and Taxation," *Proceedings of the National Tax Association,* 1944, p. 170; H. C. Sonne, *How Should Corporations be Taxed?* p. 22; Oscar F. Litterer, "Corporation Income Tax and Production," p. 204; Committee for Economic Development, *A Postwar Federal Tax Plan for High Employment,* p. 16; Beardsley Ruml and H. C. Sonne, *Fiscal and Monetary Policy,* p. 11.

[27]See Goode, "The Corporate Income Tax and the Price Level," p. 45.

[28]Professor Shoup illustrates the situation as follows: "Suppose that a concern is earning a profit of $1,000 before tax, and the corporation tax rate is raised from 38 per cent to, say, 88 per cent; its tax payment is increased from $380 to $880, an increase of $500. The concern now considers what it must do if it is to obtain its former net profit after tax (that is, $620). It finds that it must increase its profit before tax by much more than the $500 increase in tax, for some of the increase will itself be taken in tax. In this particular case, the concern's profit before tax must increase from $1,000, not to $1,500, but to $5,166.67. The spiral, or cumulative effect operates the more strongly, in terms of what has to be done to the price structure if the tax increase is to be recouped, the higher the rate of tax after the increase has been made." "Incidence of the Corporation Income Tax: Capital Structure and Turnover Rates," p. 13.

[29]During discussions with Canadian business men and members of the accounting profession, however, the writer found some evidence of a tendency to think in terms of net profit after taxes when considering corporate price policy. There

conditions increased price means a reduction in volume of sales and an increase in unit costs. This fact is likely to give him real reason to ponder before raising price for income tax reasons. Furthermore, as Goode points out, "if a tax on net profits is a cost it is indeed a strange kind of cost. It is a 'cost' which rises with success but automatically disappears when operations are unsuccessful."[30] Certainly it is not a cost in the usual accounting sense of the word.

It is sometimes suggested, however, that a tax on corporate net income does fall on certain costs, and therefore should not be considered to fall wholly and exclusively on what the economists call economic surplus. It is often concluded that at least that part of the tax which falls on costs will be reflected in price.[31]

In economic terms net profit is the surplus of a company's money receipts over its costs. Costs are defined for the individual enterprise as the money payments necessary to secure the services of the factors of production required for any given volume of output. For income tax purposes, net profit is defined as gross receipts less certain specified deductions which are deemed to be "necessary" expenses or costs for the purpose of making the income. Pages of statutory provisions and a great body of judicial decisions define the items that are to be included in receipts and deductible costs. The economic concept of net profit and the concept of taxable net income found in the tax statute, however, are not entirely comparable.

If the tax reaches certain costs, it must be because the legal definition of costs is narrower than the economic.[32] If they are

---

is no way of telling what significance should be attached to these rather isolated opinions, although a few specific cases of price policy being determined for tax recovery purposes were reported in confidence.

[30]"The Corporate Income Tax and the Price Level," p. 45.

[31]See Groves, for example, who states that the "corporate net-income tax applies to items of imputed rent and interest—items deductible as costs when management employs these factors on a contractual basis. Thus the tax does reach certain costs as well as surplus." He then makes the cautious observation: "Suffice it to say that no definite conclusion as to the incidence of the corporate income tax is possible and that not improbably the burden is divided between at least stockholders and consumers." *Postwar Taxation and Economic Progress*, p. 28.

[32]Any difference between the economic concept and statutory definition of income is not likely to have bearing on this point because the latter is more narrowly drawn and has such refinements as exempt income and the distinction between income and return of capital.

identical, or if the legal definition is broader than the economic, then all economic costs will be deductible from gross receipts, and not subject to tax. In this situation the tax falls on economic surplus in its strictest sense, and not upon any element of cost. The point to be settled here is whether there are elements of economic costs which the tax statute does not recognize as items deductible from gross receipts. If there are, then the question remains as to whether the tax on these costs is reflected in price.

The Canadian Income Tax Act provides for the deduction of direct operating cost and for the recovery of capital assets through depreciation. No allowance is made, however, for the deduction of certain imputed costs. Interest is deductible only if it is a contractual obligation. The statute makes no allowance for imputed interest on equity capital. Neither is an allowance made for imputed rent on scarce factors of production owned by the corporation and used in earning its income. Furthermore, the statute does not consider the reward for bearing uninsurable risks a cost of doing business. In the economic sense these three items are costs, and to this extent the statutory definition is narrower than the economic concept. Thus the tax can be considered, in the strictest economic sense, to fall in part upon costs. Does this involve a modification of our theory of incidence?

It will be recalled that the traditional theory of incidence is based upon the short-run effect of the tax upon supply. If demand remains constant, a price increase is possible only if there is decrease in supply.

In the short run the only costs that have bearing on output or supply are direct costs, costs which vary with the volume of current output. The tax statute provides for the deduction of all such costs in determining net taxable income. Indeed, it allows for more than this in the form of a deduction for indirect overhead costs. Thus the tax definition of costs is broader than the economic concept of costs which determine output in the short run. It follows that in the short run the tax rests on economic surplus, and there is no incentive to reduce output because of the tax. As long as there is no change in demand, a corporation is unlikely to secure a larger profit through decreased production, unless, of course, it had been producing beyond the point of maximum return. Thus it is concluded that no modification of this short-run incidence theory is made necessary by the fact that the tax reaches certain imputed costs.

In the long run the results become obscure. The distinction between fixed and variable costs disappears and all costs must be regarded as variable since in the long run the scale of plant may be changed. There are many far-reaching ramifications which have nothing to do with our short-run concept of tax incidence. Among these are the results of differentiating between debt interest and imputed interest on equity capital, the effect of the tax on sale of securities, on saving and investment, and on the capital market. Perhaps the most important aspect of this part of the problem is the result of ignoring the cost of bearing uninsurable risks. But all of these fall under the heading of "economic effects" and will be discussed as such.

It has been argued in these pages that the federal corporation income tax is not, in the usual sense of the word, a tax upon costs, but rather a tax on economic surplus. Even where a strict economic modification of this conclusion is necessitated there appears to be no reason to modify the short-run theory of incidence examined earlier in this chapter. Despite the apparent disparity between theory and practice, it is maintained that the opportunity for an individual corporation to operate outside the economic price determining laws is more or less narrowly restricted by serious obstacles.

Perhaps the greatest obstacle to shifting the tax in the form of increased price is the inability of a single producer to control his price save within relatively narrow limits. While not many industries operate under such a highly competitive price situation that all firms must adhere to a single price dictated by the untrammelled forces of supply and demand, nevertheless the scope of most producers for setting price independently of normal market price is probably circumscribed narrowly.

In the case of commodities where consumers have a wide range of choice of brand or product—and this situation is found in most consumer goods industries—an individual producer is likely to be restrained from making a price increase by uncertainty regarding the price policy of his competitors. Short of a definite agreement on price arranged through a trade association or some similar form of agreement, there is not likely to be any uniformity of thought and action in an industry.

The fact that in many industries a considerable portion of the total output is produced by firms which make no profit and pay no tax gives rise to some tantalizing speculation regarding their reaction to a price increase by the profit-making firms. Would they increase price, too, in order to make a profit, or would they maintain their old prices in order to capture a greater share of the market, thereby increase output, reduce unit costs, and perhaps make even more profit than under the other alternative? No answer can be given in such a hypothetical case because too many variables are involved. But it is this very uncertainty that is likely to act as a restrictive force in the infra-marginal firms.

Still another difficulty is attached to price raising under a tax which is restricted to the corporate form of enterprise. In the trade and service industries, and in a considerable portion of the light manufacturing industry, incorporated companies experience serious competition from partnerships and sole proprietorships on which no net profits tax is imposed. Should corporations raise their prices because of the tax, they would probably lose part of their market to their unincorporated competitors.[33] The extent of the loss would depend, of course, upon the amount by which price was raised.

It is concluded from the above argument that the corporate income tax is not a tax on cost in the usually accepted sense of the word. Since it is not a tax on cost, it is not likely to be shifted in the form of a price increase. Even where it does fall on certain imputed costs in the strict sense of economic costs which are not allowed as a deduction for tax purposes, the short-run economic theory of incidence is unaffected.

If the tax is in fact added to price, then a reduction in it or its removal should result in lower prices. Two years after the reduction in the corporation tax rate from 30 to 10 per cent on

[33]The possibility that the unincorporated units might raise price, too, should not be ignored. But unless there were a strong sellers' market with a highly inelastic demand, this would not likely happen. Concerted action is not to be expected of a large number of individual operators. Probably they would elect to retain their established price and increase their volume of sales.

profits up to $10,000 there is still no apparent decrease in prices.

The conclusions reached by the Colwyn Committee in Britain more than twenty years ago still appear sound. The Committee stated that "the broad economic argument [the one used in this study] is true over practically the whole field and for practically the whole of the time, any exceptions being local or temporary and insufficient to invalidate it."[34]

3. *The Diffusion Theory*

Falling between the two theories examined above is the theory that the corporate income tax is diffused throughout the economy and is borne by stockholders, consumers, and wage earners. A typical presentation of this view is found in the following words:

> When the tax money is traced down, corporate taxation turns out to be in part a tax upon the income of stockholders, and in part an indirect tax upon consumers, wage earners, or both. The indirect taxation occurs because such taxes are accounted as part of the costs of doing business, and soon or late some part of the tax gets passed on to consumers in the form of higher prices for the goods they buy; some part of it, also, is invisibly borne by workers in the form of lower wages and salaries than they could otherwise receive.[35]

The argument about the effect of the tax on prices has already been discussed and conclusions have been reached. It remains now to consider whether the tax has any effect on wages. This is perhaps an even more difficult analysis than the former because the price of labour, particularly in the short run, is determined not so much by the free interplay of demand and supply as by the bargaining of near-monopolistic suppliers (the labour unions) and quasi-monopolistic purchasers (large corporate employers).

The crux of the problem centres about the factors that do

[34]*Report of the Committee on National Debt and Taxation,* p. 119. The Minority Report of the Committee stated: "We are of the opinion that it is only in very exceptional cases that manufacturers and merchants are able to pass their Income Tax on to consumers through the prices of the goods that they sell." *Ibid.,* p. 378.

[35]Committee for Economic Development, *A Postwar Federal Tax Plan for High Employment,* p. 16. In another study it is stated: "The federal income tax on corporations tends (1) to raise the cost of goods and services, and in some cases to pyramid them, (2) to keep wages lower than they otherwise might be, and (3) to limit the yield on risk-bearing investment." Ruml and Sonne, *Fiscal and Monetary Policy,* p. 11.

determine wages. It is possible that in industries where labour is strongly organized union demands may be influenced by the level of corporate profits after taxes, and this factor may have a bearing on the attitude of mediation or arbitration bodies.[36]

Generally speaking, however, wage demands appear to bear a closer relationship to the general level of economic activity as reflected in the demand for labour than they bear to the level of profits. It seems quite unlikely that a sudden and sharp increase in the rate of corporation tax would be reflected in a downward revision of wage rates.[37] Such a move would be resisted strongly by the unions (and resisted effectively, too) as long as the demand for labour remained unchanged, as it probably would in the short run.

Conversely, there appears to be no sound basis for the assumption that a reduction in corporate income tax rates would be reflected in an increased level of wages. If a decrease in the tax resulted, as it most certainly would, in larger net profit, which in turn enabled labour to bargain successfully for higher wages, it appears more than likely that the extra labour cost would be reflected in higher commodity prices. Wages constitute a direct cost of production, a cost which is typically and habitually written into the price structure.[38]

From the viewpoint of our short-run incidence theory it seems unlikely that there is any significant short-run effect of the tax upon wages. Thus the diffusion theory has little, if any, bearing on the actual incidence of the tax. But the implications of diffusion in the long run are very considerable. It might be argued that in the long run all taxes are diffused through their ultimate

[36]See Goode, "The Corporate Income Tax and the Price Level," p. 56.

[37]Indeed, if the tax be extremely high, such as the 100 per cent tax on excess profits during World War II, there is likely to be a tendency towards payment of abnormally high salaries and wages in order to increase deductible costs. That this phenomenon did not materialize generally was owing, probably, solely to the wartime control over wages.

[38]This is the conclusion reached by Goode, who states that it "is supported by the remarkable stability of the past relationship between gross income produced in private business and salaries and wages paid by private business. The tentative conclusion reached, paradoxical as it may seem from the point of view of the neo-diffusionist school, is that to the extent to which it stimulates wage increases, a reduction in the corporate tax will mean higher instead of lower prices." *Ibid.*, pp. 56-7.

economic effects. As will be pointed out later, the economic effects of the corporation tax are so diffused that in all likelihood the wages of labour are affected, at least to some extent.

Summary

The approach to the problem of determining the incidence of the corporate income tax has been limited to an analysis of incidence in its usual economic meaning. This is necessarily a short-run concept, as distinguished from the long-run economic effects of the tax.

The economic analysis of short-run incidence appears to be convincing in its general conclusions that the corporate income tax is not passed to the consumer in the form of higher prices. Neither does there seem to be much likelihood that the tax has any significant short-run effects on wages. As a general proposition, the tax falls on the shareholders of the corporation. This conclusion holds under conditions of competition, monopolistic competition, and monopoly.

It is admitted, of course, that there are exceptions to the rule. At a given time there may be many. In a strong sellers' market the tax is undoubtedly shifted in many cases. The impact of the new defence economy on a full employment economy is likely, therefore, to result in considerable shifting of the corporation tax, particularly if the tax is increased. This has important bearing on the kind of tax policy that should be formulated for financing defence, a point to be developed in the final chapter of this study. We now turn to an examination of the long-run economic effects of the tax.

CHAPTER FIVE

ECONOMIC EFFECTS OF THE TAX

DOUBLE TAXATION AND REGRESSIVITY

THE DOUBLE TAXATION of corporate dividends arises from the fact that the net profits of a corporation are subject to the corporation income tax, and that dividends paid out after the payment of this tax are then subject to the individual income tax. For example, under the current rate of federal corporation income tax in Canada, a corporation earning $100,000 net taxable income pays a tax of $42,540.[1] Thus out of every $100 of profits made by the corporation, the federal tax is $42.54, and (ignoring provincial taxes) the amount available for dividends is $57.46. If the profits after taxes are paid to an individual shareholder who is subject to personal tax on his dividends at an average rate, say, of 50 per cent, that shareholder receives a net amount of $28.73 of the original corporate profit of $100. Had the business not been incorporated, but operated as a sole proprietorship or partnership, the same taxpayer would have paid a tax of $50, rather than $71.27.[2]

The extent to which double taxation exists depends, of course, upon the degree to which the tax is shifted. If, as concluded in the preceding chapter, most of the tax remains where it is placed, and is not in fact shifted to consumers, or wage earners, or both, then clearly the existing system of taxation results in the double taxation of corporate dividends.[3]

[1]The rates are 15 per cent on profits up to $10,000, and 45.6 per cent on profits in excess of $10,000.

[2]It will be noted that there is not a complete doubling of tax. The total tax rate on $100 in this case is 71.27 per cent. Regardless of rates, the combined corporate and individual rates cannot exceed 100 per cent of the original profit before tax.

[3]Despite the wide disagreement on the incidence of the tax, there is a curious unanimity in popular opinion regarding double taxation. Not infrequently those who argue that the tax is a cost and is included in price will argue that the tax

It is perhaps unfortunate that the expression "double taxation" has been used in the arguments about the corporation tax. It has an emotional content which "is enough to condemn the present system in the minds of most people without further hearing."[4] There is nothing unusual about double taxation. It is found throughout the entire tax system, and in the final analysis all taxation is in fact multiple, since practically all taxes must be paid out of income. As long as the revenue system is to be made up of diversified taxes, multiple taxation is inevitable, and there is nothing inherently objectionable about it.

Some forms of double taxation are objectionable, however, from the viewpoint both of equity and of economic effects. On the equity side two arguments against this form of double taxation are commonly found.[5] In the first place, it is argued that it is inequitable to discriminate against corporations when in so many fields of business enterprise they must compete with unincorporated business firms for both capital and customers. In the second place, it is argued that the corporation tax is regressive, in that it imposes a tax on shareholders with small incomes at a substantially greater rate than that of the tax they pay on their individual incomes.

The first of these points has been discussed in some detail in chapter III. On the grounds of equity alone there is surely no justification for penalizing the corporate form of business to the extent of taking away a half or more of its net income. This argument is particularly pertinent in the case of the small corporation which is especially subject to competition from unincorporated businesses, as well as from large corporations.[6]

---

results in double taxation. This is arrant nonsense. If the tax does not reduce the amount of profit available for dividends, the shareholder will pay only one tax—the tax on individual income. The point to be stressed is that double taxation exists if any part of the corporate tax is not shifted.

[4]Richard Goode, "The Postwar Corporation Tax Structure," *How Should Corporations be Taxed?* p. 46.

[5]See Roy Blough, "Some Aspects of Corporate Taxation," *Bulletin of the National Tax Association,* June 1946, pp. 287-91.

[6]In his 1949 budget speech the Minister of Finance recognized this situation in his announcement of a rate reduction from 30 per cent to 10 per cent on corporate profits up to $10,000. He stated: "The house will at once recognize this as tax relief for small businesses. . . . My own belief is that small businesses should be encouraged and it seems to me that a useful way to do this is to lower the tax. . . ." *House of Commons Debates,* March 22, 1949, p. 1798.

The regressivity argument is based upon the fact that the corporation tax takes no account of the differences in income of shareholders. If the tax reduces the amount of net corporate profits available for distribution as dividends, it is a tax deducted at source at a uniform rate regardless of the taxable income of the individual shareholders. The very small shareholder, who pays no individual income tax because of personal exemption and deductions bears the greater relative burden of the corporation tax, because the "deduction" of the corporation tax at source subjects him to a tax at a relatively high rate. The wealthy shareholder, on the other hand, suffers little reduction in dividend income because the high personal income tax rates to which he is subjected would have taken most of his dividends anyway.[7] From this viewpoint the tax does appear to be regressive. But other factors must be taken into consideration before final judgment is reached.

It is quite apparent that practically all of the individual taxpayers in Canada pay tax at a rate less than the corporation rate.[8] But available statistics do not indicate the extent of the regressivity because they indicate nothing of the importance of dividends to total income in different income brackets. It is probably true in Canada, as it is in the United States, that dividends con-

[7]Richard Goode demonstrates this as follows: ". . . for example, assume that the X corporation has profits of $1 per share before taxes. A 40 percent corporate tax will reduce earnings available for dividends to 60 cents per share. Assume further that stockholder A is subject to a marginal individual tax rate of 50 per cent, stockholder B to a marginal rate of 20 per cent. If all earnings available for dividends are distributed, the combined corporate and individual tax on the $1 of earned profits earned on A's share of stock will be 70 cents (40 cents corporate tax plus 30 cents individual tax). The combined tax on the $1 of profits earned on B's share of stock will be 52 cents (40 cents corporate tax plus 12 cents individual tax). If no corporate tax were imposed on distributed profits and as a result dividends paid out by the X corporation were $1 per share instead of 60 cents, the total tax on the $1 of profits earned on A's share would be 50 cents and on the dollar earned by B's share, 20 cents. Thus, the corporate tax increases total taxes on the $1 earned on A's share by 20 cents (70 cents as compared with 50 cents) and on the $1 earned on B's share by 32 cents (52 cents as compared with 20 cents)." *The Postwar Corporation Tax Structure,* p. 8, note 5.

[8]For example, in 1948 the corporate tax rate was 30 per cent on all taxable income. In that year an individual had to have nearly $16,000 of taxable income to pay a tax of 30 per cent. Of the 2,689,930 persons who paid income tax in 1948, all but 14,270 had taxable income of less than $15,000. The *marginal* rate of 30 per cent was reached on taxable income in the $6,500 to $8,500 income bracket. See *Taxation Statistics,* 1950, pp. 8, 112.

stitute a much larger proportion of high than of low incomes.[9] When account is taken of this factor, it follows that to the extent that the corporate tax does reduce dividends, it affects in the aggregate a much larger percentage of high income groups than of low.[10] This is not to say that regressivity does not exist, but in terms of statistical averages it does not appear to be as serious as often contended. It is certainly not as serious as the regressivity of a sales tax.[11]

Another factor to be considered is the so-called capitalization of the corporate income tax. As used in this sense the term means that purchasers of stock adjust the price that they are prepared to pay for shares so that the net return on the investment, after taxes, will be comparable to other alternative investment of their capital. While the extent to which this discounting of future taxes takes place is impossible to determine, it is probably considerable and has important bearing on the market price of share capital. It is probably true that most of the owners of listed shares are not the original investors, but investors who have purchased the shares from previous owners. The price at which these shares were purchased represented the expectations of buyers and sellers regarding future earnings and future taxes. The double taxation of corporate income and dividends has been a feature of the tax system for so long that a great turnover of shares has taken place, and it seems probable, as Blough says, that "under these circumstances, most owners of such securities do not present a convincing complaint regarding the inequities of double taxation."[12] The capitalization argument is not applicable, however, to new shares issued, whether by established corporations or by new ones. It applies only to issues made in the past.

From the viewpoint of equity, then, the double taxation of

[9]Randolph E. Paul states that in the United States in 1942 dividends amounted to less than 2.5 per cent of the incomes of individuals with incomes of $4,000 or less, while they accounted for nearly 54 per cent of the income of individuals with incomes of $200,000 and over. *Taxation for Prosperity*, p. 356.

[10]See Goode, *The Postwar Corporation Tax Structure*, p. 42, for statistical presentation of the burden of the United States corporate tax on shareholders by individual net income classes.

[11]If the tax is shifted in the form of higher prices, it falls in the same category as a sales tax.

[12]"Some Aspects of Corporate Taxation," p. 288.

corporate income and dividends is not as serious as it might appear from a superficial examination. But this does not imply that no serious economic effects accrue from this form of double taxation under the existing rate structure. The effect upon investment and on the method of corporate financing may be very serious indeed, and it requires careful consideration. This leads us to the most important criticism of the existing double taxation of dividends.

Effects on Saving and Investment

1. *Individual Saving and Investment*

If, as argued in this study, the corporation tax normally is not shifted, it must result in a general reduction in the yield of common shares. While the reduction will be less than proportional to the tax rate, still, any reduction in yield could be a deterrent to the purchase of such securities. It is recognized, of course, that not all share purchases are based upon any carefully calculated evaluation of risk and yield. But usually it follows that the more hazardous the undertaking, the greater must be the yield to induce investment.

It is impossible to determine to what extent the double taxation of corporate income and dividends has affected individual saving and investment, and it is also impossible to appraise with any accuracy the long-run effects of the present tax system on the economy as a whole. There is a strong temptation to conclude on pragmatic grounds that the capital market is seriously impaired and that corporations no longer can hope to do in the future as much financing through shares as they have done in the past.

One of the imponderables is the extent of the flexibility of individual investors' standards of an adequate return on their investment. These standards have certainly been subject to fairly drastic reduction over the past three decades, and perhaps they may be reduced still further. But the current state of the market may be an indication that the lower limit has been reached. The reluctance of investors to purchase shares, despite their very low average price in relation to average corporate net profit, indicates an unnatural situation. Here again it is impossible to determine to what extent this reluctance is a derivative of the tax structure *per se,* and to what extent it is simply the result of uncertainty regarding the business outlook generally and future earnings specifically. Quite possibly this uncertainty is more important than is the fact that corporate income is subject to double taxation.

It is obvious, of course, that the economic significance of the unwillingness of individual investors to purchase common shares will depend upon the extent to which corporations must resort to new stock issues for new capital requirements. Currently a very considerable part of new corporate financing is done internally, through the medium of undistributed earnings. While this will not be affected directly by an adverse effect of the tax on the capital market, the corporate tax structure as it now exists will restrict corporate saving in many cases, and thereby restrict the amount of funds available for internal financing.

Not only is the corporation tax likely to reduce individual investment in corporate shares, but because of the double taxation feature it is quite likely to reduce individual saving. If, as is probable, the great bulk of individual saving is done by persons in the highest income brackets, the present system of taxation seems certain to impair individual saving.[13] If a corporation earns 10 per cent on its investment, and the stock is held by shareholders paying tax on their dividends at an average individual rate of 60 per cent, corporation taxes at 1951 rates (federal and provincial, before the new 10 per cent credit) and the individual income tax will consume 8 per cent of the 10 per cent, leaving a net return of 2 per cent.[14] Not only does this figure show the impact of the tax system on the ability of persons in the high

[13]The Minister of Finance admitted as much in his 1949 budget speech, when he said: "My second proposal introduces a measure of reform which has long been a declared objective of this government. I refer to the removal of double taxation of corporate profits. . . . Today we find governments in this country . . . taxing away at least a third of corporate profits. In addition, the personal income tax rates apply in full to what is distributed out of the remaining two-thirds. The tax may be as high as 80 per cent upon distributions to shareholders. It seems to me that under a system of private enterprise which depends for its existence on a steady flow of venture capital we cannot afford to neglect the implication of this defect in our tax system, which has been accentuated by the increase in both corporate and personal income tax rates." *House of Commons Debates,* March 22, 1949, p. 1799. The remedial proposal made by the Minister represents a partial solution to the problem. He announced a credit for individuals against their personal income tax equal to "10 per cent of the dividends they receive from common shares of Canadian tax-paying corporations." *Ibid.*

[14]This calculation is based upon an assumed *average* corporate rate of 50 per cent (the total of federal and Ontario rates). It does not take into consideration

income brackets to save, but it also points to a marked reduction in the incentive to invest in share capital, particularly in the share capital of new corporations, the earning capacity of which is unknown. This affects the financing of corporate expansion and has bearing on dividend policy, a matter which will be discussed in the following section. It also may make it difficult to bring new enterprise into existence.

The National City Bank of New York, in its *Monthly Letter* (November 1947) stated that:

> . . . the individual investor has come close to disappearing as the source of new capital for private business. Estimates of the Securities and Exchange Commission indicate that individuals in all of 1946 added nothing, net, to their holdings of corporate stocks and bonds. The same is true for the first half of 1947. A major cause is income tax levels so high as to force continuous dissaving in the higher income brackets and shut down new supplies of saving farther down the line.
>
> The individual savings that take place today in largest volumes are either institutionalized savings, reflected in accumulations of insurance and pension funds, or savings in anticipation of consumption.

2. *Corporate Saving and Investment*

(*a*) Some Economic Aspects of Dividend Policy

Before proceeding to a discussion of the effect of the tax on corporate saving, it appears desirable to examine briefly some of the economic aspects of corporate dividend policy. If the aggregate effect of existing policy is detrimental to the economy, as is maintained by some economists, then there is a case for devising a tax system to remedy the situation. An attempt will be made here to come to conclusions regarding the economic effects of dividend policy. Then general conclusions will be drawn regarding the effects of corporation taxes.

It has been stated that expediency rather than basic conviction frequently determines policies of corporate management.[15] While this may be true, there appears to be a discernible pattern of dividend policy in both Canada and the United States which

---

the 10 per cent dividend credit. It is worth noting that the assumed average rate of 60 per cent paid by the shareholders is the 1951-2 rate on income between $25,001 and $40,000.

[15]H. E. Hoagland, *Corporation Finance*, p. 570.

is probably the result of certain basic convictions of management.

There are, of course, some corporations which plough back earnings without apparent limit and without any apparent consideration of the rights of shareholders to determine the disposition of the earnings from their investments. There are also corporations, at the other extreme, which appear to favour complete or almost complete distribution of earnings as they accrue. Neither of these groups is typical, however. Most corporations follow a policy of distributing a part of their earnings and retaining a part. "A dollar for dividends, a dollar for surplus" is an old and probably ill-founded adage.

Some of the general considerations which are borne in mind by corporation directors in deciding their dividend policy at a particular time are (1) the company's cash position; (2) its capital structure and the extent of share distribution; (3) plans for future development and expansion; (4) the possibility and/or desirability of securing new outside capital as opposed to financing internally; (5) the past record of earnings and prospects of future earnings; (6) general business conditions; (7) taxes; and (8) contingencies.

In some cases an important consideration is the apparent belief that a long record of unbroken dividend payments, through good years and poor, gives the company a relatively strong position in the capital market when new shares are offered to investors. It is argued that the stock should sell at a higher price, even though in the aggregate the rate of dividends declared might be lower than when a policy of intermittent and fluctuating dividend payments is followed.[16]

This argument for stability of dividends has probably been an important factor in the determination of the policy of public corporations. Its results are reflected in the record of dividend payments throughout the various phases of the business cycle. The general pattern has been one of paying out a greater portion of net earnings during depression than during boom.[17]

[16]E. E. Lincoln, *Applied Business Finance*, p. 738.

[17]Lincoln's analysis shows that in the United States in 1928 aggregate corporation net earnings exceeded dividends by 20 per cent for *all* corporations. From 1930 to 1934 aggregate dividend payments were much greater than net earnings. In 1934, for example, dividends were 214.5 per cent of net earnings. *Ibid.*, pp. 740-3.

In recent years perhaps one of the most important considerations determining the dividend policy of public corporations has been the difficulty of securing new capital in the capital market on terms considered suitable to the corporation. When it appears that new capital is difficult to secure for one reason or another, a company which plans expansion is quite likely to plough back the necessary capital out of earnings. Small corporations, particularly closely held family companies are, of course, almost entirely dependent upon earnings for expansion of plant. But in recent years even the large and well-established corporations have resorted to internal financing of much of their new capital requirements.[18]

Still another reason for heavy retention of earnings during periods of inflation is the need for more working capital as prices and wages rise. This is especially the case in industries with a slow turnover. Reported net profits are grossly overstated during such periods, owing to the failure of existing accounting methods to provide for price level changes. Consequently the cash position of corporations would be impaired seriously were dividends to be paid in accordance with reported net profits. This point will be expanded in the discussion of tax policy.

Still another, though less important, reason for the retention of profits is the desire to avoid the individual tax on them. This policy is more likely to be followed in small closely held corporations than in large public corporations where there is a wide diffusion of ownership. Its effects probably have relatively little significance for the national economy because the total earnings

[18]Professor Sumner H. Slichter reports that in the United States between 1909 and 1929 retained corporate earnings amounted to $37.3 billion, compared with a total issue of $48.4 billion stock, bonds and notes, and that slightly more than half (52.3 per cent) of corporate profit was kept in the corporations. In 1946 and 1947 and in the first half of 1948 corporations retained $34.9 billion of reported profits and raised $11.2 billion through the issue of new securities. United States, Congress, Joint Committee on the Economic Report, 1948, *Corporate Profits*, p. 16. This situation is currently being paralleled in Canada. It is estimated that in 1947 the total of corporate securities issued, other than for refunding purposes, was $337.1 million. Undistributed profits for that year are reported at $608 million. See Department of Trade and Commerce, *Investment and Inflation with Special Reference to the Immediate Post-War Period, Canada, 1945-1948*, Table 60, p. 143, and Table 65, p. 149. The figure for undistributed profits has since been lowered to $590 million.

of such corporations make up a comparatively small portion of the total of all corporate earnings. The problem of tax equity here is quite another matter, and one which deserves consideration by itself.

These, then, are some of the factors that determine corporate policy with respect to the payment of dividends, and at the same time determine the volume of corporate saving (the amount of earnings ploughed back into the business). Before proceeding to the discussion of the economic effects of corporate saving, it might be useful to examine the relationship between corporate and individual saving.

The volume of personal and corporate saving in Canada for the period 1938-50 is shown in Table VI. Before the war the ratio of corporate to personal saving was relatively high, 73.6 per cent in 1938 and 68.4 per cent in 1939. During the war years the ratio fell sharply despite the substantial increase in corporate saving. This was owing mainly to two factors. First, the volume of personal saving expanded enormously because wartime conditions

TABLE VI

RELATIONSHIP BETWEEN
CORPORATE AND PERSONAL SAVING IN CANADA, 1938–1948

(1) *Year*	(2) *Personal saving*	(3) *Undistributed corporate profits*	(4) *Ratio* 3 to (2)
	$000,000	$000,000	%
1938[a]	178	131	73.6
1939	320	219	68.4
1940	411	172	41.8
1941	569	304	53.4
1942[b]	1,441	374	25.9
1943	1,592	362	22.7
1944	1,683	334	19.8
1945	1,282	374	29.2
1946	857	469	54.7
1947	326	595	182.2
1948[c]	869	777	89.4
1949	838	601	71.7
1950	776	730	94.2
TOTAL	11,142	5,442	48.8

[a]Figures for 1938-41 taken from *National Accounts Income and Expenditure*, 1938-1947, p. 14.
[b]Figures for 1943-7 taken from *ibid.*, 1942-1949, p. 22.
[c]Figures for 1948-50 taken from *ibid.*, Revised Preliminary 1950, p. 7.

made it impossible to buy many durable goods, and in addition, there was the patriotic appeal to buy war bonds. Personal saving reached its peak in 1944, and the ratio of corporate to personal saving fell to its lowest point in that year. Second, the excess profits tax cut sharply into the amount of corporate earnings available for saving. It will be noted that the volume of undistributed profits fell in 1943 and again in 1944, while personal saving continued its upward swing during these two years. Immediately after the war personal saving fell sharply as consumers' goods became available again, and corporate saving mounted as profits increased after decontrol and the abolition of the excess profits tax. It will be noted that in 1947 the ratio of corporate to personal saving was 182.2 per cent. By 1949 the pre-war pattern had been resumed, but the inflationary boom since then has pushed the volume of corporate saving higher while personal saving fell in 1950.

It is extremely difficult to forecast the shape of things to come under current conditions of cold war. But it seems probable that the ratio of corporate to personal saving will remain higher than before the war, unless it is forced down by higher taxes. It may level off at a considerably higher point if, as forecast in one official document, "firms will have to continue to rely to a large extent on their own retained earnings to finance industrial growth in the near future."[19] Thus it is obvious that corporate saving is a very important part of the total saving in the economy.

Opinion is divided on what percentage of the national saving should be effected by corporate enterprise, as well as on the economic effects of it. For that matter, opinion is also divided as to how much saving is necessary for a balanced economy. The exploration of the arguments on this point would lead us too far afield for the purposes of this study. But a point which is often ignored by the economists who maintain that oversaving is typical of our kind of economy is worth mention. Imperfections in the capital market and the apparent general unwillingness of individual savers to assume the risks of ownership result in a situation in which venture capital can be scarce even at a time when there is oversaving in the economy.

[19]Department of Trade and Commerce, *Investment and Inflation*, p. 158.

The purpose of our analysis can be served by a brief glance at the economic implications of corporate saving. One observer maintains that on strictly economic grounds the reinvestment of earnings in a corporation is likely to result in malinvestment.[20] It is argued that expansion of existing enterprises is often the result of other than economic motivation and is therefore unwarranted, in fact is economically undesirable. If, as not infrequently seems the case, expansionist policy is pursued purely to achieve size and possibly power, without regard for the marginal return on capital, it must be condemned from an economic viewpoint. Another doubtful aim is that of endless expansion as an indication of sound business leadership. The North American tendency to consider size a virtue in itself is reflected in much of its business leadership.[21]

If such expansion results in the investment of capital in a way which yields a smaller than average return on the investment, then there seems no doubt about malinvestment. Had the earnings been distributed to the shareholders, they probably would not have reinvested them in that corporation, but (assuming that a considerable portion of dividends is reinvested) in some other venture. The fact that the largest average return on investments occurs not in the large but in the medium-sized corporations appears to indicate over-expansion and malinvestment.[22] How serious this is in the Canadian economy cannot be determined. But it is unlikely to be very serious, in view of the fact that, had all earnings been distributed in the past for shareholders to invest in accordance with their judgment, there almost certainly would have been a great deal of malinvestment, perhaps as much as has resulted from the decisions of corporate boards of directors.

A more serious economic aspect of the corporate propensity to save is the effect upon the supply of capital for new enterprises

[20]See N. S. Buchanan, *The Economics of Corporate Enterprise,* pp. 248 ff.

[21]Hoagland remarks, "In the absence of the laurel wreath as a mark of quality, and indeed in the absence of any definite authorized agency for bestowing rewards of any kind, American business leaders become their own judges of excellence in business leadership. As yet, qualitative measures of excellence have not been developed. Quantitative measures are more easily applied. Hence, the size of the business managed is used as the test of the capacity of the management. This helps to account for the urge to expand." *Corporation Finance,* p. 603.

[22]See Temporary National Economic Committee, *Relative Efficiency of Large, Medium-Sized, and Small Business* (Washington, 1941).

waiting to be born. If dividend income represents a sizable portion of the income available for new investment, then undue retention of corporate earnings will necessarily reduce the amount available for new investment. This is an important consideration to be borne in mind when considering the effects of the taxation of corporate income.

Another controversial issue is whether or not the retention of corporate profits at the current level is inflationary. Professor Seymour Harris states that "investment has been too high; and the moderation of the rate of profits would keep investment down and thus reduce the weight of one of the greatest inflationary factors."[23]

Whether or not the retention of corporate earnings is inflationary depends upon the purpose for which these earnings are withheld and their ultimate disposition. If profits are retained for the purpose of stabilizing dividends throughout the business cycle, and are held liquid for that purpose, the effect of such policy is deflationary at the time of retention, and counter-deflationary at the time of disbursement during a slump. This thesis has been used as an argument for the policy of dividend stabilization. The efficacy of such a policy in offsetting major upsurges and downswings in the business cycle is doubtful, to say the least. But the point should be made that the retention of profits is not *per se* inflationary.

If corporate profits are retained for the purpose of expansion during a period of inflation, then they are probably inflationary in their net effects. Had they been paid out in the form of dividends their aggregate size would have been reduced by the amount of individual tax paid on them, and pressure on the consumer and/or capital goods markets would have been reduced accordingly.

In so far as the retention of earnings is a reflection of conservative corporate policy, designed to provide adequate reserves for future contingencies, the economic effect is, on balance, more favourable rather than otherwise. Excessive payment of dividends would result in a weakened corporate position upon the arrival of

[23]United States, Congress, Joint Committee on the Economic Report, 1948, *Corporate Profits*, p. 44.

depression, and would undoubtedly entail more serious dislocation than would have taken place otherwise. It appears that the long-run economic effects of conservative oversaving by corporations are likely to be less than the effects of undersaving. This is admittedly a very broad generalization about the aggregate effects of the dividend policy of corporations considered as a whole. It cannot be as well defended as the case for conservative policy in the individual corporation, where dividend policy must be determined, not by aggregate effects on the economy, but by all the circumstances peculiar to that corporation. Tax policy that prevents the withholding of earnings to an extent that places a corporation in a vulnerable position is likely to have serious long-run results.

To sum up these economic implications of corporation dividend policy, it is concluded that the argument regarding misdirected investment is not altogether convincing, despite its apparent soundness on purely theoretical grounds. While it is probably true that a certain amount of malinvestment does occur because of the indiscriminate expansion of existing enterprise without proper economic motives, probably a similar margin of error would occur under individual investment of earnings, were they fully distributed.

A more serious indictment of existing dividend policy is the possibility of increased inflationary forces being released through overinvestment resulting from the retention of corporate earnings. But the writer is unsympathetic to any proposal for curbing such overinvestment through tax measures, even though it could be measured in time to decide upon policy, and that policy could be implemented in time to rectify the situation—both of which are unlikely. Furthermore, overinvestment is a generalization applied to the economy as a whole, and remedial measures should be just as broad. They would almost certainly work a hardship in industries where overinvestment is not a problem, and in the case of individual corporations this could be fatal.

Excessive retention of corporate profits undoubtedly results in some impairment of the supply of capital for new business ventures. But this is probably unimportant, compared with the factors that have made the investing public loath to purchase corporation stock. If the shares of tried and tested corporations with a long record of earnings cannot be sold to the public, then it is unlikely that there will be any enthusiasm for the share offerings of new corporations, the future of which is quite unknown.

The point that seems to clinch the argument for corporate saving is the obvious need of corporations, great and small, to rely upon undistributed earnings for future capital requirements. As long as this situation exists, it overshadows any of the economic effects of retaining profits enumerated above. As Professor Slichter said: "The willingness of corporate managements to plow back a substantial proportion of profits has had great advantages for the country . . . it has enabled industry to make large expenditures on much-needed increases in capacity, despite the inadequate supply of outside funds."[24]

It is concluded that something like the existing level of corporate saving is not only desirable but necessary.[25] It is important, therefore, that tax policy be framed to avoid lowering it. This is not to argue in favour of preferred treatment for corporate saving, except, perhaps, in the case of new, small enterprises. The approach seems to be equal treatment for all income. Before conclusions are reached, the effects of the corporation tax upon dividend policy and corporate saving should be considered.

(*b*) Effect upon the Distribution of Earnings

If the tax on corporate income is not shifted, it reduces the aggregate amount of net earnings available for dividends and corporate saving. The question that concerns us at this point is whether the reduction in net profits results in a reduction of

[24] *Ibid.*, p. 18.

[25] The Colwyn Committee stated that "when a company saves by retaining part of its profit, the operation is smooth and simple. In the case of a progressive business the flow of capital is just in the place where it is required; it is at the growing point of industry, enabling new needs and opportunities to be met without delay as and when they arise. This is true of the new enterprising business, which may as yet be making only small profits, as well as of the established company whose ability to save large sums for development year by year has given proof of efficiency and power of continued expansion. There are cases of course where reserves are accumulated out of caution rather than enterprise, and are invested, *e.g.*, in the preference shares of outside concerns, but generally speaking it is true that the Income Tax, when it falls upon company reserves, entrenches upon a form of saving which is of special value to the community." *Report of the Committee on National Debt and Taxation*, p. 149.

corporate saving or corporate investment, or both, or whether a greater portion of earnings is withheld in order to maintain the level of saving deemed necessary by management. A distinction will be drawn between large and small corporations because the effects may often depend upon the size and nature of the business.

It is not enough to examine the volume of corporate saving by itself and conclude, as has been done, that even very heavy taxation of corporation profits does not impair the ability of corporations to save.[26] While it does appear from the figures for recent years that corporate profits and saving have been very high despite the imposition of a 100 per cent excess profits tax, it must be remembered that these reported profits are greatly overstated, owing to failure to deduct the rise in the cost of replacing inventories, and to a lesser extent, failure to charge adequate depreciation.[27] This overstatement has undoubtedly played an important part in the determination of dividend policy.

The management of most corporations has a preconceived idea of a minimum amount of earnings which must be retained in the corporation, based upon the factors outlined above. Even if there is no capital expansion programme in sight, ordinary prudence requires the retention of some part of the earnings as a reserve for contingencies. The percentage will vary, of course, from company to company, and will also vary within a company

[26]Matthew Woll, Second Vice-President of the American Federation of Labour, states that "in spite of enormously greater taxation, corporations still managed to accumulate more than twice as much in profits after taxation in 1943, than they had in 1939. In spite of enormously high wartime taxes, they put away for corporate reserves and expansion more money in 1943, than they had accumulated in 1939 as profits before taxes. These figures, which I submit, prove conclusively that high taxation is no bar to the accumulation of high profits and high reserves for reinvestment." "Should Corporations be Taxed as Such?" *How Should Corporations be Taxed?* p. 35.

[27]Professor Slichter stated to the Joint Committee on the Economic Report of the President that American corporations overstated their profits by about $16.4 billion in the period 1946-8. As a result, 1946 profits were represented as being nearly twice as large as they actually were, and in 1947 they were overstated by about 50 per cent. He estimated that the overstatement in 1948 would be approximately 25 per cent. *Corporate Profits*, p. 3. The United States Department of Commerce estimates the profit distortion resulting from changes in inventory valuation at upwards of $5 billion in each of the years 1946 and 1947. *Survey of Current Business*, July 1948, National Income Section, Table 1. An interesting study on this problem was prepared for the Joint Committee on the Economic Report by William H. Moore, entitled "Corporate Profits and Their Measurement," October 1948; see *Corporate Profits*, pp. 229-41.

from time to time. Up to a point, heavy taxation of corporate income is likely to induce a corporation to increase the percentage of earnings retained rather than sacrifice the future security of the company. This is especially likely to happen if the company plans expansion and must depend upon earnings for its capital. A qualification of this statement will be made in the discussion of the effects of taxation upon investment.

TABLE VII

CORPORATE PROFITS BEFORE AND AFTER TAXES AND UNDISTRIBUTED PROFITS IN CANADA, 1938–1950

(1) Year	(2) *Net profits before taxes*	(3) *Income and Excess profits taxes*	(4) *Ratio of* (3) *to* (2)	(5) *Net profits after taxes*	(6) *Undistributed profits*	(7) *Ratio* (6) *to* (5)
	$000,000	$000,000	%	$000,000	$000,000	%
1938[a]	477	92	19.3	385	131	34.0
1939	618	112	18.1	506	219	43.3
1940	814	324	39.8	490	172	35.1
1941	1,124	515	45.8	609	304	49.9
1942[b]	1,314	629	47.8	685	374	54.6
1943	1,297	640	49.3	657	362	55.1
1944	1,216	598	49.2	618	334	54.0
1945	1,223	599	48.1	624	374	59.9
1946	1,450	654	45.1	796	469	58.9
1947	1,805	703	38.9	1,102	595	53.9
1948[c]	1,944	689	35.4	1,255	777	61.9
1949	1,898	727	38.3	1,171	601	51.3
1950	2,270	868	38.2	1,402	730	52.1

[a]Figures for 1938-41 taken from *National Accounts Income and Expenditure*, 1938-1947, pp. 12-14.
[b]Figures for 1942-47 taken from *ibid.*, 1942-1949, pp. 20-2.
[c]Figures for 1948-50 taken from *ibid.*, Revised Preliminary 1950, p. 9.

The pattern of corporate saving in Canada from 1938 to 1950 is shown in Table VII. In 1938, when only 19.3 per cent of corporate net profits was taxed away, 66 per cent of what was left was distributed to the shareholders, and 34 per cent was retained by the corporations. As the percentage of profits taken by taxes increased during the war years, corporations earmarked an increasingly large percentage of what was left for corporate saving, diminishing relatively the portion paid out in dividends. In the years 1942 to 1945, when income and excess profits taxes amounted to almost half the net profit of corporations, less than half of the remaining profit was paid out as dividends. In 1945 almost 60 per cent of net profits was retained.

It will be noted that in no year since 1941 have Canadian corporations failed to retain more than half their net earnings after tax, despite the fact that after the war the ratio of tax to total net earnings was reduced substantially from the wartime peak. In 1948, when the tax-profit ratio was at its lowest point (35.4 per cent) since 1939, a greater proportion of earnings was retained (61.9 per cent) than at any time during the period examined. The increased retention of profits during the post-war years is largely due to the unprecedented capital investment programme that has been taking place in Canada, much of which has been financed out of retained earnings.

The effect of the tax is likely to be much more marked on some types of corporations than on others. A distinction should be made between the larger type of well-established public corporation and the small, closely held corporation.

The large public corporation is likely to be more or less sensitive to public reaction to dividend policy, and therefore, regardless of tax, is likely to distribute earnings in sufficient amount to make future stock issues attractive to investors, and to maintain public confidence.[28] Again, there is not likely to be much incentive in this type of company to retain earnings deliberately to avoid personal income taxation of dividends. This is particularly so where ownership and management are divorced. The most important factor in the case of the large corporation is its ability, normally, to secure new capital from the investing public through the sale of shares and bonds. Thus there is not so great a need to retain earnings as in the case of small companies. For these reasons, it is likely that taxation of such companies will have less effect on their dividend policy than will the taxation of small companies.

Small companies, on the other hand, are likely to react much more strongly to the tax, especially when management and ownership are unified. Such companies cannot generally secure funds from the capital market. New funds must be provided

[28]Hoagland cites an example, extreme, perhaps, but to the point. The Pennsylvania Railroad Company paid 6 per cent on its common stock for many years. In 1921 the company reduced the dividend rate to 4 per cent, and "the effect upon its credit was almost as bad as if it actually had failed to pay all its bond interest." *Corporation Finance,* p. 576.

through the retention of profits for that purpose. For this reason such companies need not be concerned over public reaction to their failure to pay dividends, even over a long period of time. Furthermore, the small corporation is generally more exposed to unfavourable economic conditions than is the large one. It is less likely to have other income against which to offset its losses. Therefore it must usually retain a higher proportion of earnings than does the large company. Again, where the owners of a corporation are also the managers, there is a strong incentive to withhold earnings to avoid high personal income taxation of dividends, even though such avoidance is only temporary. They may pay themselves liberal salaries which are allowed as a deduction from earnings before tax, and there is thus the possibility of taking at least a part of the return on their investment in the form of salary.

For these reasons, it is to be expected that the ratio of undistributed profits to total profits is higher in small corporations than in the medium and large ones. This is very definitely the case in the United States,[29] and it seems almost certain that a similar situation exists in Canada.

It is concluded that a high corporation tax, coupled with high taxation of dividends in the hands of shareholders, probably increases the portion of net profits retained by corporations. The increase is likely to be greater in small corporations than in large. If the tax is so high, however, that it affects investment incentives adversely, the result may be reversed because corporations, particularly the large public ones, may distribute earnings rather than

[29]E. E. Lincoln compiled the following figures showing the pattern of dividend payments in the United States in 1935, the year prior to the enactment of the undistributed profits tax (*Applied Business Finance,* Table 156, p. 753):

Size of Corporation (Assets Classes)	*Number of corporations*	*Net profit after taxes*	*% of net profits retained after taxes*
Under $50,000	69,714	98.7	55.0
$50,000- $100,000	24,953	104.1	49.8
100,000- 250,000	26,138	238.5	45.2
250,000- 500,000	13,058	259.3	40.4
500,000- 1,000,000	8,255	322.7	29.9
1,000,000- 5,000,000	8,232	932.9	24.4
5,000,000-10,000,000	1,241	437.1	19.3
10,000,000-50,000,000	1,156	1,212.2	6.5
50,000,000- and over	328	2,388.6	19.1

withhold them for investment. This point will be expanded in the following section.

(*c*) Effect on Corporate Investment

The effects of the taxation of corporate income and dividends have already been discussed in connection with the investment of individuals, and it was concluded that the tax tends to reduce the aggregate supply of investment capital, as well as discourage the purchase of share capital. We turn now to the possible effect of the corporation tax on investment by corporations in plant and equipment.

Heavy taxes are undoubtedly a matter of major interest to corporate management, and the decision to go ahead or not to go ahead with new projects may be determined in the final analysis by the tax consequences of the ventures. The higher the tax, the greater will be its effect on such decisions.

The extent to which the tax affects the incentive of management to invest depends upon how it affects the return on the investment. The return on new investment should include what has been termed the "premium for risk taking,"[30] as well as interest on the capital invested.

One of the primary brakes on investment is the risk of losing the capital invested. The prospective return must be great enough to offset the possibility of loss. If a tax reduces the amount of reward for risk taking it is likely to restrain investment. It is impossible to determine how much the so-called premium for risk taking can be reduced by taxation before the effects on investment become serious. But there is little doubt that investment has been impeded to some extent by the existing level of taxation in Canada.

Even if the total reward for risk taking were to be removed through taxation, some minimum return on the investment is necessary if there is to be corporate investment. There must be some prospect of gain,[31] otherwise there can be no economic

[30]See Goode, *The Postwar Corporation Tax Structure*, p. 9.

[31]The gain may be in the form of positive cash income, or a capital gain. Or it may take the form of a reduction in losses which would have been incurred had the investment not been made. Or it may be a deferred gain to be realized in the future as a result, say, of a dominating position in the market caused by the new investment. The point is that there must be some prospect of gain if investment is to be made on a rational basis.

motivation for investment. It is improbable that possible loss offsets would compensate for a reduction in the minimum return that is determined by management. It is usually assumed that the minimum return on venture capital approximates roughly the yield on high-grade bonds. If the anticipated return on a proposed investment in plant and equipment is less than such bond interest, management is likely to invest in such bonds, or hold the funds idle, or pay out the earnings as dividends, rather than plough earnings back in the business. Management may even decide upon a policy of gradual disinvestment through cutting back inventories and neglecting to replace worn-out machinery and equipment.

No quantitative appraisal of these possible effects can be made. But it seems highly probable that some new corporate investments have failed to materialize because of the small prospective return after taxes.

Here again, the effects of the tax are likely to vary with different types of corporations. Investment by large corporations tends to be less sensitive to changes in the rate of return after tax than it is in the case of small concerns. In the large corporations decisions on investment by management are likely to involve factors other than the prospective earnings from new investment —factors such as the improvement or maintenance of market position, and the protection of existing investment. It has already been noted that there is a tendency towards expansion of business enterprises on the grounds that expansion and progress are synonymous. It is possible that some managements would elect to continue expansion through investment, even if the net return were to approximate zero.

Small corporations, on the other hand, particularly where the owners are the managers, tend to be highly sensitive to changes in the rate of investment return after tax, and are more likely to refrain from investment if some reward for risk and a minimum return are not present in the prospective yield after taxes.

3. *Conclusions*

The double taxation of corporate income at high rates appears to result in a number of changes in the pattern of individual and corporate saving and investment. The effect on individual saving and investment in turn affects corporate saving quantitatively.

If the combined corporate and personal tax is high enough to reduce the return from investments in corporate enterprise so that the risk and interest on capital are not reflected adequately in the return, it seems likely that individuals will not invest in corporation stock, and perhaps not in bonds either. At the same time capacity to save is diminished by the heavy taxation of investment income in the hands of individuals and the taxation of that income in the hands of the corporation.

This has, in turn, an important effect on corporate saving. To the extent that individuals are unwilling or unable to invest in new corporate securities, corporations must do their financing internally. That is, corporations must make up the required amount of saving by ploughing back earnings. This, of course, has the effect of reducing dividend payments still further, and of reducing individual capacity to save.

The ramifications of these long-run effects are many and they are complex. One of the most important is the difficulty of creating new corporations owing to the lack of venture capital. This means that perhaps a disproportionate share of new production facilities will be created by existing corporations out of previous earnings. Thus a still greater concentration of economic power may be fostered by a tax system which at least pays lip service to discrimination against it.

The effects of taxation on corporate investment are similar to its effects on private investment, but at a given rate they are not likely to be so great. The individual shareholder pays two taxes, and their combined effect is what must be considered in determining his investment policy. The corporation need consider only the effect of the corporate tax in deciding whether to make new investments. But if the tax results in a net return incompatible with the risk taken and no larger than the yield of high-grade bonds, there is likely to be little incentive to create new plant and equipment. The possible decrease in both individual and corporate saving and investment which might be caused by the tax as it now stands, would result in serious economic maladjustment of consumption and saving.

The present tax structure has probably caused no actual diminution in real saving. But there has certainly been a shift in individual saving away from corporate shares, and an increase in corporate saving through the retention of a greater portion of earnings. The long-run economic implications of this situation deserve careful consideration. One of these is the effects upon the methods of corporate financing, which will be considered under that heading.

Effects on Prices

In the discussion of the incidence of the tax, it was concluded that there is not likely to be any short-run effect upon prices because the tax does not tend to affect supply. In the long run, however, prices may be affected through the effects of the tax on saving and investment, and ultimately on supply.

An important point in this connection is the unlikelihood that the tax on corporate profits by itself will affect investment to such an extent that there will be any effect on supply.[32] It is the combined effect of the corporation tax and the individual tax on dividend income that is likely to impede investment.

If the combined corporate and individual tax rates are such as to result in a diminution in the supply of investment, then production will be affected. New productive capacity, both in old and in prospective companies, will not be created. If the funds that would normally have been invested are diverted to consumption, there will be a greater demand for which there will be an inadequate supply. Thus a rise in the general price level might be expected, resulting in a diffusion of the tax to the consumer.

A conditioning factor in the situation is the use to which the government puts the funds that it has taken away from individuals by the corporation and personal income taxes, and the effect this has upon the volume of money and its velocity of circulation.

If the funds are expended to achieve the ends of a welfare state through payments that will typically be spent by the recipients for consumption, inflationary pressure will be exerted if the volume of private saving has been retarded by such a tax programme. In other words, if demand outstrips supply, there will be a rise in the price level of consumer goods. At the same

[32]Were the rates to be increased very substantially, however, the effect could be detrimental to saving and investment. It seems unlikely, however, that the rate structure would be so constructed.

time there will be a dislocation in the capital goods industries. If, as was assumed, there is a decrease in investment, the demand for capital goods will decrease, and their prices will fall.

In a free enterprise economy a new equilibrium would be reached in both the consumer goods and the capital goods industries. In the former the price increase, if sustained, would call forth new capacity in the long run, supply would rise, and a new price adjustment would be reached. Similarly, in the capital goods industry low prices would result in greater demand and a corresponding price adjustment. But this situation presupposes a return on investment, after taxes, sufficient to justify investment in the minds of individuals and corporate management. If the impact of the tax system is so great as to result in no new investment or disinvestment, the maladjustment is likely to be permanent.

So much for the situation when government spending is directed largely towards consumption. If the government programme is essentially one of public investment, that investment, depending upon its nature, may to some extent replace the loss in private investment occasioned by taxation. Short of the government entering the consumer goods industry,[33] however, there will be no change in the supply of such goods. If the supply is curtailed because of the lack of private investment, prices will still rise. But the rise will be less under these conditions, because only that part of the government's expenditures that is reflected in wages, salaries, dividends, and profits will reach the consumer goods market.

The result in the capital goods industry will depend, of course, upon the nature of the government programme. There will be an increase in demand for all the capital goods required for the government programme. If this demand is not satisfied when all existing production facilities are working at capacity, price must rise because, under our original assumption, no new capital will be forthcoming to provide additional facilities and additional supply.

This analysis has been oversimplified by taking the extreme

[33]In the case of such a durable consumer good as housing, the impact of a government programme is diffused throughout a wide range of ancillary goods connected with housing. The results are so complicated that it is impossible to trace them with any degree of accuracy.

case of taxation destroying the incentive for *all* new private investment. That is hardly realistic under any conceivable situation short of a completely socialist state in the Marxian sense of the term. But to the extent that private investment is curtailed, and there undoubtedly has been some degree of curtailment under the present tax structure, results of the kind outlined above are to be expected.

Quite obviously the analysis of the long-run effects of the taxation of corporate income and dividends on prices is most complex and dependent upon many variables. The point to be borne in mind is that price must rise if taxation curtails production and supply, and it will remain high until supply is increased or demand reduced. Demand may be reduced ultimately through unemployment resulting from actual disinvestment, accompanied by a decrease in purchasing power.

On these grounds, it appears that the tax may be diffused widely if investment is affected to a serious extent. The diffusion is among investors in the form of lower returns on their investment, consumers in the form of higher prices, and wage earners in the form of partial or total loss of wages.

Effect on Methods of Corporate Financing

The double taxation of corporate income and dividends applies only to investment in share capital. Bond interest is deductible from corporate income before the corporation tax is imposed, so that the recipient of bond interest pays tax only on the interest. Dividends paid on stock are not deductible. Under a corporate tax rate of 52.6 per cent (the combined federal and provincial rate in Ontario and Quebec), a corporation with large earnings must earn approximately $2.11 in order to pay a dividend of $1 out of current earnings. It need earn only $1 to pay $1 of bond interest. The tax discrimination between dividends and bond interest is apparent, and on the surface would appear to influence individuals to buy bonds rather than shares, and corporations to react to this demand.[34]

[34]Professor Groves states, "That the present discrimination is substantial and that it does, in many cases, exercise an unfortunate influence upon corporate and individual decisions is confirmed by accountants and others close to corporate

There is some evidence that this discrimination has affected the method of corporate financing in the case of individual firms in the United States,[35] where the tax law provides for the taxation of corporate income and dividends in much the same way as in Canada, and at similar rates. But there is disagreement about the over-all effects on corporate financing. In one American study it was concluded that "statistical data on debt and equity financing over the past 25 years indicate no marked trend toward or away from long-term debt financing."[36] In a later analysis Professor Slichter states that during 1946, 1947, and the first half of 1948 issues of bonds and notes were considerably more important as compared with issues of stocks than was the case between 1910 and 1929. During these three years stock issues represented only 30 per cent of all domestic private issues (exclusive of refunding issues), compared with a ratio of 44 per cent between 1910 and 1929.[37] There was a heavy preponderance of bond issues over stock issues in Canada during 1947. A total of $246.3 million of new corporate bonds was issued (exclusive of $272.8 million for refunding purposes), while new share capital issued was only $90.8 million (27 per cent),[38] compared with 30 per cent in the United States.

There appears to be little doubt in the minds of most observers close to the situation that the existing tax structure does alter the pattern of corporation financing. Not only has it discouraged the ownership of stock in corporations, but it has at the same time forced corporations to do a considerable part of their financing through retained earnings. Whether there has been a general

---

financing. Obviously, if a company pays out to bondholders half its net income (before federal taxes and the payment of interest), it can save half the corporate tax that would be due were the company to finance itself exclusively with stock. The higher the effective rate of the corporate tax, the greater the saving." *Postwar Taxation and Economic Progress*, p. 31.

[35]J. Keith Butters, "Federal Taxation of Corporate Profits," doctoral dissertation, Harvard University, 1941, cited by Groves, *ibid.*, p. 32.

[36]Richard Goode, *The Postwar Corporation Tax Structure*, p. 11. The period studied was 1921-45. Goode concedes that "there is no way of knowing what means of financing would have been used if there had been no corporate income tax."

[37]United States, Congress, Joint Committee on Economic Report, 1948, *Corporate Profits*, p. 17.

[38]Department of Trade and Commerce, *Investment and Inflation*, p. 149.

increase in debt financing is doubtful,[39] but there is ample evidence that the favoured tax position given to bonds has had substantial effects on this form of corporate financing in a number of specific instances.[40]

This result is undesirable, since it is generally agreed that financing through stock issues is sounder, not only for the business organization itself, but for the economy as a whole. The existence of fixed charges (debt interest), which must be met regardless of the earnings of the business, results in a lack of resiliency on the part of corporations to absorb the shocks of depression in the form of sharply decreased profits, or deficits. Were a disproportionate part of corporate financing to be done through bond issues, undoubtedly the incidence of insolvency during depression would increase "with grave losses, not only for the stockholder but also for senior securities and the enterprise as a whole, through the great costs of reorganization and the inevitable disturbances of operations and business relations which insolvency involves."[41]

It is obvious that the stability of the economy would be impaired if debt financing were to assume a major role in providing new capital for corporate enterprise. It is unlikely, however, that such a situation will develop. Corporate management for the most part is probably sufficiently aware of the potential trouble occasioned by excessive debt financing to set aside the desire to achieve tax savings through the issue of bonds. Under existing conditions, management is far more likely to do most new financing through retained earnings.

One must wish that corporate enterprise were less dependent upon internal funds for expansion, and that share capital could be the most important source of funds for corporate expansion. The first step towards the achievement of this end should be reform of the federal tax system by removing the tax discrimination between

[39]Goode's study shows a very sharp reduction in the aggregate issue of new long-term bonds and notes in the United States throughout the whole period 1931 to 1945, compared with the period 1921 to 1930. *The Postwar Corporation Tax Structure*, p. 45.

[40]See Roy Blough, "Some Aspects of Corporate Taxation," *Bulletin* of the *National Tax Association*, June 1946, p. 289.

[41]Henry C. Simons, quoted by Groves, *Postwar Taxation and Economic Progress*, p. 33.

bond interest and dividends.[42] The sensible approach is that of allowing a credit against either the corporate or the personal tax for the element of duplication.[43] Pushed to its logical conclusion, this would mean that whether the corporation were financed with bonds or stocks, earnings would be subject to only one tax. This proposal will be developed in a later chapter.

Effect on the Form of Business Organization

It is often argued that because of its discrimination against the corporate form of business the corporation tax discourages the creation of new incorporated companies, and that the economic advantages of an efficient form of business organization are lost.[44] Under such conditions the tax system becomes a factor in determining the form that is assumed by business concerns. This is held by many critics to be undesirable.

It is probably inevitable that taxation on anything like its present scale with its many complexities must have some effects on the form of business organization. Many enterprises have undoubtedly been forced, for reasons of taxation, to forego the important advantages of conducting their business in the corporate form. One American writer states:

> It can be demonstrated that taxes do, in fact, strongly influence the form of business organization for thousands of enterprises. . . .
>
> Whereas, before the war, partnerships represented about one third of the total of partnerships and corporations, in 1942, when the high wartime tax rates were effective, about half of the total were partnerships. From these figures, one might estimate that from one

[42]This alone is not likely to be sufficient to solve the problem in its entirety. Slichter has pointed out that "even before the income tax became stiff and before there was double taxation of income distributed in the form of dividends, corporations found outside funds insufficient for their needs. The kind of securities which industry offers do not seem to appeal to the large number of potential investors in the middle income brackets who wish a considerable degree of security, some chance to participate in the gains of expansion and technological progress, and some protection against a possible long-run rise in prices." United States, Congress, Joint Committee on the Economic Report, 1948, *Corporate Profits*, p. 19.

[43]The Canadian government has recently gone a short step in this direction in the allowance of a credit of 10 per cent on dividends received by an individual.

[44]See Richard Goode, *The Postwar Corporation Tax Structure*, p. 11.

hundred to one hundred and fifty thousand enterprises were operating as partnerships in 1942—enterprises which would have preferred to operate as corporations had pre-war tax rates obtained.[45]

While it is probably true that many business enterprises are near the margin between operating as corporations or as partnerships or sole proprietorships, the percentage that would incorporate were the tax discrimination against corporations removed would not likely be large. Most of these concerns operate in a very small way in the retail and service trades, and would not incorporate under any circumstances. The corporate form is so fundamentally important in some lines of enterprise (for purposes of raising capital, securing limited liability, continuity of existence, etc.) that it is likely to persist regardless of tax discrimination. Quantitatively the problem may not be very important. But it may have qualitative significance for the economy as a whole if the kind of small business that is attempting to introduce new products and techniques, which may be important economically, is prevented from incorporating because of taxation.

On the other hand, there is evidence that the tax system encourages the incorporation of business concerns under certain conditions, despite the apparent discrimination against corporate profits. For example, it may be possible, through incorporation, to effect tax saving, or at least to postpone the payment of individual income tax on business profits for an indefinite period of time. If the owners of a business have sufficient individual income to place them in a bracket with a higher rate than the corporate rate, a saving can be effected by retaining the profits in the company and investing them in new plant or other assets. The saving is fully realized as far as a given individual is concerned if the corporate income is not distributed until after his death, or if it can be realized during his life as a capital gain.

This possibility has certainly resulted in the incorporation of businesses which would have been operated as partnerships or individual proprietorships under a different tax structure. The relative advantage or disadvantage of incorporation depends upon individual and corporation income tax rates, the personal

[45]Howard R. Bowen, "Optional Partnership Treatment of Corporate Earnings," *How Should Corporations be Taxed?* pp. 63-4.

income of the owners of the business, the size of the business, the amount of profits retained within it, and the length of their retention. There probably will be many more cases where incorporation is a disadvantage, from a tax viewpoint, than where it is an advantage. If there are any really serious effects on the form which business organization takes, most of them could probably be eliminated by the removal of double taxation of corporate income and dividends.

EFFECTS ON SMALL BUSINESS AND NEW ENTERPRISES

A great deal has been written about the special problem of small businesses and new enterprises under the existing system of taxing corporate profits and dividends,[46] and comments have been made on the point several times in this chapter.

1. *Definition of Small Business*

It is difficult to formulate a precise definition of a "small" company, because the terms "small" and "large" have different meanings in different contexts. The terms are necessarily relative, and they have different connotations in different industries. For example, a firm with assets of $25 million may be considered small in an industry where there are one or more companies with assets of several hundred million dollars. The smallest company in the pulp and paper industry or steel industry may be large in

[46]See Howard R. Bowen, "Optional Partnership Treatment of Corporate Earnings," *How Should Corporations be Taxed?* pp. 61-71; "The Taxation of Small Business," *Proceedings of the National Tax Association*, 1946, pp. 394-400; A. G. Buehler, "Some Comments on the Taxation of Small Business," *ibid.*, pp. 415-19; J. K. Butters, "Should the Profits of Small Corporations be Taxed Like Partnership Earnings?" *How Should Corporations be Taxed?* pp. 72-90; J. K. Butters and John Lintner, *Effect of Federal Taxes on Growing Enterprises*; W. L. Hearne, "Does the Present Tax System Discourage Business Enterprise?" *How Should Corporations be Taxed?* pp. 185-90. The majority opinion is that high taxation of corporate profits discourages business enterprise, particularly the creation of new corporations and the expansion of them. But some labour spokesmen maintain that there is no basis for such views save the desire to reduce corporate taxes. S. H. Ruttenberg, Assistant Director of Research, C.I.O., denies that there is double taxation of dividends, and states that "it is difficult for me to see how our present tax structure, in any major way, discourages American business enterprise. I personally believe that the exponents of this theory use it as a means to an end, the end being reduced tax liability." Quoted by Hearne, "Does the Present Tax System Discourage Business Enterprise?" *How Should Corporations be Taxed?* p. 191.

comparison with the largest company in the long lumber or woodworking industries. For all practical purposes, however, any definition of "small" includes the great majority of firms in most fields of business activity.[47]

For the purpose of this analysis it appears sufficient to define a small corporation as a relatively new and rapidly growing concern with promising prospects, as distinguished from the small concern with little chance or need to expand.[48] This classification is used because our primary concern over the effects of taxation on the small business is connected with its ability to expand in the economy to the point of maximum efficiency. Even more important is the need to allow the creation of such companies.

2. *Effects of the Tax*

(*a*) The Creation of New Enterprises

It has been observed that tax considerations "seldom dominate decisions to organize small, independent enterprises."[49] This is probably true, because businesses are started by men who have confidence in their ability to make them succeed, and who anticipate a considerable return on their investment. They are often started by professional promoters who have an idea for sale. In too many cases the ultimate returns are not the primary consideration. Rather, the anticipated reward for promotion is the motivating force.

Even though taxation does not impede the desire to start new

[47]See Butters and Lintner, *Effect of Federal Taxes on Growing Enterprises*, p. 9. This is an excellent study of the effect of federal taxes (United States) on growing enterprises, containing case histories of selected corporations. The writer has drawn heavily on the conclusions contained therein for the purposes of this discussion.

[48]J. K. Butters makes such a distinction in his article, "Would the Complete Integration of the Corporate and Personal Income Taxes Injure Small Business?" *Proceedings of the National Tax Association*, 1947, pp. 189-90. Typical of the group with little chance or need to expand are the corner grocery store, the filling station, small restaurant, and apartment house. These businesses have little need for the retention of earnings to any extent. Butters states (p. 189) that "as a group they are of great importance to the social and political stability of the economy, but they contribute relatively little to introduction of new products and techniques—upon which the growth of our national productivity so largely depends."

[49]Butters and Lintner, *Effect of Federal Taxes on Growing Enterprises*, p. 13. They state (pp. 13-14) that "the founders of small, independent enterprises seldom give detailed consideration to taxes in deciding whether to undertake their ventures. This conclusion holds almost without exception for the large number of such businessmen interviewed during the course of this investigation."

enterprises, it may have an important effect on the ability of promoters to create them.[50] In the promotional stages of a new enterprise, it is particularly difficult to attract outside capital. Probably most of the financing at this stage is done personally by the promoters. In so far as the combined effect of the corporation and personal income taxes reduces personal saving, there is less promotion capital available. Under the existing rate structure it is certain that there is less capital available for promotion than there was under more modest taxation. This is simply a restatement of the conclusion reached above that individual saving and investment are reduced by the existing tax system.

It is impossible to measure to what extent companies are stillborn because of the impact of the tax system on the supply of investment funds. Even in the days before high taxation of income, many a proposed venture collapsed before it could be put into production because of the lack of capital. *Risk* was then the dominant factor. It probably still is. But the very fact of high taxation lends weight to the presumption that at least some ideas possessed of merit are not made effective through the creation of a company to exploit them. It would be interesting to know how many of these ideas are taken over by large and well-established corporations able to finance them out of past earnings or by means of new security issues, or, what is more important, are taken over by large corporations and "killed" to prevent an innovation which would affect adversely their existing product.

If this situation is becoming more prevalent, and one suspects that it is, it contributes still further to the decline of competition and accentuates a problem which is already the cause of much concern. It seems fundamental that the tax system should be so devised as to encourage rather than impede new enterprises.

(*b*) Effect on Expansion of Small Companies

The over-all economic importance of the ability of small companies to expand should not be underestimated. Its significance is twofold. In the first instance, expansion of the individual company in many fields of activity is necessary, up to a point, in order to secure the advantages of large-scale production, achieve maxi-

[50]This point is admitted by Butters and Lintner, *ibid.*, pp. 15 ff.

mum efficiency of the factors of production, reduce unit costs, and secure the maximum return on investment. The desirability of expansion is obvious, for the individual firm, as well as for investors and the consuming public. In the second place, there is the fundamental desirability of stimulating the healthy growth of the economy through the competition afforded by the expansion of vigorous young enterprises.[51] This is not to say, however, that all small business concerns should become large, or even that all small concerns should expand. Probably most of them should not expand by creating new capital plant, and some which have expanded would have been better off had they remained at their former size. The important point to be made is that the tax system should not be a deterrent to expansion that is socially and economically desirable.

Taxation can curtail corporate expansion in two ways. First, it can impair the incentive to expand, and second, it can impair the availability of capital for expansion purposes.

(i) Incentives of management

While high taxes probably repress the incentive to expand less than they decrease the availability of capital needed for expansion, they do have a bearing on the incentive of management which is worth consideration.

Management of small corporations is likely to be considerably more sensitive to the effects of high taxation than that of large corporations. The small enterprise, especially the new one with which we are concerned primarily, is not likely to have much reserve, and the possibility of loss is accordingly a more important factor in policy determination than it is for a large corporation with substantial reserves and good credit standing. In other words, the risk of loss is more important to the small firm than to the large one.[52] Furthermore, a high corporate tax reduces the profit

[51]Butters and Lintner state that "it is of great social importance that small companies undertake such developments. The technological mutations which spring from them have a profound bearing on the rate of economic evolution, the vitality of the industrial competitive structure, and the level of employment and national income. A dollar spent in *developing* new products may be responsible for a hundred dollars spent in *producing* these and related products in subsequent years." *Ibid.*, p. 27.

[52]Taxation at its current level tends to increase risks more for small firms than for large. A tax on corporate income, regardless of the size of the business, di-

expectancy from an expansion made by a small firm to a greater extent than it reduces it for large companies. Butters and Lintner state that "in general, a flat-rate corporate tax would reduce the profit expectancy of a new development to a large company only in proportion to the tax rate whereas the profit expectancy of a similar development undertaken by a small firm would be reduced *much more* than in proportion to the tax rate."[53]

The combined effects of the corporate tax and personal income tax are likely to be more important for small companies than for large, because in the former there is more likelihood that ownership and management are vested in the same persons. When ownership and management are divorced, as they so often are in large corporations, less attention is likely to be paid to the results of corporate policy on the tax status of individual shareholders.

It is impossible to say how much the tax system as it now stands acts as a deterrent to the incentive to expand small businesses. Probably it does not deter as many as might be expected, because the desire to expand will likely outweigh the anticipated effects of taxation in many instances. But there is evidence of some deterrence resulting from a careful balancing of the probable costs and gains attached to expansion.

The repressive effects of taxation on initiative can be alleviated to some extent without change in tax rates. For instance, if the double taxation of corporate income were eliminated, if a more rapid write-off of fixed assets and development expenses were allowed, as well as averaging of profit and loss over a reasonable time interval, and if a basic exemption were given to corporate income, much of the incentive to expand could be maintained.

Another approach to a solution of the problem is through the use of a graduated rate structure for the tax on corporation prof-

---

rectly impairs the prospective return on a new investment. The government will share positive gain, but does not share losses. Thus, unless the company can find a way to offset losses occasioned by a new investment against profits from other sources, the result of an unprofitable expansion is pure loss. Large and well-established corporations often have relatively assured income against which to offset a loss from a new venture. But an undiversified small or new business can seldom hope to offset losses against other income. See Bowen, "The Taxation of Small Business," pp. 394-400.

[53] *Effect of Federal Taxes on Growing Enterprises,* p. 28.

its.[54] Such a proposal is predicated on the assumption that the corporation, like the individual, has taxpaying ability *per se*. But it is the writer's contention that such an assumption has no sound basis in fact. It rests upon the precarious concept of personality ascribed to the corporate form by legal fiction. Furthermore, such a proposal has no status on grounds of equity. Under a graduated rate structure a $100,000,000 corporation with a taxable income of $100,000 in an abnormal year would pay tax at a lower rate than a $1,000,000 corporation which happened fortuitously to earn, say, $200,000 in the same year. Size of net profit, taken by itself, has no meaning whatever.

The inequity is intensified because of the tendency for earnings of a small business to fluctuate from year to year more than those of a large business, due, among other things, to the fact that most small concerns are less diversified in their operations. Unless averaging of profit and loss were allowed, too great a percentage of the earnings of a good year would be taxed under rate graduation, with no compensation for loss in a poor year. For these reasons it is argued that the corporate tax be levied at a flat rate.

(ii) Availability of capital

It has been observed already that the adverse effect of the tax upon the amount of capital available to growing enterprises is greater than the deterrent to the initiative to expand. There are two possible sources of capital for the expansion of corporate enterprise—outside capital and retained earnings.

Outside capital. The availability of outside capital is limited by the size of the business itself, and most small corporations find it impossible to secure funds from the capital market. One authority has stated that in the United States an average annual income of $200,000 is a practical minimum below which public distribution of securities is not feasible.[55] Quite obviously income of this volume is above the level of what is usually considered to be "small" business. Even when securities of smaller units might be marketed, underwriters are reluctant to handle them because the

[54]See Bowen, "The Taxation of Small Business," pp. 397-8.

[55]James J. Minot, Jr., Vice-President of the Investment Bankers' Association of America, at the hearings before the Committee on Ways and Means, *Revenue Revision Laws*, 1938, p. 379. Cited by George E. Lent, *The Impact of the Undistributed Profits Tax 1936-1937*, p. 133.

issue would be small, and there would be limited opportunity for profit to the underwriter.[56] It was reported that only 40 per cent of the amount of securities registered with the Securities and Exchange Commission by small going concerns in the period 1936-9 were actually sold.[57]

The situation has been summarized as follows: (*a*) a substantial demand for capital on the part of small companies has gone unfilled; (*b*) small companies are at a severe competitive disadvantage in comparison with large companies in raising outside capital; (*c*) this disadvantage is in large part the result of the greater element of risk confronting small companies; (*d*) in contrast to small firms, large corporations have been able to raise new capital on relatively favourable terms since the late 1930's; (*e*) individual investors have increasingly entrusted their funds to safe forms of investment, such as government bonds, life insurance companies, and other major savings institutions. These institutions seldom invest in companies needing venture capital.[58]

The most important factor in the difficulty of marketing the securities of small corporations is the relatively high element of risk. The only important attraction attached to the shares of a small company with a promising future is the prospect of rapid growth, high profits, and substantial appreciation of the capital value of the stock. This is what is needed to offset the extra risk. But if taxation lowers the profit expectancy to any considerable extent, the incentive to invest is impaired seriously, or removed altogether if the profit expectancy is reduced to the average of large and well-established corporations. Thus high taxation heaps further difficulty on a situation which is already difficult.

Retained earnings. It has been indicated already that retained earnings have over the years been a major source of funds for corporate expansion, and have become still more important in the

[56]Analysis of registration statements filed with the Securities and Exchange Commission in 1938 and 1939 showed that the cost of floating new issues varied inversely with the size of the issuer. The cost of selling common stock of companies with less than $1 million of assets was on average 24.1 per cent of the amount actually sold, compared with 4.8 per cent for companies with assets between $10 and $50 million. *Ibid.*

[57]*Ibid.*

[58]See Butters and Lintner, *Effect of Federal Taxes on Growing Enterprises*, p. 90.

past few years. This is particularly the case with small corporations,[59] which depend very largely upon their own net earnings, after taxes, for capital with which to expand.

It is obvious that a high tax on corporate income, as compared with a low tax, must limit severely the rate of expansion that can be financed by an enterprise from retained earnings. Butters and Lintner state that "this restrictive effect is cumulative in character and will be greater (a) the longer the tax is in effect, (b) the higher the rate of the tax, (c) the higher the rate of profit earned by the company, and (d) the more conservative the company's dividend policy under the lower rate of tax."[60]

The net result of the tax in the case of any given corporation will depend upon the rate of profit, and the need, if any, to distribute earnings. As suggested earlier, a company earning a high return on its investment would, if possible, retain a larger percentage of its earnings, or retain them all, in order to finance desired expansion. This might offset the impact of the tax. But the over-all result of high taxation is likely to be a restriction of expansion and a decrease in profits distributed.

If, as our argument has tried to prove, the expansion of small corporations with a good prospect is important socially and economically, the case against a tax system which discourages or prevents such growth can hardly be overstated.

One of the major limiting factors working against such expansion is the difficulty attached to raising outside capital because of the high element of risk. The government should not be expected to do anything about this, and such an enterprise must continue, therefore, to finance its expansion through retention of earnings. But in this case, the government should certainly formulate its tax policy so as to place the least possible hindrance on financing expansion internally. It should be possible substantially to relieve the adverse pressure on most small, growing companies without any great effect on federal revenues. The need is apparent. Proposals for meeting the problem will be made in the final chapter of this study.

[59]See table in note 29, p. 162, *supra*. During the period 1931-40 companies with assets of less than $50,000 retained 51.13 per cent of their earnings, compared with 19.20 per cent for all companies. See Butters and Lintner, *Effect of Federal Taxes on Growing Enterprises*, Exhibit 9, p. 66.

[60]*Ibid.*, p. 70.

Summary and Conclusions

1. *Saving and Investment*

The most important effects of the corporate income tax are derived from its effects on saving and investment. The impact of the tax on saving and investment is intensified through the additional impact of the steeply progressive, high rate of tax on individual income. The double taxation of corporate income is the major factor in the impact of taxation on savings and investment.

As a result of a high rather than a low tax on corporate and individual income, the aggregate volume of saving is likely to be diminished. The impact of this diminution is conditioned to some extent by the way in which the government spends the funds which it has channelled out of the taxpayers' hands. But the general effect of taxation at a high level is still that of diminishing the volume of saving.

Individual saving is reduced because the people who do most of the saving are subject to very high rates of individual income taxation. Their ability to save is curtailed still further by the impact of the corporation tax, which diminishes the volume of investment income in their hands. Corporate saving is likely to be reduced by high corporation taxes, despite all efforts to maintain the volume by increasing the amount of profits retained instead of distributed as dividends.

The pattern of investment by individuals has changed from investment in corporate securities to investment in government bonds and institutions such as life insurance companies. Taxation has not been wholly responsible for this shift, but probably it has had an important bearing on it. The net result of the shift has been a diminution in the supply of outside capital available for financing corporations. This in turn has led to an even greater reliance on earnings for the new capital required by corporate enterprise.

2. *Prices and Wages*

The taxation of corporate income and dividends can affect prices and wages only to the extent to which supply and demand are affected. In the long run, which is a time interval sufficient to allow changes in the scale of productive capacity, taxation at a high enough level to curtail investment may reduce the supply of commodities. If the over-all volume of supply is reduced without a reduction in demand, the level of prices will rise.

The effect on the price level is conditioned by the way in which the government spends the money taken away from the taxpayers. If the funds are spent in achieving the ends of a welfare state, there will be a shift from saving and investment to consumption. The greater the proportion of the national income taxed away for such purposes, the greater will be the accent on consumption, and the greater the inflationary pressure on prices. If the supply of investment funds is impaired, it will be impossible to expand production to meet the increased demand, and a rising price level is likely to be a continuing process, until economic collapse is reached.

If, on the other hand, the greater portion of the government's spending is for capital purposes, there will be much less pressure on the prices of consumer goods. There may well be no perceptible change in the general price level over a considerable period of time.

The taxation of corporate income and dividends at the pre-1950 rates is unlikely to have any noticeable effect on the supply of labour. But if the tax burden is sufficiently great to induce actual disinvestment, the result may be unemployment, a reduction in aggregate wages paid out, and a reduction in wage rates through increased competition for jobs. Short of this there seems to be little likelihood that wages will be affected to any appreciable extent by taxation at the levels that are likely to prevail in this country. The bargaining strength of the labour unions is an important factor in offsetting any tendency towards wage reductions induced by taxation.

Thus, in the long run, the tax on corporate profits may be diffused throughout the economy, and borne in part by all consumers, but there is unlikely to be much diffusion to wage earners as such. The higher the rate of taxation, the greater will be the diffusion.

3. *Corporate Financing*

The tax discrimination against dividends makes debt financing more attractive than equity financing. There has long been a reluctance on the part of the investing public to purchase equity securities for other than tax reasons. The fact that the present tax system now discriminates heavily against such securities makes it all the more difficult for even large corporations to finance new ventures through the issue of stock. Only the rare small corporation can hope to secure new venture capital through the sale of equity securities. But there does not appear to be any marked trend in the direction of bond financing, save in the case of a limited number of companies. The problems inherent in excessive debt financing are apparently well recognized by management, and act as a deterrent to an increase in bond issues. The trend is strongly in the direction of internal financing by retained earnings. This results in the distribution of a smaller portion of earnings as dividends, which may have the cumulative effect of discouraging the purchase of equity securities still further. It is desirable to eliminate the double taxation of dividends.

4. *Form of Business Organization*

It is concluded that the tax does not affect the form of business organization to such an extent that there are serious implications for the economy as a whole. Most large businesses have to use the corporate form, regardless of tax discriminations. Most of the small concerns which are not incorporated have no need to incorporate and would not incorporate, even if there were no tax discrimination. There are some businesses, of course, which would be incorporated were it not for taxation, but it is difficult to see what over-all effect their incorporation would have on the economy.

5. *Small and Expanding Enterprise*

Generally speaking the effect of the tax is greater on small corporations than on large because it discourages (*a*) their creation, and (*b*) their expansion once they have been put on an operational footing.

This is the most serious indictment of the present system of taxing corporate profits. It accentuates the trend towards concentration of productive capacity in the hands of a relatively small number of large corporations, thereby reducing competition, creating an unhealthy price rigidity under conditions of near monopoly, and resulting in public reaction against the private enterprise system, which, if strong enough, would result finally in its elimination.

The tax discourages the creation of new corporations because of its impact on the prospective return from venture capital. The tax restricts the growth of small corporations (*a*) by reducing the attractiveness of risky expansion to management; (*b*) by adding to the difficulties of acquiring outside capital on satisfactory terms; and (*c*) by curtailing the amount of capital available from retained earnings.

Since retained earnings are of critical importance to the expansion of small companies, the method of taxing corporate income should be revised so as to have the minimum effect on the earnings of small enterprises. It is possible to provide substantial relief to small, growing companies without any serious loss in federal revenues. Such relief should not be given in the form of a graduated rate structure, but be effected through the elimination of the double taxation of dividends and through special depreciation allowances.

CHAPTER SIX

THE PROBLEM OF BUSINESS LOSSES

THE PROBLEM

IT HAS BEEN STATED that "Business men and economists who have studied the subject agree that the importance of losses in the business calculus has been and is likely to be much underemphasized."[1] The economic implications of business losses are quite obvious, and need no detailed discussion. They reduce the income of investors and cause loss of capital in cases of bankruptcy. This in turn results in a loss of investors' confidence and affects the willingness of investors to buy corporate securities, particularly shares of stock. Business losses reduce the income of wage earners. The reduction of purchasing power, if extensive enough, results in further business losses, and engenders a deflationary spiral which may have very serious results for the economy.

The effects of business losses are more serious for small enterprises than for large. Small businesses, as a group, are less profitable than larger concerns, and the range of profit and loss is considerably greater.[2] The business mortality rate is greatest in the small business group, and heavy among enterprises still in their infancy. This is in large part a result of the following factors: (1) The large and well-established concern is likely to have a more diversified business than small and new enterprises. Losses from one venture can be absorbed, at least in part, by profits from more successful ventures. (2) The large concern is likely to have substantial reserves for loss contingencies, and is thus able to

[1]Harold M. Groves, *Postwar Taxation and Economic Progress*, p. 130. He states further: "The degree and scope of corporate losses, both in good and bad years, are rarely fully appreciated. . . . Had all American corporations been allowed to file a joint consolidated return with an unlimited carry-over and carry-back of losses from 1922 to 1939, their net income would have been reduced 45.7 per cent." *Ibid.*, p. 131.

[2]*Ibid.*

withstand losses over a considerable time before facing bankruptcy. In so far as these reserves are invested outside the business, they provide a source of investment income with which to balance losses on operating account. (3) Large and well-established businesses are likely to have very much better credit than small concerns, both for short- and for long-term borrowing.

For these and perhaps other reasons, the impact of business losses is likely to be much greater on small than on large businesses. If it is socially and economically desirable to foster the development and growth of small business, as argued in the preceding chapter, then tax policy should be designed to take cognizance of the vulnerability of small businesses to losses. A strong case can be made for the view that the same level of net income in a given year (even expressed as a percentage return on investment) for a small corporation as for a large one, does not reflect at all their comparative taxpaying capacity.[3]

Another important point in connection with the problem of business losses is the fact that some industries are affected more than others by fluctuations of general business activity. It is well known, for example, that the incidence of cyclical losses is much greater in the capital goods industries than in the consumer goods industries.[4] This is because the demand for capital goods is derived from the demand for consumer goods. During depression the demand for capital goods often approaches zero, and will remain very low until the demand for consumer goods has risen sufficiently to be reflected in the demand for new capital goods. The purchase of capital goods such as machinery can be and is postponed indefinitely.

The implications for tax policy are clear. If the income of a business fluctuates from year to year, resulting in net losses in some years and net profits in others, the tax burden of that business will not correspond, over the years, with the tax burden of

[3]This viewpoint has sometimes been used to support the argument for corporate income tax rate progression. As argued elsewhere in this study, however, the size of a corporation's income is no criterion of its taxpaying capacity in any particular year.

[4]This has been demonstrated statistically by the Machinery and Allied Products Institute in its study, *Capital Goods Industries and the Federal Income Taxation.*

another business with the same aggregate income, but receiving it in regular and stable amounts. It will be obvious that such a discrepancy would be intensified under rate progression.

Several careful studies have been made of the discrimination resulting in the United States. In 1939, Mr. J. Keith Butters published the results of an analysis of the situation in that country during the periods 1922-35 and 1929-37.[5] His figures show a definite and sometimes extreme discrimination between corporations, with the greatest discrimination being against those most sensitive to business cycle fluctuations.[6]

Professor Groves published the results of his study of the problem in 1946. The period analysed was 1922-39.[7] He states:

> From 1922 through 1939, agricultural and related industries paid a sizable net-income tax on an actual net deficit; and the service industry paid 149 times more in taxes than the actual net income, or a tax rate of 14,920.6 per cent. Public utilities, on the contrary, paid only 18.3 per cent of their actual net income in taxes. Even though there is a much greater degree of homogeneity among manufacturing industries, there is still a wide range in the tax rate on the actual net income. The forest-products industry paid slightly over one-half, or 51.3 per cent, of the actual net income in taxes, and the food-products industry paid only 16.2 per cent.[8]

The results of basing the corporate income tax on the annual

[5]"Discriminating Effects of the Annual Computation of the Corporate Income Tax," *Quarterly Journal of Economics*, Nov. 1939, pp. 51-72.

[6]In an analysis of forty corporations in eight industries between 1922 and 1935 it appears that only 60 per cent of them paid taxes at approximately the statutory rate. Six of them paid tax on a net deficit for the period, while three paid taxes from one-half to four times their net income for the period. In the retail trade 8 per cent paid taxes amounting to over 50 per cent of their actual net income, or paid taxes out of capital. Of twenty-two corporations in the iron and steel industry, 27 per cent paid taxes of over 50 per cent of actual net income, or paid taxes even though they showed a net loss over the period. *Ibid.*

[7]*Postwar Taxation and Economic Progress*, pp. 135-8.

[8]*Ibid.*, p. 136. Professor Groves examined 60 corporations operating in Wisconsin to determine the discriminatory effects of the federal income tax as a result of the variation in business losses among individual firms between 1930 and 1942. He concluded: "On the basis of a strictly annual assessment, 10 corporations, or 16.7 per cent, would pay a tax on an actual net deficit for the period; 15 (including these 10), or 25 per cent, would pay a tax of more than 15 per cent over (*i.e.*, more than double) the average legal rate; and 19, or 31.7 per cent, would pay a tax of 10 per cent or more above the basic rate. On the other hand, 23 corporations, or 38.3 per cent, would have been subject to about the average legal rate—less than 14.0 per cent." *Ibid.*, pp. 137-8.

accounting of profit and loss appear quite obvious,[9] and indicate that the tax should not be so levied for reasons of tax equity and the economic effects of such a system.

1. *Equity Considerations*

From the standpoint of equity the basic consideration is the definition of net taxable income in such a way as to provide equal treatment of stockholders in different companies. Taxation of net income on an annual basis results in inequity because of the fact that in some industries, over a period of years, losses are much greater than in others. The annual reporting of profit and loss is only an accounting convention resulting from management's desire to have periodic reporting of the results of business operations. It is quite meaningless, however, in terms of the impact of taxation which is supposed to be based upon the real net income of the business. As indicated in the analyses made by Butters and Groves, in many cases corporations pay tax, over a period of years, at a very much higher rate than that provided by law. In some instances, the tax is paid when there is a net loss, and thus becomes a tax upon capital. Moreover, when the tax is based upon net income for a single accounting year, companies showing a loss for that period receive less than full income tax credit for the wear and tear on their capital. A depreciation allowance which only adds to a loss is, as Groves has said, "gone and gone forever so far as the income tax base is concerned."[10]

The inequities arising out of basing the corporate income tax on the income of a single accounting period require some corrective measure or measures.

2. *Economic Considerations*

The most important economic considerations connected with business losses and taxation concern risk-taking and the stimulation of new business enterprises.

It has been argued earlier in this study that one of the unfortunate characteristics of the contemporary economic scene is the scarcity of risk or venture capital. While the cause of this situa-

[9]The argument applies equally, of course, to the taxation of income of unincorporated business.

[10]*Ibid.*, p. 144.

tion cannot be ascribed entirely to taxation,[11] it certainly can be traced in some considerable measure to taxation. The reduced return on investment, caused by high taxation of corporate income and dividends, coupled with the fear of loss of capital, are important determinants of the situation. Since a corporation which has impaired its capital through business losses has no real net income until that impairment is recouped from subsequent profits,[12] a tax system which ignores cumulated losses is likely to be even a greater deterrent to investment because of the very high tax rate which may be imposed. If the tax system were to provide for the offset of losses in one period against profits in another, it seems likely that some encouragement would be provided for risk-taking, since in some fields of economic activity the aggregate tax burden would be reduced considerably.

The case for stimulating the creation and growth of small businesses has occupied a central position in this study. The problem of business losses has particular importance for this type of enterprise because (1) losses are more likely to occur in the early stages of business development, and (2) they are likely to be much more serious for the small or new enterprise than for the larger well-established concern with diversification of sources of income. Recognition, for tax purposes, of the principle of offsetting losses against profits over a period of years should encourage the development and expansion of new enterprises, which often need several years to establish themselves in a profitable position.

Another economic consideration is the tendency of taxation based upon income received in a single accounting period to accentuate business instability. In years of depressed business activity, when profits are low and losses heavy, corporate expenditures are held to a minimum. But if the cost of expenditures could be used, through loss offsets, to reduce future taxes or secure refunds from past taxes, business expenditures might be stimulated enough to have a counter-cyclical effect. This point will be developed later.

[11]See Michael Young, "Is a Lower Income Tax the Answer to the Risk Capital Shortage?" *Saturday Night*, Sept. 6, 1949, pp. 22-3.

[12]See Norris Darrell, "How Long Should the Accounting Period be for Corporate Income Tax Purposes?" *How Should Corporations be Taxed?* p. 138.

Approach to the Problem

There are three different approaches to the problem of adjusting the tax structure to provide for offsetting losses against profits. They are (1) the use of a longer accounting period, (2) averaging devices, and (3) carry-over of business losses. They will be discussed in turn.

1. *Longer Accounting Period*

Perhaps the most obvious way to meet the problems inherent in the twelve-month accounting period is to extend the period over which profit and loss are computed. It would be possible to adopt a six-year period, for example. Tentative profit and loss statements could be drawn at the end of each twelve-month period, and tax instalments paid annually. At the end of the period the final return could be made, and the final tax liability computed.

There are several objections to a plan of this kind which need little elaboration. The most important is the undesirability, from the viewpoint of both the government and business, of leaving tax liability open and unsettled for a long period of time. The longer the accounting period, the greater is the period of undetermined liability. It does not appear that the results obtained from this approach merit the abandonment of the present accounting practice which is almost universally followed.

2. *Averaging Devices*[13]

A second alternative to meet the problem of fluctuating in-

[13]The discussion of averaging will be summary and confined to averaging applied to business income as distinct from personal income, because different problems are involved. A considerable volume of literature has developed on this subject in recent years, but most of it applies to the averaging of individual income. Among the better material are the following: Roy Blough, "The Averaging of Income for Tax Purposes," *Taxes—The Tax Magazine,* Oct. 1944, p. 448; Groves, *Postwar Taxation and Economic Progress,* pp. 226 ff.; B. L. Klooster, "Averaging Constructive Base Period Income," *Taxes—The Tax Magazine,* Jan. 1947, pp. 37-40; C. R. Maxwell, Jr., "Averaging Fluctuating Income of the Individual for Income Tax Purposes," *Washington Law Review and State Bar Journal,* April 1945, pp. 105-111; R. E. Slitor, "The Flexibility of Income Tax Yield under Averaging," *Journal of Political Economy,* June 1946, p. 266; William Vickrey, "Averaging of Income for Income-Tax Purposes," *Journal of Political Economy,* June 1939, p. 379; "The Effect of Averaging on the Cyclical Sensitivity of the Yield of the Income Tax," *Journal of Political Economy,* Sept. 1945, p. 275; *Agenda for Progressive Taxation,* chap. vi, pp. 164-97.

come is the adoption of a system under which the annual tax payment would be based upon the average annual profit and loss over a period of years, or even over the cumulative life of the corporation.

Several methods of averaging have been used in various tax regulations, and still others have been advocated by authorities on taxation. Among these are the simple average, the moving average, and the progressive average. Almost any method of averaging will alleviate to some extent the inequities attached to the annual accounting system, and averaging has the advantage of interfering in no way with the generally accepted accounting procedure. But there are inherent difficulties attached to all forms of averaging which deserve attention.

(*a*) Length of the Averaging Period

Several reasons have been advanced for making the averaging period as long as possible. It has been argued that the only system of averaging that really discloses the taxpayer's "true taxable capacity" is one which covers the span of his income-earning life. From this premise it follows logically that shortening of the period must result in a departure from true taxable capacity. The shorter the period, the greater will be the divergence.[14] Vickrey has stated:

> Obviously, the longer the period, the smaller will be the administrative task of valuation and checking valuations. If the ends of the averaging periods of different individuals are staggered, lengthening the averaging period will reduce the amount of taxpayers' assets to be valued at any one time, and the effect of the valuation date upon the security and capital markets will thus be minimized. The incentive for the taxpayer to shift his income from one period to another will be smaller the longer the averaging period, since it will be more difficult for him to forecast over the longer term what the size of his income will be and to what rates he will be subject; moreover, actual variations in average income and rates between one period and another are likely to be smaller. . . . In general, the increase in equity afforded by the

[14]This was the argument advanced by the majority of the members of the Australian Royal Commission on Taxation, *First Report,* 1921, p. 64. Three members disagreed, stating: "Our conception of taxable capacity is that on the whole it is likely to be more accurately reflected in the 'annual net income.'" *Ibid.,* p. 58.

averaging method of assessment will become greater as the period is made longer.[15]

If there is any case for lifetime averaging, it applies to individual, not to corporate income. On the face of it, the cause of tax equity would not be served by lifetime averaging of corporate income, and from an administrative viewpoint it simply would not be practicable. Indeed, a strong case may be made against its use with respect to personal income,[16] both on grounds of equity, and in terms of the heavy revenue loss that would result from it.

If there is no case for long-term averaging of corporate income, what of an average covering a short-term period? The most obvious problem involves the selection of a time interval over which business income may be averaged so as to meet the underlying problem of business loss. If the average is to be effective in ironing out peaks and troughs of business income, it should be geared to the cyclical movement of business activity. But there is no established business cycle pattern that fits all cycles, so that the results obtained from trying to fit the corporate income tax to a hypothetical cycle seem hardly to warrant the intellectual exercise involved. Furthermore, there are different cycles for different types of business activity, and this opens broad horizons in the pursuit of tax equity. From a practical viewpoint the interval chosen for short-term averaging must be purely arbitrary. This is illustrated in the experience of the United Kingdom, Australia, the State of Wisconsin, and Canada,[17] and it should not be surprising that refinements have been introduced to provide different periods for different types of business. Moreover, in the

[15] *Agenda for Progressive Taxation*, p. 185.

[16] Louis Shere has stated: "I cannot accept as equitable a tax philosophy which would permit the refund of taxes collected from fortunes extracted in a brief few years by the lucky, or even the skilled, from sporadic economic situations like Florida land booms, stock exchange and commodity speculative orgies, wars, and, as an economist might say, quasi-wars to be enjoyed over the remainder of their potentially inactive and useless lives. . . . Averaging of the type that spans relatively short periods, a business cycle or so, would improve equity in taxation. But lifetime averaging, or averaging that covers long periods, would on this account destroy the equity of a tax system." "Federal Corporate Income Tax—Revenue and Reform," *National Tax Journal*, June 1949, p. 117.

[17] In the United Kingdom the period was three years for business profits, five years for mining profits, and seven years for manorial profits. Australia used a uniform period of five years. In Wisconsin it was three years. In Canada fishermen and farmers have the option of paying tax on an annual basis or averaging income over a five-year period.

search for equitable treatment of fluctuating income various types of averages have been employed or advocated. Three of these are worth consideration. Each has its advantages and disadvantages, and various modifications have been proposed by averaging enthusiasts to meet the disadvantages.

(*b*) The Simple Average

This is a simple arithmetic average applied to a given period of years without reference to years preceding or following those contained in the averaging period. Such is the average introduced recently in Canada with respect to farmers and fishermen, and known in this country as the "block system." It applies to both individual and corporate income within the statutory definition of farming and fishing. It is optional to the taxpayer, and he may average his income for any five-year period, provided that he does not bring into the averaging period income made in a year which has already been used for averaging purposes. In effect this method permits the taxpayer in a given year to average his income of that year and the previous four years (if he has not already used any of them in an average). He may then recalculate his tax bill in accordance with the rates and exemptions prevailing in each year, as though his income in each year had been equal to the average income over the five-year period. If, on the basis of the recalculation, the tax already paid exceeds what is required under the averaging system, a refund or a credit is obtained.[18]

[18]The following example illustrates the procedure. Suppose that an incorporated farming enterprise has taxable income in the period 1946-50 as shown. (Note: It is assumed that the company's fiscal year ends on December 31, and the 1950 tax was computed on the following *pro rata* basis: 243/365 of the income was assessed at the old rates, and 122/365 at the new rates, made effective on September 1.)

	Income	*Tax rate*	*Annual tax*	*Average income*	*Tax based on av. income*	*Actual tax*
	$	%	$	$	$	$
1946	6,500	30	1,950	7,800	2,340	1,950
1947	3,500	30	1,050	7,800	2,340	1,050
1948	5,000	30	1,500	7,800	2,340	1,500
1949	4,000	10	400	7,800	780	400
1950	20,000	10, 15 33 & 38	4,634	7,800	910	3,810
	39,000		9,534	39,000	8,710	8,710

Had the income been earned in a steady stream of $7,800 per year, the total

The block average has the advantage of being simple and readily understood by the taxpayer. It removes, in the period averaged, the tax inequality between sharply fluctuating and stable incomes (the tax cannot be greater than the amount payable on the average income during the period), and it does not involve any drastic changes in the law. Furthermore, the tax is paid annually at the going rates, so that the taxpayer is always paid up. In general, averaging might also have the economic effect of encouraging the investment of capital in businesses with fluctuating incomes. It has found support on these grounds.[19]

The simple average has several disadvantages, however. In the first place, in terms of equity a convincing case can be made against averaging, especially of corporate income. On an optional basis, as the average is used in Canada, the plan favours unduly the taxpayer who has had high income during low-rate years and low income in high-rate years, and it discriminates against the taxpayer in the opposite position. It is a curious inversion of the ability theory of taxation to impose heavier taxes when income is falling and lighter taxes when it is rising. It has been stated that "it has often proved impossible to collect a tax in a given year

---

tax payable over the period would have been $8,710. The tax already paid between 1946 and 1949 was $4,900. If the taxpayer elects to average over this period, he will pay $3,810 ($8,710—$4,900) in 1950, thus effecting a net saving of $824. Had the sequence of earnings been reversed, as follows, the result would have been very different.

1946	20,000	30	6,000	7,800	2,340	6,000
1947	4,000	30	1,200	7,800	2,340	1,200
1948	5,000	30	1,500	7,800	2,340	1,500
1949	3,500	10	350	7,800	780	350
1950	6,500	10 & 15	759	7,800	910	—340
	39,000		9,809	39,000	8,710	8,710

In this case $9,050 would have been paid during the first four years. Since $8,710 is the tax liability over the five-year period, there would have been a refund or credit of $340 in 1950.

[19]See Henry C. Simons, *Personal Income Taxation*, pp. 153-4, and Groves, *Postwar Taxation and Economic Progress*, pp. 226-8. To meet the objection that averaging would involve administrative trouble because of necessary refunds, both of these writers advocate that the refund or credit be limited to cases where the actual taxes paid exceed the taxes payable under the averaging system by 5 or 10 per cent. Perhaps a better way of avoiding the problem of refunds would be to carry over the excess paid as a credit against future tax liability, with an appropriate rate of interest. But this would complicate matters for the administration.

(when there was little or no income) based on income earned two years before, which income has since vanished."[20] On an optional basis the taxpayer must contend with the imponderable problem of future rate and earnings probabilities. He is always confronted with the gamble of averaging now or deferring until later in order to secure the maximum tax advantage offered by the plan. As pointed out above, the period chosen for averaging may make considerable difference to the taxpayer.

In the second place, the plan necessitates the maintenance of special records, makes assessments complicated, adds to administrative costs, and results in loss of revenue. While its use with respect to income derived from farming and fishing operations in Canada may work reasonably well, its extension to all types of income, corporate and individual, would undoubtedly result in serious complications. A plan substantially like the Canadian block system was proposed to the Australian Royal Commission on Taxation in 1921, but was rejected because it was considered to be "neither in accordance with sound principles nor reasonably practicable in administration."[21] As far as corporate income is concerned, the simple average is not recommended.

(*c*) The Moving Average

The moving average, in contrast to the simple or block average, is computed by taking each year the average of the income of that year and a certain number of preceding years. The number of years included in the moving average is always constant. Thus under this system, the three-year moving average of taxable income for 1950 would be the average of the years 1948, 1949, and 1950. In 1951 it would be the average of 1949, 1950, and 1951, and so on. The moving average has been used for income tax purposes in the United Kingdom, Australia, and Wisconsin. But it has been discarded by Britain and Wisconsin, and modified in Australia for reasons which will now be discussed.[22]

[20]United States, Congress, Senate, Special Committee on Post-War Economic Policy and Planning, *Post-War Tax Plans for the Federal Government*, p. 47.

[21]*First Report*, 1921, p. 14.

[22]The United Kingdom and Wisconsin used a three-year moving average. It was used in the former from 1799 to 1926, when it was abolished. This move had been recommended by the Royal Commission on the Income Tax in 1920. Wisconsin introduced the three-year average in 1927 and abandoned it in 1931 because of the difficulties attached to it. Australia used a five-year moving average

The chief difficulty with the moving average is that the tax based upon it does not correspond closely enough to the income in a given year. The result is that at one time the taxpayer may receive great advantage at the treasury's expense, while at another time he may suffer serious hardship. Unlike the block system, the moving average never allows the taxpayer to get in the position of being paid up. Because the average constantly moves forward one year at a time, dropping a year in the process, his tax liability is never determined finally as long as he is earning income. In a year of low income following high earnings the squeeze may be severe. Thus, under a three-year moving average, in the case of a company earning $60,000 in 1948, $80,000 in 1949, and only $10,000 in 1950, the 1950 tax would be computed on an income of $50,000 (the three-year average) instead of on $10,000 (the actual amount earned). At the current level of Canadian corporate income tax rates, the 1950 tax would be $16,700 instead of $1,500, and it will be noted that the $16,700 tax would be imposed in a year when the total net earnings were only $10,000. This possibility would require the prudent taxpayer to set up substantial reserves, in a year of high earnings, against potentially heavy taxes in the next year or two, when earnings may be low. Such a requirement may be entirely undesirable from the viewpoint of the small business particularly, when a year of high earnings may well be the long-awaited opportunity to buy more assets and expand operations. It appears to this observer that the moving average may be definitely undesirable in terms of its economic consequences for small business.

But, of course, the plan works the other way, too. Should the company in question go on to earn $20,000 in 1951, and $60,000 in 1952, the 1952 tax would be computed on a base of $30,000 (the new average) instead of on $60,000, the actual earnings in that year, a tax saving of $11,400 at the current rates.

It has been the experience under the moving average that demands from taxpayers for relief were widespread during depressions or periods of declining income. In response to this

---

from 1922, but in 1938 it was abandoned save in the case of primary producers. This was the result of the unanimous recommendation of the Royal Commission on Taxation, 1934.

demand the United Kingdom employed a complex and constantly changing system of reliefs from 1842 to 1907, and they were revived again in 1914.[23]

Because of this serious problem due to the time lag, and in view of the experience of three different taxing jurisdictions with the moving average, it is not recommended for use in Canada.[24]

(*d*) The Progressive Average

Another type of average was proposed several years ago in the United States by William Vickrey,[25] which he termed the "cumulative method." It is now popularly termed the progressive average. While this plan is primarily designed to iron out unequal tax treatment of individual incomes, it is worth a brief discussion here, as an example of the refinements that have been developed in an attempt to meet the shortcomings of averaging.

Vickrey developed the concept of "adjusted total income," designed to place all taxpayers on the same tenable footing. "Adjusted" income is the total income received during the period plus compound interest on the taxes already paid. The final tax payment for the period is "the difference between a total liability

[23]An excellent summary of the experience in the United Kingdom may be found in an article by Martin Atlas, "Average Income and Its Use in Taxation," *Accounting Review*, June 1938, pp. 124-31.

[24]Returning to our hypothetical company in the last part of note 18, *supra*, the following example indicates the results of paying an annual tax, using the Canadian block system, and a three-year moving average under one set of conditions:

	Income	*Annual tax*	*Block average*	*Three-year moving average*
	$	$	$	$
1946	20,000	6,000	6,000	3,500*
1947	4,000	1,200	1,200	3,400
1948	5,000	1,500	1,500	2,900
1949	3,500	350	350	416
1950	6,500	759	−340	583
	39,000	9,809	8,710	10,799

*Assuming earnings of $5,000 in 1944, and $10,000 in 1945.

Under this set of conditions the moving average obviously penalizes the taxpayer, while the block system gives him an advantage. Under other circumstances the results could be reversed. Because of the uncertainty of the results from using the moving average there is bound to be widespread dissatisfaction with the system.

[25]"Averaging of Income for Income-Tax Purposes," pp. 379-97, and *Agenda for Progressive Taxation*, pp. 172 ff. Detailed examples are given in the latter, Appendix III, pp. 417-27.

computed from the adjusted total income and the present value (with accumulated interest) of previous tax payments made on this income."[26] The procedure for computing the tax in a given year has been summarized as follows: "To the sum of the income for all years of the averaging period (including the current year), add compound interest on all taxes previously paid. From tables supplied, compute the present value of taxes that would have been paid had the income been equally divided between the years. Then compute the present value of all taxes actually paid (i.e. add compound interest to such taxes), and deduct such taxes from the taxes computed as per the tables above noted, in order to find the tax due for the current year."[27]

From the viewpoint of pure theory, this plan is superior to both the simple and the moving averages. It meets the basic objection to them, because it places the taxpayer with a given total income on exactly the same footing with all other taxpayers having the same total income, regardless of what year, during the period, the income is earned. But the proposal is more than a little complicated, and it would certainly be unintelligible to the average taxpayer.[28] From an administrative viewpoint, the plan involves wholesale changes in existing tax law concepts, and requires complicated tables for the computation of present values of taxes. One is inclined to agree with Maxwell that it "would put an impossible burden on administrative agencies."[29] It is not recommended for use in Canada.[30]

(*e*) Conclusions

The fundamental difficulty connected with averaging income for tax purposes is that of finding an averaging device which will go well along the road to achieving tax equity without, at the

[26]*Agenda for Progressive Taxation*, pp. 173-4.

[27]United States, Senate, *Post-War Tax Plans for the Federal Government*, p. 48.

[28]Not to mention the difficulty of trying to explain a bill providing for this plan to a parliamentary committee.

[29]"Averaging Fluctuating Income of the Individual for Income Tax Purposes," p. 110.

[30]There are other plans for meeting the difficulties embodied in the simple and moving averages, two of the most intelligible being the "Braveman" and "Silverson" plans. They are intended for individual income, however, and need not be considered here. They are discussed fully by Professor John Willis in a forthcoming study to be published by the Canadian Tax Foundation.

same time, becoming so complicated as to cause confusion for taxpayers and serious administrative problems.

From the viewpoint of equity and administrative feasibility the simple average is the best. The moving average has such serious effects in a period of declining income after high earnings that it has been abandoned in the United Kingdom and Wisconsin, and retained in Australia only for primary producers. Most of the proposals designed to remedy the defects of the simple and moving averages are so complicated that they are not feasible.

Even the simple average has its disadvantages, and its results depend upon the particular period over which the taxpayer strikes the average. For this reason, if averaging of income is used, it should be made optional, as it is in Canada, and not mandatory, as it was in the United Kingdom. The average is not a specific cure-all, and the taxpayer should approach it on a *caveat emptor* basis.

The Canadian provision for averaging farmers' and fishermen's income is probably helpful to many taxpayers in those industries. The question arises as to whether this relief should be extended to all taxpayers. From the viewpoint of tax neutrality, a strong case may be made against the practice of selecting certain classes of taxpayers for preferred treatment and ignoring others who have just as strong a claim for similar treatment. If the average were made universal, as advocated by most of its proponents, it would apply to corporate and individual income. This would raise a host of new administrative problems, and it is by no means certain that a commensurate gain in equity would be achieved, because of the inherent defects in the average.

It must be remembered that most of the inequity attached to sharply fluctuating incomes arises out of the steeply graduated rate structure applying to individual income. In the case of corporate income taxed at a flat rate, a sharp increase in earnings results only in a proportionately greater tax.[31] In the case of corporations,

[31]This is shown in the following comparison of the tax results of a sharp increase in income for an individual and a corporation (assuming constant rates):

	Taxable income	*Individual tax*	*Corporate tax*
1947	$10,000	$ 2,934	$ 3,000
1948	$40,000	$18,726	$12,000
% Increase	300 %	538 %	300 %

the problem is not so much that of inequity arising out of fluctuating income *per se*. Indeed, there are good grounds for arguing in favour of letting the chips fall where they may as long as taxable capacity is indicated in the form of net earnings. Rather, the problem is really one of business losses. The basic inequity arises out of the fact that many corporations do have, at times, negative income, and therefore special treatment to take this into consideration is indicated. In this writer's view there is a better approach to the problem than the use of any averaging device,[32] and this brings us to the principle of loss carry-over.[33]

3. *Carry-over of Business Losses*

There appears to be general agreement among students that for corporations the carry-over system of business losses is the best approach to the problem created by the use of the twelve-month accounting period.

The provision of loss offsets simplifies some aspects of tax administration and tends to complicate others. It has been stated that, "Loss offsets, by reducing the significance of the annual accounting period, tend to reduce the number of points in time in which controversies over valuations and accruals may arise. However, unless the system of loss offsets is perfect and complete, these points in time may actually be increased, particularly in periods of consecutive losses."[34] Furthermore, incomplete loss offsets may make the problems connected with the tax-benefit rules (e.g., bad debt deductions) even more complicated, "since the deduction would have to be chased through several years of

[32]It is interesting to note the comment made in a joint submission by the Association of British Chambers of Commerce and the Federation of British Industries to the Board of Trade Committee on Taxation of Trading Profits (the Tucker Committee). It was stated: "The basis of an average of three preceding years was abandoned after prolonged consideration by Section 29 of the Finance Act 1926 and there is a general desire on the part of business not to return to it, nor to any system of averaging as a general basis." *Definition of Taxable Profits*, 1950, p. 34. The Institute of Taxation stated: "In our opinion, it would be a grave mistake to re-introduce the average system, with all the complications which that would necessarily entail." *Recommendations by the Council of the Institute of Taxation to the Committee on Taxation of Trading Profits*, p. 19.

[33]This is not to suggest, however, that some type of averaging is not desirable for individual income tax purposes. The present provisions of the Canadian Income Tax Act, Sections 39 (1) and 129 (11), providing for averaging the income of farmers and fishermen, appear to be constructive.

[34]United States Treasury Department, *Business Loss Offsets*, p. 3.

income to see if a tax benefit from it had arisen."[35] Again, the auditing problem is increased with the length of the carry-over period. On balance, however, the equity and economic considerations in favour of the loss offset system outweigh the administrative complications arising out of it.

The carry-over of business losses for tax purposes raises several points on which there is difference of opinion. Among these are (1) the direction in which losses should be carried: (2) the period of the loss carry-over; (3) the kind of loss to be carried over.[36]

(*a*) The Direction in which Losses Should be Carried

The argument of "carry-backs" versus "carry-forwards" involves considerations of equity, economic effects, and administration, and the point will be discussed within this framework.

As indicated above, the equity consideration is that of defining taxable net income accurately enough over a period of years to ensure similar treatment of stockholders in different corporations. A case can be made for the carry-back as well as for the carry-forward of losses,[37] in order to attain the most accurate measure of net income.

Considerations of economic effects and problems of administration, on the other hand, indicate that the carry-forward is preferable to the carry-back. From the viewpoint of stimulating new business enterprises the carry-forward is much more important. The initial losses of a new enterprise are really capital costs of earning future income. The carry-back of such losses is meaningless, because the losses can only be recovered when they are carried forward against profit when it is realized.

Another point in connection with new enterprises was made by the United States Treasury:

> Moreover, so long as a carryback is permitted, even if a carryforward can also be made, the new enterprise would be at a disad-

[35] *Ibid.*

[36] Mr. Darrell discusses some others, e.g., "Should the carry-over right be limited to the same corporation which suffered the loss, or should it be regarded in a sense as a corporate asset available to a successor in reorganization?" and "What safeguards are necessary to prevent abuses of the carry-over?" "How Long Should the Accounting Period be for Corporate Income Tax Purposes?" pp. 142-3, 147-51.

[37] Groves states that "if both were allowed without limitation, the income tax would be confined to the real earnings of a company during its life operation." *Postwar Taxation and Economic Progress*, p. 145.

vantage. If the entry of such an enterprise were followed by sharp competitive warfare which results in losses in the industry, the established company would be able to recoup a portion of its losses from the Government by way of the carryback, but the new enterprise could not. The latter would have to wait for future profits to recover a portion of its losses. Yet the prospect of future profits is made more uncertain because the Government would partially underwrite its competitors.[38]

The use of the carry-back would also result in government budgetary uncertainties. Tax returns of past years must be kept open, or reopened, if closed, for purposes of applying the carry-back of later losses.[39] This would result in continuous refunds, the aggregate of which might be very considerable after a year of heavy business losses.

The carry-back might have the further effect of opening up new avenues of tax avoidance through manipulations such as the shifting of new and profitable operations from one affiliated company to another so that the former could recover past taxes paid by it. Moreover, since an operating loss in a given year would affect the amount of tax paid in previous years, there might be an incentive deliberately to create a loss in order to secure a tax refund.

On the other hand, the counter-cyclical effect of a carry-back is more certain than that of a carry-forward, although both will have some such effect because of the opportunity of offsetting expenditures made in a loss year against taxable income. Under a carry-back allowance, a company can be certain that the expenditures made during a loss period will reduce taxes already paid. A carry-forward would result in tax reduction only if the operations of future years resulted in taxable net income. Because of this greater certainty, the carry-back might stimulate expenditures during a depression to a greater extent than the carry-forward. It is difficult to say, however, to what extent this greater certainty has any real significance. Probably it has very little. The United States Treasury study states: "It appears that carrybacks may stimulate business expenditures during a depression to a slightly greater extent than carryforwards. It seems

[38]*Business Loss Offsets*, p. 6.

[39]The longer the period of the carry-back the longer will be the period in which previous returns must be kept open, and the longer the period during which government revenue from the corporation tax is tentative and uncertain.

unlikely, however, that the difference between carrybacks and carryforwards in this respect will be very great, or that either carrybacks or carryforwards will have an important countercyclical effect."[40]

It is more difficult to justify the carry-back than the carry-forward, since most losses are forward looking. Most expenditures made by business are for the purpose of bringing in future income and are not related to past income. They should be deducted, therefore, from future rather than past income.

It is recognized, of course, that there are costs which should properly be charged, at times, against past income. For example, the cost of a capital asset should be spread over its useful life. If obsolescence of the asset occurs, such a loss is properly deductible from past, not future, income. Similarly, losses arising from incorrect valuation of inventories are chargeable against past income, and the same is true of bad debts arising from sales made in an earlier accounting period. Furthermore, the carry-back is, as Mr. Darrell has pointed out, "a useful means of remedying defects of the annual accounting system with respect to many types of business transactions requiring more than a year for completion, and as to which profits may have to be reported initially under technical tax accounting rules though the transaction may eventually end up with a loss."[41]

While the carry-back can act as a corrective in these particular cases, perhaps a better approach would be through increased depreciation, a different method of spreading capital costs, and improved methods of inventory valuation. Special difficulties are attached to these problems, and they will be discussed later.

The general consensus appears to favour the carry-forward plan against the carry-back. In view of the greater administrative difficulties connected with the carry-back, its effect on budgetary stability, and its possible use for tax avoidance, most observers oppose it, or recommend a very limited use of the plan.[42]

(*b*) The Period of the Loss Carry-over

While there appears to be no theoretical limit to the length

[40]*Business Loss Offsets*, p. 7.

[41]"How Long Should the Accounting Period be for Corporate Income Tax Purposes?", p. 143.

[42]Groves, writing in 1946, did not recommend it beyond the first two years of the post-war period. *Postwar Taxation and Economic Progress*, p. 146. Darrell

of time over which losses should be carried forward,[43] there are serious administrative objections to lengthy carry-forwards. The carry-forward requires audits of losses previously passed over, and audits of losses sustained over a considerable period in the past are difficult. Furthermore, it is doubtful if an indefinite carry-over period would provide any more incentive to risk-taking than would a period sufficiently long to allow a business to recover from the effects of cyclical business fluctuations, and to allow a new business to become established.

There are no available data indicating conclusively the effectiveness of different periods of loss offsetting.[44] For the present it is necessary to select a period long enough to offset most losses and still fall within the limitations of administrative feasibility. Since the average business cycle has a length of about eight years, it is argued that a five- or six-year carry-forward period

---

states that "it seems preferable to abandon the system of carry-backs even though its presence would afford greater equality in taxation. There seems to be general agreement also on this. It would appear that the elimination of the carry-back can be substantially made up for by extending the period for the carry-forward of losses, especially if this can be supplemented by more liberal methods of accounting for business transactions requiring more than a year for completion." "How Long Should the Accounting Period be for Corporate Income Tax Purposes?" p. 144. The United States Treasury study recommended the repeal of the two-year carry-back. *Business Loss Offsets*, p. 2. The 1947 Conference of the Canadian Tax Foundation recommended a two-year carry-back (a minority favoured one year). *Conference on the Income Tax Bill: Report of Proceedings*, p. 9. It was argued that "extension of the carry-back would make relief available sooner when several loss years occur in succession, and would allow for the fact that tapering of profits on a downswing reduces the benefit obtainable from the last profitable year alone." *Ibid.*, p. 10.

[43]Professor H. L. Lutz has recommended an indefinite carry-forward period. *Guideposts to a Free Economy*, cited by Darrell, "How Long Should the Accounting Period be for Corporate Income Tax Purposes?" pp. 144-5.

[44]A study of four hundred large United States corporations for the period 1929-38 by the Machinery and Allied Products Institute indicates that 42 per cent of the companies would have had complete loss offsets with a two-year carry-forward in that period, but only 19 per cent of the capital goods companies in the sample would have had complete loss offsets. Under a five-year carry-over period, 70 per cent of the companies studied would have had full loss offsets. *Capital Goods Industries.* The United States Treasury study of aggregate data for all corporations for the period 1921-42 indicates that a two-year carry-over would have offset from 3 to 26 per cent of the losses of a given year, depending upon whether depression or an upswing followed the year of loss. Under a five-year carry-forward from 10 to 41 per cent of the losses would have been offset. *Business Loss Offsets*, pp. 8-9, 23-4. Groves's study of sixty corporations in Wisconsin during the period 1930-42 indicates about one-half the companies would have offset their losses over a three-year period or less, and slightly more than two-thirds over a six-year period. *Postwar Taxation and Economic Progress*, p. 140.

would be sufficient to allow the losses attributable to depressions to be offset against income of prosperous years.

A six-year carry-forward period has been allowed in the United Kingdom since 1926, and the same period has been recommended by Butters[45] and Groves.[46] The United States Treasury study recommended a five-year carry-forward.[47] Canadian opinion is reflected in the views expressed at the 1947 Conference of the Canadian Tax Foundation. "It was the unanimous opinion that five years is too short particularly for capital goods industries in the light of past experience. A seven-year period was regarded as more realistic."[48] The Minister of Finance stated in his 1949 budget speech that the loss carry-forward period would be lengthened from three to five years,[49] and the Act was so amended. In effect, a Canadian company now may average earnings over a seven-year period (one-year carry-back and five-year carry-forward). Final judgment as to the "best" period over which losses should be carried forward should be deferred until experience under the present plan indicates the effects upon Canadian business and revenues. It may develop, after sufficient experience through the various phases of the business cycle, that the present system is quite adequate. On the other hand, it may be that an unlimited carry-forward would not be so impracticable as it now appears. Indeed, there is a body of responsible opinion in favour of extending the carry-forward indefinitely. In its submission to the Tucker Committee in the United Kingdom the Society of Incorporated Accountants and Auditors made the following statement: "It is also suggested that there should be no time limit on the carrying forward of losses and that losses should be carried back for one year. There appears to be no justification for the present provision whereby the carry forward of losses is restricted

[45]"Discriminating Effects of the Annual Computation of the Corporate Income Tax."

[46]*Postwar Taxation and Economic Progress*, p. 145.

[47]*Business Loss Offsets*, p. 9.

[48]*Conference on the Income Tax Bill: Report of Proceedings*, pp. 9-10. The Conference recommended, however, a four-year carry-forward (in conjunction with a two-year carry-back). A minority favoured a five-year carry-forward and a one-year carry-back. *Ibid.*, p. 9. A formal submission was made to the Minister of Finance in April, 1948, recommending a loss carry-over of seven years, two back, and four forward. *Memorandum of Recommendations on Bill 454, "An Act Respecting Income Taxes," submitted to the Minister of Finance*, p. 19.

[49]*House of Commons Debates*, March 22, 1949, p. 1799.

to six years, while wear and tear allowances may be carried forward indefinitely."[50]

(*c*) The Kind of Loss to be Carried Over

There are two conflicting approaches to the kind of loss and the kind of income that should be used to calculate the loss offset. These approaches may be called (1) the taxable income approach, and (2) the total income approach.

The taxable income approach holds that the loss to be carried over should be computed in the same way in which taxable income is determined. Under this method, exempt income, such as intercorporate dividends and capital gains in Canada, would be excluded from the calculation. It is argued that since such income is excluded from the calculation of taxable income, it would be inconsistent not to exclude it from the calculation of a loss which is to be carried over. This method places all corporations on the same footing, whether they have tax-free income or not.

The total income approach holds that a loss offset should not be allowed unless there is an actual loss—unless the total net income of a business is negative. It follows from this that such a "true" loss should be offset against "true" profit—the total net income of the company, irrespective of tax exemption—and not against taxable income. This method favours the company that derives its total gross income from its operations, and discriminates against the company which has substantial income from tax-exempt dividends. For example, a company which has no exempt income and shows an operating loss in a given year would pay no tax in that year, and, under a carry-forward system, would offset that loss against the succeeding year's profit, if any. But a company with sufficient tax-exempt income to offset its operating loss in a given year would not only pay tax in that year, but would have no loss to carry forward against later profits.

The choice of approach depends in large part upon the basic considerations underlying the use of the loss carry-over device. If the purpose of the loss offset is to prevent the taxation of capital as income, then that objective is achieved through the total income approach. The discrimination against companies with sub-

[50]*Taxation of Trade Profits*, p. 11. The Institute of Taxation stated in its submission that, "Losses should be carried forward either for six years as at present, or indefinitely." *Recommendations to the Committee on Taxation of Trading Profits*, p. 19.

stantial investment income is incidental only. But if the purpose of the offset is fundamentally one of solving the tax base inequities inherent in the one-year accounting system, then exempt income should logically be excluded.

On balance, the argument appears to favour the taxable income approach because it places all corporations on the same footing. The Canadian legislation has been amended recently to provide that loss is to be computed in the same way as taxable income is computed, excluding intercorporate dividends which are normally exempt from tax.[51]

(*d*) Conclusions

The carry-forward of losses is preferable to the carry-back, which should be used over a very short period. The period of the loss carry-forward should be sufficient to allow depression losses to be offset against boom profits. The current legislation in Canada is constructive, and probably meets the problem of most corporations. But there is a good case for the extension of the loss carry-forward over an indefinite period, if all profit and loss contingencies are to be taken into consideration. On logical grounds there is no reason to limit the period. Business losses should be determined in the same way as taxable income is determined. Here again, the Canadian legislation is sound.

It is concluded that the loss carry-over device is the best approach to the problem of business losses. Under this approach a corporation is taxed only on the aggregate of net income over the period of the loss carry-over. If the tax is not based on a graduated rate structure, and if the rate does not change, the fact that income may fluctuate sharply does not increase the aggregate tax burden. Thus substantial tax justice is achieved without the complications arising out of any system of averaging. The loss carry-over does not, of course, solve the problem of fluctuating income of non-incorporated businesses, because the proprietors are subject to the steeply graduated rate structure applied to personal income. That is a problem beyond the scope of this study, and it deserves careful consideration.

[51]Section 127 (1)(*w*). This conforms with the recommendation to the Minister of Finance made by the Canadian Tax Foundation in 1948. *Memorandum of Recommendations on Bill 454*, p. 19. The opposite view is taken editorially in the *Accountant*: "The whole system of loss relief—if it can be called a system—should be replaced by a single omnibus provision . . . to cover all income of the taxpayer without regard to source or schedule." April 8, 1950, p. 374.

CHAPTER SEVEN

THE PROBLEM OF THE VALUATION OF ASSETS

IT WAS OBSERVED in the introduction to this study that income is the best conceivable measure of taxpaying ability, but at the same time the inherent difficulties attached to computing it for tax purposes make it a yardstick on which we cannot read the scale accurately. The problem of measuring taxable income applies both to individual and to business income, but it is much more difficult in the latter case because of the complications attached to computing expenses incurred in earning the income. This raises the whole question of what expenses should be allowed in the computation of true net income or profit.[1] Strict application of economic principles to the problem results in one set of conclusions,

[1] So serious is the problem in an inflationary period that the British Chancellor of the Exchequer appointed a special committee (the Tucker Committee) in 1949 to study the matter. The Committee conducted a long series of public hearings, and is now preparing its report. The *Economist*, May 20, 1950, made the following comment: "The Tucker Committee now has the task of finding some single guiding principle that will give an equitable basis for computing the taxable profits of such diverse organisations as the Mersey Tunnel, whose chief asset is a hole in the ground, and crematoria, whose assets do not rank as industrial buildings. Without doubt, the touchstone ought to be that taxable profits should conform as closely as possible to commercial profits arrived at by using the best accounting principles with a few safeguards for the Revenue to limit the taxpayer's discretion in writing off assets, in providing for vague contingencies, or in charging expenses only remotely connected with the business. Unfortunately, there is no such test to apply, because the whole concept of 'profit' is undergoing a change and there is today no unanimity on what constitute the 'best accounting principles.' . . . If the Committee can persuade the Business community and the legislature that surpluses which are the by-product of inflation are not profits at all, and if it can lead the Revenue to understand that as a sleeping partner, it enjoys a majority share in the profits of industry and should, therefore, be more interested in commercial wellbeing than in forcing up the amount of taxable profits by meticulous and exacting applications of old rules of thumb, then it will have done its task well."

and involves highly theoretical determination of what constitutes net profit in the economic sense.[2] The accounting approach to the problem results in a different set of conclusions, primarily because of a different concept of income. For income tax purposes it is essential that general accounting practices be followed in the determination of taxable income. Any attempt to translate into tax legislation the theoretical economic concept of proper charges against income would result in complications of an imponderable nature to the taxpayer. This should certainly be avoided since one of the goals of tax legislation ought to be the greatest simplicity consistent with equity.

Of course the income tax laws do not follow accounting practice in all respects in connection with expenses deductible from income. They cannot, because accounting practice is by no means uniform from industry to industry, or even within a single industry. For this reason the legislation frequently gives rise to dispute, as evidenced by the long record of litigation. Perhaps the most vexatious problem connected with the taxation of corporate income is the computation of taxable profits. It is beyond the scope of this study to probe the whole problem of what costs should constitute a proper deduction from income. That would involve a study in itself. This chapter will be confined to the problem of asset valuation as it affects capital costs. It is a particularly urgent problem now, and has received a great deal of attention in all countries taxing business profits.

The Problem

The problem of asset valuation derives its urgency from the deflated purchasing power of money which has become progressively greater since 1939. It has serious implications, the ramifications of which spread in several directions. Essentially the problem centres on the distortion of the reported net profits of corporations caused by price inflation. If the profits are overstated, management is confronted with many problems, not the least of which is taxation. This situation arises, it is argued, out of the

[2]For example, an economist would say that such items as imputed interest on equity capital, imputed rent on scarce factors of production owned by a corporation and used in earning its income, and the cost of bearing uninsurable risks are properly chargeable against gross income in order to determine "real" net income.

fact that accounting based upon past costs is unrealistic in terms of present costs. It is claimed that balance sheets and profit and loss statements do not present fairly the financial position of companies or the results of their operations. One writer takes the position that (*a*) financial statements give only relative figures, which are misleading; (*b*) the investor cannot secure an accurate estimate of either the true value of the business or its earnings, although the arithmetic used in the calculations encourages him to believe that he can; (*c*) the shareholder is misled about the amount available for distribution as dividends and, to a lesser extent, about the success or failure of management; and (*d*) in or after a period of rising prices, labour is encouraged to believe that corporate earnings are much higher than they actually are, and that consequently wages can be increased without necessitating an increase in prices.[3]

The tax implications are clear, if these charges are warranted. If corporate profits are in large part fictitious, then heavy taxes levied on these so-called profits are in part a levy on capital which must result in impairing the capital position of corporate enterprise.[4] To take a simple and exaggerated example, suppose that a

[3]Roy A. Foulke, *A Study of the Theory of Corporate Net Profits.* Mr. Foulke lays the blame for these results on the following accounting practices: (1) the valuation of fixed assets at cost of acquisition, plus improvements at cost as of the date of purchase, less depreciation based on the costs of acquisition thus recorded; (2) the deduction of depreciation based on this mixture of costs from receipts in current dollars in determining net profit; and (3) the personal judgment of the accountant: (*a*) in determining the useful life of depreciable assets; (*b*) in deciding which of several approved methods of allocating the costs of these assets over their useful lives shall be used; (*c*) in determining the cost value of inventories; and (*d*) in deciding the method of computing balance-sheet values of inventories after costs have been ascertained. Thus he makes the valuation of assets the focal point of the problem.

[4]A British view (*Economist,* June 12, 1948) is that ". . . the weight of taxation on high 'profits'—as the accountant defines them—represents a levy on 'capital'—as the economist understands that term. . . . For several years past, industry has been distributing to the tax collector and its shareholders more than the real profits which it was earning. . . .

"The extent to which a defective economic outlook and accounting technique clouds the true measurement of profits is considerable, even in the United States. Accounting opinion in the United Kingdom has even more to learn on this problem. It will have to be solved from first principles, for there are few reliable statistics to illustrate the point. . . . This argument about the nature of profits, though it is apparently only statistical in character, has most important repercussions on national policy. . . .

". . . Already there is increasing evidence from recent company reports that

merchant, whose business is increased, begins the fiscal year with $100,000 of inventory valued at cost. Suppose further that at the end of the year he has sold the entire stock for $150,000. Ignoring the selling cost and other expenses, his profit is $50,000 and it is still intact. But during the year the cost of this inventory has risen by 50 per cent so that he has to pay $150,000 to acquire the same amount of the same kind of stock for the next year. After replacing his stock he finds that his $50,000 has disappeared and at the same time he must pay a federal corporation tax of $16,700. If he has no liquid earned surplus, he will have to borrow to pay this tax. His capital position has been impaired in any event.

Taking another simple case, suppose that a manufacturer has machinery which he purchased for $100,000. It has an estimated life of ten years. By charging $10,000 a year against income he will, in ten years, have recovered the total cost of the machinery. But suppose that when it has to be replaced it costs $200,000. Until the actual replacement his financial capital is still intact, but after replacement his capital position is impaired to the extent of $100,000. In other words, it is argued that profits over the ten years of the machinery's life were overstated by $100,000. This argument is based upon a special concept of depreciation which will be discussed later.

The extent to which corporate profits have been overstated in the United States was indicated by Professor Sumner H. Slichter in 1948. Appearing before the Joint Congressional Subcommittee investigating prices and profits he stated American corporations had overstated their profits by $16.4 billion in the period 1946–8. In 1946, profits were represented as being nearly twice as large as they really were; in 1947, profits were overstated by about 51 percent;

liquid resources for new capital investment are being rapidly exhausted; the pinch is coming when it is too late to rectify the over-taxation of past years. But businessmen and accountants . . . should have made their mental adjustments long ago, and recognized that a business is a continuing thing from which no profit arises until the cost of keeping it going has been met in full."

An American interpretation of the result of inflation is indicated in the statement of E. Stewart Freeman: "While there is no appreciation of the assets in terms of dollars, there is depreciation of the dollar capital in terms of what the dollar will buy. There can be no net gain to the corporation until enough additional dollars have been provided out of gross income to offset the depreciation of the dollar previously invested by the stockholders." "Budgetary and Financial Policies for Industrial Corporations," *N.A.C.A. Bulletin,* Aug. 15, 1944, p. 1286.

in 1948, profits will be overstated by approximately 25 percent. Naturally, it is highly misleading to stockholders, employees, customers and the public to have the amount of income available for dividends, plant expansion, wage increases, or price reductions so greatly overstated.

In 1946, the actual amount of corporate income available for dividends, wage increases, plant reductions, expansion of plant, or price reductions, was about 6.4 billion dollars instead of 12.8 billion dollars as actually reported. In 1947, the amount of corporate income available to pay dividends, increase wages, reduce prices, or expand plant was approximately 12.0 billion dollars instead of 18.1 billion dollars as actually reported. During the first 6 months of 1948, reported profits have been running at the annual rate of 19.8 billion dollars a year.[5]

Slichter attributed the overstatement to two things: (1) failure to deduct the rise in the cost of replacing inventories, and (2) failure to charge adequate depreciation. Most of the distortion was due to the inventory factor, which over the three-year period accounted for 79 per cent of the overstated profits.[6]

The United States Department of Commerce estimated "the profit distortion resulting from changes in inventory valuation at upward of 5 billion dollars in each of the years 1946 and 1947. That is to say, had the corporations charged the same sales prices that they did charge in 1947, but had they universally followed the practice of charging to expense the amounts needed to replace the physical volume of inventory used up, corporate 'profits' would have been 5.1 billion dollars less than they were."[7]

No estimate appears to have been made of the amount by which profits have been overstated in Canada. But the Royal Commission on Prices made what it called "a very rough guess" as to the amount by which inventory profits increased total profits be-

[5]United States, Congress, Joint Committee on the Economic Report, *Corporate Profits*, p. 3.

[6]His figures (pp. 4, 6) are as follows (in billions):

	1946	*1947*	*1948*
Overstatement due to inventory factor	$5.0	$5.1	$3.0
Overstatement due to depreciation factor	1.3	1.0	1.0
Total overstatement	6.3	6.1	4.0

[7]United States, Congress, Joint Committee on the Economic Report, Subcommittee on Profits Hearings, *Profits*, p. 37.

tween 1945 and 1947. The estimate was $250 million, slightly more than 20 per cent of the total reported profits, before tax, during the period.[8]

It was remarked earlier that the cause of the disparity between profits as measured by the accountant and "true" profit hinges on the concept of income that is used. There is need for a clear understanding of what is meant by the term income, and one's views on the controversy raised by inflated profits will be determined in large measure by one's approach to income. If we could decide and agree upon what business income should mean, then the implications for tax policy would be reasonably clear.

CONCEPTS OF INCOME[9]

It would be better, perhaps, if the term "trading profits" or "business profits" were used instead of income. What we are interested in primarily is the net profit of a business operation after all expenses made to earn that profit have been deducted from gross income.

In facing the problem of profit determination the objective should be to decide upon the concept of income that is most useful for corporate reporting. It is desirable, of course, that the concept be generally acceptable, although that appears to be a most unlikely achievement. It has been suggested that "there are four basic concepts interwoven into one fabric of reporting of earnings: (1) accounting, (2) tax, (3) legal, and (4) economic."[10] For our purposes, (1), (2), and (4) merit discussion. The legal concept, important as it is, is primarily an expression of judicial opinion on the tax law.

[8]*Report of the Royal Commission on Prices*, II, 193.

[9]I have deliberately avoided entering the long and murky trail of discussion concerning the meaning of income. That would lead us too far off course, and it is extremely doubtful that any useful purpose would be served. An extensive and specialized literature has been developed over the years by economists, accountants, lawyers and the tax specialists. No attempt has been made to compile a bibliography on this matter. All that this Section pretends to do is examine some of the problems connected with defining business income, and indicate the basic difference between the accounting and economic concepts. Therein lies our problem. A useful study on this point has been prepared by Arthur H. Dean, *An Inquiry into the Nature of Business Income under Present Price Levels.*

[10]George D. Bailey, "Concepts of Income," *Harvard Business Review*, Nov. 1948, p. 687.

1. *The Accounting Concept*

The accounting concept[11] is based on "money" profit, and it ignores changes in the value of money. This concept has often been defined as the matching of costs against related revenues. The matching cannot be precise, of course, because of the need to defer some costs already expended against revenues yet to be determined. In essence, conventional accounting practice sets up a balance sheet which is a statement of costs (prudently adjusted for anticipated losses), not a statement of values.[12] Therefore if profit gained in a given period is thought of as the increase in proprietorship that has taken place during the period (after making due allowance for any part of such increment as may have been distributed), it is a cost concept completely independent of the current economic value of assets.

2. *The Tax Concept*

Some distortion of the accounting concept has been created under the tax law.[13] The Income Tax Act recognizes and is based upon the fundamentals of the accounting concept, although it does not say so. It starts with "profit" as the point of departure and then lays down rules for the computation of taxable profit. They are found under five headings:

[11]It is not strictly accurate to refer to *the* accounting concept. Accounting practice is undergoing some fundamental changes, and there are various refinements now applied to the traditional practices.

[12]This is precisely the reason why the accounting concept of income has been so exposed to attack. See, for example, Roy A. Foulke, who says: "This practice by which assets are carried on the books of account, and in balance sheets, at digits which are different from their actual economic values at any particular date after purchase, is the result of what is known as an 'accounting' convention and represents one of the present-day mathematical limitations to existing accountancy. Accounting, as practiced, has not reached the point in its development where variables, that is, fluctuating economic values of assets, are taken into consideration except in the case of inventories." *A Study of the Theory of Corporate Net Profits,* p. 15.

[13]George D. Bailey states: "The tax laws have set up an entirely different concept of income, perhaps roughly differentiated from the accounting concept by tests of final determination as well as by certain almost whimsical departures caused by court decisions, statutes or government policy." "Concepts of Income," p. 688. This seems to be an overstatement of the situation. If attention is focused on the similarities of the two concepts instead of on the differences, they will appear closely related. Indeed, the two concepts have a common heritage. An excellent discussion of this point may be found in Dan Throop Smith and J. Keith Butters, *Taxable and Business Income,* chap. I.

(*a*) "Amounts Included in Computing Income"
(*b*) "Amounts Not Included in Computing Income"
(*c*) "Deductions Allowed in Computing Income"
(*d*) "Deductions Not Allowed in Computing Income"
(*e*) "Miscellaneous Rules for Computing Income"

While not all of these specific provisions are designed to impose restrictions on usual accounting practice, some of them are deliberately restrictive; others provide for a more narrow concept of income than is used by either the accountant or the economist. Perhaps the greatest difference in the concept of profit provided under the Canadian tax law is the implicit understanding that only income is taxable. Capital and capital gains are excluded from the tax base. The Act does not say this, and there is no definition of a capital gain. Most of the problems inherent in the distinction between income and capital gain are left for the courts to solve. Needless to say, this feature of the Canadian (and the British) law gives rise to a serious controversy in drawing the line between taxable income and non-taxable capital gain, which has been discussed in chapter II.

The provisions of the law that deviate from the accounting concept of business profits fall into two broad categories: (1) those resulting in timing of various income and expense items, and (2) those resulting from policy decisions designed (*a*) to prevent tax avoidance, and (*b*) to accord special treatment to certain types of income or expense.

The different emphasis on timing in the computation of business profits and taxable profits results in different treatment of several income and expense items when there is doubt regarding the accounting period to which they might best be assigned. Conservative accounting practice requires the postponement of doubtful income items and the inclusion of doubtful expense items in order to avoid the overstatement of profit for the current period. For tax purposes, however, the policy is to maximize immediate profits. Thus, the tax law may require the inclusion of some income items at an earlier date than accounting practice would normally allow, and conversely, expenses are not allowed until they can be determined accurately.

The tax treatment of reserves is a case in point. Conservative accounting practice sanctions the creation of precautionary and contingency reserves, representing management's best judgment as to probable or future losses. But the tax law is niggardly in its treatment of such reserves. Section 12 (1) (*e*) provides that no deduction shall be made in respect of "an amount transferred or credited to a reserve, contingent account or sinking fund except as expressly permitted by this Part." The only provisions for deductible reserves are found in Section 11 (1)(*d*) which provides for a deduction of a "reasonable" reserve for doubtful debts. Such a reserve charged in a given year will be added to taxable income in the following year. Bad debts actually written off are deductible, but bad debts recovered in the future must be written back into income upon recovery. Special provision is made in Section 11 (4) for the deduction of certain reserves set up by banks. No provision is made regarding any other reserves.

An example of the limitation imposed upon the accounting concept of profit by the tax law to prevent tax avoidance[14] is found in Section 12 (1) (*a*), which states that "In computing income, no deductions shall be made in respect of (*a*) an outlay or expense except to the extent that it was made or incurred by the taxpayer for the purpose of gaining or producing income from property or a business of the taxpayer."[15] This provision has resulted in a very considerable amount of controversy over items of expense which are border-line cases. The further restriction, found in Section 12 (2), that an expense is not deductible unless it is reasonable involves more difference of opinion. Still another limitation provides that an expense made for the purpose of gaining exempt income is not deductible.[16]

The Canadian tax law contains many examples of special

[14]More attention has been paid to the individual taxpayer in this respect, and the whole theme of constructive dividends represents an interesting and far-reaching deviation from standard accounting practice.

[15]The analogous section of the old law (Income War Tax Act, Section 6), provided that "a deduction shall not be allowed in respect of (*a*) disbursements or expenses not wholly, exclusively and necessarily laid out or expended for the purpose of earning the income; . . . (*e*) carrying charges or expenses of unproductive property or assets not acquired for the purposes of a trade, business or calling or of a liability not incurred in connection with a trade, business or calling."

[16]Section 12 (1)(*c*). Intercorporate dividends are normally exempt in Canada. Thus, if a Canadian corporation receives $2,000 in dividends on shares of another Canadian corporation, but has borrowed the money to buy those shares and paid

policy decisions designed to accord special treatment to certain types of income and expense. One example is the exemption of intercorporate dividends, designed to prevent double taxation. Another is the special allowances for depletion to mining companies. Still another is the new special treatment accorded to the undistributed surplus of companies, which was discussed in chapter II. Further examples are the averaging of income from farming and fishing operations, and the carry-back and carry-forward of business losses.

Thus the tax concept of business profits differs in several respects from the accounting concept. Each has been influenced by the other. The tax concept in Canada depends to a great extent upon British judicial opinion regarding the meaning of profit, and to a lesser extent upon judicial opinion in Canada. Were it not for that vast body of opinion in case law, the Canadian statute would necessarily be much more detailed in spelling out the meaning of profit.

3. *The Economic Concept*

It is not proposed to examine the extensive volume of literature indicating the opinions of various economists on the economic concept of capital and income. There are many versions of the economic concepts, and elaborate refinements have been made by contemporary theorists.[17] It is perhaps fair to make a very generalized statement to the effect that the economic concept of business profit involves matching current replacement costs against sales income. It will be seen that, in this sense, the economic concept stresses current replacement costs, as contrasted with the traditional accounting accent on historical cost. As long as price levels are reasonably stable, there is little difference in the results obtained from applying the accounting concept in profit determination. But when price levels change as substantially as they have over the past decade, the difference becomes very important.

$2,500 interest in that year on that debt, no part of the $2,500 would be deductible. Following the usual accounting concept the whole expense would be charged against income.

[17]See, for example, John Maynard Keynes, *The General Theory of Employment, Interest and Money*, pp. 52 ff.; and J. R. Hicks, *Value and Capital*, pp. 172 ff.

4. *Conclusions*

Whether or not there can or should be a reconciliation of the accounting and economic concepts of business profit is a matter of opinion. It seems highly improbable that there will be any generally acceptable answer to the query "How should business income be defined?" A glance at the extraordinary volume of literature concerning this problem which advances so many different viewpoints is sufficient to indicate the sharp cleavage of informed opinion. One view is that accounting practice should be changed and based upon current replacement costs. And there are various other views, ranging from adherence to traditional principles to modifications of them designed to meet the contemporary problem of inflated price levels. A few of the proposals will be examined in the following pages.

Elements of the Problem

As indicated at the outset of this chapter, the two elements in the problem of distorted earnings to be discussed are the valuation of current assets on the one hand, and fixed assets on the other. Essentially the problem boils down to the valuation of inventory and the depreciation of fixed assets. These two points will now be discussed in turn.

1. *Inventory Valuation*

(*a*) The Problem

The valuation of inventory is a major factor in the determination of annual net profit. The conventional accounting practice of valuing inventory at the lower of cost or market value exaggerates the statement of profits and losses in periods of sharp changes in the price level. Thus, in a period of sharply increasing prices, for example the post-war period, profits have been greatly overstated because the cost of merchandise, matched against income, has been understated. The result of understating these charges has been an overvaluation of inventories. Conversely, during a sharp decline in the price level, profits are understated, or losses overstated.

While these fictitious paper profits and losses may cancel out over a long period of time, they have very important and serious short-run results, not the least of which is the accentuation of the business cycle through the exaggeration of profits and losses during "boom and bust" periods.[18] Our concern here is specifically the problem as it affects the tax base. It can be illustrated by a simple example of the result of failure to charge increases in the cost of replacing inventories against profits. Assume that a company is making no operating profit in a given period. Suppose further that during this period the price of raw materials has advanced so that the cost of replacing the inventories consumed during the period increases by $1,000,000. Then suppose that the company is able to increase its selling price by exactly enough to offset the rise in the cost of inventory replacement.[19] Under the usual practice of reporting profits, the company would not charge the $1,000,000 increase in the cost of replacing inventories against the $1,000,000 gain resulting from its increased selling price. Instead of showing no operating profit, as assumed, a profit of $1,000,000 would be reported. There is really no profit, and, assuming that inventories are replaced in the same volume, there is no cash available for dividends or for taxes. Yet, under the Canadian income tax law, the company would be required to pay $377,700 in federal tax, and from $50,000 to $70,000 in provincial tax, according to the province in which it is located. The funds for paying the tax must come from surplus, or they must be borrowed. In any event, the problem is serious, and requires careful consideration.[20]

(*b*) Alternative Approaches

There is no intention here of becoming embroiled in the

[18]For a discussion of the economic results of inadequate accounting methods, see N. S. Buchanan, *The Economics of Corporate Enterprise*, pp. 271 ff.

[19]This is not likely to happen, of course. In most cases selling price is unlikely to be increased by the whole amount of the increase in the cost of replacing inventory. It may not be increased at all. The Royal Commission on Prices stated, for example, that "retail shoe stores in the autumn of 1947 continued to sell their stock on hand with little advance in price even though replacement cost of shoes had advanced substantially." *Report*, II, 192.

[20]Charles A. Bliss queries this viewpoint in a provocative article, "The Reality of Inventory Profits," *Harvard Business Review*, Sept. 1948, pp. 527-42. This is well worth reading, because it presents the opinion that "inventory profits do not arise out of the methods of inventory accounting, and in fact do not exist at all in many areas of the economy where changes in prices and costs are not nicely correlated" (p. 542). The arguments used in support of this view deserve attention.

dispute over accounting technicalities which at times obscures the real issue. The accounting treatment of inventories has been much discussed,[21] and it has been modified considerably in the last decade. This is in large part a result of the increasing burden of taxation on business, and the need for more accurate annual reporting of net earnings. This section will deal only with objectives and principles which seem fundamental, but which appear to be forgotten in the scramble to face the tax difficulties of individual taxpayers. With these principles stated, a cursory examination of the more important proposals will follow.

In the first place, it seems important that tax legislation provide for as much consistency as possible in the treatment of fixed and circulating capital. This is inherent in the underlying theme of tax neutrality contained in this study. The acquisition of assets, both fixed and circulating, represents a cost (within limitations) properly chargeable against revenue in order to determine taxable income. The basic difficulty is, of course, that of applying such costs to revenue in a way which reflects most accurately the earnings position of the company. Unhappily the accounting technique which favours a taxpayer at one point in the business cycle injures him at another, and the inevitable result is a not unnatural desire to change accounting practice in accordance with changing price levels. This type of proposal is resisted, of course, by tax administrators, and the conservative flank of the accounting profession likewise opposes it. While a foolish consistency may be the hobgoblin of little minds, it is by no means foolish to advocate consistency in accounting practice.

This leads to the second and more fundamental point, whether the tax system should be adjusted from time to time to take into consideration sharp changes in price levels. It has been argued in the introduction to this study that the tax system should be designed primarily for revenue purposes, and that it should not be considered an instrument for economic control. It now seems quite consistent to argue vigorously against cluttering up the income tax structure with special relief provisions because of

[21]An example of the technical discussion among accountants is to be found in National Association of Cost Accountants, *Year Book, 1940: Proceedings of the Twenty-first International Conference,* Sessions I and II, pp. 1-172.

price inflation. In short, why impose upon the tax structure the penalty accruing from the failure of monetary management? Income tax legislation should be simple, allowing the taxpayer to use that accounting system most suitable to his business, and showing most accurately his profit and loss position.

The traditional practice of valuing inventories at the lower of cost or market value is based upon a first-in first-out presumption. This rule, which has always been allowed in Canada, is a concession from the criterion of strict realization. It allows a shifting of the valuation base from one method of costing to another in accordance with the ups and downs of the price level. It is biased in favour of the taxpayer and against the treasury, because it allows for the deduction of unrealized losses, while it does not give corresponding recognition of accrued gains. Furthermore, this method of inventory valuation is not as simple as it appears to be. The various ways of determining "cost" and "market" used by Canadian business concerns are an indication of the divergent practices connected with it.[22] In this connection it is interesting to note the recommendations of the Institute of Chartered Accountants in England and Wales, which are in part as follows:

(1) The basis of valuation for stock-in-trade should normally be the lower of cost or market value, calculated as in (2) and (3) below.
(2) Cost should be calculated on such a basis as will show a fair view of the trend of results of the particular type of business concerned. Indirect or overhead expenditure, if included as part of the cost of partly processed or finished products, should be restricted to such expenditure as has been incurred in bringing the stock-in-trade to its existing condition and location.
(3) Market value should be calculated by reference to the price at which it is estimated that the stock-in-trade can be realised, either in its existing condition or as incorporated in the product normally sold, after allowing for expenditure to be incurred before disposal. In estimating this price, regard should be had to abnormal and obsolete stocks, the trend of the market and the prospects of disposal.
(6) Whatever basis is adopted for ascertaining cost or calculating market value, it should be such as will not distort the view of the real trend of trading results and should be applied consistently regardless

[22]See the analysis prepared by the Dominion Bureau of Statistics, *Inventory Accounting Methods of Canadian Manufacturers,* 1949.

of the amount of profits available or losses sustained. Any reduction in stock values which exceeds the provisions embodied in the above recommendations is a reserve and should be shown as such in the accounts.[23]

This is a clear exposition of the objectives to be kept in view under conventional accounting practice, but the fundamental difficulty arising out of sharply fluctuating price levels remains unsolved. It is the inability to apply, in many cases, specific costs to revenues that has resulted in the various proposals for costing on the basis of a pattern of flow.

(i) The base stock method

The base stock method has been used most commonly by the extractive and processing industries that always maintain a certain minimum inventory of raw materials.[24] It consists in adopting a quantity of stock that is the minimum that the business must have to keep in production. This inventory is valued at a constant price over a long period of years. All new stock purchased is promptly written down to this valuation, by debit to the profit and loss account (usually there is a write-down, because the practice is to value the base stock at a figure well below cost). As the stock is used in production and sold, the full difference reverts to the profit and loss account. Thus there is a tax deferment on the amount of the write-down until the stock is all disposed of. The argument used to support this practice is that changes in the value of the minimum or normal inventory should no more be reflected in income than changes in the value of fixed assets.

The base stock method offends the principle of showing a fair and true result of the year's operations, because in a year of heavy purchases there would be a disproportionate write-down charge, with a corresponding disproportionate reduction of income. When purchases are unusually light, the reverse would be true. But it does solve for the taxpayer the problem connected with rising prices. In their joint submission to the Tucker Committee the Association of British Chambers of Commerce and the

[23]*Memorandum for the Committee on Taxation of Trading Profits appointed by the Chancellor of the Exchequer,* Appendix I, pp. 33-4.

[24]See Smith and Butters, *Taxable and Business Income,* p. 97.

Federation of British Industries stated that the method "may be a suitable basis for some particular industries and particularly for by-products for which no reliable cost can be ascertained and which have no established market value. It should not be ruled out as being wrong in principle[25] but rather studied with a view to perfecting it as a stabilizing factor without being a cloak for hidden reserves."[26]

(ii) Lifo

Lifo (last-in-first-out) is based upon the assumption that the cost of sales should be measured by the purchase costs of the latest inventory additions. In other words, it assumes that the stock on hand consists of the oldest purchases. That such an assumption is not always valid is quite obvious. But one of the principal advantages claimed for Lifo is that it tends to produce a desirable levelling of peaks and valleys of profits exaggerated by price fluctuations. Its most ardent proponents claim for Lifo the distinction of being the solution to the inventory valuation problem for tax purposes. That view must, however, remain a matter of opinion, because no method of inventory valuation is the best in all circumstances. But Lifo deserves the close attention that has been focused upon it.

The time at which the system is applied to a company's accounting practice is important. It has been pointed out that "If it is commenced in a period of high costs the stocks remain at that high cost so long as they remain at the same volume or less. If the system is commenced in a period of low costs the stocks remain at a low value so long as they remain equal in quantity or less."[27]

But at all times Lifo causes materials to be charged out nearer to current market prices than do either the Fifo (first-in-first-out) or Average Price methods. Thus the system does mitigate severe fluctuations of inventory values, and, to that extent, it approaches

[25]Very early in United States income tax history the Advisory Tax Board ruled (1917) that the method was not in conformity with the revenue acts on the ground that it did not conform to the best accounting practice, that it disregarded the annual accounting period, and that it ordinarily tended to understate profits. T.B.R. 65, *Cumulative Bulletin*, 1, p. 51 (1919), cited by Smith and Butters, *ibid.*

[26]*Definition of Taxable Business Profits*, p. 29. [27]*Ibid.*

the requirement of business that current material cost be kept in line with current market replacement prices.[28]

In view of the initial difficulty of starting Lifo, however, and the recurring difficulty of catering for movements in the volume of inventory, it is questionable whether Lifo is the most equitable method of valuing inventory. There has been considerable controversy over Lifo, the details of which need not concern us here.[29] Its critics argue that it does not conform to the logical flow of costs to revenues, and that it does not show inventory at its current purchase price for balance sheet purposes. The chief difficulty with Lifo is the same one attached to lower of cost or market value and Fifo, i.e., that all these systems pinch at one point or another on the scale of sharply fluctuating prices.[30] One wonders whether some of the ardent Lifo enthusiasts of today would not become Fifoists during a major depression. All these new schemes are a derivative of the upward spiralling of prices since 1939, and it might well be that interest in them would go into a sharp decline should severe deflation occur. The danger of allowing the

[28]Cf. Cecil A. Ellis, "The Financial Effects of Inventory Methods," *Canadian Chartered Accountant*, Jan. 1948, p. 39.

[29]A sample of the pros and cons will be found in articles by Jerome Tannenbaum, "The LIFO Method," *Taxes—The Tax Magazine*, June 1947, p. 492, and "Inventorying Raw Materials under LIFO," *ibid.*, July 1947, p. 601; Leo W. Crown, "Inventory Pricing," *ibid.*, April 1948, p. 318; Maurice E. Peloubet, "Inventory Methods in the United States," *Canadian Chartered Accountant*, Jan. 1948, p. 8, and "Has LIFO Fallen?" *Journal of Accountancy*, April 1948, p. 298; E. B. Wilcox, "The Rise and Fall of LIFO," *Canadian Chartered Accountant*, April 1948, p. 201; and R. M. Parkinson, "The LIFO Method of Inventory Valuation," *ibid.*, May 1950, p. 206.

[30]Lifo has been made respectable in the United States under the Internal Revenue Code, 22 (*d*)(1), which allows inventories generally to be valued on the Lifo basis. This provision was enacted in 1939, and it has been observed: "The last-in-first-out option was of great significance for many companies during and immediately after the war. . . Inasmuch as the trend of prices was steadily upwards after 1939, companies that elected the last-in-first-out option benefited greatly. These benefits will, of course, be partly or conceivably even wholly, offset by any future price declines. Therefore future price changes and future tax rates should be considered before the last-in-first-out method is adopted." Smith and Butters, *Taxable and Business Income*, p. 95. A nonconformist tax authority in the United States, the late Henry Simons, in discussing the use of Lifo to mitigate the serious overtaxing of corporate income, made this pungent remark: "The expedient, moreover, indicates alarmingly the route ahead if we continue such *ad hoc* tinkering and keep on trying to get a satisfactory tax edifice by forever adding gadgets and superstructure instead of repairing the foundation." *Federal Tax Reform*, p. 106.

taxpayer to play hide-and-go-seek with inventory valuations is too obvious for comment, and it should be apparent that he cannot have his cake and eat it. One of the critics of Lifo has remarked: "It begins to appear that we have inadvertently opened Pandora's box when we tried to improve income determination with LIFO. Certainly there are grounds for the fear that it has done more harm than good to the cause of income determination. It has greatly defeated that purpose to which the accounting profession in the United States has dedicated itself in recent years, to narrow the areas of inconsistency in financial statements."[31]

If inventories are to be reflected in income statements as though their cost had been incurred at current levels, then it would be only logical and equitable to extend this treatment to fixed assets, because outlays on inventories and fixed assets are both deferred charges. But the implications of such a procedure would probably be too dramatic even for the most ardent Lifo partisans.[32]

The official tax viewpoint in Canada was enunciated clearly by Mr. Charles Gavsie, of the Department of National Revenue:

In the past the taxing authorities have looked unfavourably in varying degree upon such rules of presuming identity of inventory as "basic stock", "Lifo" and "Average Cost". The fundamental reason for disfavour of these presumptions may be attributed to the fact that the taxing authorities considered that the basis of these rules is the very antithesis of sound business procedure inasmuch as most things deteriorate through age and consequently every business is desirous of moving its old stock first. Some persuasive arguments have been advanced from time to time to show that in particular businesses the application of one or other of the "basic stock", "Lifo" or "Average Cost" theories for presumption of inventory identification more nearly corresponds with reality than the "Fifo" theory. The taxing authorities are not beyond sound argument in support of any such contentions on the part of taxpayers and are prepared to treat cases upon their merits. The test, however, must continue to be: "In the absence of positive identification of the inventory on hand, which rule of presump-

[31]Wilcox, "The Rise and Fall of LIFO," pp. 203-4.

[32]But see Paul Graely, "Impact of Economic Income, or Replacement Costs, on Public Utilities," *Replacement Costs and Depreciation Policies*, pp. 29-37. He would accept provision for plant exhaustion at current price level similar to Lifo, if estimates are determined objectively and the method is followed consistently.

tion is most likely to present the result most closely akin to reality?"

Once having determined the identity of the inventory, the time honoured rule for valuation, now incorporated into legislation, may be applied.[33]

The Lifo method of inventory valuation has merit, and is used by many corporations in the United States, and by some in Canada. It does not appear, however, to be a panacea, and certainly there are cases in which it would represent no improvement over the traditional accounting practice. If the Canadian legislation provided that the valuation of inventories was to be made in accordance with generally accepted accounting practice, the courts might rule that Lifo should be allowed under the law, provided that the taxpayer established that it was used consistently.

(*c*) The Canadian Legislation

Prior to 1948 the Canadian income tax law made no specific reference to the method by which inventory was to be valued. But it was the practice of the Department of National Revenue to value inventory at the lower of cost or market value. The new Act (1949) provides in Section 14 (2) that "For the purpose of computing income, the property described in an inventory shall be valued at its cost to the taxpayer or its fair market value, whichever is lower, or in such other manner as may be permitted by regulation." Section 1800, Regulations, Part XVIII, provides that, "For the purpose of computing the income of a taxpayer from a business (*a*) all the property described in all the inventories of the business may be valued at the cost to him, or (*b*) all the property described in all the inventories of the business may be valued at the fair market value."

Thus the taxpayer is given three alternatives. He may (1) value each inventory at the lower of cost or market value, (2) value all inventories at cost, or (3) value all inventories at market value. No reductions from cost are allowed if method (2) is chosen, or from market value if method (3) is chosen. There is no definition of cost or fair market value. The taxpayer may not change from one method of valuation to another without the Minister's permission.[34]

[33]"Some Aspects of Income Taxation in Canada," *Canadian Chartered Accountant*, Oct. 1949, pp. 164-5.

[34]It has been observed by one tax official that "the taxing authorities regard

There is certain to be a wide range of opinion as to whether the new statutory provision and the regulations covering inventory valuation represent any constructive improvement. Section 14 (2) avoids definitions, and allows the Department unlimited scope for providing through regulation any special treatment of inventory valuation. One writer has interpreted the new law as follows: "If, however, accounting and commercial principles may be relied on—and they have the great weight of British practice behind them—it may be said that sec. 14 (2) of the Canadian Act already gives recognition to the base stock method, Fifo, Average Cost and Lifo, in appropriate circumstances, for the determination of 'cost' under the well-known formula."[35]

It seems unlikely, however, that any such broad recognition of these costing methods will be given by the Department of National Revenue. The principle of inventory reserves becomes involved when closing inventories are valued *below* the lower of cost or market value; because such a practice automatically provides a "hidden" reserve against a future decline in inventory values. But the Canadian income tax law allows no reserves of any kind save those expressly permitted for doubtful debts, depreciation, depletion and to banks. It appears certain that the Department would disallow any method of inventory valuation which establishes in effect a hidden reserve or contingent account for a decline in future values.[36]

---

consistency in method of inventory valuation as of primary importance and, generally speaking, changes of method once adopted and accepted will not be sanctioned without some adequate reason and then subject only to any adjustment in taxes which may be required to offset any profit change resulting from the change of method of valuation." *Ibid.*, p. 165.

[35]Editorial comment, "Valuation of Inventories for Tax Purposes," *Tax Review*, March 1949, p. 29. J. G. Glassco states: "I suggest, however, that you cannot dismiss it [Lifo] as merely a device to reduce taxable income and I would venture to predict that, in time, it will find its proper place in Canadian accounting. I also suggest that if the income tax administration rejects the method, it will have to explain to the Courts why it is not an acceptable method of determining cost, rather than merely demonstrate that the method is outlawed because the administration has not sanctioned it by regulation." "Changes in Income Tax Law," *Canadian Chartered Accountant*, Feb. 1949, p. 54. There is now an appeal pending before the Exchequer Court as a result of the Department's refusal to allow Lifo. It will be interesting to see what the Court's decision will be.

[36]The Canadian law did provide, however, for an inventory reserve for excess profits tax purposes. It was confined to businesses subject to the 100 per cent rate on excess profits, and was limited to inventory not in excess of that on hand during the standard period.

At first glance it might appear that the Regulations, Section 1800, constitute an application of the global method of inventory valuation, as required by the Inland Revenue authorities in the United Kingdom, and against which the Court ruled in *I.R.C.* v. *Cock, Russel & Co. Ltd.*, ([1949] 2 All E. R. 889). There was an almost unanimous protest against this system in the submissions to the Tucker Committee. Apparently, however, the Canadian regulation was designed to give legal status to the well-established practice used by security dealers for valuing inventories. Without the regulation, Section 14 (2) would have outlawed the existing practice.

(*d*) Conclusions

There is no unanimity among accountants regarding a solution to the problem of inventory valuation, and probably there is no one approach that would satisfy the diverse requirements of all types of business. An interesting proposal has been made by Professor Groves:

> Inventory accounting is badly in need of better and more standardized practice. Perhaps it is even in order to suggest that, within a given type of industry, business or trade, an appropriate inventory procedure should be determined and made mandatory for income-tax reporting and reports to stockholders. Determining the one best way for a given industry to evaluate its inventory and state its profits, and drafting this into an amendment to the Revenue Act, is a matter for a representative group of business men, accountants, and tax experts. A complete manual of inventory valuation procedures and the specific mandatory application of a certain method to certain businesses would go a long way toward eliminating tax discriminations and providing comparable profit-and-loss data for similar enterprises.[37]

While this plan would undoubtedly produce intra-trade uniformity and thereby achieve a considerable degree of equity, the price paid seems to be too great. It would result in complicated tax legislation, and would impose an undesirable rigidity on

[37]*Postwar Taxation and Economic Progress,* pp. 152-3. He goes on to say: "One of the objectives in this reform should be the elimination from the current income account of profits due to cyclical price fluctuations. That techniques can be found to accomplish this objective perfectly is extremely doubtful, to say the least. Nevertheless, the trend toward 'lifo' and reserve accounting can be recognized as a hopeful one, and efforts to further the trend are very much in order."

accounting and tax practice. Regardless of how painstaking the draftmanship might be, one wonders how many business concerns in a trade would think the pertinent schedule equitable in their particular case.

Informed opinion in Canada appears to favour general rather than specific legislation on this point. A group of experts recommended that the Canadian Act be amended to read: "For the purpose of computing income goods held for consumption or resale shall be valued in accordance with generally accepted accounting practices appropriate to the business and consistently applied. . . ."[38]

Since the problem of inventory valuation in Canada is parallel to that in the United Kingdom, it is worth considering the proposals made in that country to the Tucker Committee. There was marked uniformity in the recommendations made by several groups. Apparently there is little sympathy for the kind of measure advocated by Groves. The British want flexibility, and the joint submission of the Association of British Chambers of Commerce and the Federation of British Industries is typical as far as basic principles are concerned. This proposal is as follows:

[38]Canadian Tax Foundation, *Conference on the Income Tax Bill: Report of Proceedings*, 1947, p. 7. The failure of the government to adopt this recommendation is consistent with its attitude on computation of income. When the present Act was in bill form, Section 4 read as follows: "Subject to the other provisions of this Part, income for a taxation year from a business or property shall be determined in accordance with generally accepted accounting principles." This provision was deleted before the bill was passed, and the section now reads: "Subject to the other provisions of this Part, income for a taxation year from a business or property is the profit therefrom for the year." It was probably wise to avoid the expression "generally accepted accounting principles," because while the general intention is obviously sound, the legal interpretation of the term could easily open up a wide field of argument. See Canadian Tax Foundation, *The Income Tax Bill: A Review and Analysis*, p. 14.

It is interesting to note the recommendation of the United Kingdom Income Tax Codification Committee in 1936. Referring to a long line of tax cases, the Committee said: "We considered in detail these and other judicial pronouncements, and we decided that, in dealing with the computation of profits from businesses, our draft Bill should first contain a statement that the computation is to be made on ordinary commercial principles, and should then set out a list of specific matters allowed or disallowed in computing profits for income tax purposes, introduced by words making it clear that, if there is in any case a conflict between ordinary commercial principles and the provisions of the Bill, the latter are to prevail." *Report*, vol. I, p. 49. The Act was not amended in accordance with this recommendation.

Subject to the observations below in relation to inflated prices it is considered that precise rules of stock valuation are not required. The trader's method of valuation should be accepted provided that it satisfies three tests as follows: (1) that the method adopted by him is in accordance with the custom of the particular trade, (2) that he has adopted it consistently over the relevant periods, and (3) that it expresses a fair view of the balance of profits or gains of the relevant periods. The final decision on stock valuation should be for the appeal Commissioners as a question of fact which cannot be upset in a court of law unless it can be shown that there was no evidence to support the decision. Where the taxpayer's method of valuation is vulnerable on any of the three grounds stated above, it would be for the Commissioners to prescribe the adjustment which in their view would have the result of fairly expressing the profits of the period. This adjustment might involve altering the method of valuing the opening stock as well as the closing stock so as to bring them on to the same basis.[39]

The Institute of Chartered Accountants in England and Wales stated that "owing to the varying circumstances of different businesses . . . it is therefore not desirable to frame special income tax rules for the valuation of trading stocks." It was recommended, "That the method of valuation should be that adopted by the business, provided it is applied consistently from period to period and is based on accepted accounting principles."[40] The Society of Incorporated Accountants and Auditors stressed that "no special rules should be introduced in regard to the valuation of trading stocks for taxation purposes. The valuation of stock is primarily a commercial matter, and if the basis of valuation is one which is acceptable on commercial principles, it should be equally applicable for taxation purposes. There are no grounds for adopting a separate set of stock valuation rules purely for the purpose of ascertaining taxable profits."[41] The Association of Certified and Corporate Accountants stated that: "While the basis of cost or market value has much to commend it, any insistence on a particular method of calculating either appears to be misplaced. . . . In our opinion, there is no ground for questioning any method of valuation that is reasonable, although it is desirable that a method once adopted should be adhered to consistently

[39] *Definition of Taxable Business Profits,* p. 28.
[40] *Memorandum for the Committee on Taxation of Trading Profits,* p. 18.
[41] *Taxation of Trade Profits,* p. 10.

in the absence of special circumstances which might justify variation."[42] The Joint Committee of Councils, Chartered Accountants of Scotland,[43] and the Institute of Taxation[44] made similar recommendations. The British view is therefore very clearly in favour of any method of inventory valuation which is based upon proper accounting principles.[45]

This appears to be the most sensible approach to the problem, and might well provide a point of departure in reaching a conclusion regarding policy for Canada. The Canadian legislation provides that inventory shall be valued at the lower of cost or market value, or in any manner prescribed by regulation. This limits the taxpayer to such valuation methods as the Department of National Revenue cares to allow, and it has been seen that in two years of operating under the new section only one regulation has been issued, which was simply a relieving provision for one class of taxpayer. As long as the law and the regulations are specific, there is less chance for relief in the courts than there would be in the absence of a statutory provision. Under the present law the admission of Lifo, for example, would have to turn upon the question of whether or not it is a cost within the meaning of Section 14 (2).

In other words, provision for the valuation of inventory under statute law and regulations imposes a degree of rigidity upon the taxpayer's accounting procedure that is considered by many people as undesirable. If an attempt is made to liberalize the statute by providing that inventory may be valued according to generally accepted accounting principles, it would have to contend with the serious difficulty of deciding what these principles really are.

There is a good case for making no statutory provision at all for inventory valuation. The Income War Tax Act was silent on this point, but it was the practice of the Department to value inventories at the lower of cost or market value. Under these circumstances the taxpayer's relief from a refusal by the Depart-

[42] *Memorandum*, Item 5.

[43] *Representations to the Tucker Committee on Taxation of Trading Profits*, p. 10.

[44] *Recommendations by the Council of the Institute of Taxation to the Committee on Taxation of Trading Profits*, p. 17.

[45] The Council of Retail Distributors, however, wanted "clear and specific rules" laid down by statute for valuing inventories. *Memorandum on the Taxation of Trading Stocks*, p. 3.

ment to allow a specific method of valuation lies clearly in the courts, and eventually a body of judicial opinion will be formulated which would provide recognized precedent on the admissible methods of inventory valuation.

In summing up, the most likely approach to the problem of inventory valuation is the consistent use of any recognized accounting procedure. The writer is unprepared to come to any hard and fast conclusion as to whether, for tax purposes, the Income Tax Act should try to lay down the procedure to be followed in broad terms,[46] or whether it should resume its former silence on the matter. A compromise would be to leave the matter to ministerial discretion, but that, too, is not always the happiest solution.

All that one can be certain of is that the problem will remain serious as long as inflationary pressures exert themselves upon the general level of prices.

2. *Valuation of Fixed Assets*

The next element of the problem of measuring business profits involves the valuation of fixed assets, which revolves around the problem of measuring the impairment of such assets.

Impairment of capital assets may take place in several ways. They wear out with use, or depreciate in value. They may become outmoded, or obsolete. And they may be depleted through piecemeal sales, such as occur in the case of mineral and timber assets. Hence the expressions depreciation, obsolescence, and depletion.

Since capital assets are impaired in one or more of these ways, it is necessary to take this impairment into consideration in computing net profit. The amount of impairment during an accounting period is a cost of doing business, just as much as the cost of labour and raw materials. Thus it should be charged against gross income. There is no confusion up to this point, and most income tax laws[47] provide for deductions which purport to show the

[46]I think, however, that if statutory provision is to be made covering the matter, it should be in general rather than specific terms. The difficulty here, though, is that of accomplishing a generality which will be meaningful.

[47]For a comparative description of depreciation for tax purposes in the major English-speaking countries, see Raymond E. Manning, "Depreciation in the Tax Laws and Practice of the United States, Australia, Canada, Great Britain, New Zealand and South Africa," *National Tax Journal*, June 1948, p. 154.

amount of capital impairment in the tax year. The difficulty arises when an attempt is made to measure the amount of impairment in a given period, and the failure to provide accurate measurement may have serious economic effects. This is the underlying problem, and the failure to achieve a generally acceptable solution has resulted in widespread dissatisfaction with the accounting treatment of capital impairment, especially in the post-war years. Each of these three types of impairment will be discussed in turn in order to indicate the complexity of the problem, and this discussion will include an examination of the way in which the impairment of capital assets is treated in Canada for tax purposes.

(a) Depreciation

(i) The problem

It is quite obvious that depreciation, unlike such costs as raw materials and wages, must be a matter of estimate, because the amount of capital impairment caused by wear and tear during an accounting period cannot be measured accurately.[48] There is not only the problem of determining the useful life of the asset (which cannot be forecast accurately); there is also the problem of determining what depreciation reserves are designed to do—recover the original cost of the asset, or provide for replacing it when it is worn out. This latter objective involves another imponderable because of the difficulty attached to forecasting (*a*) the life of the asset, and (*b*) the cost of replacing it at some future point in time. Moreover, the calculation of depreciation is affected by the maintenance policy of the company.

It has been said that "depreciation is a puzzling, prorated annual deduction of the original costs (or other bases) of consumable, and deteriorating properties spread over the assets' estimated useful lives."[49] Because it is necessarily an estimate, depreciation has been a cause of perennial controversy among manage-

[48]Groves has stated that, "The process [of estimating depreciation] involves so many variables and imponderables that it may be closer to guess-work than to estimating." *Postwar Taxation and Economic Progress*, p. 156.

[49]J. H. Landman, "The Old and New Depreciation Problem," *Taxes—The Tax Magazine*, Oct. 1949, p. 911.

ment, labour, investors, and particularly the tax collectors.[50] In recent years, with the sharply increased price level, the depreciation problem has taken on a new complexion. Traditional accounting practice treats depreciable capital assets as prepayments of future charges to the revenue of those years that they will service. No consideration is given to any variation in the replacement cost of an asset from one year to another. This practice results in little difficulty during periods of relatively stable price levels,[51] but the short-run implications for a given business in a period of inflated prices may be serious.

Since capital assets normally have a long life (one estimate is that fixed assets are turned over on the average of once in twenty-five years)[52] there is ample opportunity for a discrepancy to arise between original cost and replacement cost. This, then, is certainly a different problem to that of inventory valuation, since inventory turns over one or more times every year.

There are several important implications of depreciation policy, apart from its tax aspects. It may play an important role in decisions concerning (*a*) replacement of assets, (*b*) expansion of existing plant, and (*c*) creation of new enterprises. There is no need to expand upon these implications,[53] because it is apparent that decisions of this kind depend to a large extent on estimates of financial gain and the availability of funds. If a restrictive depreciation policy affects estimates of gain or the ability to finance plant expansion, then there is likely to be a lag in new capital formation. This raises another point that may be of major

[50]It has been stated that, in the United States, depreciation allowances occasion more controversy between taxpayers and the Bureau of Internal Revenue than any other. Financial executives participating in a questionnaire opined that controversies over depreciation provide, with one exception, the most troublesome aspect of federal tax administration. This is confirmed officially in the statement: "The determination of a fair allowance covering wear and obsolescence of assets has been one of the most troublesome problems of tax administration." United States, Congress, Joint Committee on the Economic Report, Subcommittee on Investment, *Factors Affecting Volume and Stability of Private Investment,* pp. 159-60.

[51]It has been pointed out by A. R. Prest that accountancy crystallized into a profession and accounting conventions were elevated into principles in the latter part of the nineteenth century, a period of relatively stable prices. "Replacement Cost Depreciation," *Accounting Research,* July 1950, p. 387.

[52]J. Frank Gaston, *Effects of Depreciation Policy,* p. 8.

[53]For fuller treatment of how depreciation policy affects business decisions, see Lewis H. Kimmel, *Depreciation Policy and Postwar Expansion,* pp. 32-41.

importance. The productive and taxpaying capacity of the nation depends upon capital formation—the creation of the physical factors of production. But it is difficult to determine how much capital formation is taking place if there is no accurate measurement of the capital used up in current production. The conventional measurements use two different scales on the yardstick. Capital consumption is valued at its original cost, while capital formation is valued at current cost. Thus, the accounting figures may indicate a positive increment of capital formation during an accounting period, while in reality there may have been a net capital impairment during the period.[54]

(ii) Alternative approaches

As a result of the problems inherent in the traditional historical approach to depreciation, various other proposals have been advocated in an effort to secure a method which would reflect more accurately the economic facts of a business operation. The discussion[55] has been focused, for the most part, on original cost

[54]It is not suggested that such is the case in Canada, although the quotation from the *Economist*, p. 208, above, indicates that there are grounds for real concern over this matter in the United Kingdom.

[55]Hundreds of articles and pamphlets on the problem have appeared in the last few years. They will be found in both accounting and economics journals, business periodicals and official papers. A sample of this material may be found in the following: Harold Benjamin, "A Diminishing Depreciation Method Based on a Sine Curve Works with Any Scrap Value," *Journal of Accountancy*, April 1950, p. 303; William Blackie, "What is Accounting Accounting for—Now?" *N.A.C.A. Bulletin*, July 1, 1948; S. J. Broad, "The Impact of Rising Prices upon Accounting Procedures," *Journal of Accountancy*, July 1948, p. 10; E. C. Brown, "Tax Allowances for Depreciation Based on Changes in the Price Level," *National Tax Journal*, Dec. 1948, p. 311; E. C. Brown and Gardner Patterson, "Accelerated Depreciation: A Neglected Chapter in War Taxation," *Quarterly Journal of Economics*, Aug. 1943, p. 630; M. A. Copeland, "Suitable Accounting Conventions to Determine Business Income," *Journal of Accountancy*, Feb. 1949, p. 107; J. L. Dohr, "The Next Step in Depreciation Accounting," *ibid.*, Feb. 1950, p. 114; A. C. Ellis, "Cost Basis in Accounting Must be Used or We Upset Whole Business System," *ibid.*, July 1950, p. 40; J. F. Gaston, *Effects of Depreciation Policy*; H. M. Groves, *Postwar Taxation and Economic Progress*, pp. 153-160; *Production, Jobs and Taxes*, chap. VI; Lewis H. Kimmel, *Depreciation Policy and Postwar Expansion*; J. H. Landman, "The Old and New Depreciation Problem," p. 911; J. K. Lasser and M. E. Peloubet, "Tax Accounting v. Commercial Accounting," *Journal of Accountancy*, April 1949, p. 279; George Moller, "Historic Costs—The Lesser Evil," *Canadian Chartered Accountant*, July 1949, p. 21; W. A. Paton, "Measuring Profits under Inflation Conditions: A Serious Problem for Accountants," *Journal of Accountancy*, Jan. 1950, p. 16; R. E. Paul, *Taxation for Prosperity*, chap. XL; A. R. Prest, "Replacement Cost Depreciation," p. 385; T. H. Sanders,

versus replacement cost as the basis of depreciation. But other proposals, such as accelerated depreciation and the diminishing balance method, have also received close attention—close enough, in fact, to result in specific legislation. These methods of depreciation will be discussed in turn.

Historical cost—the accounting approach. Depreciation, in the accounting sense of the word, has been defined as follows: "Depreciation, as applied to fixed property, is now a word of art, used to describe broadly the cost or expense due to all the factors which cause the ultimate retirement of property in so far as that cost is not included in current maintenance. Annual depreciation charges are an amortization of cost over useful life; they are *not* an attempt to measure a change in value; *they have nothing to do with replacement*."[56] Much of the controversy over the conventional accounting practice would be avoided if this last point were clearly understood. A prevalent misconception of the accounting use of the term is that it purports to recover the original cost of an asset in order to have the funds with which to replace it when worn out. J. H. Landman states: "In fact, it is neither a recovering nor a replacing operation. The depreciable property is in reality consumed and expended during its useful life, and it is not ordinarily replaced with the identical item because the new asset is usually more efficient and productive than the one which became

---

"Depreciation and 1949 Price Levels," *Harvard Business Review*, May 1949, p. 293; T. H. Silcock, "Accountants, Economists and the Valuation of Fixed Assets," *Economic Journal*, Sept. 1949, p. 343; and George Terborgh, *Depreciation Policy and the Postwar Price Level*.

[56]George O. May, *Financial Accounting*, p. 118; italics mine. Defined in this way, depreciation must include obsolescence, a fact recognized in the recent Canadian income tax legislation. Lewis H. Kimmel states: "The relationship between depreciation and replacement is not recognized from the strictly accounting point of view, which holds that the purpose of depreciation is merely to account for the cost of depreciable assets. According to this view, the depreciation allowance is not inherently a provision for replacement." *Depreciation Policy and Postwar Expansion*, p. 11. Another authority states that depreciation "is the accounting for a past expenditure, not a provision for a future one. The relationship between depreciation and replacements is purely coincidental—most assets are replaced at the time of retirement." Perry Mason, "Depreciation and the Financing of Replacements," *Accounting Review*, Dec. 1935, p. 320. This position indicates clearly that depreciation policy should be determined regardless of whether or not the asset would be replaced when worn out. This, to me, is entirely sensible, because who can tell at the time of acquiring a new asset whether it will ever be replaced?

worn out and obsolete. As a rule, the new assets are betterments and expansions."[57]

A better expression than depreciation, for accounting purposes, would be amortization of capital costs.[58] The term depreciation more accurately denotes the economic concept, which implies the current social value of assets.

The typical application of this principle of amortizing the cost of a depreciable asset over its useful life is the straight-line method based upon original cost. This method is predicated on the assumption that depreciation accrues at a uniform rate throughout the life of the asset. Such an assumption is quite unwarranted, of course, because it ignores the relationship between wear and tear and the volume of output, in the case of machinery, and ignores the relationship between wear and tear and maintenance. But it is defended on the grounds that it is simple, convenient, and understandable.[59] The longer the anticipated useful life of the asset, however, the less realistic this basis becomes. When an asset has an expected life over a very long period, perhaps there are good grounds for disallowing depreciation on any basis.[60]

[57]"The Old and New Depreciation Problem," p. 912.

[58]It will be noted that the new Canadian legislation makes no mention of depreciation as such. It refers only to capital cost. Section 11 (1) (*a*).

[59]Cf. May, *Financial Accounting*, p. 146, and W. A. Paton, who said that the straight-line method of depreciation "represents a consistent, understandable and highly convenient plan of procedure, and it is not surprising that it is in almost universal use. Further, in view of the fact that at best the depreciation charge is nothing more than a careful estimate the use of the straight-line method would seem to be fully justified for a great majority of cases." *Accounting*, p. 340. But Professor Paton stated in 1948, in his testimony before the Joint Committee on the Economic Report of the President, that corporate earnings are generally overstated to a significant degree. In an article written in 1949 ("Measuring Profits under Inflation Conditions: A Serious Problem for Accountants") he supports the thesis favouring a "fresh start and formal accounting adjustment" (p. 25). Mr. May also stresses the need for a fresh start because of the significant change in the value of the dollar. See *Business Income and Price Levels*.

[60]It is interesting to note the recommendation of the British Royal Commission on the Income Tax: ". . . as all material assets waste, and as no income emerges from a source which is so permanent as not to be subject to the possibility of wastage in capital value, there shall be a time limit to the recognition of wastage. In fixing this time limit regard should be paid, we think, only to that wastage which is important when considered in relation to human life and human expectation. If a man has an income which will apparently last for 60 years it is to him practically a permanent income. Contingencies happening after the lapse of a period of time exceeding 35 years appeal very little to the mind of the average

The historical cost straight-line basis of depreciation comes under the greatest and most telling attack by those who assume that depreciation is designed to create a sinking fund for the replacement of capital assets when they are worn out. Under this assumption it is quite accurate to state that during a period of sharply rising prices the reserve for replacement of assets is entirely inadequate. The argument is familiar, and goes as follows: A company which purchased assets in 1939 having an estimated life of ten years, would have charged depreciation at an annual rate of 10 per cent. In 1949 the depreciation reserve for these assets would have amounted to the original cost. But if the replacement cost of the assets were twice the original cost, the reported profit during the decade was overstated by the amount of the deficiency in depreciation charges. If such profits had been distributed as dividends, the company would have been distributing part of its capital.[61]

---

individual; for example, it is only when the period of deferment is something less than 35 years that reversionary interests begin to have any appreciable value. Moreover, the longer the life of the asset the greater the difficulty of estimating it with any reasonable approach to accuracy. These considerations, amongst others, have led us to recommend that NO ALLOWANCE SHOULD BE MADE WHEN THE LIFE OF THE WASTING ASSET IS ESTIMATED TO BE 35 YEARS OR LONGER. This is no doubt an arbitrary time limit without any special intrinsic merit, but if some period of time beyond which wastage will not be recognized is not fixed the number of minute adjustments in every class of income will become so great that it will almost disintegrate the administration of the tax. We think that a period of time which approximately covers a generation is a fair time limit to impose." *Report,* 1920, p. 42.

[61]Mr. George D. Bailey, a past president of the American Institute of Accountants, told the Joint Committee on the Economic Report of the President: "In my experience as an accountant I have seen the cash reserves of many companies eliminated and borrowings required because the necessary replacements of plant had to be made at current high prices." National City Bank of New York, *Monthly Letter on Economic Conditions,* Jan. 1949, p. 6. The extent to which depreciation is understated in the United States is indicated in a widely quoted estimate by George O. May, who said that in 1947 depreciation provisions fell some $2 billion short of the amount required to cover depreciation on current replacement costs. "Restudy of Concepts and Terminology of Business Income," *New York Certified Public Accountant,* Jan. 1948. Professor Slichter's estimate was $1 billion for 1947, and $1.3 billion for 1946, *supra,* p. 212.

Mr. E. M. Voorhees, Chairman of the Finance Committee, United States Steel Corporation, told the Joint Committee on the Economic Report: "It is a very real and very simple fact that corporate understatement in costs of the worth of the tools of production that are consumed in production can mean in the end nothing but hidden and serious erosion of the Nation's tools of production. Yet these tools are vital to the welfare of all of us. They should be expanded, or at the very least, they must be kept intact.

It is concluded that straight-line depreciation based on historical cost is a simple and rough allocation of capital asset impairment over the life of the asset. It is not meant to provide a fund for replacing the asset when it is worn out, and during an inflationary period it certainly does not provide for such replacement because of the wide spread between original and replacement cost.

There are serious implications attached to this method both for the individual business and for the national economy. In the first instance, the failure to understand the real nature and results of this method of depreciation may result in capital impairment as taxes are paid on and dividends paid out of the fictitious profits calculated on the historical cost basis. In the second instance, the method probably affects the volume of capital replacements, the volume of capital additions, and the incentive to invest in new enterprises.

Accelerated depreciation has been proposed as a measure to allow corporations (and other businesses) to charge against income an amount of depreciation sufficient to offset rises in the replacement cost of equipment, regardless of the actual impairment of assets during an accounting period. Advocates of accelerated depreciation have made proposals ranging from complete freedom for the business man to select and perhaps vary his annual charge from year to year, to a more restricted form of depreciation which would shorten the period over which the asset is written off, and would limit the freedom to vary the annual charge.[62] Conceivably an asset might be written off completely in

---

"I can understand the committee's very serious interest in proper accounting for the cost of the tools of production consumed, for the present nonrecognition of part of that cost in computing taxable income means that the Federal Government itself is participating in, and even forcing, the erosion of the Nation's tools of production. More than that, those who would avoid that erosion in the management of their own enterprises are compelled not only to provide against it, dollar for dollar, but for every dollar of disallowed cost they must find an additional 67 cents for the Government in taxes." *Corporate Profits*, pp. 597-8.

[62]One proposal, made by Admiral Ben Morell of the Jones and Laughlin Steel Corporation, would permit companies to write off up to one-half the cost of equipment within one to five years as they choose, and to claim this amortization charge as a deductible item for tax purposes. A limit to the annual charge would be set at one-half the taxable income before any charge for depreciation for the year. Cf. Gaston, *Effects of Depreciation Policy*, p. 21. It is interesting to note the steps taken by some American companies. The United States Steel Corporation in

one or two years, thus reducing taxes and enhancing the cash position of the company while the heavy depreciation charges were being made.

Accelerated depreciation circumvents the criticism that has been made of most of the plans devised to alleviate the depreciation problem under conditions of changing price levels because it is based upon historical cost, and the amount that can be charged against income cannot exceed the original cost of the asset.

It is argued that accelerated depreciation promotes investment in the following ways: (1) it reduces the risk of investment and encourages capital outlays which otherwise would not have been made, thereby stimulating employment and business activity; (2) it speeds up replacement of plant and machinery, not merely when it is physically obsolete, but also when it is economically obsolete, thus promoting new techniques and innovations; (3) in certain forms it spreads replacement and additions more evenly over the different stages of the business cycle; and (4) it stimulates investment by small and growing enterprises.[63]

It is by no means self-evident, however, that the use of accelerated depreciation would stimulate business investment. One view is that the only condition under which accelerated depreciation would have a stimulating effect would be a general anticipa-

---

1947 charged extra depreciation in the amount of 30 per cent of the normal depreciation (this amounted to an extra charge of $26.3 million), and in 1948 another extra charge was made amounting to 60 per cent of the normal charge (this amounted to an extra charge of $55.3 million). *Annual Report,* 1948. More recently the Corporation has adopted an accelerated rate of 10 per cent of the cost of equipment in the first two years. No acceleration is used if operations fall below 70 per cent of capacity. Gaston, *Effects of Depreciation Policy,* p. 36. Effective January 1, 1948, the du Pont Company instituted a policy of accelerating depreciation of the cost of post-war facilities. The amount of accelerated amortization was $17.9 million in 1948. *Annual Report,* 1948. The Chrysler Corporation in 1947 increased its depreciation charges by about 60 per cent, in accordance with a policy of accelerated depreciation determined on the basis of amortizing over a three-year period a portion of the cost of post-war facilities. See May, *Business Income and Price Levels,* p. 51. This extra depreciation was not, of course, deductible for tax purposes. Indeed, in view of the disapproving attitude of the Securities and Exchange Commission, the du Pont Co. filed an amended *Report* for 1947, showing income greater than that shown in its regular report to the shareholders by $20.9 million.

[63]See Randolph E. Paul, *Taxation for Prosperity,* p. 378.

tion of lower tax rates in the future.[64] This judgment is probably over-conservative. It seems quite obvious that the risk incurred through expansion could be reduced if a large part of the cost of new equipment could be written off during the early years of its use. But the possibility of increases in the tax rate is an important factor in determining whether accelerated depreciation really will reduce risks.[65] If a company's fixed assets are charged off early in their lives, and taxes are increased substantially at a later period, when no depreciation charges remain, the company then will have been penalized by acceleration, assuming that the assets are still used in the company's operations. A way out of this situation would be to dispose of the assets after they had been charged off, and replace them with new and depreciable items. Whether this would result in long-run saving would depend upon a number of variables. But there are presumptive grounds for believing that management might well be advised to consider all aspects of the question in deciding upon policy.

It is quite possible that the use of accelerated depreciation would induce companies to replace old equipment sooner than they would under straight-line depreciation. The lower the figure at which assets are carried on a company's books, the less is likely to be the resistance to replacement. In the United States, during the thirties, depreciation allowances were tightened considerably by the Bureau of Internal Revenue. As a result of this policy it is alleged that asset replacements were deferred.[66]

A number of objections have been made to the use of accelerated depreciation. For instance, Mr. Randolph Paul writes:

The American Institute of Accountants fears that high initial depreciation rates on new machinery might lead to unnecessary abandonment

[64]See Brown and Patterson, "Accelerated Depreciation: A Neglected Chapter in War Taxation," pp. 630-45. Cited by Groves, *Postwar Taxation and Economic Progress*, p. 159.

[65]There seem to be good grounds, however, for maintaining that the accelerated depreciation policy of the federal government during the war and post-war years was an important factor in the expansion of physical plant. For an American view, see the National Industrial Conference Board's study, *Effects of Taxes upon Corporate Policy*, pp. 35-6.

[66]Professor Groves indicates that in 1941 "70 per cent of machine tools on hand were 10 years of age or older, and the average age was high even in the modern factories." *Postwar Taxation and Economic Progress*, p. 157.

of much useful equipment, cause unforeseen competitive advantages and "influence businessmen to undertake transactions with an eye to tax savings rather than sound economic policy." The institute holds that when costs properly attributable to a future year are permitted to be anticipated for tax purposes, taxable income is understated for the earlier year and overstated for the later year. If tax rates go down, the businessman will have enjoyed a subsidy at the expense of taxpayers in general; if they go up, he will have suffered a penalty. The institute believes that present disparities between taxable income and business income have brought about an undesirable condition which "will not be improved by introducing new subsidies or incentives into the tax system."[67]

The opposite view is taken by Mr. W. L. Hearne, Tax Supervisor of the United States Steel Corporation, who states: "I urge, then, for your consideration that taxpayers should be allowed to take whatever amount of depreciation they wish, and in whatever year they wish, so long as it is against taxable income, and so long as it does not exceed one hundred per cent."[68]

The truth of the matter probably lies somewhere between these two viewpoints. The experience gained from the wartime use of accelerated depreciation indicates that it merits careful consideration as a peacetime measure. In most cases the treasury would suffer a postponement rather than a loss of tax revenue. But the postponement of taxes on income currently earned would have effects on the current budgetary position of the government. Careful estimates of the impact of any proposal for depreciation acceleration on the current government revenue position are an indispensable component of policy making.

A limited use of accelerated depreciation is allowed under the Canadian tax law. Double depreciation is permissible in the case of certain types of assets constructed between 1944 and 1949. This policy was designed to facilitate rehabilitation and avoid a post-war slump by encouraging capital expenditures. Whether there is real justification for a reapplication of the double depreciation policy now is a point over which there is bound to be disagreement. On strictly economic grounds, there are good reasons for avoiding it, which apply also to the other proposals for

[67]*Taxation for Prosperity*, pp. 378-9.

[68]"Depreciation, Depletion, and Research and Development Costs," *How Should Corporations be Taxed?* p. 153.

new depreciation policy. They will be discussed in the concluding remarks in this section. One is inclined to agree with Professor Groves's sensible comment that accelerated depreciation "might be used effectively as a depression remedy, and it should be held in reserve for application in extreme cases."[69] Accelerated depreciation does accomplish the immediate need—the correction of the overstatement of income—and still pays lip service to the conventional rule of original cost. But it is not a permanent solution, because its correction of profit overstatement is accomplished by increasing at an accelerated rate the understatement of capital that occurs when it is held that there has not been any change in the value of the dollar.

Depreciation based on replacement cost. A much discussed proposal emanating out of the depreciation controversy is the substitution of replacement cost for original cost as the basis of computing depreciation. This proposal is resisted generally by members of the accounting profession[70] and by the tax administration. The pros and cons are worth examination.

The reasoning behind the proposals favouring the replacement cost method is based, consciously or otherwise, on the presumption that there should be a change in the concept of depreciation. As indicated earlier, the traditional accounting concept is that depreciation is designed to recover the original cost of a depreciable asset. It is now argued that depreciation should, in one way or another, effect the recovery of the replacement cost. The fact that this proposal would result in tax reductions lends it popular support, and perhaps the tax aspects of the proposal are not so incidental as some writers appear to believe.

This new conceptual approach is played in two keys, one of which is a highly refined theoretical (economic) variation on the theme, based upon the economic concept of income and capital. It embraces the problem of estimating capital consumption. Since

[69]*Production, Jobs and Taxes*, p. 65.

[70]But a minority, including some of its leaders, advocate replacement cost. See, for example, George O. May, "Should the LIFO Principle be Considered in Depreciation Accounting When Prices Vary Widely?" *Journal of Accountancy*, Dec. 1947, p. 453; W. A. Paton, "Depreciation and the Price Level," *Accounting Review*, April 1948, p. 118, and "Measuring Profits under Inflation Conditions: A Serious Problem for Accountants," p. 16 (in this article he says that "the profession has missed the boat in this matter," p. 19).

the economist is interested in estimating national income, he must make corrections for price level changes. Strict accounting practice is inadequate from his viewpoint. It is argued that the kind of adjustments that have to be made in order to determine real social income should be applied in the computation of the profits of a business.[71]

The other line of argument is based on the sinking fund theory of depreciation, and points at the direct consequences resulting from failure to provide for the replacement of capital assets. It is argued that management should always accumulate sufficient funds by depreciation charges to replace depreciable assets when they are worn out or obsolete.[72]

From the economists' viewpoint, replacement cost accounting is indeed quite likely to provide a more accurate measurement of national or social income than is the ordinary accounting practice. Moreover, the economic concept of income certainly has relevance for the individual corporation, because any measure of income from current output must take into account the implications for future production, just as the measurement of national income must take into account any implied encroachment on future income. But there are limitations to the complete extension of the economic concept of income to the individual business unit even though it is a "microcosm of society." As Prest has pointed out,

> It is *not* good economics to apply a social concept of income *simpliciter* to the business corporation. From the viewpoint of society the structure of debits and credits so characteristic of modern economies cancels out (apart from loans from or to foreigners, of course), and therefore the relevant concept of "capital" is the sum total of physical assets. But for the individual firm the position is not the same, and the simple fact that the firm has obligations to its shareholders—the principal one being to assure the solvency of the firm rather than the extent of its

[71]A. R. Prest, in an excellent article, summarizes this viewpoint in the following words: "In other words one can regard business corporations today as a microcosm of society at large and therefore the principles relevant for measuring capital consumption in a social sense are directly relevant to business enterprise too." "Replacement Cost Depreciation," p. 388.

[72]George Terborgh has proposed a more subtle version of this argument by stating that depreciation should be designed to preserve intact the real value of the money capital originally subscribed, in terms of some index of purchasing power, rather than the stock of physical assets corresponding to that money capital. *Depreciation Policy and the Postwar Price Level.*

future operations—as well as to society as a whole, must always be remembered. Indeed, it can reasonably be maintained that many, if not all, firms when faced with a difficult decision ask themselves primarily the effect on the structure of their assets, as measured by, for example, the ratio of current assets to current liabilities or the effect on their relations with their shareholders rather than the effect on income from trading ten years hence.[73]

It seems neither desirable nor possible to invoke the economic concept of social income in the attempt to measure business profits. The two things are essentially different, and it should be kept in mind that the national income is not the aggregate of all personal and business incomes. When corrections have been made for transfer payments and receipts (and this is necessary for national income purposes), the basic difference is apparent. The practical difficulties of trying to effect a reconciliation of two fundamentally different concepts rule out this argument for measuring depreciation on the basis of replacement cost.

The argument that corporations should follow a policy designed to preserve intact their supply of physical assets (or the real value of the original money capital) has an attractive appeal. But the use of this argument to support a particular depreciation policy is a clear indication of the confusion that exists over the real nature of depreciation. The accounting and tax concept of depreciation is not concerned with the capital assets required for future production. It is not concerned with whether a company will continue its operations indefinitely, requiring capital replacements and additions, or whether it will wind up shortly, or reorganize. It is concerned only with amortizing the cost of these depreciable assets that have been used *in the past.* So that any attempt to use depreciation as an instrument with which to prepay uncertain future charges clearly violates the amortization principle of depreciation. The sinking fund concept of depreciation is therefore unacceptable.[74]

[73]"Replacement Cost Depreciation," p. 390.

[74]I find it extremely difficult to rationalize the deduction of depreciation on assets not yet built from current income for tax purposes. There is definitely a real problem connected with the computation of taxable profits in an inflationary period, but to approach it from the viewpoint of replacement cost depreciation seems to me to be putting the cart before the horse. Furthermore, the possibility of charging off more than 100 per cent of an asset's cost smacks of legerdemain that had better

Even if depreciation were admittedly a proper means of providing for replacement of assets, it is by no means certain that the replacement cost basis is the best or even a manageable way to achieve that end. The argument is based on the thesis that the corporation should place its accounting on a replacement cost basis in order to be certain of having "sufficient" cash for future replacements of assets. This argument is something of a red herring, when it is remembered that depreciation funds are only one of several means of financing replacement of capital equipment.[75] Companies usually have liquid resources available through capital or earned surplus, and of course many companies have access to the capital market for funds for this purpose. One further observation is that if depreciation charges on a replacement cost basis are not earned, there might be no liquid funds available for replacement, despite the most meticulous and conscientious accounting.

The practical difficulties of developing a workable method of applying price changes to fixed asset accounts are very considerable. Since the depreciation of existing assets will have been based upon original cost, during a period of rising prices provisions for subsequent years will have to be increased, not merely to the full proportionate amounts due for such subsequent years, but to amounts which will compensate for the deficiency during the earlier years. This may result in very high depreciation provisions if the greater part of the asset's life has expired prior to the adjustment.

If a system of depreciation based upon replacement costs were

---

be kept out of accounting practice. George Moller's views are worth noting: "What do those enterprises with cheaply bought fixed assets really want? They want to retain part of their profits which they feel they will need for replacing their cheaply bought, outworn assets in times of high prices.

"There are two fallacies in the problem: 1. At the time when they will actually replace the assets, which may be anytime from 1 to 49 years from now, prices may have come down, perhaps to pre-war level and lower. In Canada they can retain their profits less 35% or 37% taxes. What they really want therefore is a relief from the 35%-37% taxes. Why not call a spade a spade and ask for such a relief?" ("Historic Costs—The Lesser Evil," p. 24).

[75]George Terborgh indicates that only about 50 per cent of the cost of capital replacement in the United States is financed in this way. *The Bogey of Economic Maturity*, p. 127, cited by Prest, "Replacement Cost Depreciation," p. 393. Quite obviously corporations do not maintain liquid depreciation reserves in anything like the amount of depreciation charged.

introduced, it might cause serious difficulties during a downward swing in the price level. A company which had been charging high depreciation in anticipation of high replacement costs might find that on the downswing its past depreciation charges had in the aggregate exceeded the cost of replacement, and thus be penalized with heavier taxes.

On balance, both from a theoretical and a practical viewpoint, the disadvantages of replacement cost seem to outweigh the advantages claimed for it by its advocates.

The revaluation of fixed assets. Another proposal[76] for dealing with profit overstatement is the revaluation of fixed assets in accordance with their current "value." The newly determined values would then be used as the basis for depreciation. In a period of inflation the book values of assets would be written up, and presumably they would be written down under conditions of serious deflation.

In addition to the inherent weakness of the proposal, it would be extremely difficult to carry out, on a physical appraisal basis or by means of index number adjustments. Physical appraisals are costly and time-consuming, and, of course, represent only the appraiser's best judgment in the final analysis. The use of some index number adjustment would be less difficult, but it presupposes the availability of satisfactory indexes, and that they would be satisfactory for adjusting the values of assets acquired over a long time interval.

The arbitrary write-up of assets is not novel. The accounting profession in the United States countenanced the write-up of assets in the inflationary period of the twenties, and their write-down in the depressed thirties. Fixed assets were written up in Austria between 1922 and 1924, in Germany in 1924, in France in 1945,[77] and in Italy in 1946. But the procedure has had little

[76]See Bernard M. Berry, "Appreciation of Fixed Assets," *Accountant*, Feb. 21, 1948, p. 138; E. B. Nortcliffe, "Revision of Balance Sheets in France," *ibid.*, June 25, 1949, p. 532; and H. W. Sweeney, *Stabilized Accounting*, pp. 219 ff.

[77]The 1945 revision was followed by two further upward revisions in 1948 and 1949. Businesses generally have been empowered, but not required, to revalue their fixed assets. Even assets which have been written off completely may be revalued if still usable. There is no fixed plan of revaluation, but the law lays down a maximum amount of revaluation. The maximums are expressed in terms of coefficients, which are different for each year, and range from 1 in 1948 to 108

success in correcting the evils which follow monetary inflation.[78]

About the only point that can be made in favour of revaluing fixed assets in a period of inflation is that the greater depreciation charges resulting from the increased valuation would reduce corporate profits and taxes. The method does not solve the problem of replacing assets, and the basic principle of allowing management to alter balance sheet valuations of capital assets seems repugnant to currently accepted accounting concepts.

The diminishing balance: The Canadian approach. The diminishing balance method of depreciation introduced into the Canadian law in 1949 is based on historical or original cost. Each year a fixed percentage is charged for depreciation, but it is not a percentage of the original cost. It is a fixed percentage of what remains of the original cost after deducting the depreciation of preceding years. Thus, an asset costing $1,000 and depreciated at the rate of 10 per cent would be depreciated $100 in the first year, $90 in the second year (10 per cent of $1,000 – $100), $81 in the third year, and so on. An asset can never be completely written off under this plan, but eventually it can be reduced to an amount which approaches zero. There is no need for depreciation reserves under this system.

The use of the diminishing balance method involves substantially higher depreciation rates than used under the straight-line system because of the diminishing base to which the rates are applied. A substantial part of the cost of an asset is thereby charged off in the early years of its use. The new rates in Canada are, generally speaking, double those used under the old straight-line system, so in the early years an asset is depreciated at a much higher rate than formerly. For example, a comparison of the 5 per cent rate under the new method with the 2½ per cent rate

---

for 1914 and earlier. The original cost of an asset is multiplied by the factor applying to the year of its purchase. Thus, an asset acquired in 1940 at a cost of a million francs could be revalued at thirteen times its cost. For details of the plan, see Nortcliffe, "Revision of Balance Sheets in France," p. 532.

[78]See Landman, "The Old and New Depreciation Problem," p. 917. S. J. Broad says in opposition to the plan, "Economic adjustments following World War I resulted in the appraisal write-up of the 1920's and the write-downs of the 1930's. This solution brought as many new problems as it solved and its imperfections have led most of us who went through those eras to say 'Never again.'" "The Impact of Rising Prices upon Accounting Procedures," p. 17.

under the old method indicates that higher annual charges accrue under the new method for the first fourteen years, resulting in progressively lower undepreciated capital cost. After fourteen years the relatively higher annual charges under the straight-line method narrow the divergence, and the balances are approximately equal by the end of the thirty-second year.

Prior to 1949 the Canadian tax law specifically disallowed the deduction of capital costs from income, and then made exceptions to the general rule by providing for such depreciation and depletion deductions as the Minister in his discretion might allow.[79] The regulations drawn up by the Department of National Revenue followed very closely the established principles of good accounting practice,[80] and provided for depreciation rates applicable to the original cost of depreciable assets in accordance with the straight-line depreciation method. This method possessed all the disadvantages that were discussed earlier. One especially inequitable feature of it was the inability of the taxpayer to charge off obsolete, idle, or discarded capital assets. No allowance was provided for obsolescence.

The new legislation does not provide specifically for depreciation or obsolescence as such. Indeed, there is no mention of the word depreciation in the law. The governing principle is the amortization of the costs of depreciable capital assets.[81] The law now provides under Section 11 (1)(*a*) for the deduction of "such part of the capital cost to the taxpayer of property, or such amount in respect of the capital cost to the taxpayer of property,

[79]There was always objection to this principle of ministerial discretion. A. W. Gilmour writes: "For many years the old *Income War Tax Act* and the procedure thereunder were subject to strong criticism on the grounds that many allowances were only made by virtue of the exercise of ministerial discretion, and many of us felt that perhaps our competitor was getting a better deal than we were." "Diminishing Balance Depreciation under the Income Tax Act," *Canadian Chartered Accountant*, June 1950, p. 274.

[80]To such an extent, says Gilmour, "that most taxpayers and accountants simply set up their records to conform to these rules, and seldom gave a thought to whether the maximum rates of depreciation established for tax purposes bore any reasonable relationship to the rates required for their own business." *Ibid.*, p. 273.

[81]The intention of the new legislation is to provide for the amortization of all *depreciable* assets. It does not provide for the amortization of all capital outlay. For example, the cost of land may not be charged against income, and property not acquired by the taxpayer to produce income may not be depreciated.

if any, as is allowed by regulation."[82] The details are provided by regulations,[83] which establish twelve classes of assets to which the diminishing balance system applies. The depreciation rates range from 4 per cent in Class 1, to 100 per cent in Class 12.[84]

An important feature of the system is that when a taxpayer has a number of assets in the same class, all the assets in that class are grouped together as one unit for depreciation purposes, and all losses and all gains on disposal apply, not to the asset disposed of, but to the relative group asset account.

Since virtually all capital outlay may now be charged against income, it is only reasonable to ensure that the deductions for amortizing the cost of an asset will not exceed the final proven cost of the asset to the taxpayer. Clearly the proper amount of an asset's cost that a taxpayer should be allowed to amortize is the final net cost of that asset. The principle involved is simply that the taxpayer may recover its net cost to him, and no more.

An entirely new section was, therefore, written into the Income Tax Act to provide for recapture of excessive amortization. Section 20 provides that when a capital asset is sold for a price in excess of the undepreciated capital cost immediately before the sale, the taxpayer pays on the lesser of (*a*) the excess of the selling price over the undepreciated capital cost, or (*b*) the excess of the original cost price over the undepreciated capital cost. Thus, if a taxpayer acquires an asset at a cost of $100,000 in 1950, charges off $50,000 in depreciation by 1960, and sells the asset in that year for $120,000, he would pay tax in 1960 on $50,000.[85]

[82]This represents a marked change from the former treatment of depreciation. It is a decided departure from the engineering concept of depreciation as compensation for the physical wear and tear on assets actually in use and being worn out, which implies that no depreciation accrues unless the assets are in use.

[83]Embodied in Parts XI and XVII of the Income Tax Regulations, published in the *Canada Gazette*, Dec. 28, 1949; Feb. 22, April 12, and June 14, 1950.

[84]There are in addition three other classes, dealing with leasehold property; patents, franchises, and licences; and property acquired for the purpose of removing timber from a timber limit of no further use to the taxpayer after completion of that specific operation. Property in these three classes is not depreciated on a strictly diminishing balance basis.

[85]The formula works as follows:

(*a*) Selling price	$120,000	(*b*) Original cost	$100,000
Undepreciated capital cost	50,000	Undepreciated capital cost	50,000
Excess	$ 70,000	Excess	$ 50,000

The extra $20,000 received by the taxpayer is pure capital gain and not taxable. It is important to note that this provision does not represent the introduction of an element of capital gains taxation. It is merely a levy to recover excessive depreciation charged in years past.

The new system is effective for 1949 and subsequent years. It is not retroactive, so that all depreciable assets acquired prior to 1949 are deemed to have been acquired at the beginning of the 1949 taxation year at a cost equal to their undepreciated capital cost. No recapture of depreciation will be claimed prior to 1949.

In summing up his remarks on the diminishing balance system, the Minister of Finance said: "I believe that these principles which I have outlined will mean a great improvement over the old system and will be a further step towards greater simplicity in our system of taxing business profits. There should be a real reduction in the accounting work both for business concerns and the tax department as well. The system will likewise be more equitable to the taxpayer and to the treasury."[86]

It is too early to secure an over-all picture of the results of this new policy. In the case of taxpayers whose assets are relatively new, the initial result will be a substantially greater depreciation, with a corresponding reduction in tax. But in the case of taxpayers who have already charged off more than half the cost of their assets, their annual depreciation will now be less than before 1949. Since the depreciation rates were doubled in most cases, the break-even point is roughly where 50 per cent of the cost has already been written off. In view of the very heavy new capital formation in Canada since the war, it appears that for the first few years of the new plan total depreciation charges will be greater than before. But this will gradually be reduced as the balances are diminished. If the corporate tax rate continues to rise, the diminishing balance system as it is applied to old assets will result in proportionately heavier taxes than would have been paid under the straight-line system.

The diminishing balance method does ensure that the capital cost of a depreciable asset is recovered by the taxpayer by deducting it from income, regardless of whether or not it is in use.

[86]*House of Commons Debates*, March 22, 1950, p. 1800.

Moreover, the obsolescence problem is solved. But it does not touch the basic difficulty of inflated profits resulting from undervaluation of fixed assets, since it is based upon original and not replacement cost. It has been criticized as being a deviation from "good" accounting practice,[87] for being inappropriate,[88] and for being complex.[89]

The diminishing balance method has been used in the United Kingdom for a long period of years. In 1945, commenting on the new proposals for depreciation made by the Council of the Institute of Chartered Accountants in England and Wales, the *Accountant* stated (January 13, 1945):

> The outstanding point that will at once catch the attention of every reader is that the time-honoured reducing balance system is now so thoroughly deposed from its former popularity that it is not admitted even to be a second-rate alternative; it disappears from the scene, unwept, unhonoured and unsung. A long time has elapsed since an authority attracted the criticism of the incredulous by remarking that the plan had 'not one redeeming feature.' . . . Even the walls of the citadel at Somerset House now show signs of crumbling and it is high time that accountancy science should lead the Inland Revenue rather than follow an obedient lamb to the slaughter.
>
> Pride of place is therefore now given to the straight-line method whereby the total foreseen depreciation is allocated equally to successive periods of time.

[87]". . . the new regulations concerning deduction of capital cost are purely taxation regulations and in many instances have departed a long way from what most of us consider to be good accounting treatment of depreciation." A. W. Gilmour, "Diminishing Balance Depreciation under the Income Tax Act," p. 274.

[88]Gerhard J. Mayer says, "With its effect of rapid write-down during the first years, it must be considered a relic from the days when balance sheet presentation was the primary objective and conservatism a cardinal virtue of accountants. It is out of date at a time when comparability of income statements occupies the foreground. . . . It may be doubted even whether that application satisfies the basic requirement that it clearly reflect income. The idea that years of high earnings or productivity should bear a larger share of depreciation, loses sight of the rule that depreciation comes not after, but before, profits." "Declining Balance Depreciation," *Taxes—The Tax Magazine*, Feb. 1947, p. 170.

[89]George Moller, in commenting on the new Canadian law, said that "generally speaking, one is tempted to question the point whether there were not simpler ways and means available to the Department to implement the basic idea of the taxpayer being entitled to the recovery of his total capital outlay, but not to tax free capital gains out of depreciation provisions. The burden on the accountant in carrying out the involved procedure may not be commensurate to the advantages ostensibly granted the taxpayer." "The New Income Tax Regulations on Allowance of Capital Cost (Depreciation)," *Cost and Management*, Jan. 1950.

The British income tax law now allows the taxpayer to depreciate either on a diminishing balance basis or on a historical cost straight-line basis. It is doubtful if the accountants' criticism of the British plan would have been levelled at the Canadian legislation, because the latter, through its unique grouping of all assets in a given class into one account against which depreciation is charged, makes the Canadian procedure very simple.

It is too early to appraise the results of the new Canadian legislation. On balance, however, it appears to be constructive. It is simple, and on the face of it, seems to provide considerably more equity than the old law.

(iii) Conclusions

The problem of computing depreciation accurately enough to reflect the actual impairment of capital in a given year is difficult, to say the least. Its seriousness is intensified during a long period of rising prices and high taxes because of the overstatement of profits and the resulting increase in the tax burden. Inadequate depreciation charges result in the failure to recover impaired capital, and when this happens, part of the corporate income tax falls on capital or surplus instead of on income.

There is no magic formula which can convert monetary accounting, on which the corporation tax is based, into economic accounting, and much of the controversy over depreciation hinges upon the meaning given to the term depreciation. Much, if not all, of the agitation for replacement cost depreciation and the other proposals of like nature springs from an understandable desire to secure tax reductions. But it does not appear that the problem is serious enough in Canada to warrant any such concession.

The economic consequences of allowing additional depreciation before tax merit consideration. Any of the plans examined above would, of course, reduce tax payments and increase the working capital of companies. This might result in increased inflationary pressure, depending upon how the funds were used. If they were used for debt retirement or the building up of cash balances, the result would be non-inflationary. But if, as appears more likely, these funds were used to finance accumulation of inventories and capital goods, or for increased dividend payments, the net result might be the addition of considerably more inflationary pressure.

The argument used by the Government when it provided for accelerated depreciation in 1944 may now be used to oppose any further extension of the principle. The Minister of Reconstruction and Supply made the following statement:

> Among fiscal incentives was the provision introduced on November 10, 1944, for special depreciation under the Income War Tax Act for industrial investment primarily designed to aid the conversion, modernization and expansion of Canadian industry in the transition period. The purpose of this provision was to encourage industrial growth by reducing the tax load of investing companies at a time when income and excess profit taxes were high, investment costs were rising, and the risks involved in making large capital outlay were considered great because of the uncertainty of the future.[90]

Thus, government policy was frankly designed to stimulate private investment, and the special depreciation allowance effecting a tax credit was one of the weapons employed. The current inflation now appears to dictate a policy of high taxation rather than a lower burden. For this reason any change from the historical cost basis of depreciation for tax purposes seems at this time to be unwise.

Even if it were possible to work out the appalling complications of the adjustment of fixed asset valuation for price level changes, there would still be disadvantages attached to the principle. From the viewpoint of equity, it would increase the capricious differences between companies attributable to price level changes. From the economic viewpoint, it would probably release further inflationary pressures. And from the fiscal viewpoint, it would entail substantial revenue loss at a time when government requirements are rising sharply because of defence commitments.

This is not to say, however, that companies should not create special reserves for the purpose of replacing capital equipment.

[90]Department of Reconstruction and Supply, *Encouragement to Industrial Expansion in Canada: Operation of Special Depreciation Provisions*, p. 3. Between November 10, 1944, and March 31, 1947, special depreciation was approved for a total investment expenditure of $1.4 million. This was almost three times as much as was approved during the war years. *Ibid.*, p. 4.

In many instances such provision might well be a "must" of sound managerial policy. But there seems to be no sound reason for extending a tax credit for such special reserves at this time. The taxing authorities should keep clearly in mind, however, the desirability of allowing a company to have enough net profit, after taxes, to provide for the maintenance and replacement of its capital assets, and to pay a reasonable dividend to its shareholders.

(*b*) Obsolescence

Obsolescence occurs when a capital asset becomes out of date, or obsolete. For accounting purposes, obsolescence may be said to take two forms, normal and abnormal. Normal obsolescence is treated as part of depreciation. It is the impairment of capital resulting from predictable changes or improvements that will occur in an industry. Abnormal obsolescence, on the other hand, is the result of a sudden and unpredictable invention or innovation, or change in demand, which decreases the value of an asset. Most obsolescence is of this kind, and quite unpredictable.

Obsolescence is likely to be important in industries with a high risk factor, and a proper allowance for extraordinary obsolescence should be provided for such types of business. It is a charge which should properly be made against past rather than future income, and is an argument for the principle of loss carry-back. The carry-back of losses occasioned by extraordinary obsolescence would involve reopening of dead accounts, and the administrative inconvenience involved would probably be prohibitive. Therefore it does not seem feasible or wise to adopt the carry-back system simply because of obsolescence. It would be better, probably, to charge obsolescence against future income. In reality it is a special kind of depreciation, and so long as this form of capital impairment is recovered, it does not make much difference at what time the recovery takes place. The important point is the need for recovery.

Until 1949 the Canadian tax law took no cognizance of obsolescence. But it is now recognized under the decreasing balance depreciation procedure, which guarantees to the taxpayer the recovery of the capital cost of an asset. Since assets are now depreciated heavily during the early years of their use, the obsolescence factor is given early recognition. One of the most attractive features of the new legislation is that it does meet this problem.

(*c*) Depletion

Depletion is a special type of capital impairment resulting from the piecemeal sale of a wasting asset, or, to put it another way, resulting from the exhaustion of natural resources through extractive processes. Depletion is thus distinct from depreciation, because it applies only to certain types of assets, i.e., those used in the extractive industries, the chief of which are mining and lumbering. It also differs from depreciation in that it relates to property that has not been created by an expenditure of capital.

Quantitatively depletion is, of course, much less important in accounting than depreciation, but it presents more points of interest and raises problems in the proper determination of taxable income which are very formidable indeed. The calculation of depletion is complicated in many cases, because of the virtual impossibility of forecasting the life of the asset, as well as the uncertainty of future prices and production costs. For accounting purposes it might be just as useful sometimes to make no provision for depletion. Where the mineral content of a property is highly uncertain, any estimate of depletion is wholly conjectural, and the accounting statement resulting from the inclusion of depletion may be of no greater use than a statement omitting a calculation for depletion, and saying so explicitly. There are cases, such as many iron and coal mines, which form the basis of the steel industry, where the minerals are measureable, and may be considered as analogous to inventories. Depletion is meaningful in such cases, and should be charged.

Depletion, being the recovery of the impairment of a wasting asset due to the process of extraction, raises much the same problems concerning the method of recovery as were discussed in connection with depreciation. It has been suggested by one authority that, "It can fairly be argued that for the purposes of amortization, a mine may be regarded as analogous to a terminable annuity. This would mean that the amount to be written off in the first year of n years of assumed life would be the difference between the value of an annuity of n years and the value of one for $n-1$ years. However, the perhaps less logical but more conservative alternative of amortizing the investment on the basis of a uniform rate per unit is almost universally employed in practice."[91] This method of charging depletion on a basis of a fixed charge per unit may very well be excessive in the case of a property with a long probable life. As suggested above, there may be no reasonable ground for charging depreciation on an asset with a life expectancy of, say, more than fifty years. The same view may be taken with respect to depletion.

The inherent difficulty attached to a proper or reasonable determination of depletion is that of determining the true value of a mining property and forecasting its life. In the case of some mining properties, the problem cannot be resolved accurately. On the other hand, it is possible to secure reasonably precise depletion figures in the case of timber limits.

The depletion regulations in Canada accord different treatment to different extractive industries, and two different methods of depletion are used. The first of these is related to capital cost, as in depreciation. It is designed to allow the taxpayer to recover his capital cost, and recapture provisions ensure that the treasury recovers any excessive depletion upon the ultimate disposal of the property. The second method has no relation to capital cost, and there are no recapture provisions for this type of depreciation.

Capital cost depletion. This method is applied to taxpayers working timber limits or industrial mineral mines based on bedded deposits. Such property is capable of a physical survey, and a close estimate can be made of the output that can be produced commercially.

In the case of timber limits, depletion may be computed on the basis of a rate per cord or board foot of timber cut during the taxation year. The rate is determined by dividing the undepreciated capital cost of the property, less the residual value, by the estimated number of board feet or cords. This rate is then applied to the number of board feet or cords cut in the taxation year. The other class of property to which this method is applied is called industrial mineral mines, or bedded deposits. This group

[91]May, *Financial Accounting*, p. 152.

includes clay, gravel, gypsum, sand, sodium sulphate, and peat.[92] The depletion rate is determined by dividing the capital cost of the property, less its estimated residual value, by the estimated number of commercially mineable minerals in the property. This rate is applied to the annual output of the mine.

The method of capital cost depletion is reasonably accurate, and allows the taxpayer to recover the capital cost of his property, less the residual value. It is consistent as far as the types of property to which it is applied are concerned, and appears to be a fair and equitable method of applying depletion to determine net business profit.

Flat rate depletion. This method is applied to oil and gas wells, base and precious metal mines, and some industrial minerals. There are two classes of general deductions. One applies to all the properties entitled to use this method of depletion, and is a deduction of 33 1/3 per cent of the profits attributable to the production of the mineral. The other applies only to coal mines, and is a flat rate deduction of 10 cents for each ton of coal mined in the year. Special provision is made for gold mines in which 70 per cent or more of the value of the total output is gold, allowing a deduction which is the greater of 40 per cent of the profits attributable to the production of gold or $4.00 per ounce of gold produced during the year.

Further special "incentive" deductions are allowed in the case of coal, base metal, or industrial mineral mines of a non-bedded nature. The operator may deduct an amount not in excess of 25 per cent of the amount expended in the mine prior to bringing it into commercial production. A special deduction of all such expense incurred in prospecting, exploration, and development in searching for minerals during the calendar years 1950 to 1952 is also provided. Finally, provision is made for special treatment of dividends received by shareholders of a mining company. A deduction ranging from 10 to 20 per cent of the dividend is allowed to the shareholder.

The flat rate deduction method thus has no relationship to

[92]Certain industrial minerals, such as barite and limestone, occur either in bedded or non-bedded deposits, so that the method of depletion to be used in their extraction depends upon how they are classified by the Department of National Revenue.

capital costs. It represents a completely arbitrary determination of depletion which has no implied relationship to actuality. The rate is continued as long as the property remains in production, and the cumulative write-off for depletion purposes may exceed by far the capital cost of the property. For obvious reasons there is no recapture provision connected with this method, so that a taxpayer operating a gold or coal mine, for example, may well receive a tax concession far more liberal than that received by any other type of taxpayer. On the other hand, in the case of a marginal producer, the capital cost may never be recovered.

It is difficult to see how any real improvement could be made in providing for depletion where the value of the property is so difficult to determine. The rate must be arbitrary and discriminatory, and seems inevitably to be the net result of the demands made by the industry and the administration's views regarding what is reasonable.[93]

CONCLUSIONS[94]

The problem of asset valuation is directly a derivative of sharply fluctuating price levels. As long as prices remain relatively stable, conventional accounting practice reflects the profit and loss position of business operations with a sufficient degree of accuracy for all purposes.

Under conditions of inflation (or deflation) there is a degree of distortion in the reporting of profit and loss which is claimed to have serious effects on the capital of companies. The very considerable amount of soul searching that has taken place in recent years by accountants, business men, economists, lawyers, and legislators has resulted in a variety of accounting proposals designed to effect a neutralization of the effects of inflation on the income statement of corporate enterprise. Much of this so-called remedy is aimed directly at tax relief.

[93]When the federal income tax was first imposed in 1917, the depreciation rate for all mines was 50 per cent of the net profit. In 1933 the rate was reduced to 33⅓ per cent. By 1946 a Senate standing committee recommended a return to 50 per cent, which has not been adopted.

[94]Since this chapter was written a new concept has been introduced in Canadian tax practice, "deferred" depreciation. This is part of the government's fiscal policy to combat inflation. It is discussed in chapter IX.

The problem is monetary, and the writer has strong views on the undesirability of trying to effect compensatory results through income tax legislation designed to reduce the tax burden on corporations. The tax law should be simple, it should provide similar treatment for similar taxpayers, and it should not impose unnecessary rigidity of accounting procedure upon taxpayers. If inflation becomes so serious as to imperil the capital of business concerns, the proper remedy lies in the direction of tax abatement[95] rather than in amendment of the statute on such matters as inventory valuation, depreciation, depletion, and obsolescence, which are in themselves likely to be inflationary in the final analysis. But there is no indication that Canadian business has been hurt to the extent of a net impairment of the productive capacity of the nation because of the tax burden on overstated profits. The investment boom and inflation still continue unimpeded.

It is concluded that the most desirable approach to the problem of asset valuation is to allow any accounting practices that are suitable to an industry or a given type of business operation, provided that the taxpayer is compelled to use his system consistently. In that way the statute provides a desirable degree of flexibility, and rough justice appears to be an inherent result of it.

The Canadian tax legislation is generally sound, constructive and forward-looking in treatment of asset valuation. It might be better to avoid any reference at all to the method of inventory valuation, and the diminishing balance method of depreciation might better have been made optional. As far as depletion is concerned, no constructive conclusions can be drawn by this writer. This is a problem deserving serious attention, although work already done on the subject indicates that it may indeed be one of the imponderables connected with the taxation of business profits.

[95]But the abatement should not take the form of changing the measurement of income.

CHAPTER EIGHT

THE INTEGRATION OF CORPORATION AND PERSONAL INCOME TAX

THE MAJOR CONCLUSIONS reached in the foregoing chapters are as follows: (1) Despite the theoretical arguments against the taxation of corporate income at the existing high level, it is not practical to advocate outright repeal of the tax. It is such an important revenue source that its abolition would result in serious dislocation of the entire revenue structure. (2) There is, in fact, double taxation, because under normal conditions the incidence of the corporation tax is likely to be partially if not wholly upon the shareholder. (3) The unintegrated corporate and personal income taxes have tended to discourage individual investment in the shares of corporations, forcing them to rely on bond financing or the retention of earnings for new capital requirements. (4) This has resulted in the problem of undistributed earnings, a serious problem which has vexed both the tax administration and the taxpayer. (5) There has been real tax discrimination between the publicly owned and the private or family type of corporation, favouring the former in the tax treatment of undistributed profits. This problem has now been met in part by the 1951 legislation, but it is complicated and does not reach the core of the problem. (6) The results of any serious bias in favour of large public companies are economically undesirable because such a bias accentuates the trend towards undue concentration of productive capacity and economic power in the hands of a relatively small number of large companies and discourages the growth of new enterprise, thus precluding the development of a more competitive economic system.

It now remains to examine various proposals for ameliorating the present situation. Most students agree that the method of taxing profits in Canada and the United States should be revised. The Canadian government has already provided some measure of reform, such as the allowance of a 10 per cent credit on dividends received by all shareholders, the reduction of the corporation tax rate to 10 per cent (later raised to 15 per cent), on the first $10,000 of corporate profit, and the extension of the loss carry-over period from three to five years. This is a beginning, and has been commended by many American students,[1] but few observers will be of the opinion that the fundamental problems have been solved. Furthermore, there will be little agreement among business men and tax students regarding the specific direction which future tax reform should take, and how it should be effected. One fundamental point to be settled is whether tax relief is indicated, or whether there should be integration of the corporate and individual income taxes.

The views that one takes should be governed by the objectives that one believes should be attached to the tax system. The writer's basic views on the objectives of the tax system were indicated in the introduction to this study as follows:

1. The raising of the necessary revenue with which to meet the expenses of government.

2. The fostering of production through (*a*) the maintenance of a balanced relationship among consumption, saving, and investment; (*b*) the conservation of national resources through their more efficient exploitation; (*c*) the preservation and development of incentive to produce on the part of both labour and management.

3. The spreading of the tax burden in the most equitable manner possible, consistent with the above objectives.

As indicated in the preceding chapters, the existing method of taxing corporate income and dividends does not conform to the principles of taxation outlined above. More than tax relief is indicated. Fundamental changes are needed in order to approach what the writer believes to be the minimum requirements that will satisfy these basic principles.

[1]See, for example, John W. Hanes, Chairman of the Tax Foundation, "A Tax Policy for Enterprise," *Fortune*, June 1949, p. 70.

Accordingly, the following are considered to be the objectives of any tax reform proposals: (1) The income tax should, on grounds of tax equity, be the foundation on which the federal tax structure is built, because it is the best tax yet devised to measure taxpaying ability. (2) The efficiency of the income tax should be improved so that it can provide a large revenue with the least inequity and the least damage to the economy. (3) Some remedial measure should be applied to the taxation of the corporate income stream at two points to eliminate or alleviate a basic inequity and the economic defects of the existing system.

The two major defects in the Canadian income tax are first, the double taxation of corporate income and dividends, and second, the inherent confusion in the law itself which leads on the one hand to attempts to avoid taxation by methods "improper but not illegal," and on the other to counter measures of a notional and artificial character which are a hazard to ordinary business men. The solution of the problem appears to lie in the direction of integration of the corporate and personal income taxes, and the following discussion will be devoted to the principles of integration and a critical analysis of the various integration proposals that have been put forward.

Total or Partial Integration?

On theoretical grounds there should be complete integration of the corporate and personal income taxes in order to eliminate the difference in the tax treatment of the income of incorporated and unincorporated businesses, as well as to eliminate the difference in the tax treatment of income derived from corporations and income derived from other sources. Thus total integration implies the taxation of corporations in exactly the same way as unincorporated businesses are taxed.

There has been much discussion of (and as little agreement about) integration in recent years,[2] and it is quite apparent that

[2]See the following, which is a representative list of recent American material: E. C. Alvord, "Would Integration of Corporate and Individual Taxes Injure Business?" *Proceedings of the National Tax Association*, 1947, pp. 175-9; J. Keith Butters, "Would the Complete Integration of the Corporate and Personal Income Taxes Injure Small Business?" *ibid.*, pp. 189-93; "Should the Profits of Small Corporations be Taxed Like Partnership Earnings?" *How Should Corporations be Taxed?* pp. 72-90; John L. Connolly, "Alternative Methods of Taxing Corporate

all the implications of integration are not understood fully. Indeed, the writer has many reservations regarding these implications, and his conclusions should be regarded as tentative only. The following discussion will deal with complete versus partial integration, lay down some criteria for an acceptable plan of integration, and then appraise several alternative approaches in terms of those criteria. We begin with the assumption that some form of integration is desirable.

1. *Total versus Partial Integration*

The case for total integration rests upon grounds of equity and consideration of the economic effects of the tax system before and after total integration.

(*a*) Equity Considerations

It was concluded in chapter III that there is no case either from the viewpoint of equity or on economic grounds, for taxing corporations as such, distinguishing them from other forms of business enterprise.[3] The only argument for the corporation tax is the very formidable one of its heavy yield. From the viewpoint of theoretical tax equity and the concept of neutrality in taxation, the tax discrimination against the corporate form is unjustified and should be discontinued.

In chapter IV it was concluded that the tax on corporate income normally falls almost wholly upon the shareholders. If this conclusion is correct, then the tax is regressive in the case of shareholders who pay no personal income tax or who pay at a rate lower than that applied to corporations. A further inequity is created through the double taxation of corporate income and

---

Earnings at the Personal Level," *Proceedings of the National Tax Association*, 1947, pp. 146-50; Richard B. Goode, "Alternative Approaches to the Integration of Corporate and Individual Income Taxes," *ibid.*, pp. 134-45; Harold M. Groves, *Postwar Taxation and Economic Progress*, chaps. II and III; George E. Lent, "Alternative Methods of Taxing Corporation Earnings at the Personal Level: The Withholding Approach," *Proceedings of the National Tax Association*, 1947, pp. 151-60; Louis Shere, "Federal Corporate Income Tax—Revenue and Reform," *National Tax Journal*, June 1949, pp. 110-21; William Vickrey, "The Effects of Integration of Corporate and Individual Income Taxes on Business," *Proceedings of the National Tax Association*, 1947, pp. 179-88.

[3]It is conceded, however, that a special tax on corporations might be justified as a payment for the privilege of doing business in the corporate form. But this would surely be a modest tax, such as was imposed in the early days of Canadian income taxation.

dividends, which discriminates between the shareholder and the bondholder since bond interest is deductible from corporate income before tax. In this case, however, the equity argument is not as strong as the argument based upon the economic effects of the discrimination, because double and multiple taxation are inherent in any diversified tax system, particularly under the federal form of government.

Complete tax equity can be secured only through total integration, and if equity is considered as a fundamental of sound taxation, the case for total integration is very strong.

(*b*) Economic Considerations

It was argued in chapter v that the most important economic effect of the unintegrated corporate and individual tax structure is its effect on investment and the availability of risk capital, especially when tax rates are high. The combined tax on corporate income and dividends has probably had an adverse effect on the accumulation of capital by individuals. Even if the aggregate of individual saving has not been reduced, the pattern of that saving has been changed, and, because of different investment habits in different income brackets, the pattern of investment has been changed. Relatively more saving now appears to be done by corporations. But this is not so important a consideration as the undoubted effect of the two taxes on the incentive of investors to invest their savings in corporate share capital. The combined impact of the tax on corporate income before its distribution and the high rate of personal tax paid by most investors on their dividend income tend to make the net return on such capital incommensurate with the risk of capital loss. This risk is likely to be much more pronounced in the case of the small and growing enterprise than in the case of the large corporation with a long record of profitable operations. The fundamental desirability of encouraging expansion of the economy through new enterprise rather than expansion through increasing concentration in old companies is the strongest argument for total integration.

If total integration is to achieve the desired end of stimulating the volume of saving and its investment in new corporate enterprise, it must involve one or the other of two things. Either the total taxes collected must be reduced, or the over-all progressivity of the tax system must be reduced without affecting the total yield.[4] The simple approach would be to reduce governmental expenditures. But wars and the threat of wars, along with the welfare state philosophy, seem to preclude that approach entirely. We are in the position of trying to have our cake and eat it at the same time. If the latter result is achieved, it means a redistribution of the total tax burden among the various classes of taxpayers through changes in other taxes. This should be recognized clearly as a fundamental effect of integration on the distribution of income. The problem of striking a balance between the progressivity of the tax system and the volume and pattern of private saving and investment required to allow the normal expansion of a private enterprise system is another of the imponderables connected with fiscal policy.

Many advocates of complete integration base their argument on the assumption that the equalization of taxes on corporate profit and other kinds of income would stimulate investment. If such a proposal involves no major reduction in the rate progression of the individual income tax, complete integration would increase the current rate of tax on reinvested corporate profits in the case of corporations owned by high-income shareholders, and there is likely to be a greater deterrent to investment than at present. For example, under the existing Canadian corporation taxes (federal and provincial) corporate earnings can be reinvested in a corporation after payment of a tax in excess of 45 per cent. Under complete integration, where the shareholders would pay tax on their corporate earnings at the current individual rates, a tax as high as 80 per cent would be paid before such earnings could be reinvested.

Total integration is aimed at placing corporate income on the same footing as income from partnerships and sole proprietorships. In other words, its aim is to treat the stockholder in the same way as the partner or proprietor. But this cannot be

[4]Of course the entire revenue loss occasioned by eliminating the corporation tax (it would have been $810 million in 1950) could be recovered in theory by increasing the rate progression of the individual income tax. But this would hardly solve the problem of stimulating the saving and investment done by persons in these income brackets. More likely it would have the opposite effect. Furthermore, it would probably be impossible to secure public support for such a plan.

done simply through the taxation of the corporation in the same way as unincorporated businesses are taxed. In the first place, such a procedure would involve the taxation of corporate earnings in the hands of shareholders, whether or not they had been distributed. In the case of undistributed earnings, the shareholders would be required to pay tax on income which they had not received. This undoubtedly would have an adverse effect on the market for share capital, unless all corporate profits were distributed, a situation which is neither practical nor desirable. A further problem arises in the case of shares which change hands during the year. If there were undistributed earnings of $10 on a share of stock in a given year, and that share had changed hands five times during that year, there would be the problem of deciding whom to tax. Whatever decision was made, there would almost certainly be general dissatisfaction.

In the second place, no method of integration which does not involve full taxation of capital gains can be really effective in placing the stockholder, the partner, and the sole proprietor on the same footing. The elimination of the present tax on corporations would result in substantial windfall gains to stockholders, and therefore create new inequities, unless such gains were taxed on the same basis as earned income. But the many problems connected with the taxation of capital gains impel one to ponder carefully if the cause of tax equity can justify the price to be paid for it. Perfect equity can never be attained, and simplicity of the tax structure is so desirable as to outweigh the futile pursuit of an ephemeral goal.

Despite the strong case for complete integration on grounds of equity, practical necessity appears to dictate a compromise—limited or partial rather than complete integration. The form that such a middle of the road procedure should take will be conditioned to some extent by economic considerations, and administrative considerations will enter as well.

2. *Criteria of an Acceptable Plan for Integration*

There is a wide area of disagreement over the extent to which the taxes should be integrated (if at all), as well as disagreement over the method of integration that should be adopted. Before examining the various alternatives it appears necessary to outline the characteristics and requirements of an acceptable plan for integrating the corporate and personal income taxes. In view of the impracticability of achieving total integration, minimum requirements for a satisfactory compromise should be formulated in accordance with the basic objectives to be attained, which have already been indicated in terms of equity, economic effects, and administrative feasibility.

Richard Goode has suggested the following minimum requirements, and they provide a good point of departure for the discussion of the alternative plans that have been proposed:

(1) It should provide equitable taxation of dividend income of stockholders in all income groups.

(2) It should prevent undue tax avoidance or postponement by stockholders with respect to their share of undistributed corporate profits.

(3) It should minimize adverse effects on investment.

(4) It should be administratively feasible.[5]

It will be noted that there is no provision in this proposal for the complete equalization of the treatment of stockholders on the one hand and partners and sole proprietors on the other. The first minimum requirement outlined here provides only for the elimination of the double taxation in all income groups. Thus the same proportion of the corporate tax load would be removed from every dollar of dividends. While this requirement falls short of meeting the equity problem of treating corporations on the same basis as other businesses, it does seem to be a realistic compromise approach to one of the worst features of the present tax system.

The treatment of undistributed earnings is a thorny problem that has bedevilled all tax students, and is fraught with difficulties of an administrative as well as an economic nature. At this point all that is necessary is to indicate that the problem of tax avoidance or tax postponement by shareholders in the higher income brackets requires full recognition under any method of integration. Care should be exercised to avoid opening any new loopholes, and yet at the same time to avoid prejudicing the ability

[5]"Alternative Approaches to the Integration of Corporate and Individual Income Taxes," p. 135.

of corporations to retain earnings for legitimate expansion. This problem will be discussed under a separate heading.

The extent to which the availability of investment funds and the incentive to invest in corporate securities are affected by integration must depend, of course, upon the extent of the integration, the method employed, and the resulting tax rates. It is quite possible that different results would be secured for different enterprises under any of the integration plans generally proposed. As pointed out before, the complete integration of corporate and personal income taxes would result actually in higher taxes on reinvested earnings in the case of corporations owned by wealthy shareholders. In the interest of stimulating rather than retarding investment ability and incentive, such a result should be avoided. Compromise plans for partial integration may deal either more or less severely with reinvested earnings than is done under the existing system. A minimum requirement for any such plan is that it consider carefully its effect on investment.

The fourth of the minimum requirements, administrative feasibility, should be carefully considered. Administrative problems associated with any integration plan should be weighed against the advantages accruing from it.

3. *Special Problems*

There are two particularly vexatious problems connected with the integration of corporate and individual income taxes that must be given careful consideration before any decision can be reached regarding the type of integration to be used in accordance with the minimum requirements discussed above. They are (*a*) the treatment of undistributed profits, and (*b*) the problem of capital gains.

(*a*) *Undistributed Earnings*[6]

Taxation of undistributed corporate earnings is required for purposes of tax equity. Savings are not exempted under the per-

[6]For discussions of the problem from various viewpoints, see E. C. Alvord, "The Taxation of Undistributed Profits from the Business Point of View," *How Shall Business be Taxed?* pp. 90-112; Harold M. Groves, *Postwar Taxation and Economic Progress*, pp. 40-73; George C. Haas, "The Taxation of Undistributed Profits from the Point of View of the Federal Tax Structure," *How Shall Business Be Taxed?* pp. 113-24; George E. Lent, *The Impact of the Undistributed Profits Tax, 1936-1937*, particularly chap. IX; Carl Shoup, "The Taxation of Undistributed

sonal income tax, and since the undistributed profits of companies represent savings of the equity shareholders in varying degree, undistributed profits should be taxed concurrently with dividends. Our primary concern is that of preventing shareholders from using the corporate form as a device for avoiding personal income tax on business earnings, or postponing it indefinitely, while proprietors and partners are taxable at once on their total current net business profit.[7]

Few advocates of integration, and even those people who want outright elimination of the corporate income tax, deny the need for a tax on undistributed corporate profits.[8] The question

Profits from the Theoretical Point of View," *How Shall Business Be Taxed?* pp. 125-34; Othel D. Westfall, "Integrating Federal Income Taxes on Corporations and Their Shareholders," *Taxes—The Tax Magazine,* March 1949, pp. 236-57.

[7]It will be noted that the point stressed here is not that of placing proprietors and partners on the same footing with shareholders for the purpose of providing equity through equal treatment. This objective was discarded in our minimum requirements for an acceptable partial integration programme. Had it not been, one proposal would be that of allowing proprietors and partners the option of being taxed as corporations are taxed, thus enabling them to withhold earnings and to postpone the payment of personal income taxes on them. The effect of such a plan would depend upon the corporate and personal income tax rate structures. Under a flat rate corporation tax and a steeply graduated personal rate structure, the benefits of the plan would accrue only to proprietors and partners in the higher income brackets who own businesses earning considerably more than their personal annual income requirements. Small taxpayers owning small businesses would not be likely to elect to pay taxes under such a plan.

Professor Shoup argues (p. 132) that tax should be paid on all business earnings as they accrue, because "the owner does experience an increase in his economic power to support the government, and the increase occurs when the earnings are made, since it can be realized in cash by a sale of part of the investor's stockholding in a corporation, or by withdrawal of funds from a proprietorship or partnership, or by borrowing on the increase in the assets of the company." He concedes possible exception, but states that "practically all current earnings must be taxed." On straight equity grounds, if savings in general are taxed as income, there should be no exemption of the savings of certain individuals whose investments take the legal form of shares in corporations which do not distribute their earnings promptly and completely. See "Final Report of the Committee on Federal Taxation of Corporations," *Proceedings of the National Tax Association,* 1939; Gerhard Colm, "Conflicting Theories of Corporate Income Taxation," *Law and Contemporary Problems,* Spring, 1940, pp. 285 ff.

[8]In recommending the abolition of the American corporate income tax, two of its most unequivocal critics write: "Such a reform should not occur without concurrent provision to prevent the corporate form from being used as a refuge from the personal income tax, from building up uninvested and untaxed corporate surpluses, and from securing undue advantages over partnerships and unincorporated businesses." Beardsley Ruml and H. C. Sonne, *Fiscal and Monetary Policy,* p. 10. They propose a tax of 16 per cent on undistributed earnings. More recently Mr. Sonne has proposed a surtax of 60 per cent on any part of earnings retained by a

is how to impose such a tax. There are two major difficulties, the first involving equity considerations, the second a matter of economic effects.

From the viewpoint of equity, the extent to which the undistributed profits of a company are properly considered as the savings of the shareholders varies considerably. Typical cases range from that of a large publicly owned corporation having many shareholders who do not participate in management's decisions as to dividend policy, to the small privately owned or family corporation, in which ownership and management are identical. Falling between these two extremes are all the intermediate cases. In the case of the large publicly owned company, many shareholders would not concede that retained earnings represent savings attributable to them in anything more than a theoretical sense. In the case of the family company, however, profits kept in the business certainly represent real savings of the owners.

From the economic viewpoint, the purposes for which earnings are withheld, and the form of the assets representing them, are equally divergent. The motive for retaining earnings may be a desire to avoid or postpone personal income taxes, or it may reflect a real need of the company for increased capital. Earned surplus may be represented by assets of a liquid nature held available for future distribution without disturbance of the business, or, at the other extreme, it may be represented by permanent fixed investment in fixed assets analogous in every functional sense to the investment of additional capital subscribed by the shareholders for that purpose. Here, again, no clear and objective lines of division can be drawn.

These difficulties, involving such a subjective matter as motivation, as well as the very real differences between shareholders of various types of corporation, require distinctions which no income tax law anywhere has managed to make successfully. These distinctions also raise the fundamental question whether

---

corporation in excess of 25 per cent, or $50,000, whichever is larger. This is in addition to the normal 16 per cent, so that "a large business would have to pay out at least 75 per cent of its earnings." "How Should Corporations be Taxed?" *How Should Corporations be Taxed?* p. 23.

legislation which seeks to tax corporations as a general class of taxpayers in omnibus fashion is realistic, let alone fair. In any event, it must surely be realized that whatever approach to these difficulties is adopted, it will accomplish only rough justice at best. It appears, therefore, all the more desirable that at least the general intention of the law should be clear in principle. The Canadian law, as it now stands, is deficient.

Two main lines of approach to the problem of undistributed earnings are open as alternatives. For the present it is necessary only to summarize them in terms of principle. A more detailed examination of alternative proposals and their variants will be made later.

The first alternative is that of looking through the corporate entity and taxing shareholders on their imputed share of the profits, whether distributed or not. Some bold spirits have advocated that this be done across the board, as is now done in the case of personal corporations. But the obstacles are so great, and the economic results of such a policy likely to be so intolerable, that the proposal is not considered feasible. This principle has, however, been applied up to a point in Australia by drawing an arbitrary line across the classification of ordinary incorporated business and treating all companies below that line as though they were partnerships.

The other approach is that of disregarding considerations of ownership and control, except where the corporate form is obviously used as a cloak, and taxing all companies on their undistributed profits at a flat rate which compensates roughly in aggregate effect for the amounts of personal tax which would have been paid on such profits had they been distributed as dividends.[9] Double taxation is avoided either directly, through the exemption of dividends, or indirectly, as in the United Kingdom, by an adjustment to shareholders with respect to the tax paid on dividends

[9]The comments of the late Professor T. Adams, made thirty years ago in an address to the American Economic Association, are still very much to the point. He stated: "Corporations, in order to be placed on something like an equality with individuals and partnerships, must bear an additional tax roughly equivalent to the surtax on undistributed profits paid by sole proprietors, the members of partnerships, and the stockholders of personal service corporations. This additional tax should apply only to undistributed profits." "Immediate Future of the Excess Profits Tax," *American Economic Review, Supplement*, March 1920, p. 16.

at the source. The essential feature of this approach is the operation of a compensatory tax confined to undistributed profits, as contrasted with a comprehensive tax levied on all profits, as provided under the Canadian system.

The whole problem of undistributed earnings can, of course, be ignored by methods of taxation which fail to meet it, or it can be concealed by methods which go beyond it. Furthermore, it can be by-passed in theory at least by the taxation of capital gains.

It is suggested that the Canadian income tax system conceals the problem by overreaching it. Undistributed profits are taxed, but distributed profits are also taxed to the company at the same rate. There is, therefore, no compensatory factor, and the existing general corporate tax rate is so high that no room is left for introducing this factor. Any attempt to do so might have disastrous results on the financial position of incorporated companies, unless accompanied by a substantial reduction in the rate on distributed profits or the elimination of that part of the tax altogether.

The conclusion is reached that the treatment of undistributed profits is the root of the problem of integration, and that the existing method of taxing corporate income and dividends makes it impossible to deal with them effectively. Before examining the Canadian legislation, it seems useful to review the experience of the United States, where various devices have been tried.

(i) Experience in the United States

Prior to 1921, American legislation to check tax avoidance through the withholding of corporate earnings was designed to strike at the shareholders rather than attack it through the corporation itself. This was done by taxing the shareholders of companies accumulating unwarranted surplus on their pro rata shares of the corporation's earnings. After a decision of the United States Supreme Court (*Eisner* v. *Macomber*, 252 U.S. 189) in 1920 some doubt existed regarding the constitutionality of this procedure, and subsequent legislation imposed penalty tax rates directly on the corporation for improper accumulation of earnings.[10]

[10]For a brief history of American tax legislation regarding undistributed earnings, see Lent, *The Impact of the Undistributed Profits Tax, 1936-1937*, chap. I. This is the source used for the above material.

In a special message to Congress, March 3, 1936, President Roosevelt announced a new proposal for the taxation of undistributed earnings which represented a revolutionary change in the corporate tax system, and was designed "to provide a fairer distribution of the tax load among all the beneficial owners of business profits whether derived from unincorporated enterprises or from incorporated businesses and whether distributed to the real owners as earned or withheld from them."[11] While the details of the plan were not disclosed in the President's message, a plan had been worked out by the Treasury Department, and the Subcommittee on Ways and Means presented a detailed report supporting the President's proposal.

It was proposed that the tax on undistributed profits would replace the old corporate income tax as well as the capital stock and excess profits taxes. Thus it would be the only tax on corporations. Professor Lent states: "The rate schedules, applied to the entire net income of the corporation, were graduated with the percentage of net income retained. Corporations distributing all of their income would be free of taxes. Preferential rates were prescribed for small income corporations (with incomes of less than $10,000) which ranged from one per cent of net incomes of which 10 per cent remained undistributed, to 29.7 per cent on incomes of which 70.3 per cent or more was retained."[12] Under this proposal, a corporation which retained 30 per cent of its earnings would pay the same effective rate on its profits to which it was then subject under the 15 per cent normal corporate tax.

This proposal, which would have been a step towards integration, contained much merit, and is still worth careful consideration as a major tax reform measure. It was never put into

[11]*Message from the President of the United States Transmitting Additional Information Concerning the Budget for the Fiscal Year 1937*, H. Doc. no. 418, 74th Cong., 2nd Sess. Cited by Lent, *ibid.*, p. 17.

[12]*Ibid.*, p. 19. The effective tax rates on corporations with net income in excess of $10,000 were as follows:

Percentage of income undistributed	*Tax rate*
0	0
10	4
20	9
30	15
40	25
50	35
57½	42½

effect in the United States because it was mangled beyond recognition by Congress. The bill that was finally adopted, after amendments by both House and Senate, retained the graduated normal tax on net income, the capital stock tax, and the excess profits tax. The rate of surtax on undistributed profits was graduated with the percentage of the adjusted net income that remained undistributed at the end of the taxable year. The rates varied from 7 to 27 per cent.

The legislation proved to be most unpopular, for the reasons enumerated by Groves:

> Particularly annoying was the pressure to distribute earnings, under threat of taxation, in the case of corporations which had accumulated deficits from past operations and which were not allowed, under many state laws, to declare dividends. The absence of any carry-over provision for losses aggravated this grievance. The law did include a relief provision for companies having contracts restricting the payment of dividends, but the proviso was strictly interpreted and not often effective. The requirement that distribution be made before the end of the taxable year was unfortunate since corporations could not always determine that early what their net income would be. The law also brought into sharp focus the differences involved in taxable income, book income, and cash available for distribution. Inventory profits afforded an undistributed income-tax base but no money for distribution to stockholders.[13]

Some of the technical faults were corrected in 1938 and then very low rates were applied, virtually removing in practice the effect of an undistributed profits tax. It was eliminated entirely in 1939.

The present provisions of the American legislation regarding undistributed profits (Section 102) make accumulation of surplus beyond the reasonable needs of the business the equivalent of tax avoidance, unless the corporation can prove otherwise. It has been stated that "it is generally recognized that this feature of the revenue law is feeble."[14]

The problem of handling the taxation of undistributed profits has not been solved in the United States.[15] The American ex-

[13] *Postwar Taxation and Economic Progress,* pp. 50-1.

[14] *Ibid.,* p. 43.

[15] The Committee of the National Tax Association on Federal Taxation of Corporations stated that "Congress merely retreated from this problem without solving it." *Final Report,* p. 49.

perience in attempting to superimpose an undistributed profits surtax on the normal corporate income tax indicates that this is not the approach to the problem. It must lie in the direction of integration in one form or another.

(ii) Situation in Canada

Until 1950 the situation in Canada closely resembled that in the United States after the elimination of the undistributed profits tax in that country. As indicated earlier,[16] there had been a long and complicated series of amendments to the Income War Tax Act designed to prevent tax avoidance through the retention of corporate earnings. This was necessitated by the decision taken in the mid-twenties to tax corporate income as a separate thing from dividend income. There was no problem of undistributed profits prior to that time, when there was almost total integration of the corporate and personal income taxes.

The new legislation provides that undistributed profits accrued prior to 1950 may now be capitalized and distributed upon payment of a special tax of 15 per cent. The disbursements of tax-paid surplus are free of further tax. Accumulations from 1950 on may be so distributed, at the 15 per cent tax rate, in amounts not exceeding the dividends paid in a completed taxation year. The plan was originally restricted to private corporations, but was extended to public companies in June 1951.

As indicated in chapter II,[17] special treatment is accorded to personal corporations[18] and certain investment companies, both of which are exempt from the corporation tax.[19] In both cases

[16]The history of the tax is developed in some detail in chapter II, and the new legislation regarding undistributed profits is discussed in some detail.

[17]*Supra*, pp. 84–6.

[18]Until 1932 "family corporations" were given similar treatment. A family corporation was defined as a company, 75 per cent of the stock of which is owned by the members of one family, at least one of whom takes an active part in the business, or a corporation in which 80 per cent of the stock is owned by persons actively employed in the business, or by them and their families. Such companies were given the option to elect annually whether to be treated as a partnership (i.e., with all earnings taxed in the hands of the shareholders regardless of whether distributed), or as ordinary corporations.

[19]There were 1,164 personal corporations listed in the 1948 taxation year, and they showed an aggregate profit of $7.1 million on which no corporate tax was paid. See *Taxation Statistics*, 1950, Table C, p. 29.

such companies may elect to pay the corporation tax, upon notice to the Minister. In this way the shareholders qualify to claim the 10 per cent dividend credit. One of the major reasons for providing for exemption of these companies is undoubtedly to prevent their use for tax avoidance purposes.[20] Where no corporate tax is paid, there is no problem of double taxation and no problem of undistributed profits.[21]

The chief objection to the classification of corporations for separate tax treatment is the necessity of drawing an arbitrary distinction between one corporation and another. The Ives Commission stated: "When a definite class of corporation is provided for in the law there are immediately raised a number of borderline cases, and without any real justification in equity one corporation will be entitled to the special arrangements established for the class and another will be excluded."[22] Groves suggests that an improvement could be made, applying both to personal holding companies and to those subject to penalty for unwarranted accumulation of earnings "by requiring that the stockholders be taxed on their prorata share of undistributed income. . . . This would avoid pressure to distribute earnings and would apply tax burdens most equitably among stockholders. The option of using the prorata method should be open to all concerns at all times."[23]

This proposal might have merit as a compromise, but it has the weakness of imposing taxation on accrued but unrealized income. It would in many cases be a hardship for a taxpayer to pay perhaps a substantial tax on income he has not received.

While there was no theoretical difference in the tax treatment of corporations prior to 1950 (save for those singled out for special treatment), there was a very real practical difference. In the

[20]The stipulation that they may elect to be taxed as ordinary corporations indicates, however, that the way is still open to such abuse. The high rates of corporate tax, coupled with the progressive personal rate structure, make it unlikely that many companies would find it profitable to exercise this privilege.

[21]In contrast with the Canadian treatment of personal holding companies, it is interesting to note that the United States imposes special and severe corporation taxes on such companies.

[22]*Report of the Royal Commission on the Taxation of Annuities and Family Corporations*, p. 66.

[23]*Postwar Taxation and Economic Progress*, p. 44.

case of the closely held company the day usually comes when retained earnings are distributed, or deemed to be distributed, and are therefore subjected to personal income taxation. When substantial earned surplus has been accumulated over the years, its complete distribution, such as occurs in winding up or reorganization, may well result in very heavy personal taxation. Should the distribution coincide with the shareholder's death, the additional burden of death duties may amount to virtual confiscation.[24]

In the case of publicly held companies, liquidation or winding-up seldom occurs, except in the event of financial difficulties, when there are not likely to be any undistributed earnings. Thus, that part of the earnings retained in the company accrues to the shareholders' benefit as a non-taxable capital gain, because they can sell the stock at any time, and its market price will probably be affected by the amount of the earnings retained by the company. The Ives Commission stated that "if the reinvestment in the enterprise of some part of the earnings of a corporation is a sound principle, it should be available on the same basis to the small and to the large corporation, and the objective in taxation should be to place no undue burdens on the shareholders of a prudently administered business."[25] The case for tax equity cannot be stated more clearly.

(iii) Conclusions

Undistributed corporate earnings are the focal point in the problem of formulating an equitable and realistic programme for the taxation of corporate income and dividends.

The present Canadian system taxes both undistributed and distributed profits at the same high rate without distinction. It thereby excludes compensatory treatment of undistributed profits; even a rough approach to equity might be made in the concurrent taxation of realized income in the form of dividends, and of attributable income in the form of actual or imputed savings retained by corporations. Indeed, the Canadian system tends to

[24]The extent of the problem is indicated by the number of closely held companies. The Ives Commission estimated that in 1945 some 10,000 of the 28,000 corporations filing income tax returns were closely held. *Report*, p. 62, and Appendix B, pp. 97-8. In 1948 there were 35,710 private companies compared with 3,049 public companies. *Taxation Statistics*, 1950, p. 29.

[25]*Report*, pp. 66-7.

operate in the opposite direction by showing greater severity towards distributed profits, because the taxation of declared dividends is immediate and more certain than the taxation of income not yet distributed. The corporation tax is accordingly prevented from being an equitable adjunct of the personal income tax.

The law is thus left to straddle a fundamental inconsistency. While it appears to rely on the doctrine that the corporation and the shareholder are separate taxable entities, it is obliged to assert an uncompromising claim on the retained earnings of companies in the name of the beneficial owners. It says in effect, having taken two bites out of profits that are distributed, we must insist that undistributed profits shall not escape a second bite sooner or later. Hence the need for complicated and artificial provisions designed to enforce a tax lien on deferred distributions in any form.

The Report of the Ives Commission demonstrated clearly how far the consequences of this position differ for private and public companies, and how much more serious they have been for the former. The fact that private companies are much more manoeuvreable for purposes of tax avoidance has resulted in a running challenge to the national revenue which was met over a period of time by Sections 14 to 19 of the Income War Tax Act, brought together and reinforced in Sections 8 and 9 of the revised legislation in 1949. Section 9 was repealed in 1950 when the new legislation covering private companies was enacted. These devices have been developed over the past twenty-five years and the present culmination of the struggle between the taxpayer and the administration is represented in Section 126. In the absence of a new approach to the taxation of corporate income, the struggle is likely to go on inconclusively and with increasing irritation all across the board.

The results of the road-blocks placed in the legislation to prevent tax avoidance have been found to be untenable in the case of private companies, as indicated in chapter II. In 1930 relief was introduced and was continued for four years. Distribution of surplus accumulated prior to that year was allowed free of tax on the winding up, discontinuance, or reorganization of a company. In 1945, on the recommendation of the Ives Commission, special provision was made for the capitalization or distribution of surplus earned up to 1939 on the payment of a special tax by the company. The same situation has now developed once again. In the budget speech of March 22, 1949, the Minister of Finance, referring to the excessive tax burden on many family-owned businesses, and the resulting loss of revenue through complicated devices for legal tax avoidance, said that the problem is an exceedingly difficult one, and stated: "We have been considering a plan under which a straight percentage tax paid by such a corporation at the time of winding up or at the time of capitalization of earned surplus will relieve the earned surplus of tax liability in the hands of the eventual recipient. Whether this would be equitable and, if so, what the flat tax should be, are questions which require the most careful consideration."[26]

It is doubtful whether the fundamental problem can be solved satisfactorily through any adjustment which leaves the present basis of the law unchanged, because any such remedy will encounter the objection that it represents a special privilege, and the making of exception is not likely to be a durable method of securing fair tax treatment.

It should be noted that the remedies introduced or proposed to date, including the concessions of 1930 and the second (majority) recommendation of the Ives Committee which the government was not prepared to accept, have the following features in common: (1) they constitute a limited application of the principle of compensatory treatment of undistributed profits either on the strength of corporation taxes paid previously or on the strength of a special corporation tax to be paid currently; and (2) they appear against the background of the existing system as exceptional relief to be granted reluctantly, if at all.

This experience suggests that nothing short of a bold and fresh approach to the whole question of the proper relationship between the corporate income tax and the personal income tax will really solve the problem of undistributed earnings. When the Canadian income tax system was placed on its present course

[26] *House of Commons Debates*, March 22, 1949, p. 1800.

in 1925, no one foresaw where it would lead, and quite possibly no one had very clear ideas as to where it should lead. If we can now decide where we want it to lead, and bearing in mind that the personal income tax must be utilized to the limit of its efficient capacity, then hesitant respect for the work of earlier parliaments should not stand in the way of revision. If a more easily enforceable income tax law can be developed as a by-product, this in itself will constitute a considerable gain.

The new legislation regarding undistributed profits does meet the problem part way, in that it provides a means, though complicated, of releasing all of the pre-1950 accrual of income at a price. But the provisions for future accruals, limited as they are, fail to cut through to the heart of the problem.

(*b*) Capital Gains

The problem of capital gains and losses from transactions in investment assets is one of the most controversial issues connected with the taxation of income. A strong theoretical case can be made for the inclusion of capital gains in the concept of taxable income, because a realized capital gain does enhance the recipient's economic position and thus adds to his taxpaying ability. There are far-reaching implications in the preferential tax treatment of capital gains now granted in the Canadian legislation. Such treatment tends to aggravate certain refractory problems of tax avoidance, and is an incentive to resort to new forms of avoidance.

It is not proposed to pursue the various arguments for and against the taxation of capital gains here.[27] But it does seem necessary to explore the problem as it applies to the equitable integration of the corporate and personal income taxes. The problem of capital gains is tied closely to the problem of undistributed earnings. Our immediate concern is to determine whether the exclusion of capital gains from the tax base has any serious

[27]Professor Henry C. Simons has developed the case for their taxation in his *Personal Income Taxation*, chap. VII, pp. 148 ff. See also Arthur H. Kent, "The Question of Taxing Capital Gains—The Case for Taxation," *Law and Contemporary Problems*, Spring 1940, pp. 194-207. For the opposite view, see G. N. Nelson, "The Question of Taxing Capital Gains—The Case against Taxation," *ibid.*, pp. 208-16; and Morris Tremaine, "The Capital Gains Tax," *Tax Magazine*, vol. XV, 1937, pp. 517 ff.

equity implications as far as the treatment of undistributed profits is concerned.

Under the existing system of taxing corporate income and dividends the exemption of capital gains may provide an opportunity for tax avoidance under certain circumstances. For example, the owner of an unincorporated business which has taxable income of $100,000 would pay a personal tax of $51,660 on that income (ignoring his basic exemption and deductions for dependents). If he wanted to reinvest $30,000 in the business, his net income would be $18,340 ($100,000 – $51,660 – $30,000). If he incorporated the business, the net result of exactly the same operation in the tax year would leave him with a net income of $23,144,[28] or $4,804 more than under the proprietorship.

The only possibility of bringing the net income from the two operations into rough equity under the present tax structure is the taxation of the $30,000 of undistributed corporate profits upon distribution. Under the new Part IA legislation this surplus can be distributed later on payment of the 15 per cent tax. The special tax would be $4,500, so that the total corporation and personal taxes on the $100,000 profit would be $51,356, compared with the tax of $51,660 paid by the proprietorship. This result has the appearance of a close approach to perfection in terms of tax equity.

If, however, as alleged, the shareholder may avoid taxation of his equity in the company's undistributed profits by recovering it through selling the shares,[29] he is in a distinctly advantageous position compared with the proprietor of an unincorporated business, or for that matter, compared with a shareholder who cannot recover his enhanced equity by sale of his shares. But there is no certainty that the market value of shares will reflect undistributed

[28]The corporation tax would be $35,700. After retaining $30,000 in the business, he could receive a dividend of $34,300. On this he would pay a normal tax and surtax of $14,586, and offset his dividend credit of $3,430, leaving a net tax of $11,156. The total corporation and personal taxes would therefore amount to $46,856, leaving him a net income of $23,144.

[29]See, for example, Arthur H. Kent, who says "this appreciation in the value of corporate equities is in substantial measure the result of accumulation of corporate earnings. Such retention of corporate profits swells corporate surplus and enhances the value of the assets underlying the securities." "The Question of Taxing Capital Gains—The Case for Taxation," p. 202.

surplus.[30] So many other factors are involved in determining the market price of share capital that conclusions must be drawn carefully. It is apparent that the undistributed profits of corporations are not necessarily reflected in the value of their stock, so that there is no guarantee that tax liability on such surplus can be avoided by means of a tax-free capital gain. Moreover, in the case of a private company such as that used in our example, there is often such reluctance to part with the control of the company that a sale of the shares is not considered a practical alternative to paying taxes.

It can hardly be denied that there are many cases where taxation can be and is avoided through the retention of corporate earnings and the sale of securities, the value of which does in fact reflect at least part of the earnings retained. Perhaps this is more likely to be the case in closely-held family corporations.[31] Thus the exemption of capital gains from income taxation may well provide an incentive to retain earnings when the tax rate on corporate income is substantially lower than the rate applicable to the owners of the corporation. One is inclined to agree with Professor Kent, when he says that "it is difficult to believe that corporate shareholders will not prefer, as time goes on, to realize their profits on corporate investment, so far as practicable, through the sale or exchange of his shares at a profit created by the retention of corporate earnings rather than through the receipt of dividends out of such earnings."[32]

There appear to be strong theoretical grounds for including capital gains in the tax base in order to prevent tax avoidance

[30]Keith Butters has pointed out the case of the Lockheed Aircraft Corporation in which the cumulated retained earnings from 1939 through 1943 amounted to well over $30 per share of common stock. Yet the market value of these shares declined from about $34 per share at the beginning of 1939, to $16 at the end of 1943. He states that this illustration "could be multiplied many times by similar examples from many industries occurring during any major bear market period." "Should the Profits of Small Corporations be Taxed Like Partnership Earnings?" *How Should Corporations be Taxed?* p. 74.

[31]Butters says, however, that "the available evidence indicates that the value of the stock of many small companies fluctuates much more markedly and erratically than does that of most large companies. It, therefore, seems reasonable to believe that the correlation between corporate savings and the realizable value of the securities of small, closely held corporations would be no better than that of the large, listed companies." *Ibid.*, p. 75.

[32]"The Question of Taxing Capital Gains—The Case for Taxation," p. 202.

and to secure greater tax equity. But the practical difficulties attached to the taxation of capital gains are very considerable, as indicated in American experience.[33] Bearing in mind that one of our declared objectives is to make the income tax as simple as possible, consistent with the objective of tax equity, capital gains taxation is to be avoided if substantial tax equity can be secured in another way.

Ignoring consciously the fact that capital gains do represent income, and in theory should be taxed as such, attention is concentrated upon the treatment of undistributed profits in order to achieve some semblance of tax equity. If some new approach can be devised which does not need to use the capital gains tax, then the immediate difficulty is solved, and the highly contentious problem of capital gains can be by-passed. Bearing in mind the minimum criteria for a satisfactory plan of integration outlined earlier, attention can now be turned to the principal alternative approaches to integration.

Alternative Approaches to Integration[34]

1. *Repeal of the Corporate Income Tax*

Outright repeal of the corporate income tax would eliminate the double taxation of distributed earnings, and would achieve the integration ideal of equal taxation of dividends and other types of personal income. But it would not meet the problem of undistributed earnings. Rather, it would accentuate it by permitting the accumulation of untaxed corporate earnings, and thus increase tax avoidance or tax postponement. Serious inequity would result if this plan were adopted without taxation of capital gains at the normal personal income tax rate. But even this would

[33]Nelson, "The Question of Taxing Capital Gains—The Case against Taxation," pp. 208-16.

[34]For a discussion of various proposals for integration, see Richard Goode, *The Postwar Corporation Tax Structure*, pp. 16-41. This is an outstanding contribution to the critical analysis of the more widely discussed proposals. See also Goode's "Alternative Approaches to the Integration of Corporate and Individual Income Taxes," *Proceedings of the National Tax Association*, 1947, pp. 134-45; John L. Connolly, "Alternative Methods of Taxing Corporate Earnings at the Personal Level," *ibid.*, pp. 146-50; George E. Lent, "Alternative Methods of Taxing Corporation Earnings at the Personal Level: The Withholding Approach," *ibid.*, pp. 151-60; Groves, *Postwar Taxation and Economic Progress*, pp. 55-73.

not solve the problem of tax postponement, or complete avoidance through the use of "wash sales." Furthermore, the loss of revenue entailed by the plan would necessitate serious adjustments in the national budget, transferring the tax load ($800 million in 1951) either to the personal income tax or to consumption taxes, or both. The plan is not practical, nor is it likely that it is politically feasible.

2. *Exemption of Dividends from Personal Income Tax*

This plan would eliminate the double taxation of corporate income and dividends, and it would deal with undistributed profits as effectively as the present system. But it would be a grossly inequitable way of taxing distributed corporate earnings.

Dividend income would be removed from the progressive income tax and would pay tax at the going corporate rate (47.6 per cent on all income above $10,000). In the case of stockholders in the high personal rate brackets, the exemption of dividends would be a valuable concession, while it would be worthless in the case of stockholders in the lowest brackets. If rate progression on personal income is a sound principle, then it is violated by taxing dividends at a flat rate regardless of the other income of the shareholder. This plan must be rejected because it does not comply with our objective of equality in the taxation of all forms of income.

3. *The Partnership Approach*

The proposal to tax corporate income in the same manner as the income of a partnership is taxed, i.e., by looking through the corporate form and taxing corporate income in the hands of the shareholders, whether distributed or not, is the most logical, direct, and uncompromising approach to the integration problem. This plan was recommended by a Committee of the National Tax Association a decade ago, as the ideal method of achieving tax equity in accordance with ability to pay.[35]

This plan has the important advantage of simplicity. There is no differentiation between corporate income and other business income. It conforms to our concept of tax equity. It solves

[35]See "Final Report of the Committee on Federal Taxation of Corporations," *Proceedings of the National Tax Association*, 1939, pp. 534-99.

once and for all the problem of undistributed earnings. It eliminates the need for a tax on capital gains to equalize the taxes on corporate income and other business income. Finally, it eliminates the long-standing controversy about the tax treatment of co-operatives.

The objections to the plan are that it is based upon the false assumption that the receipt of earnings by a corporation represents the actual receipt of those earnings by the corporation's shareholders. It fails to recognize the fact that, while the shareholder has a beneficial interest in the corporation's retained earnings, he may have no voice in the company's dividend policy. The distribution or retention of earnings is the act of corporate management, which may be completely divorced from the corporate ownership. As Groves has said, "The taxation of corporations as partnerships violates the popular conceptions of income and of the relations of stockholders to corporations. Through decades of custom, corporations have come to be considered as institutions apart from their stockholders, and the income of the former is not regarded as belonging to the latter until dividends are declared."[36]

A very real objection to the taxation of corporate earnings in the hands of shareholders, whether distributed or not, is the hardship imposed on shareholders taxed on earnings which have not been distributed. This procedure clashes with the realization concept of taxable income, and unrealized income is certainly no indication of taxpaying ability. Under this plan a shareholder might have no alternative but to sell shares in order to pay a tax on income which he has not received and may never receive.[37]

Professor Groves has pointed out that corporations could overcome this problem to some extent by distributing cash dividends to meet the shareholders' tax liability, but the personal requirements of the shareholder are not always a determinant in corporate dividend policy.[38] It is also possible for corporations to distribute earnings through stock dividends or other securities and still retain the cash profits for reinvestment. But the capital structure of corporations should not be determined by tax avoidance considerations.

[36]*Postwar Taxation and Economic Progress*, pp. 56-7.
[37]*Ibid.*, pp. 56-7.
[38]*Ibid.*, p. 57.

Another defect in the general plan of taxing all corporate net income in the hands of shareholders involves the several administrative problems inherent in the plan. These problems fall into two groups, (1) those of determining to what classes of securities there should be an allocation of undistributed earnings in a given tax year, and (2) specific allocation problems arising after the classification of securities has been made.

Problems of the first group do not arise in the case of a corporation having only one class of common stock and no debt. But when a company has outstanding preference shares and bonds, the situation may be complicated,[39] especially when the company is not in a strong financial position. Under these circumstances, the bondholders and the preferred shareholders may benefit just as much as, or more than, the common shareholders when earnings are retained by the company. The risk attached to the senior securities may be reduced substantially by the transfer of earnings to surplus account, whereas the common shareholder may never actually receive any part of this income in the form of dividends. As earned surplus is swollen through repeated retention of earnings, it is conceivable that the value of the senior securities might appreciate by as much or more than the appreciation in the value of the common shares. This complication has such grave implications for tax equity that it rules out the general use of the plan for all corporations.

The second type of administrative difficulty involves the problems arising out of the allocation of undistributed earnings among the common shareholders. Among these problems are the following: (1) The first problem is connected with the allocation of the year's corporate profit when there is active trading of the shares. If an attempt were made to assess each owner of stock on his share of the earnings in accordance with the length of time the stock was held during the year, the administrative procedure would be terribly complicated. Any other allocation method would be inequitable in the case of undistributed earnings. (2) The second problem has to do with the treatment of special types of income,

[39]It would be particularly complicated where several holding companies lie between the operating company and the individual shareholder. Earnings allocated to common shares in a given year might actually be distributed a year later to the preference shares.

such as tax-exempt inter-corporate dividend payments. This is not as serious a problem as the first, because special provision could easily be made on the tax form to provide for the deduction of such income. (3) A particularly vexatious problem would be encountered should it be necessary to reaudit a corporate return, and thus reopen the shareholders' individual returns. A field audit of a given company some years after individual income tax assessments had been made could entail changes in thousands of individual income tax returns. While Groves suggests that this problem might be "minimized . . . by altering taxpayers' current income rather than reopening past returns,"[40] this is still no answer to the basic problem. The individual has a right to expect early clearance of his individual tax liability, and it would be most inequitable to have possible upward tax readjustments hanging over him indefinitely because of the fact that he owns shares of stock in a corporation.

Enough has been said, perhaps, to indicate some of the problems that would be encountered in an effort to treat all corporate income in the same way as the income of unincorporated business. These problems apply particularly, however, to the large, publicly held company, with a complicated financial structure and a widespread ownership. For this reason it has been argued:

> The situation might warrant a classification according to size, with small companies being treated like partnerships and large ones paying a compensatory undistributed-profits tax, adjusted as nearly as feasible to exact from the corporation the equivalent of what stockholders would pay were all earnings distributed. But the compensatory undistributed-profits tax would not be a very satisfactory means of tax integration, and chances are that it would incur the same political hostility heaped upon the "noble experiment" of 1936. If undistributed earnings are to receive any favours, it should be in the case of new small companies especially dependent upon this source for new equity capital.[41]

Mr. H. R. Bowen also argues for the use of what he calls the "partnership option" in the case of "small" corporations.[42] He

[40]*Ibid.*, p. 56.
[41]*Ibid.*, p. 59.
[42]"Optional Partnership Treatment of Corporate Earnings," *How Should Corporations be Taxed?* pp. 61-71.

states that "this measure would be a desirable first step in a long-term program for integrating the corporate and personal taxes,"[43] that "it would reduce discrimination against corporate as compared with noncorporate enterprises, that it would help smaller businesses to secure the benefit of operating under the corporate form . . . that it would be part of a program of tax relief for small business, and that it would not be very costly in terms of revenue."[44]

The very fact that the plan can be applied to certain corporations, i.e. small companies with a relatively simple capital structure and whose managerial policy is closely allied to the shareholders' interests, necessitates an arbitrary dividing line between corporations. This in itself creates the special problem of border-line cases. Such a plan would, of course, cover most Canadian corporations, but it would apply to a relatively small proportion of the total corporate profits earned in Canada.

The establishment in Canada of a dual system such as is found in Australia and Great Britain, with the partnership method confined to "private" companies would be likely to result in serious inequities and undue complications in the taxation of corporate earnings.[45] This method was introduced in Canada for "family" corporations in 1926 on an optional basis, but it was abandoned in 1932, when such companies were placed on the same footing with other corporations.[46] It still applies, however, to personal corporations and investment companies, as defined, on an optional basis.

If the taxation of certain corporations on the partnership basis were made compulsory, the effects would be serious for many small companies. Instead of helping them, as suggested by Groves and Lent, it might place them in a much worse position than under the present system. It is the small corporation that is so dependent upon retained earnings for expansion. Yet in many

[43]*Ibid.*, p. 67. [44]*Ibid.*, pp. 69-70.

[45]See Lent, *The Impact of the Undistributed Profits Tax*, pp. 152-3.

[46]The Ives Commission indicated that it would be an unwarranted departure from the established principle of corporate income taxation to resume this practice in respect of family corporations, unless it were part of a basic change in the whole field of the taxation of corporate profits. "Presumably this factor was of importance in the decision to rescind the provisions previously applicable to 'family corporations.'" *Report*, p. 69.

cases the personal tax paid on the income of a family corporation by a small number of shareholders would be higher than the corporate tax paid on retained earnings. Professor Butters states that "Probably there is general agreement that such a tax policy would be intolerable."[47]

If the plan were made optional, the corporations concerned would presumably select the tax basis more favourable to them. The very principle underlying a plan to allow certain companies to choose a method of taxation which allows the shareholders to select one tax that is lower than another violates all the canons of tax equity and tax neutrality. Furthermore, it is doubtful that such a plan would provide general relief to small corporations. If they elect to be taxed as partnerships, undistributed earnings are likely to be taxed at high rates, though the double taxation feature is eliminated. If they elect to be taxed as corporations, they are no better off than they now are. Such relief as would be provided would result almost entirely from the elimination of the double taxation of dividends. The partnership option for selected corporations appears to be an awkward means of mitigating the double taxation of dividends, and moreover, it is discriminatory in that it fails to reach the problem of double taxation in the case of corporations excluded from the partnership option.

It appears better, therefore, to approach this problem from the viewpoint of a dividend credit or some other device for retaining the tax on corporate income and eliminating the present double taxation. A plan of this kind has the added advantage, as compared with the partnership method, of not subjecting the retained earnings of the small corporation to the highly progressive rates of the personal income tax.

4. *The Dividends-Paid Credit Approach*

The plan involves the retention of both the corporate income

[47]"Should the Profits of Small Corporations be Taxed Like Partnership Earnings?" p. 79. In rejecting the partnership approach, the National Tax Association's Committee on the Federal Corporate Net Income Tax said "Like almost all committees that have investigated this subject, our Committee considered this ideal solution hopefully. And like most other committees we concluded regretfully (and with some dissent) that in our modern era this solution is not feasible. . . . Surrender of this ideal solution relinquishes the one hope of precise equity and neutrality in the tax system. Having burned this bridge, we may as well face up to the fact that what remains are only expedients qualifying, better and not so well, under the heading of 'rough justice.' " *Final Report*, p. 7.

and the personal income taxes. Corporations, however, would be granted a deduction or credit for dividends actually paid, in addition to the deduction now allowed for bond interest paid.

This approach, supported by Professor Butters,[48] is in reality a tax on undistributed profits. It is the plan recommended by the United States Treasury in 1936 for the repeal of the corporation income tax and the substitution therefor of a tax on undistributed profits. It removes effectively the double taxation feature of the existing Canadian or United States system, it places a premium on the distribution of corporate earnings because no corporation tax is paid on distributed earnings, and it provides the same treatment for dividend income and other forms of personal income.

Inasmuch as this plan removes the double taxation of corporate income and dividends, it should provide a stimulus to investment in equity securities. From a tax viewpoint, shares and bonds would be placed on the same footing. Furthermore, there is no administrative problem connected with this approach.

Up to this point, the dividends-paid credit plan appears to conform to the three minimum criteria of an acceptable approach to integration outlined above.[49] First, it provides equitable taxation of dividend income for shareholders in all groups. Second, the fact that declared dividends are deductible from the company's taxable earnings should go part-way towards meeting the

[48]"Should the Profits of Small Corporations be Taxed Like Partnership Earnings?" p. 83, and "Would the Complete Integration of the Corporate and Personal Income Taxes Injure Small Business?" p. 192. The most recent National Tax Association Committee on the Federal Corporate Net Income Tax, states: "On balance, and reserving the right to change its mind, the committee has expressed preference for the dividend deduction at the corporate level. *Preliminary Report*, July 1949, p. 17. In its *Final Report*, Aug. 1950, the Committee made the following recommendations (pp. 11-12):
"1) That the corporate tax be raised from 38 to 45 percent providing that the privilege of deducting dividends from the base be allowed to the extent of one-third of such dividends; or (stating differently what amounts to the same thing) we would change the corporate levy from its single rate of 38 percent to a dual charge, one of 45 percent on retained earnings and one of 30 percent on dividends;
"2) That small corporations (ranging, perhaps, to incomes of $250,000) be allowed the lower of the two rates on at least half of their income regardless of the disposition of such income (that is, a rate of 30 per cent would be applied to half their current income or to dividends paid, whichever were higher); and
"3) That in the present or any future use of graduation of the corporate levy, substantially the above differentials be applied in proportion to rates lower than the highest (for example, rates of 24 and 17 might be applied in lieu of the present 21 percent on the first $5000 of corporate income)."

[49]*Supra*, p. 262.

problem of tax avoidance or tax postponement fostered under the existing system. It does not, of course, solve completely the problem of undistributed profits, because the single rate at which undistributed income is taxed, whatever that rate be, cannot compensate for the range of rates that would apply to such income taxable in the hands of the shareholders. Third, it should minimize any adverse effects on investment that accrue under the current tax system. And fourth, it is feasible from an administrative viewpoint.

But this method of integration has an important defect in that it tends to discriminate against small and expanding corporations. Large and well-established corporations having access to the capital market would be likely to distribute a large part of their earnings, thus avoiding the tax on distributed corporate income, and finance any further expansion through the sale of new shares or bonds. But most companies have at best a limited access to the capital market, and must rely upon retained earnings to provide funds for expansion. Under the dividends-paid credit plan, these companies would be forced to pay the corporation tax on earnings retained, even though the retention of such earnings were desirable from the viewpoint of the national economy. The extent to which concentration of productive capacity in the hands of the large corporations would be stimulated under this plan would depend in large part upon the rate of tax levied on undistributed earnings.

From the Canadian viewpoint, however, there is a special problem attached to the dividends-paid credit approach, and that is the fairly heavy revenue loss that it would entail. It is reported that the total of corporate profits in Canada for 1948 was $2,174 million before taxes. The total corporate income and excess profits taxes amounted to $744 million. Undistributed profits amounted to $890 million,[50] leaving dividend payments of $540 million. Had full credit been given in that year for all dividends paid, the $540 million would have been deducted from the total net income of $2,174 million, leaving $1,634 million. At the prevailing corporate rate of 30 per cent, the normal tax would have

[50]See *National Accounts Income and Expenditure,* 1947-1948, Revised, Table VI, pp. 12, 13.

been $490 million, or $162 million less than it actually was. But it seems likely that complete deduction of all dividends for corporate tax purposes would have resulted in greater dividend payments, and thus the revenue loss on corporate account would have been substantially larger.

Part of this loss would have been recovered through increased individual income taxes, resulting from the greater distribution of earnings. A substantial portion of the dividend payments made to individuals in Canada is received by people who pay personal tax at rates much higher than the corporate rate.[51] But a large part of the total dividend payments are made to other corporations, and are not normally taxable. In 1947 Canadian corporations reported a total of $165 million in non-taxable dividends, compared with only $111 million of taxable dividends reported by individuals resident in Canada.

Furthermore, a very large portion of the dividends paid by Canadian corporations are received by non-residents, particularly in the United States. It is difficult to get precise figures on the amount of such dividend payments, but the total of dividend and interest payments to American investors in 1947 amounted to $222 million. Probably more than half of this was in the form of dividends. It was reported that in 1945 the total earnings, after corporation and withholding taxes, on common stock of Canadian companies held in the United States was $129 million, of which $59.6 million was reinvested.[52] Such dividends paid to non-residents are subject to a 15 per cent withholding tax. Were they to be deductible from corporate income, there would, of course, be

[51]In 1947, for example, over half the taxable dividends paid to individuals in Canada were received by persons who paid tax at a rate greater than 40 per cent. The data for this compilation were provided by Mr. Mark F. Sprott, Director of Economics and Statistics, Department of National Revenue, in a letter to me dated July 21, 1949.

[52]United States, Department of Commerce, *International Transactions of the United States during the War, 1940-1945,* Table 15, p. 73. It was estimated that about one-third of the investment in all Canadian manufacturing companies was American-owned in 1939. See Report of the Commissioners, Combines Investigation Act, *Canada and International Cartels,* Oct. 10, 1945, p. 41. It is estimated that in 1948 about 32 per cent of the ownership of Canadian industry was in the hands of non-residents. See Dominion Bureau of Statistics, *Canada's International Investment Position, Selected Years 1926 to 1949,* p. 10. The total value of the capital stock of Canadian companies held by non-residents was $3,680 million, of which $2,615 million was held in the United States. *Ibid.,* p. 35.

an absolute revenue loss, unless the withholding rate were increased. This is not considered desirable, however, because an increase in this rate might have an adverse effect upon the investment of American capital in Canada.

Thus the dividends-paid credit approach, while theoretically attractive, would entail a substantial revenue loss if applied in Canada.

5. *The Withholding Tax Approach*

This plan involves the levy of a tax on all taxable corporate income, whether distributed or retained. The tax is regarded as being paid by the corporation on behalf of its shareholders. When dividends are distributed, individual shareholders include in their taxable personal incomes the cash dividends actually received plus the withholding tax paid on their behalf by the corporation. This is necessary because the tax paid by the corporation is used to meet part of the shareholders' tax liabilities. It is properly regarded, therefore, as part of the shareholders' income. After computing his personal income tax on this basis, the shareholder takes credit for the amount of tax withheld at the corporate level. This is the system used in Great Britain.

The withholding approach is designed to reduce or eliminate the double taxation of distributed profits by applying all or part of the tax paid by the corporation on such profits against the tax liability of the shareholders. For this reason, the shareholder is not required to pay a tax on his dividends, unless his individual tax liability exceeds the amount already paid by the corporation on his behalf. If the corporate tax rate is lower than the upper rates on personal income, there will be cases in which further tax liability accrues to the shareholder in respect of his dividend income. If, on the other hand, the amount paid by the corporation is greater than a shareholder's personal tax liability (because the corporate rate is higher than that person's individual rate) the shareholder is entitled to a refund. Thus, in Britain, where the corporate withholding rate is 45 per cent, if the corporate profits were £100, and the entire earnings £55 after taxes were paid as a dividend, the shareholder would include £100 in his gross income, and deduct £45 from the total tax due on his total income. If his total tax liability is £60, he must pay an additional £15. If it is only £40, he receives a refund of £5.

Theoretically the withholding tax might be considered to achieve the same uniformity in the tax treatment of dividends and other forms of income as is achieved under the dividends-paid credit approach. But there are several administrative complications attached to the plan which make the results of its application fall short of the uniformity of treatment required by the ideal of equity. The more important administrative considerations are as follows:

(*a*) Rate of Tax

The rate of the withholding tax on corporate income is important from the viewpoint of both equity and revenue yield. If tax avoidance or postponement through retention of corporation profits is to be prevented, the withholding rate would have to be as high as the highest rate on personal income. But under the present personal income tax rate structure, with a top bracket rate of 80 per cent, it would not seem possible or practical to equate the corporate rate with the top individual rate. The economic effects on corporate enterprise would likely be disastrous. If, on the other hand, the withholding rate strikes an average of the rates on different levels of personal income, considerable tax postponement and tax avoidance through the retention of corporate earnings is likely to result. The lower the withholding rate, the greater the discrimination between the tax on undistributed corporate earnings and the tax on the earnings of unincorporated businesses.

(*b*) Refunds

Since considerations of equity demand the refund of withholding tax payments in excess of the individual shareholder's personal tax liability, the number of such refunds must vary inversely with the withholding tax rate. If the withholding rate were equated with the lowest personal income tax rate (at present 15 per cent in Canada), refunds would be few. But the problem of undistributed profits would be greatly magnified, and revenue reduced sharply. If the existing corporate

rate structure were retained many refunds would be necessary, and these would cause administrative expense as well as additional trouble in auditing income tax returns.

(*c*) Problems Related to the Method of Withholding

A particular difficulty connected with the withholding device is the method employed in adding the amount of the withholding tax, already paid by the company, to the cash dividends received by the shareholder for the purpose of computing total individual tax liability. It can be done either through the uniform mark-up of cash dividends, which is the easiest and simplest method, or through refinements which complicate the administration of the tax.

In Great Britain the uniform mark-up is used. Shareholders are required to increase their cash dividends by a uniform fraction to reflect the current rate of withholding at the corporate level. If this were adopted in Canada, and if the combined federal and provincial taxes were considered exclusively as withholding taxes, each recipient of dividend income would include in his taxable income roughly $1.45 for each $1 of cash dividends received.

The first problem arising from this simple mark-up is the treatment of dividends on preference shares. If a corporation's net income after taxes is large enough to meet preferred dividend payments, and they are in fact paid, the withholding tax would not be borne by the preferred shareholders. Accordingly, should the preference shareholders be given the same tax credit as the common shareholders, they would receive a windfall. As the residual equity holder in the corporation, the common shareholder normally would bear the corporate tax, and he is not recompensed by the uniform mark-up and credit system described above.[53] As Professor Goode has pointed out, "mere denial of a withholding credit to preferred stockholders would not meet

[53]Goode makes this point with the following example. Assume corporate profits of $100, withholding tax of $40, preferred dividends of $50. There would thus be only $10 available for common dividends. The withholding tax would have occasioned a $40 or 80 per cent reduction in income available for common dividends, but the 67 per cent mark-up would give common shareholders credit for a maximum of $6.70 of withholding. *The Postwar Corporation Tax Structure,* p. 30, note 60.

the problem."[54] One procedure would be to require corporations to reduce contractual dividends on preference shares by the amount of the withholding tax. Another would be to grant corporations a credit for preferred dividends paid before arriving at the amount of net earnings subject to the withholding tax. This, of course, combines the general withholding approach with a feature of the dividends-paid credit plan discussed in the preceding section.

The second problem arises in connection with dividends paid from income that was not earned in the current tax year. Two different situations arise here. First, in the case of earnings accumulated but not distributed prior to the adoption of a withholding tax, discrimination would result if dividends paid out of such earnings were not placed in a separate category. If dividends paid from previously retained earnings are treated as though they had been subject to a withholding tax, the shareholders of corporations which had retained earnings would be favoured over those of corporations which did distribute their earnings. In the case of the latter, the full corporate tax has been on earnings, and the full tax paid on that part of them distributed. If earnings that had been retained under the old tax system were distributed under the withholding system, the shareholders would receive a credit for a corporation tax paid in the past when it was not in fact a withholding tax. The second situation arises when the withholding rate is varied from time to time, resulting in many cases of understatement or overstatement of actual withholding. Under the withholding system, changes in the withholding rate should be geared to changes in individual income tax rates. That is to say, the withholding rate should be changed in accordance with changes in individual rates in order to minimize the number of overstatements and understatements of personal tax liability. Goode has pointed out that "if rates fluctuated widely, this defect would seem to be serious enough to require some refinement of the simple system already described."[55]

A third problem arises out of dividends paid from corporate income which is tax-exempt, such as intercorporate dividends and

[54] *Ibid.*
[55] *Ibid.*

capital gains. Such income must be deducted from net income before taxable income is established as the base for the existing income tax. But in the case of a complicated holding company corporate structure, where the operating company paid the withholding tax, it would be necessary to trace back intercorporate dividend payments through the different corporate layers in order to determine what tax had been paid by the operating company so that the proper credit could be allowed to the shareholder of the holding company with respect to dividends received by him.

From the cursory examination of some of the major problems arising out of the use of the uniform mark-up of cash dividends, it is apparent that this approach does not lend itself to anything like complete satisfaction of our basic equity requirements. The most serious difficulties arise in connection with the treatment of (1) dividends paid from earnings received, accumulated prior to the adoption of the withholding plan, (2) dividends paid when different withholding rates were in effect, and (3) dividends paid out of intercorporate dividends, which are tax-exempt.

Further difficulties arise out of the current provisions for the carry-forward of losses, and result in the changing of the amount of net taxable income at the corporate level and, of course, corresponding changes in the credit allowed to shareholders with respect to the withholding tax paid on their behalf.

While these and other problems could be met with arbitrary rulings of the Department of National Revenue, or through specific provisions of the Income Tax Act, such provisions would serve only to add complications to an already complicated statute and the administrative procedures applicable to it.

Summarizing the withholding approach, the following observations may be made: (1) In theory the withholding approach eliminates the double taxation of corporate income and dividends, in that the amount of tax withheld by the corporation on the shareholder's account is credited to the shareholder for personal income tax purposes. But, because of the impracticability of equating the withholding rate with the highest personal income tax rate,[56] the withholding approach would not equalize the taxa-

[56]Complete integration of income taxes could, of course, be achieved only when the withholding rate was equated with the highest personal income tax rate. But not only would this magnify the refund problem, it would place undue pressure

tion of distributed and undistributed profits. This is the same defect as was noted in the case of the dividends-paid credit approach. (2) The administrative complications involved in the necessity for refunds, in the treatment of dividends paid out of earnings retained before the utilization of the withholding approach, in the treatment of dividends paid out of tax-exempt income, in the treatment of dividends paid out of earnings accruing under a different rate structure, all would add unnecessarily to an already complicated tax structure. (3) The British system ignores conveniently changes in withholding rates, thus avoiding the problem arising from them. But it is doubtful if such a practice would be acceptable in Canada. (4) The withholding approach, while perhaps better in theory than the dividends-paid credit approach, has administrative difficulties attached to it which require most careful consideration in terms of achieving the kind of tax equity deemed desirable in an approach to integration.

6. *The Dividends-Received Credit Approach*

Under this approach a tax would be levied on corporate income, but an exemption (partial or total) or a tax credit would be applied to dividends when received by shareholders. While it is not a necessary feature of the plan, it is often contemplated that the corporate tax rate would be reduced to the level of the lowest personal income tax rate, and that dividends would be exempt from the first bracket rate of the individual tax rate.[57] This approach is similar to the system used in the United States prior to 1936,[58] and a modification of it was introduced in Canada

on the small and medium-size corporations to distribute rather than reinvest their earnings. See Lent, *The Impact of the Undistributed Profits Tax, 1936-1937*, p. 157.

[57]See Goode, "Alternative Approaches to the Integration of Corporate and Individual Income Taxes," p. 138. See also the Committee on Postwar Tax Policy, *A Tax Program for a Solvent America*, 1947, p. 119, who state that "The ultimate goal, not presently in sight, should be a corporation tax rate identical with the first bracket rate on individual income."

[58]This approach was recommended in the United States by a Committee on Postwar Tax Policy, of which Mr. Roswell Magill was Chairman. See the committee's report, *A Tax Program for a Solvent America*, 1945, pp. 98-103. But the National Tax Association's Committee on the Federal Corporate Net Income Tax referred to above rejected this plan because "(1) it calls for no refunds in case the stockholder's tax liability is less than the credit; and (2) it fails to include the corporate tax in the measure of the personal tax liability." The plan was damned

in 1949, when a credit of 10 per cent was extended with respect to dividends received by shareholders.

The dividends-received credit approach resembles the withholding approach in some respects, but in several important respects it is quite different. It resembles withholding in that the reduction of the personal income tax on dividends is justified on the grounds that the corporate tax should be looked upon as a partial payment of the individual shareholder's tax liability in respect of his portion of the earnings. But it does not achieve equity among shareholders in different income brackets, as is done in the dividends-paid credit approach and the withholding approach. For example, under the existing corporate rate in Canada (federal and provincial) of approximately 45 per cent, taxes on dividends and other income would be equalized only in the personal income bracket where the top individual tax rate of shareholders amounted to 45 per cent (the $15,000-$25,000 bracket). All shareholders whose top income tax rate is lower than the corporate rate would be unable to take full advantage of the exemption. Shareholders who have no personal income tax liability at all would get no advantage whatever from the exemption. On the other hand, shareholders whose income is in brackets bearing a higher rate than the corporate rate would receive a tax reduction which would more than offset the net burden of the present corporate tax. Goode states: "By its nature, the dividends-received-credit approach would not benefit low-income stockholders, but it would offer substantial advantages to stockholders with high incomes."[59]

One problem attached to the dividends-received credit approach involves the type of dividends to which a credit is attached. When the Minister of Finance presented his budget speech in March of 1949, announcing a 10 per cent dividend credit to shareholders, he stated that "the law will actually confine the credit to the most junior class of shareholders of a company, and it will not be granted in respect of shares that enjoy any special preference. Generally speaking, the incidence of the corporate

in these words: "There seems little to be said for it except that it is administratively simple. The Committee does not regard this advantage as convincing. Indeed none of our members except one had any kind words for the dividend-received credit." *Final Report,* p. 10.

[59]*The Postwar Corporation Tax Structure,* p. 35.

tax is upon the common shareholders, and I believe that they rather than preferred shareholders should be granted such relief as can be given at this time."[60]

The Minister's argument was not acceptable to some observers. Typical comment is found in an editorial in the *Financial Post*:

> Why the Abbott concession was offered on common stock only has never been satisfactorily explained. The same arguments that apply to the common stock apply with almost equal force to the preferred. Dividends for both come from the same source, the profits of the company which have already been taxed heavily before one cent of dividends are paid. To partially exempt one and not the other, creates all sorts of complications, but it also debases a security which is supposed to rank ahead of the other and has long been sold on that understanding.[61]

The opposite viewpoint was expressed in another editorial which supported the reasoning behind the discrimination between common and preference shares as follows:

> We cannot share the view of the *Financial Post* that the income tax concession already proposed on common stock dividends should be extended to preferred dividends. If they are receiving the dividend rate stipulated in the preference arrangement, preferred shareholders are in no way suffering from the income tax collected on the company's earnings; while the common shareholders are suffering from the company's having paid income tax not only on the part of its income distributed to, or held for the future equity of, the common shareholders but also on the part distributed to the preferred shareholders.
>
> If the preferred shareholders are not getting their stipulated dividend, and yet the company is paying income tax on its earnings, they are perhaps being slightly damaged by that taxation, but we cannot see by what method of computation their loss could be estimated and exemption granted to them, not to mention that if they are getting no dividend at all there is nothing to exempt. Where there is a supplementary distribution to the preferred beyond the stipulated rate it ceases to be a preferred dividend and should of course be treated in exactly the same way as the common, and we presume will be so treated.[62]

This indicates the intricate nature of the problem and the

[60]*House of Commons Debates,* March 22, 1949, p. 1799.
[61]*Financial Post,* Aug. 13, 1949.
[62]*Saturday Night,* Sept. 13, 1949.

administrative difficulty that is attached to any attempt made to apply different treatment to preferred dividend payments in excess of the stipulated rate. The simple approach is either the complete exclusion or the complete inclusion of preferred dividends in the tax credit allowance. In his second budget speech of 1949, the Minister of Finance announced that the credit would be extended to include dividends from all classes of shares, both common and preferred. He stated: "This change will remove a great many technical difficulties and anomalies which would have risen in attempting to administer my original proposal of limiting the tax credit solely to shares 'having no preference of any kind.' "[63] It is worth noting that this problem does not arise in the dividends-paid credit approach.

The dividends-received credit plan does not treat all shareholders in all income brackets alike, as is done under both the dividends-paid credit and the withholding plans. It does not, therefore, achieve as much equity. A modification of the plan recommended in the United States to the Ways and Means Committee of the House of Representatives[64] makes the net effects of the plan less apparent, but it does not obviate them.

The dividends-received credit approach does not qualify completely as an acceptable method of integration because it fails to achieve as much equity as some of the alternative approaches, and because it could not very well be employed to achieve full elimination of double taxation. If the tax credit were to be set at 100 per cent of the dividends received, equity in the individual income tax structure would be distorted completely. In effect the recipients of dividends from Canadian companies would pay no tax on them. Despite the fact that a corporation tax has already been paid, it seems inequitable that dividend income should be exempt. In short, the cart has been put before the horse.

[63]*House of Commons Debates*, Oct. 20, 1949, p. 978.

[64]The proposal was as follows: "The stockholder includes in his table income the amount of dividends actually received by him, and, after computing his tax, takes a credit on account of the tax paid by the corporation with respect to his dividends. This credit would be calculated by multiplying his dividends by the initial or lowest-bracket rate of the individual income tax (normal tax rate and surtax rate combined). In order to avoid refunds, it should be provided that the credit should in no case be greater than the total tax due. This plan would not result in complete elimination of the double tax, but it would result in a great improvement. We recommended it for adoption." United States, Congress, House of Representatives, Committee on Ways and Means, *Revenue Revisions*, p. 3622.

How far the dividend credit can be extended without serious distortion of the personal income tax structure must remain a matter of conjecture. But it cannot be extended very far, and this is the fundamental weakness of the plan. The best that can be said for it is that it does provide some measure of tax relief.

Summary and Conclusions

The existing system of taxing corporate income and dividends is inequitable in that it does not accord dividend income the same tax treatment as other income, and it does not reach the problem of undistributed corporate profits, thus perpetuating the discrimination between incorporated and unincorporated businesses. Furthermore, it has adverse effects on investment in equity shares, making it difficult for any save the large and well-established business units to secure new capital for expansion requirements. The core of the problem appears to be that of undistributed profits. Integration of the corporate and personal income taxes is necessary, therefore, on grounds both of equity and economic considerations. The minimum requirements for an acceptable integration plan are: (1) the equitable taxation of dividend income of shareholders in all income groups; (2) the prevention of undue tax avoidance or postponement by shareholders through the retention of corporate earnings; (3) the least possible adverse effect on investment and incentive; and (4) administrative feasibility and simplicity.

1. *Approaches to Integration*

The simplest approach is the outright repeal of the corporate income tax. In order to meet the problem of undistributed profits, however, such a programme requires the use of a capital gains tax at the prevailing personal income tax rates. This is not considered feasible for two reasons: (1) the immediate revenue loss would be intolerable, and (2) even though the accrual of undistributed profits would eventually be taxable on realization of the capital gains, the administrative difficulties would outweigh any advantage, practical or theoretical, derived from the use of a capital gains tax.

The exemption of dividends from personal income taxation, while it would result in a very serious revenue loss, would result in serious inequity among shareholders in different income brackets. Therefore this proposal is discarded.

The partnership approach, which would include all undistributed corporate profits in the individual tax base, would equalize completely taxes on undistributed profits and other forms of income. This approach is logically the line of uncompromising insistence on equity at all costs, but it has no recommendation beyond the realm of pure theory. As a complete solution it is ruled out on practical grounds by the character of the modern corporation and the varied patterns of financial structure and stock ownership, which present insoluble difficulties. It is not realistic to ignore the corporate entity entirely. As a partial solution this approach is unsatisfactory because of the many complications involved in drawing the line between corporations which are to be treated as partnerships and those which are to be taxed as corporations.

From a theoretical viewpoint, both the dividends-paid credit approach and the withholding approach are feasible and equitable methods of reducing the existing differences in the taxation of distributed corporate earnings and other forms of personal income. Neither approach, however, presents a really effective solution to the problem of achieving equitable taxation of undistributed corporate earnings because of the difference that must exist between the tax rate on such earnings and the upper rate of a steeply progressive rate structure applied to individual income. Of the two approaches, the dividends-paid credit plan presents less administrative difficulty, does not involve the refunds necessitated under the withholding approach, and seems, therefore, to merit more support. But it has the drawback of costing a substantial revenue loss.

The dividends-received credit plan, whether based on a complete credit allowance or a modified version, such as proposed by the Committee on Postwar Tax Policy, does not conform to our minimum requirements for an acceptable integration plan. It is not an equitable method of taxing undistributed profits, and it discriminates in favour of high income shareholders and against low income shareholders. Professor Goode has summarized the case against this approach neatly in these words: ". . . as a means of increasing the equity of the tax system, there seems to be almost nothing to be said in favor of the special tax scale that would result from the dividend-received credit approach."[65] It is concluded that the partial approach proposed by the Minister of Finance in 1949 is a move in the wrong direction, judged by standards of theoretical tax equity. But considering the possible alternatives, perhaps the practical justification of this policy overrides its theoretical defects. It does provide relief, although it can never be extended far enough to remove the double taxation of corporate income.

2. *The Problem of Small Business*

The type of approach to the problem of integration that satisfies the minimum requirements as laid down in this study appears to be in the direction of the dividends-paid credit plan. But it is recognized that such an approach does not result in a real solution to the undistributed profits problem. Neither does it provide direct help to the small and growing business at the point where it needs it most. Such companies usually have to rely upon funds from internal sources with which to finance expansion.

[65]"Alternative Approaches to the Integration of Corporate and Individual Income Taxes," p. 145. Goode shows (p. 142) the comparative results of the existing United States system and the chief alternatives to it in the following tabulation (these figures are roughly applicable to the Canadian situation):

Stockholder's marginal individual tax rate	*Total tax*[a]		
	Present system[b]	Dividends-paid credit plan[c] and withholding plan[d]	Dividends-received credit plan[e]
%	$	$	$
0	38.00	19.00	38.00
19	49.78	34.39	38.00
30	56.60	43.30	44.82
40	62.80	51.40	51.02
50	69.00	59.50	57.22
60	75.20	67.60	63.42
70	81.40	75.70	69.62
80	87.60	83.80	75.82

[a]The combined corporate and individual income taxes on $100 of distributed profits.

[b]38 per cent corporate income tax.

[c]38 per cent corporate tax; corporations receive a tax credit equal to 19 per cent of dividends paid.

[d]38 per cent corporate income tax, of which one-half is considered withholding.

[e]38 per cent corporate income tax; individuals receive a tax credit equal to 19 per cent of dividends received.

It must be conceded, of course, that small growing companies would benefit to some extent from the partial integration resulting from an approach such as the dividends-paid credit plan. But the fundamental problem of this type of enterprise is not solved by this approach. What is required is a plan which would increase the funds available from retained earnings. In short, measures designed to eliminate or reduce the double taxation of dividends will not meet the problem of the small corporation.

While the case for the small growing corporation seems clear, it is difficult to reconcile through tax policy two conflicting objectives. On the one hand, it is desirable from the viewpoint of tax equity to treat corporate income in the same way as other income. The practical approach appears to lie in the direction of a compromise which imposes a fairly severe tax on undistributed income. On the other hand it is desirable to allow small corporations to retain earnings (their major source of capital) without incurring a penalty which would discourage their expansion. What is needed is policy which is designed to prevent the use of the corporate form for tax avoidance purposes, and at the same time would encourage small enterprises. In short, we want to prevent "improper" accumulation of undistributed corporate earnings, and yet make possible "proper" accumulation of such earnings. The task of distinguishing between proper and improper accumulations is one of the imponderables attached to the formulation of equitable tax policy. Whatever is done, only rough justice can be achieved.

There are several approaches to this problem of the small corporation. The first attempts to meet it through graduation of the corporate rate structure. This was the approach adopted in 1949 by the Minister of Finance, when he announced that the corporate tax rate would be 10 per cent on the first $10,000 of corporate profits, and 33 per cent on all profits in excess of $10,000.[66] This plan has much to commend it, despite the fact

[66]On September 7, 1950, the Minister of Finance announced in his budget speech an upward revision of the rates to 15 per cent on the first $10,000 and 38 per cent on the amount in excess of $10,000 of corporate profits. This was necessary because of Canada's increasing defence commitments. On April 10, 1951, he announced a 20 per cent defence surcharge on profits in excess of $10,000. On October 15, 1951, he announced another 2 per cent tax on all corporate income for old age security.

that there is no theoretical justification for rate progression in the case of corporate income. As used in Canada today, it represents a concession to small business. The Minister said so in his budget speech of March 22, 1949: "Our country as a whole owes a great deal to the small family type of business. They have to struggle along, grow and develop in competition with large and well financed corporations whose activities may be nation-wide. My own belief is that small businesses should be encouraged and it seems to me that a useful way to do this is to lower the tax and take less out of the funds they need for growth and expansion."[67]

The second approach involves a basic exemption applicable to the corporate income tax, such as is provided under the individual income tax. This plan would cause a greater revenue loss than results from the application of a low rate on small profits. Regardless of the amount of the exemption allowed, many corporations would be removed completely from the corporate tax structure. If any significant exemption were provided in Canada, a large number of corporations would pay no tax. Suppose, for example, that a flat exemption of $1,000 had been allowed in the 1946 tax year, 3,355 corporations would have paid no tax. An exemption large enough to be really effective, say $25,000, would have removed 17,917 corporations (out of a total of 23,166) from the tax base, causing a revenue loss of $20,067,000 in that year. Were the exemptions to be extended to all corporations, regardless of size (as is done under the individual income tax), the revenue loss would be very much greater.

Neither of these approaches is selective enough to assist the growing small enterprise without giving at the same time a windfall concession to corporations which do not need it because they have no reason or desire to expand, or which can expand without such assistance. If the concession is substantial enough to give real assistance to companies with a legitimate claim for aid, it is likely to increase further unwarranted retention of corporate earnings.

Better than either of the above plans is the direct one of allowing accelerated depreciation designed particularly to aid growing enterprises, as well as special obsolescence and depletion

[67]*House of Commons Debates,* March 22, 1949, p. 1798.

allowances, and special consideration of expenditures made for research and development.

3. *General Conclusions*

On both economic and equity grounds, integration of the corporation and personal income taxes seems necessary. No one method of integration appears to be entirely acceptable, however, because special problems are attached to each. From a theoretical viewpoint, the withholding and the dividends-paid credit approaches are the most attractive. But the former would involve a large number of refunds because of the wide differential between the corporate and individual tax rates. The latter avoids this, but runs headlong into the serious problem of non-resident shareholders. Perhaps this could be overcome through a partial credit with respect to dividends paid. The problem would be circumvented were the credit allowed only on dividends paid by Canadian companies to individuals resident in Canada. Such a procedure is, of course, discriminatory. Perhaps the implications of such discrimination are such as to condemn it.

Regardless of the integration plan adopted, the problem of small and growing enterprise still remains one requiring special attention. While the rate graduation introduced in the 1949 budget accords some relief to small companies, a better approach appears to be in the direction of accelerated depreciation allowances, and perhaps, in the case of new companies, complete exemption for the first few years of their existence, as is now granted to co-operatives.

In conclusion, it should be stated that the whole problem of taxing corporate income and dividends so as to minimize the adverse effects upon the national economy and secure some measure of rough justice is so complicated that there is no one answer that excludes all others. All that one can hope for is a careful balancing of the special features, both good and bad, of the various approaches to a solution, and an intelligent compromise which will come closest to the target of revenue requirements and tax justice.

CHAPTER NINE

DEFENCE FINANCING AND THE CORPORATION TAX

INTRODUCTION

SINCE the original text of this study was completed, the outbreak of war in Korea has necessitated an unprecedented peacetime defence programme. Canada proposes to spend $5,000 million on defence during the next three years. The estimates tabled in the House of Commons by the Minister of Finance on March 12, 1951, provided for an expenditure of $1,664 million for defence in the fiscal year 1951–2, which is $893 million more than the total defence outlay in 1950–1. On April 10 the Minister brought down a budget providing for a total expenditure of $3,700 million on current account, or $1,290 million (51.2 per cent) greater than the previous year's budget.

It seems likely that defence expenditures will be increased even beyond the existing average annual commitment of $1,666 million, and that they will continue over an indefinite period of time. This means that a heavy defence programme must be accommodated as a way of life. Since government policy is to pay for it out of current revenues, heavy taxation is clearly indicated. Taking into account the universal old age pension plan that will be implemented in January of 1952, the next Canadian budget will call for an expenditure of about $4,225 million.

Nothing like this situation has ever confronted us before. We are living in a twilight zone which is neither peace nor war. Actual war has at least the advantage of being relatively brief because the requirements of modern war are so intolerably heavy that no nation can endure them long. But our present situation can be prolonged indefinitely, accompanied, of course, by increasing economic strain and falling standards of living.

The defence programme is certain to exert pressures on the national economy which have little in common with our experience in World War II or in the immediate post-war period. We entered the late war with a great deal of slack in the economy, and for this reason the effect of rearmament was not felt for some time. Moreover, there was a considerable time lag before the economy was converted to full war production and full employment of our resources, human and material.

In the immediate post-war period there was fear of a recession in industrial activity as a result of the cessation of war production and the anticipated difficulty of converting the nation's industrial plant to peacetime production. Official economic planning was accordingly based upon a "cheap money" policy aimed at promoting capital investment and industrial expansion. Now, however, we are embarking upon heavy unproductive government expenditure in a situation of full employment where inflationary pressures are already very strong. Inflation has made serious inroads into the living standard of many Canadians. Unless the new inflationary pressures released by defence expenditures are deliberately checked, the prospects of most of the Canadian people are very unpleasant, to say the least.

The situation is so serious that it may properly be termed a crisis. In times of crisis conventional ways of thought and action must be adapted to meet the emergency. There was little criticism of the extreme measures, some of which verged on authoritarianism, that were employed during the war. We were governed to a large extent by decree. Price, wage, manpower, and commodity controls were imposed. Compulsory saving was introduced, and the tax burden was crushing. Certainly the wartime policies were filled with inequities, and their economic effects were profound. But these policies, or something very much like them, were necessary, and they served their purpose. They were tolerable because they were temporary. Canada emerged from World War II in a strong economic position which has been maintained up to this time.

Now we are faced with the urgent need of turning out vast

quantities of war material again, and the success of this programme involves the attainment of two objectives. The first, of course, is increased production. The second is economic stability. They are really inseparable, because stability means an underlying balance between spending and supply. The allotment of commodities, productive capacity, and manpower to defence production will certainly receive first priority. Consequently, civilian supply of many commodities is likely to be reduced. But civilian demand for goods will be increased as defence spending increases. Herein lies the potential disaster of uncontrolled inflation.

Indicated Policy

It is most important to formulate and implement policy designed to prevent the results of a programme that will certainly lead to further inflation and the very real danger of frustrating defence production, to collapse of public morale, and possibly to ultimate economic collapse. The choice of methods by which to avert disaster is of critical importance. It has been stated:

> At first sight there may seem to be a choice of two methods. One is to impose direct controls over prices and wages, and to allocate resources by government direction. The other is to encourage the vitality of an open economy, relying on its productive power and allowing the price system to do its work properly, protecting it from inflation and distortion by means of the indirect methods of fiscal and monetary control.
>
> There is really no choice. Comprehensive direct controls would defeat the purpose in the following ways: they would drive the economy into a regime of black markets and administrative paralysis, would destroy public morale and the incentive to produce, and would conceal inflation without preventing it. They would in any event require crushing taxation to be practicable at all.[1]

It is conceded, of course, that direct controls will be necessary in the case of some strategic commodities and that the extent of their use will be conditioned partly by what is done in the United States, in view of our joint supply arrangements with that coun-

[1]Monteath Douglas and J. R. Petrie, "Taxation for Defence," *Financial Post*, Dec. 9, 1950. The complete text of this paper appears in Canadian Tax Foundation, *Report of Proceedings of the Fourth Tax Conference 1950*, p. 49.

try. But if Canada can maintain economic stability on the home front, the use of such controls may well be held to a bare minimum.

The only alternative to direct commodity, price, and wage controls is the bold use of the indirect controls of fiscal and monetary policy. If this is done, inflation can be checked, and we can operate within a relatively free price economy. There is no need here to embark upon a discussion of the monetary policy required to meet our objectives. It is the fiscal policy that concerns us now.[2] It is strictly necessary for the government to conduct its budgetary operations in such a way that they add least to the existing inflationary pressures, and exert the greatest possible stabilizing influence. This means that the whole of the government's outlay on current account throughout the entire rearmament period should be financed from current revenues without recourse to borrowing. Probably this alone is not sufficient. Each budget should provide for a substantial surplus.

In view of this policy proposal it becomes necessary to restate the objectives of tax policy that were outlined earlier. It will be recalled that three objectives were laid down in order of their importance: raising revenue, fostering production, and attaining the greatest equity consistent with the first two. The objectives are now restated as: raising revenue, fostering production, main-

[2]For more complete treatment of the over-all problem in Canada, see Canadian Chamber of Commerce, "Inflation—The Problem," *News Letter*, Nov. 1950; Monteath Douglas and J. R. Petrie, "Taxation for Defence," *Financial Post*, Dec. 9, 1950; J. R. Petrie, "A Tough Budget?" *Canadian Business*, March 1951, and "What Kind of Taxes?" *ibid.*; Graham Towers, *Expectations and Events*, Address to the Empire Club of Canada and the Canadian Club of Toronto, Nov. 9, 1950; Kenneth R. Wilson, "Next Year's Taxes May Not be So Bad, *Financial Post*, Nov. 18, 1950. For material on the situation in the United States, see B. H. Beckhart, "Financial Implications of Rearmament," *Commercial and Financial Chronicle*, Oct. 26, 1950; Roy Blough, "An Anti-Inflation Program," *ibid.*, Oct. 5, 1950, and "Fiscal Policy as Inflationary Curb," *ibid.*, Nov. 9, 1950; W. Randolph Burgess, "Financing Defenses," *ibid.*; Committee for Economic Development, *Economic Policy for Rearmament*, and *Paying for Defense*; Peter F. Drucker, "This War is Different," *Harper's Magazine*, Nov. 1950; Marriner S. Eccles, "The Defense of the Dollar," *Fortune*, Nov. 1950; Leon H. Keyserling, "What Controls Do We Need?" *Commercial and Financial Chronicle*, Oct. 26, 1950; Roswell Magill, "Rearmament Poses Need for Sound Tax Program," *Tax Review*, Oct. 1950; Sumner H. Slichter, "Likely Characteristics of Our Defense Economy," *Commercial and Financial Chronicle*, Aug. 31, 1950, "Economic Problems of a Defense Economy," *ibid.*, Oct. 19, 1950, "Some Current Economic Misconceptions," *ibid.*, Nov. 16, 1950, and "Business and Rearmament," *Atlantic Monthly*, Nov. 1950.

taining economic balance by controlling inflation, and attaining the greatest equity consistent with the first three. Raising revenue still ranks first in importance. Fostering production and maintaining economic balance are inseparable and carry the same weight. Considerations of equity, while still important, inevitably must give way to the exigency of the situation, and tax equity will certainly be distorted when taxation is used as an instrument of control.[3]

It is of fundamental importance to the effectiveness of fiscal policy as a means of curbing inflation that the money taken away from the taxpayers for this purpose be not spent by the government. The theory of curbing the inflationary pressure caused by excessive demand for consumers' and producers' goods by taxing away a substantial part of the excess demand for scarce goods is clear enough. But surely the principle involved indicates that this excess purchasing power is taken out of circulation. If the money is spent by the government the end result can be little different from what would have happened had it been spent by the taxpayers. In other words, if this kind of fiscal policy results merely in shifting spending from private to public account, there can be no net change in the inflationary pressures caused by a volume of purchasing power in excess of the supply of goods.[4]

Similarly the application of budgetary surpluses to debt re-

[3]This is one of the reasons why I dislike the use of taxation as a control measure. I am prepared to accept it now only as a choice of evils. It is a blunt and discriminatory instrument which inevitably results in inequity. One of the chief difficulties is determining how much taxation, and what kind, is necessary to curb inflation. The following statement, made in an address to the 36th Annual Conference of the Association of Canadian Advertisers on May 2, 1951, sums up my views: "We must deal with so many variables, including the human one, that it is impossible to forecast with precision what the effects of given monetary and fiscal policies will be. The economic effects of taxation are so diffused that it is virtually impossible to trace them in detail. The imposition of indirect controls must be a trial and error process involving the best possible judgment. It is for this reason that I have long argued for tax neutrality and opposed the use of taxation for anything but raising revenue. Controlling the economy by taxation looked too much like making the tail wag the dog. But we are now faced with a serious economic emergency, and something has to be done about it. . . . I believe that the indirect controls of monetary and fiscal policy, if applied intelligently, have a better chance of curbing inflation than any conceivable alternative."

[4]It is conceded, of course, that the pressures may be changed from consumers' goods to capital goods, or vice versa, because the pattern of government expenditure would not be the same as private expenditure of these funds. But the fact remains that the excess purchasing power is still operative.

tirement, despite the convincing arguments in its favour, must frustrate the purpose of taxing in excess of revenue requirements. The retirement of government bonds forces liquid purchasing power into the hands of the holders of such bonds. They may spend it or reinvest it. If they spend it, there is an additional inflationary pressure on the supply of consumers' goods. If they reinvest, as most of them would, then there will be new pressure on the capital goods market, the most critical inflationary pressure point.

This indicates the need to freeze or sterilize the excess purchasing power taken away from taxpayers in order to curb inflation. The important point is that this money must be taken out of circulation.

The success of fiscal policy as an instrument of control depends very largely upon statesmanship as opposed to political expediency. Herein lies one of its inherent weaknesses. In the first place, the imposition of a considerably greater tax burden than is necessary to meet current cash requirements is most difficult for the government to rationalize to the public.[5] Secondly, the existence of a substantial unused surplus might be an inducement to raids on the treasury for political purposes. Despite these difficulties, the possibility of a reasonably effective fiscal policy for curbing inflation still seems attractive.

In designing a policy of fiscal control there arises immediately the problem of deciding what taxes lend themselves best to this purpose. Probably the personal income tax, the sales tax, and excise taxes fall more directly upon the individual consumer's

[5]Typical criticism of the policy is to be found in the editorial columns of the *Gazette* (Montreal) and the *Globe and Mail* (Toronto). For example, the former states (May 29, 1951): "These bloated surpluses, occurring year after year, are actually a symptom of fiscal unhealthiness. Their consequences are being everywhere felt in the bloated cost of living and high taxes. Yet, with a truly remarkable irony, they are being sold to the people of Canada as though they were indispensable to keep the cost of living down." On May 28, 1951, the *Globe and Mail* stated: "When Mr. Abbott's actual revenues of the last few years are set beside his estimated revenues, it is hard to understand how he can command the confidence of Parliament or the public. Yet here he is manipulating our fiscal policy in a most critical period, and at this very moment is asking the House of Commons for extraordinary powers to fiddle around with corporation tax. How, in all conscience, can the House grant such powers to a Finance Minister who has shown himself the worst guesser in Canada's history?"

pocketbook than any of the other major taxes.[6] For this reason, these are the taxes that should be used in the main frontal attack on inflation.[7] They will certainly reduce living standards. They are meant to. What the Canadian people need to understand is that their living standards are going to be reduced anyway. If they are not lowered deliberately and with some semblance of equity by means of personal taxation,[8] they will be lowered by the strictly impersonal and grossly inequitable results of inflation.

Government Policy: The 1951 Budget

The government has decided to rely upon the indirect controls of monetary and fiscal policy as the means of curbing inflation. In his Budget Speech of April 10, 1951, the Minister of Finance stated that "the three principal inflationary forces presently at work in Canada are the rising prices outside Canada, the domestic capital investment boom which shows no signs of abating, and the fact that consumer spending power is outrunning the flow and production of consumer goods and services. There is little we can do about rising external prices, but we can do a good deal about the two domestic pressures and we have already done a good deal."[9]

[6]I concede that perhaps many qualifications are necessary here, but do not intend to be sidetracked into a theoretical discussion of the ultimate incidence of all the taxes in the federal revenue system. I admit that some groups in a strong bargaining position may in fact secure higher wages to offset increased income and consumption taxes. This is a possibility which must be kept in mind constantly by the framers of fiscal policy. Were it to materialize on a broad front it would be a serious threat to the whole programme of using fiscal policy as an instrument of fiscal control.

[7]No attempt is made here to indicate the relative weights that should be attached to the personal income tax, the sales tax, and excise taxes. All that is implied is that they should be used as intensively as the unfolding situation appears to demand. In the case of goods which may be in short supply, I would advocate very high excises in order to curb demand effectively.

[8]The argument that there is equity in using taxation to curb purchasing power is, after all, rather thin. *Ad valorem* taxes designed to achieve this end must result in leaving the available supply of scarce and heavily taxed goods to consumers in the higher income brackets who are able and willing to pay the enhanced prices. I am fully conscious of this, but maintain that if it be possible to control inflation by means of fiscal policy, the end justifies the means. If the cost of a man's food, shelter, and clothing could be stabilized for the price of heavy taxation of a wide range of the gadgets of modern civilization, then the sacrifice of tax equity appears to be a reasonable charge, compared with the dire effects of uncontrolled inflation on the one hand, and the results of over-all direct controls over prices, wages, and commodities on the other hand.

[9]*House of Commons Debates,* April 10, 1951, p. 1808.

1. *Tax Policy*

He pointed out that consumer expenditures were being restrained by consumer credit regulations, and then announced his tax programme to restrain them still further. The general sales tax was increased from 8 to 10 per cent. The excise tax on automobiles, radios, household electric appliances, jewellery, and cosmetics was set at 25 per cent. A tax of 15 per cent was imposed on electric refrigerators, on washing machines, and on all cooking stoves save those designed to use only coal or wood. A 20 per cent "defence surtax" was levied on personal income. So much for the attack on inflationary consumer purchasing power.[10] The attack on inflationary capital investment is being made by means of a higher corporation tax and in the deferment of depreciation on certain types of assets.

The corporation tax rate has been increased by a 20 per cent surcharge on income earned after January 1, 1951. The surcharge does not apply to the first $10,000 of income, which is taxed at 15 per cent. The effect of the surcharge is that the rate on income in excess of $10,000 is now 45.6 per cent. In Ontario and Quebec, where the provincial rate is 7 per cent, the total tax on corporate income is 52.6 per cent. In the other provinces, where the rate is 5 per cent, the total tax is 50.6 per cent.

The Minister made the following comment when he introduced the new rate:

> The field of the corporation income tax is a difficult one, and one which I have to approach with a particularly keen sense of responsibility for the real national interest, because the general public does not, I am afraid, fully understand the implication of these taxes. It would be only too easy to take a superficially popular line and increase these taxes to a point which while yielding large immediate revenues would do grave damage in the longer run to the economy as a whole . . .
>
> There is also the point that corporation taxes involve double

[10]I do not intend to discuss this policy here. My views have been expressed elsewhere. See "Inflation and the Budget," *Canadian Business,* June 1951, pp. 48-50; "Taxation in Relation to Defence Production and Inflation," *Industrial Canada,* July 1951, pp. 130-2; "Canada Tries Indirect Control of Inflation," *Tax Policy,* May-June, 1951; "Inflation," Canadian Tax Foundation, *Inflation and Price Control,* 1951, pp. 1-6.

taxation; we tax the corporation on its profits, and then we tax the shareholder again on his dividends.[11]

He then introduced a relief provision under which the 20 per cent surcharge would "not operate so as to reduce the net income after federal tax, but before any provincial income taxes, of any company to a point below a five per cent return on capital employed."[12] He rationalized this proposal as follows:

I am conscious of the fact, however, that this 20 per cent surcharge will weigh very heavily on those kinds of companies which for a variety of reasons, public control of rates or otherwise, are never able to earn more than a very modest rate on their capital. To such companies the next few years can offer little expectation of increased profits, yet many of them are engaged in activities which will require them to raise very large sums of additional capital for essential expansion. If we are not to cripple their borrowing capacity we must not cripple their capacity to earn their normal profits after tax.[13]

When the bill[14] amending the Income Tax Act was tabled a month later, it contained no definition of "capital employed," and after acrimonious debate in the House of Commons, the Minister of Finance withdrew the relief proposal because he had been unable to draft a satisfactory definition. He said in part:

I have not been able to evolve a formula, empirical or otherwise, which would be appropriate. A formula which would be appropriate as related to one taxpayer, let us say, would be completely inappropriate for another. I can only assure the house we have looked at the operating results of public utility and other companies and have endeavoured to apply this formula and that formula. All I can say is that for this year I am not prepared to recommend such a measure. Therefore I am forced reluctantly to withdraw the proposal I made.[15]

From the outset it was obvious that this relief provision would be difficult to implement. Apart from the difficult problem of placing a valuation on capital, there is the more serious problem of deciding what really constitutes a company's capital. Perhaps the core of this problem is whether to include borrowed capital,

[11]*House of Commons Debates,* April 10, 1951, p. 1809.
[12]*Ibid.*, p. 1810. [13]*Ibid.*
[14]Bill 296, introduced on May 18, 1951.
[15]*House of Commons Debates,* June 13, 1951, p. 4059.

and if so, what kind of borrowed capital. If borrowed capital is excluded (as it was in the Excess Profits Tax Act), then the relief provision would mean little to public utilities and other companies which rely heavily upon borrowed capital for their financing. But if it is included in the definition of capital, then the question arises as to whether interest should be allowed as a deduction from taxable income, as it now is.

While the proposal looked attractive, it raises so many problems of application that its soundness is questionable.[16] Furthermore, in effect it would have made the 20 per cent surcharge a tax on "excess" profits—profits in excess of 5 per cent return on capital employed. The provision represents a sharp departure from the established practice of imposing the corporate tax on profits without regard for the net income position of any company after tax. The real point to be considered is whether the corporation tax is so high that future capital investment will be prejudiced in some lines of enterprise because the earnings after taxes are too low to attract investors. If this be so, the answer is a lower tax rate rather than the introduction of complicated and clumsy relief provisions.

2. *Deferred Depreciation*

A unique feature of the 1951 budget affecting corporation taxes is the provision for deferred depreciation, aimed at curbing capital expenditures. The Minister said: "What we need is a stiff financial deterrent that will affect particularly the businessman who is considering the kind of investment which is attractive, not because of its long-term soundness, but because it can be written off out of the expected high profits of the next few years at a time when he expects the rate of corporate income tax to be abnormally high."[17] The deterrent measure is the deferment for a period of four years of the right to charge depreciation on all capital assets acquired after April 10, 1951, except certain classes of assets defined by regulation.[18] Assets are grouped in three

[16]The complexity of the concept of capital employed is well illustrated by what has happened in the United States. A short review of the development of the concept under three excess profits tax acts appears in an appendix at the end of this chapter.

[17]*House of Commons Debates*, April 10, 1951, p. 1808.

[18]See the *Income Tax Regulations*, Part XI, Section 1107.

classes: (1) those which are denied depreciation; (2) those on which depreciation may be charged if given a certificate of eligibility; and (3) those which are unaffected by the regulation.

Assets on which depreciation is denied for four years include hotel property, and property used primarily for the purpose of office use, commercial or financial services, wholesale or retail trade, or renting for other than residential habitation.

Assets for which a certificate of eligibility may be granted fall into two groups: (*a*) property necessarily acquired for the fulfilment of a defence contract or subcontract or for a purpose which contributes to the defence of Canada; and (*b*) property acquired by a taxpayer for carrying on certain businesses.[19] It is to be noted that these assets may be depreciated if certified, but there is no guarantee that a certificate will be issued. The granting of it is wholly a matter of ministerial discretion.

The principal classes of assets which remained unaffected by the original regulation[20] were all assets acquired prior to April 11, 1951, and assets acquired subsequent to April 10, 1950, and used by individual farmers, fishermen, and professional men; residential property; bridges, dams, culverts, and canals; pipe lines and certain plant connected with the production or distribution of electrical energy, gas, and water; assets used for purposes of transportation and communication; automotive equipment; certain assets with a limited life and which can be depreciated entirely within one year; and property acquired to replace property which had been destroyed by fire, flood, wind, lightning, or other act of God.[21]

It is to be noted that the responsibility for the certification of assets is vested not in the taxing authorities, but in the Department of Trade and Commerce, where this function is associated with powers of allocation of critical materials. The wide discre-

[19]Section 1107 (6) of the *Regulations* lists the businesses that may be certified as eligible for depreciation of assets necessary to the carrying on of those businesses. Included are primary industries such as mining, farming, fishing and logging; secondary industries engaged in processing or refining raw materials; transportation businesses, including air, water, bus, truck, railway, and pipe line transportation; public utility businesses; businesses producing filaments, fibres, or yarns; ship-building and ship repairs; and hospital or sanatorium service.

[20]Subsequent amendments will be noted presently.

[21]Details of the classes of exempted assets may be found in *Regulations*, Section 1107 (2).

tionary powers given to the Minister of Trade and Commerce make the measure flexible. This measure represents a short cut to the desired restrictions which avoids the difficulties of direct government interference in the plans of business to engage in capital expansion. It does not deny business the right to expand if it is prepared to pay the tax penalty implied in deferred depreciation. Obviously this measure has no more relationship to recognized accounting principles than the accelerated depreciation which is allowed on certain assets purchased for defence production.[22]

It is noteworthy that the measure was not a budget resolution, and did not involve an amendment to the Income Tax Act. It was given the force of law by means of an order-in-council, and in effect is a tax measure provided without reference to Parliament.

Three chief cases of hardship were created under the original regulations contained in order-in-council P.C. 1778, April 10, 1951, and they were caused by the simple test of the date of an asset's "acquisition."[23] First, in the case of an undepreciable asset when acquired after April 10, a tax penalty has been imposed on a taxpayer who had placed a firm order for capital equipment prior to April 10, but who had not taken delivery of it by that date. A penalty has also been imposed in the case of a taxpayer who had, say, an office building under construction but not completed on April 10. The result of the regulations is unequal between taxpayers committed to capital expansion prior to April 10 and those who were not, and in the case of the committed taxpayers, the result is unequal between those in a strong working capital position and those who are not. In the case of the latter, who probably planned to finance the acquisition partly by means of depreciation, serious financial embarrassment could result. De-

[22]See *Regulations,* Section 1100 (1)(*k*). From a long-run viewpoint it is regrettable that such departures from accounting practice are written gratuitously into income tax practice. I have long believed that the latter should conform to the former to the greatest possible extent.

[23]The Minister of Trade and Commerce said: "Determination of the date of acquisition will be made by the Department of National Revenue in accordance with *its usual practice in such cases.*" (Italics mine.) *House of Commons Debates,* April 12, 1951, p. 1941.

ferred depreciation is then in effect a tax on working capital.[24]

In the second place, it seems unfair to deny depreciation on property transferred from one owner to another after April 10 when it had been depreciable in the hands of the former owner. Probably deferment of depreciation on used assets was designed to prevent the development of a black market for "depreciable" assets, and connivance between taxpayers in turning an undepreciable new asset into a depreciable used asset. But it is unfortunate that honest taxpayers must be penalized because of the fear that unscrupulous citizens would circumvent the regulations by means of legerdemain.

In the third place, the original regulations applied to property acquired after April 10 by gift or bequest, and to a change of title involving no real change in the character or capacity of the undertaking. Thus, the incorporation of a partnership or a sole proprietorship after April 10 would have resulted in a tax penalty in the case of assets excluded from depreciation for four years. This is needless tax discrimination which serves no useful purpose in combating inflation.

Various representations were made to the government regarding these difficulties. On June 11 the Canadian Tax Foundation made a submission to the Minister of Trade and Commerce recommending four changes in the regulations,[25] as follows: (1) That in the case of capital equipment ordered prior to April 10, but not delivered, and the case of construction projects incompleted on April 10, a taxpayer be entitled to a certificate of eligibility provided that he can furnish evidence satisfactory to the Minister that such property was covered by a firm purchase order or contract;[26] (2) That exemption from the regulations be provided in the case of property acquired after April 10 which

[24]For example, suppose that a corporation acquires an asset after April 10 at a cost of $250,000, and this asset is ineligible for depreciation for four years. If the asset falls in Class (6) of Schedule B, the normal depreciation rate would be 10 per cent. Now, if taxable income *after* depreciation were $100,000, the total tax would be $56,040. But if depreciation is deferred, $25,000 is added to taxable income, and the tax is $67,440. Thus the tax penalty in the first year is $11,400.

[25]See the Foundation's *Tax Bulletin*, vol. I, no. 4, July-Aug. 1951, pp. 107-8.

[26]It will be noted that the recommendation is not for automatic exemption of such assets, but for a certificate of exemption to be granted in the Minister's discretion.

had been disposed of by a taxpayer who had used it for the purpose of his business and was allowed depreciation on it; and (3) That property acquired after April 10 by gift or bequest, or by virtue of a transaction which did not alter the character of the business undertaking (such as the incorporation of a proprietorship) be exempted from the regulations.[27]

On June 28 the Minister of Trade and Commerce announced several amendments to the regulations in the House of Commons which met some, but not all, of the hardships.[28] He followed the Tax Foundation's recommendation (3), by exempting property acquired by inheritance and property whose title is transferred by incorporation of a sole proprietorship or partnership. He compromised in the case of used assets, by providing for depreciation of assets acquired after April 10 by a taxpayer in an arm's length transaction in which the taxpayer acquired the business of the vendor and all the depreciable property of the business.[29] But the relief was extended only to assets acquired in an *in toto* purchase of a business as a going concern, and the Minister must be satisfied that the property so acquired was depreciable property of the vendor on April 10, 1951; he may still in his discretion deny a certificate. No relief has been provided in the case of individual used assets acquired after April 10. He rationalized this restriction as follows: "A number of representations have been made that deferment should not apply to properties which were in existence on April 10 and which merely change hands. The problem is exceedingly complex because of the ease with which such a change if it were adopted could be used to circumvent the purpose of the regulations. The further away we move

[27]The Tax Foundation's submission ended with these words (see p. 108): "Our recommendations are supported by an important consideration which we note in conclusion. The announcement in the Budget Speech of the Government's intention to introduce the system of deferred capital cost allowances immediately was the first intimation to the public that projects of the classes now excluded would be discouraged. While we believe that taxpayers have readily understood and accepted the reason for these measures following the Government's explanation of their purpose, they did not share beforehand the Government's closer knowledge of the trend of developments in the economy and the prospective impact of the defence programme which dictated the decision to adopt these measures. Evidence that they are proving to be effective encourages us to hope that some transitional relief on the lines proposed above can now be granted to taxpayers who made their plans in good faith."

[28]*House of Commons Debates,* June 28, 1951, p. 4817.

[29]*Regulations,* Section 1107 (8), added by P.C. 3237, June 26, 1951.

from April 10, 1951, the more difficult the problem would become."[30]

No relief was provided in the case of capital expenditure commitments entered into prior to April 10 and where "acquisition" had not occurred on the cut-off date. In commenting on this point, the Minister said: "The government is not yet in a position to reach a definite decision on this point. Where genuine commitments were made before April 10, 1951, and must be proceeded with a good case for relief can be made. However, the variety of circumstances is extremely broad and requires careful study. I am not yet in a position to say what can or should be done. Probably the government will not be able to go as far as some taxpayers would wish; on the other hand it should be possible to work out something that will give a measure of relief where the taxpayers had no option but to carry out commitments made before April 10, 1951."[31] Accordingly, there still remained for some taxpayers the serious discrimination resulting from the deferment of depreciation on assets contracted for in good faith prior to April 10 but not acquired on that date.

On November 27, 1951, the regulations were amended once more by P.C. 6384. This time relief was provided in cases where a genuine commitment had been made before April 11, 1951, and acquisition not effected until after April 10, 1951. Section 1107 (9) of the regulations now authorizes the Minister of Trade and Commerce to grant a certificate of eligibility in three types of cases. First, in the case of new structures depreciation may be allowed if the taxpayer proves that he had entered into a contract with a contractor prior to April 11, 1951, according to plans and specifications adopted before that date, and provided that the structure is completed before April 1, 1953. In explaining this amendment, the Minister of Trade and Commerce said:

> The certificate will be granted after the property is acquired. One of the tests of a genuine contract in existence on April 10, 1951, will be the fact that the work on the structure will be undertaken and completed within a reasonable time. A period of two years has been considered as a reasonable time in the light of present and foreseeable supply conditions. This explains the provision requiring completion of

[30]*House of Commons Debates*, June 28, 1951, p. 4817.
[31]*Ibid.*, pp. 4817-18.

construction before April 1, 1953. Therefore a taxpayer who has a valid contract as of April 10, 1951, but who has decided to postpone construction for say two years, would not be eligible for a certificate, since the purpose of the amendment is to provide relief to those who not only have a contract but who have also either commenced construction before April 11, 1951, or were obliged to do so, within a short time after that date.[32]

Relief is also provided where the taxpayer is doing his own construction and therefore has no contract as proof of a commitment prior to April 11, 1951. In such cases a certificate of eligibility may be granted if the taxpayer can prove that construction was actually commenced prior to April 11, 1951, in accordance with plans and specifications adopted by the applicant prior to that date.

The second group of properties covered by P.C. 6384 covers structures completed before April 11, 1951, and acquired after that date. In such cases a certificate of eligibility will be granted if the taxpayer can prove that he was obligated under a binding contract to acquire the property. But it is to be noted that an option which gives a potential purchaser a right to acquire property without legally binding him to purchase does not make the property eligible for a certificate.

The third group covers "property other than a structure which the taxpayer was obligated to acquire under the terms of a contract entered into prior to April 11, 1951. . . ."[33] This group covers machinery and equipment, both new and old. A certificate will be granted if the applicant can prove that he was obligated under a contract entered into prior to April 11, 1951, to acquire the assets in question. No final date of acquisition has been set in this case. The Minister explained that "it has been presented to us that in some cases of complicated pieces of equipment which are made to order and according to specifications set out by the purchaser, the period required to complete the equipment might involve several years."[34]

These amendments cover most of the cases where firm commitments had been made prior to the cut-off date, and hardship

[32]*House of Commons Debates,* Nov. 27, 1951, p. 1352.
[33]*Regulations,* Section 1107 (9)(*c*).
[34]*House of Commons Debates,* Nov. 27, 1951, p. 1352.

was created by the deferment of depreciation. About the only assets now to be denied depreciation are that limited group contracted for and acquired after April 10, 1951.

It is still too early to reach a final opinion as to the effects of the deferred depreciation regulations, and to decide whether such an arbitrary tax provision is warranted. Between April 11, 1951, and November 16, 1951, there were 928 applications for certificates of eligibility. Of these, 342, involving capital expenditures of $269.9 million, were approved. Assets on which depreciation has been granted include properties acquired by defence and defence-supporting industries, properties acquired by basic industries for carrying out their business, properties acquired by inheritance, and properties acquired when the whole of a business was taken over in an arm's length transaction. Certificates were denied on 175 applications, involving $27.7 million, and the remaining 411 were pending as of November 16, 1951. Many of these will probably qualify under the latest amendments to the regulations.

Speaking on June 28, 1951, the Minister of Trade and Commerce said:

> There is no direct way of measuring the results of the plan. We know how many applications have been received, how many certificates have been issued, and how many have been denied. What we do not know is how many plans have been changed because the businessman knew that depreciation would be deferred for four years. . . . From information available to the government from various lines of business I think it is fair to say that while the results cannot be measured precisely, they are substantial. The government believes that the plan has contributed in some measure to the recent reduction of inflationary pressures. It has been a useful supplement to other fiscal and monetary measures and credit restrictions.[35]

When he introduced the amendments to the regulations in November and gave the statistics on applications for certificates of eligibility, he said: "Of course the impact of the provisions is not fully reflected in the figures I have given, for two reasons. First, there will be many cases where the taxpayer has not applied for a certificate of eligibility because his project clearly does not comply with the exceptions that can be granted under the

[35]*Ibid.*, June 28, 1951, pp. 4816-17.

regulations. Secondly, there are many cases where businessmen have decided to postpone capital projects and they would therefore have no cause to apply for a certificate."[36] In reply to a question from Mr. J. M. Macdonnell, the Opposition's financial critic, the Minister said "My own opinion is that it [deferred depreciation] has been a very effective deterrent. The amount of new private construction has been materially reduced since this provision came into effect."[37]

Whether the government's views are correct will at this time remain necessarily an open question. Since the measure does not apply to capital expansion of defence and defence-supporting industries, primary industry, housing, automotive and other transportation equipment, and most public utility property, it seems as though most of the projected $5,973 million capital programme for 1951 would be unaffected. The details of this programme are shown in Table VIII.

TABLE VIII

FORECAST PRIVATE AND PUBLIC INVESTMENT IN CANADA, 1951
(millions of dollars)

Type of expenditure	*Construction*[a]	*Machinery and equipment*[a]	*Total*[a]
Business:			
Primary industries[b] and construction	213	680	893
Manufacturing	296	772	1,068
Utilities	703	688	1,391
Trade, finance, and commercial services	229	239	468
Total business	1,441	2,379	3,820
Other:			
Institutional services[c]	272	38	310
Housing	1,028		1,028
Government departments	731	84	815
Total	2,031	122	2,153
GRAND TOTAL	3,472	2,501	5,973

Source: *Private and Public Investment in Canada Outlook*, 1951, p. 13.
a Includes new investment expenditures and repair and maintenance expenditures.
b Includes agriculture, fishing, forestry, mining, quarrying, and oil wells.
c Includes churches, hospitals, schools, and universities.

[36] *Ibid.*, Nov. 27, 1951, p. 1353. [37] *Ibid.*

About three-quarters of the total projected capital investment is automatically unaffected by the deferred depreciation regulations. Only about 7 per cent of the total (the $468 million for trade, finance, and commercial services) is automatically denied depreciation, and now such projects contracted for prior to April 11 will be given normal depreciation. It seems likely that much of the estimated $1,068 million in the manufacturing industry will be given depreciation because the investment is for defence or defence-supporting purposes. Even investment projects which are denied depreciation under the regulations are not likely to be postponed unless the business is in a marginal working capital position. In essence deferred depreciation is a tax on working capital and the measure will probably affect only businesses which are not in a fairly strong liquid position. This probably means that deferred depreciation is effective only in the case of the smaller operators whose capital expenditures represent a very small portion of the total expenditure programme. It may well be that deferred depreciation will have little significance as an element of fiscal policy designed to combat inflation.

Fiscal Control and the Corporation Tax

We come now to the point of drawing conclusions regarding the corporation tax as an effective means of combating inflation. It appears that high corporate profits certainly provide inflationary pressure because they enable companies to increase their inventories, enlarge their physical plant, pay out more dividends, and increase other expenditures. In 1950 corporate profits before taxes amounted to $2,270 million (an increase of 20 per cent over the volume in 1949), and they will probably be still greater in 1951. After taxes in 1950, net corporate profits amounted to $1,402 million, of which $672 million was paid out in dividends and charitable donations,[38] and $730 million was retained as undistributed profits.[39]

The inflationary pressure resulting from high corporate profits is derived from (*a*) increased dividend payments, and (*b*) from

[38]Charitable donations amounted to $25 million.

[39]See *House of Commons Debates,* April 10, 1951, Budget Papers, Table 7, p. 12.

undistributed profits. In the case of increased dividend payments, even if they are, dollar for dollar, just as inflationary as increased wage payments, the quantitative position of dividends in relation to salaries and wages makes them relatively unimportant in the over-all picture. In 1950 dividends amounted to only 5.1 per cent of total personal income, and 8.3 per cent of the total salary and wage payments.[40] Even though dividend payments increased by 17.8 per cent between 1949 and 1950, compared with an increase in salaries and wages of 6.2 per cent, the aggregate dollar increase of the former was only $102 million, compared with a salary and wage increase of $470 million. When it is remembered that some 60 per cent of the dividends paid by Canadian corporations goes to non-residents,[41] the net payment in Canada probably amounted to less than $270 million in 1950, and the net increase of dividends paid to Canadian companies and individuals was only $40.8 million (6.6 per cent of the increase in total personal income). The inflationary effect of increased dividend payment is therefore surely of minor importance.

[40]Comparative figures for 1949 and 1950 are as follows:

DIVIDENDS, SALARIES AND WAGES AS COMPONENTS OF TOTAL PERSONAL INCOME, 1949 AND 1950

Item of personal income	1949 *Total personal income*	*% of total*	1950 *Total personal income*	*% of total*	*% Increase or % Decrease*
	$000,000	%	$000,000	%	%
Salaries and wages[a]	7,562	59.5	8,032	60.2	6.2
Dividends[b]	570	4.5	672	5.1	17.8
Other personal income[c]	4,579	36.0	4,623	34.7	− .9
Total personal income	12,711	100.0	13,327	100.0	4.8

Source, *ibid.*, Table 3, p. 8, and Table 7, p. 12.

[a]Excluding contributions to social insurance and government pension funds.

[b]Including corporate charitable contributions of $23 million in 1949 and $25 million in 1950.

[c]Including net income to agriculture and other unincorporated business.

[41]In 1948, the last taxation year for which detailed income tax figures are available, Canadian companies paid out $614 million in dividends (*Taxation Statistics*, 1950, p. 69). Total dividends reported for personal income tax purposes in that year amounted to $129 million—21 per cent of the total dividends declared (*ibid.*, p. 119). $174 million of non-taxable dividends (inter-company Canadian dividends) was reported by corporations. Allowing for dividends received by Canadians from foreign companies, the indication is that well over one-half of the dividends paid by Canadian companies goes to non-residents.

In the case of earnings retained by corporations, the extent of the inflationary pressure depends upon the use to which such profits are put. They can be used (*a*) for plant expansion (inflationary), (*b*) for additional inventory purchases (inflationary),[42] (*c*) for the maintenance of a liquid working capital position (non-inflationary), and (*d*) for increased salaries and wages, advertising and other expenditures (more or less inflationary, in accordance with the nature of the expenditure).

To the extent that a considerable portion of retained corporate earnings is ploughed back in the form of plant expansion, the net effect of the current investment boom is inflationary. Undoubtedly part of new industrial expansion in Canada is being financed from retained earnings, but a limiting factor is at once apparent. In 1950 new investment expenditure by business enterprises in plant and equipment was $1,945 million,[43] and this included investment by all unincorporated businesses and agriculture. Bearing in mind that the total undistributed corporate profits in that year amounted to only 58 per cent of this sum, and for the most part was not represented in capital expansion, the total impact of undistributed profits could not have been as important as might appear at first glance.[44] Other sources of financing new capital expansion, i.e., bank credit, stock and bond issues, seem to have been more important than reinvested earnings in 1950.

It seems most likely that a substantial part of the undistributed profits reported in 1950 was invested in inventories. The increase in business inventories from 1949 to 1950 was $697 million[45] (645 per cent), but again, this included inventories of all partnerships and sole proprietorships, as well as corporations. This over-all increase was in large part the result of panic buying after the outbreak of the Korean War. Quantitatively, the increase in busi-

[42]By this I mean the expansion of a firm's inventory position beyond the level of the preceding year. During price inflation it will, of course, cost more to maintain a constant inventory position from one year to the next. But the maintenance of a constant inventory should not be considered inflationary.

[43]*Private and Public Investment in Canada, Outlook*, 1951, p. 11.

[44]This conclusion is borne out further in the light of projected new investment expenditures for 1951. Slightly over 50 per cent of the total is attributed to business enterprises, and of this amount, much is for expansion essential to our defence requirement. The balance is made up of institutional and housing investment, and government investment. *Ibid.*

[45]*House of Commons Debates*, April 10, 1951, Budget Papers, Table 8, p. 12.

ness inventories between 1949 and 1950 was more than nine times the increase in new plant and equipment,[46] so that the greater pressure seems to have been the increase in inventories. But in terms of relative weights, the outlay on new plant and equipment in 1950 was nearly 65 per cent greater than the outlay for inventories ($1,256 million, compared with $805 million).

While the level of corporate profits is high and is obviously a factor contributing to inflation, it must be remembered that a considerable part of reported business profits is fictitious because of the problems inherent in asset valuation (discussed in chapter VII). High profits, like high wages, are a result of inflation, and both will continue to rise as long as dollars become cheaper. But it does not follow that vast new taxable capacity has been created because reported business profits are higher. An increasing part of corporate profits is required to maintain Canada's industrial plant at a high level of efficiency because the cost of replacing equipment has been rising sharply.

Despite these arguments it is not advocated that the corporation tax rate should remain constant while other taxes rise sharply as a result of defence expenditures and the use of fiscal policy to maintain economic stability. Such a viewpoint would be completely unrealistic. The existence of increasing corporate profits not only places greater purchasing power in the hands of corporations and their shareholders, but it also tends to promote demands for wage increases. Therefore it seems essential that there should be some limitation placed on corporate profits.

If taxation is to be the chief means of limiting corporate profits, there is the difficult problem of deciding how much corporate taxation should be imposed.[47] Moreover it is not certain how effective the corporation tax really is in curbing profits. Under conditions of the very strong sellers' market that has prevailed in

[46]The increase in inventories was $697 million, compared with an increase of $73 million in new plant and equipment.

[47]It has been well said that "Profit limitation plays an important part in *economic stabilization;* profit incentives play an important part in *economic mobilization.* The proper balance between these conflicting objectives must be sought in the adjustment of corporate taxes, for they are the main fiscal instrument affecting profits. Precisely what type and amount of profits taxes should be imposed is a delicate and difficult problem in readiness economics, about which there is room for argument." A. G. Hart and E. Cary Brown, *Financing Defense,* p. 112.

Canada it seems likely that much of the tax on corporate profits is shifted to the consumer in the form of higher prices.[48] If this is the case, an increase in the tax results in a reduction of consumer purchasing power, one of the objectives of fiscal policy aimed at economic stability. But the way in which this shifted tax would achieve such a result is objectionable. Unlike sales and excise taxes, which can be made selective by exempting the necessities of life, the shifting of the corporation tax would be entirely unselective both as to persons and as to commodities. It would affect basic foodstuffs as well as luxuries. In short, a shifted corporation tax is the most regressive and inequitable form of sales tax.

High corporation taxes may actually defeat the purpose of reducing corporate expenditures. If the tax actually results in curtailed net earnings, there will be an incentive to reduce capital expenditures,[49] but there may also be an incentive to increase tax-exempt expenditures—expenses which are deductible before tax, such as salaries and wages, advertising, plant maintenance, insurance, and so on. Under heavy corporation taxes management may prefer spending more money on such items to paying it to the government as taxes. The net result of such action is, of course, inflationary.

All of what has been said about the standard corporation tax applies with greater force to an excess profits tax. The argument in favour of excess profits taxation is largely emotional. On economic grounds there is nothing in its favour. An excess profits tax imposes a high tax rate on a part of business profits instead of collecting the same amount of revenue by means of a less extreme rate applied to all profits. If the excess profits tax were

[48]As explained in chapter IV, it is extremely difficult to demonstrate empirically where the corporation tax rests. The National City Bank of New York has published some interesting data. Comparative figures for 1929 and 1949 indicate only a small decrease in the ratio of net corporate earnings after taxes to the sales dollar in the United States. In 1929, when the federal income tax rate was only 11 per cent, all non-financial companies in the United States paid about $1,100 million in taxes, and their net income was about 5.4 cents per sales dollar. In 1949, when the federal tax rate was 38 per cent, and total tax payments were nine times as great, net income was 4.4 cents per sales dollar. *Monthly Letter,* July, 1951.

[49]But they may not actually be reduced because such expenditures are not normally made out of current income. They are financed out of past earnings, equity capital, or borrowed capital.

low, it would accomplish no more than would a suitable increase in the normal rate, and it would not accomplish it as well. If the rates were high, the tax would destroy the very incentives that are vital to the achievement of our defence objectives. It is impossible to devise an excess profits tax which does not have discriminatory effects as between new firms and old ones, firms with small capital and those with large, and growing firms and declining ones. The basic inequities and serious economic effects of excess profits taxation should rule it out under any conditions short of total war.[50]

Conclusions

It is concluded that the corporation tax is not a good instrument of fiscal control. Indeed, it is probably the worst of all taxes from a control viewpoint. In the first place, much of the tax appears to be shifted to the consumer and recovered by business in higher prices. To the extent that this occurs, the tax fails as a control measure. In the case of companies which have to bear the tax, ability to spend is reduced, but the inequity of controlling some companies while others remain unaffected is an indictment of the tax as a control measure. In the second place, the unpredictable effects of a high tax for control purposes on management's incentives to spend and save make it a weak prop in the control programme. It may, in fact, produce an inflationary rather than a stabilizing result, while at the same time it may have a dislo-

[50]The Minister of Finance stated in the House: "We have, of course, given thought to suggestions that we should reintroduce an excess profits tax, but I think members in all parts of the house who had experience with our wartime excess profits tax will agree that such a tax is not desirable under present circumstances. To be efficient and fair an excess profits tax needs a recent base period representing normal operating conditions for various classes of business, and a tax related to the average profits of the last three years would not be likely to yield much revenue during the next year or two. But the more important objection at this stage is that an excess profits tax, particularly one at a high rate, becomes an invitation to extravagance and waste in corporate management, whereas, as I have already said, what we need most urgently now is maximum efficiency and production. I have no doubt that all hon. members know or will have heard of cases of such waste and extravagance. Furthermore, in spite of our best efforts to make an excess profits tax as fair as possible there are bound to be severe inequities under this kind of legislation. Under conditions of total war, many businesses would be compelled to accept these inequities and hardships. I am reluctant, however, to impose this severe type of regulation under present circumstances." *House of Commons Debates*, Sept. 7, 1950, pp. 422-3.

cating effect on key industries, particularly railways and utilities whose rates are controlled. Certainly careful consideration should be given to the effects of the tax on production, which is the primary objective of all defence policy.

The argument points to using the corporation tax solely as a revenue measure. Such refinements as deferred depreciation and other departures from accepted accounting practice have no place in the corporation tax structure. The inflationary pressure of heavy capital investment and inventory purchasing are better attacked by the use of credit restrictions and the imposition of direct controls in allocating materials.

APPENDIX

Notes on "Invested Capital"

The problem of defining "invested capital" for income tax purposes has generally been connected with an excess profits tax under which excess profit was considered as an amount in excess of an allowable return on invested capital. The major problems inherent in the drafting of a definition of investment capital are (1) whether borrowed capital, in addition to equity capital, should be included; and (2) how the value of invested capital should be determined. An examination of the experience under three excess profit tax laws in the United States is a good indication of the confusion that exists in trying to secure a workable definition of invested capital.

World War I

The Revenue Act of 1917 (March 3, 1917) introduced the excess profits tax in the United States. It was based on net income in excess of 8 per cent of the "actual capital invested." Section 202 of the Act defined "actual capital invested" to mean (1) actual cash paid in, (2) the actual cash value, at the time of payment, of assets other than cash paid in, and (3) paid in or earned surplus and undistributed profits used in the business. It is to be noted that money or other property borrowed by the taxpayer was specifically excluded from the definition of invested capital. In short, generally speaking, invested capital was considered to be paid-in capital plus paid-in capital surplus plus earned surplus.

The definition of "actual capital invested" later was amended, over the Senate's objection, to provide for the inclusion of good-will, patents, franchises, etc., but only to the extent that they were actually paid for in cash or tangible property. Other modifications were introduced subsequently to cover situations where changes were made in capital structure and for new companies.

In 1918 invested capital was defined to include (1) actual cash paid in, (2) actual cash value at the time of payment of tangible property, other than cash, paid in for corporate shares, (3) paid-in or earned surplus and undivided profits (exclusive of earnings during the tax year), and (4) intangible property paid in for shares in an amount not exceeding (*a*) the actual cash value of such property at the time paid in, (*b*) the par value of the shares issued therefor, or (*c*) in the aggregate 25 per cent of the par value of the total outstanding shares. Borrowed capital was still excluded specifically from invested capital.

World War II

The first excess profits tax legislation of World War II was enacted on October 8, 1940. The House Ways and Means Committee proposed to include borrowed capital in the concept of invested capital, at varying rates. The recommended percentages varied from 33⅓ to 100 per cent in accordance with the ratio of equity capital to borrowed capital. The Senate changed this proposal to the inclusion of borrowed capital at a flat rate of 50 per cent, and this is the way the legislation finally passed. There was a corresponding disallowance of 50 per cent of the deduction of interest paid on borrowed capital.

Invested capital was defined to be the sum of the "equity investment capital" and 50 per cent of the "borrowed invested capital," less an adjustment for "inadmissibles." The determination of invested capital for the tax year involved three steps: (1) the determination of the "daily invested capital" for each day of the tax year (this was the sum of the equity invested capital and the borrowed invested capital at the beginning of each day); (2) the determination of the average invested capital for the tax year by dividing the aggregate daily invested capital by the number of days in the tax year; (3) reducing the average invested capital for the tax year by the amount of any "inadmissible assets" owned by the taxpayer during that year.

Equity Invested Capital

The determination of equity investment capital involved primarily the investment by shareholders. It was the so-called "historical capital" approach, involving in general a determination of the money and property (including goodwill and other intangibles) originally paid into the corporation for stock, plus paid-in surplus, plus net accumulations of earnings, less any distributions of capital. The equity invested capital for any day was determined as of the beginning of such day. The basis or starting-point was the amount of money and property previously paid in for stock, or as paid-in surplus, or as a contribution to capital. The value of property paid in was the unadjusted basis to the taxpayer for determining loss upon a sale or exchange under the law applicable to the tax year for which the invested capital was being computed. Unrealized increase in value of property owned by a taxpayer was not included in invested capital.

Borrowed Invested Capital

Borrowed invested capital included 50 per cent of the taxpayer's outstanding indebtedness (except interest) evidenced by a bond, note, bill of exchange, debenture, certificate of indebtedness, mortgage, or deed of trust. It was necessary to include amounts that qualified as borrowed capital, even though the corollary disallowance of interest resulted in tax disadvantage to the company. The regulations provided that an indebtedness be bona fide, and not incurred merely to increase the amount of capital invested.

Inadmissible Assets

"Inadmissible assets" were defined as (1) corporate stock (except non-capital assets and foreign personal holding company stock), and (2) wholly or partially tax-exempt securities. The latter could be treated as "admissible" if the taxpayer elected to subject the interest therefrom to excess profits tax. If it was impracticable for the taxpayer to determine admissibles and inadmissibles as of the beginning of each day in the tax year, he was allowed to determine an average for each month by adding the amounts at the beginning and end of such period and dividing by two.

E. P. T. 1950

The chief difference between the 1950 treatment of invested capital and its treatment under World War II E.P.T. is the introduction of the so-called "asset approach" as an alternative to the "historical capital approach."[1] The recent legislation introduces

[1]The House Committee on Ways and Means reported: "Your committee's bill shifts from the historical capital approach to the asset approach because it is believed that it will be much easier for the taxpayer to determine the basis of his

the concept "adjusted investment capital," which is defined to be the equity capital as of the beginning of the tax year, plus the capital addition for the year, plus 75 per cent of the average borrowed capital for the year, plus the "recent loss adjustment," which is any net deficit in the periods 1946-9 or 1940-9, whichever is greater.

Equity Capital

As indicated above, the equity capital and retained earnings of a corporation are generally determined by deducting from its total assets on its books at the end of the base period the sum of the liabilities on its books at the same time, plus any net deficit in the periods 1946-9 or 1940-9.

Except for cash, the term "assets" applies only to property having a basis for gain or loss upon sale or exchange. The value of all assets (save intangibles[2]) is determined by taking their "adjusted basis for gain," which is the higher of their cost or March 1, 1913, value, plus or minus adjustments for depreciation and capital improvement since their acquisition or since March 1, 1913. This is the value used for depreciation purposes and the value that is placed on an asset for tax purposes when it is sold at a gain. The value of intangible assets is determined without regard to the value of the property as of March 1, 1913. Intangibles are defined as "secret processes and formulas, good will, trade-marks, trade bands, franchises, and other like property." Assets which are not held in good faith for the purposes of the business are excluded from the computation of invested capital.[3]

The term "liabilities" means all liabilities of the corporation, absolute and not contingent, and includes liabilities assumed by

present assets than to determine the amount originally paid in for stock and surplus. A special advantage of the particular asset basis used is that the basis for gain is readily available for depreciable assets." United States, Congress, House of Representatives, Committee on Ways and Means, *Excess Profits Tax Act of 1950*, p. 10.

[2]This exception was written into the Bill by the Senate Committee on Finance, "because most of these assets, not being subject to depreciation, have not been valued as of March 1, 1913, and to do so would be quite difficult." United States, Congress, Senate, Committee on Finance, *Excess Profits Tax Act of 1950*, p. 9.

[3]This provision was added by the Senate Committee, which stated: "The purpose of this limitation is to disallow in computing invested capital those assets which are not required in the business and which have the principal effect of reducing excess profits tax." *Ibid.*

the taxpayer whether or not in connection with assets it holds. Included under liabilities are reserves for bad debts referred to in the Code, Section 23 (*k*). The determination of the date upon which a liability is incurred is to follow sound accounting principles and rules similar to those applicable in the computation of the taxpayer's profits.

The House Ways and Means Committee made no provision in its bill for the computation of invested capital under the historical capital approach used during World War II, but the Senate Committee added this alternative, under which the equity capital and retained earnings represent the money and property previously paid in for stock or paid in for surplus, plus the accumulated earnings of the corporation at the beginning of its tax year.

The major difference between this approach and the asset approach is the treatment of deficits. Under the historical capital approach a net deficit (that is, any deficit remaining after offsetting deficits of loss years against earnings of profitable years) does not decrease paid-in capital or paid-in surplus. Under the asset approach, a net deficit incurred prior to 1946 or 1940 (depending on which is more advantageous to the taxpayer) has the effect of reducing capital or surplus paid in prior to that date.[4]

Under the asset approach, corporations with recent losses are treated more favourably than under the historical capital approach, while taxpayers with net deficits over the whole span of their existence are treated more favourably under the historical capital approach. The Senate Committee stated: "Your committee recognized that it was desirable to provide favourable treatment for corporations with net deficits since 1940 or 1946 even though they had earnings prior to that time which would offset these deficits, since such corporations are likely to have a very unfavourable average earnings base and also are likely to find their invested capital base depleted as a result of these losses."[5]

Borrowed Capital

The House Committee's bill defined borrowed capital as a

[4]But the asset approach for the period since 1940 or 1946 reduces neither capital nor surplus paid in at any time, nor does it reduce earnings and profits prior to 1940 or 1946.

[5]*Excess Profits Tax Act of 1950*, p. 10.

company's indebtedness (not including interest) which is evidenced by a bond, note, bill of exchange, debenture, certificate of indebtedness, mortgage, deed of trust, or conditional sales contract and is employed in the trade or business.[6] The Senate Committee added bank loan agreements, and the limiting clause "incurred in good faith for the purposes of the business."[7]

Inadmissible Assets

The new law makes no major change in the World War II treatment of admissible and inadmissible assets except to deny and partially exempt government obligations as admissible assets. In short, corporate shares and all American bonds the interest on which is tax-exempt are inadmissible assets.

Net Capital Changes

(*a*) Capital Additions

The capital addition for the tax year is the aggregate of the daily capital addition for each day of the tax year divided by the number of days in the year. The daily capital addition for each day of the tax year is the aggregate of the money and property paid in after the beginning of the tax year and prior to the particular day for stock, or as paid-in surplus, or as a contribution to capital. After the end of the tax year in which additions are made, the equity capital at the beginning of the next tax year will reflect any such addition remaining in the taxpayer's hands.

(*b*) Capital Reductions

The capital reduction for the tax year is the aggregate of the daily capital reduction for each day of the year divided by the number of days in that year. The daily capital reduction for each day of the tax year is the amount of the distributions previously made during the tax year, and not paid out of current profits. Dividends are presumed to be paid out of most recent earnings.

Main Points in Testimony at Hearings on H.R. 9827

(*a*) Basis

There was little discussion by witnesses appearing before the House Committee as to the proper basis for valuing invested

[6]This is substantially the same definition used in the World War II law, except for the addition of conditional sales contracts.

[7]See *Excess Profits Tax Act of 1950*, p. 10.

capital. Railroad representatives suggested that the law provide for the use of either the historical capital or the asset basis. This alternative is provided in the bill as finally enacted.

The Association of the Bar of the City of New York pointed out that the historical method of determining invested capital imposes a heavy burden on corporations whose shares were issued prior to March 1, 1913, and recommended as an alternative that the taxpayer be permitted to include in invested capital as money and property paid in with respect to such shares an amount equal to the fair market value of those shares on March 1, 1913.

One witness, appearing before both House and Senate committees and representing certain real estate corporations, pointed out that many real estate properties had been acquired at depressed prices, and recommended that current valuations be employed in determining invested capital. He suggested (*a*) local tax assessment values, (*b*) local real estate market values, and (*c*) rent control valuations.

Another witness before the House Committee suggested that under appropriate circumstances invested capital should be increased by the difference between the cost and replacement value of the operating assets as of the end of the base period.

Witnesses representing the regulated public utilities objected to applying the minimum rates of return provided in the Bill to the adjusted tax basis of their assets. It was pointed out that state and federal agencies used numerous different bases upon which to allow a rate of return in fixing utility rates. Some use "present fair values"; others use "original cost" (meaning the cost to the person first devoting the property to public use); other bases are "reproduction cost new less depreciation," and the so-called "prudent investment." The Federal Power Commission uses "original cost." It was stated that no regulatory authorities use income tax cost to establish a reasonable utility rate.

The Edison Electric Institute and the National Association of Railroad and Utility Commissioners recommended that invested capital be the total of outstanding borrowed capital, capital stock, and surplus as reflected on the corporate books of account.

(*b*) Borrowed Capital

The Treasury proposed, with respect to borrowed capital, to

allow the full interest deduction in computing net income for excess profits tax purposes, and to provide for an addition to the credit of a fixed percentage of the interest payments. This would make the credit for borrowed capital proportionate to the amount of interest in each case.

Substantially all witnesses were opposed to the treatment accorded borrowed capital in H.R. 9827. There was substantial unanimity among business representatives that a preferable method would be to include 100 per cent of the borrowed capital in the invested capital base, with no allowance for the interest deduction. The borrowed capital so included would then be allowed the same rate of return as equity capital.

It was stated that the World War II law was too limited in its definition of borrowed capital, which restricted allowable debt to that which was secured. It was pointed out that many businesses borrow on unsecured open accounts. It was also recommended that the definition of borrowed capital include (*a*) all borrowed funds (including advance, partial, and progress payments) regardless of the sources of the funds or the method of repayment; (*b*) indebtedness represented by conditional sales contracts; and (*c*) debt borrowed on a short-term basis to purchase operating equipment.

Summary

Under the World War I excess profits tax law the historical capital approach was applied to invested capital, which was defined to mean paid-in capital plus paid-in capital surplus plus earned surplus. Borrowed capital was specifically excluded, and interest payments were deductible from income.

In World War II the historical capital approach was retained, but the definition of invested capital was broadened to include 50 per cent of the borrowed capital. A corollary provision limited interest deductions from income to 50 per cent. Invested capital was defined to be the equity investment capital plus 50 per cent of the borrowed invested capital minus inadmissible assets.

The 1950 legislation provides for both the historical approach and the asset approach, and the inclusion of 75 per cent of the borrowed capital. "Adjusted invested capital" is defined to be the equity invested capital at the beginning of the year plus the capital addition for the year plus 75 per cent of the average borrowed capital for the year plus the "recent loss adjustment," which is any net deficit in the periods 1946-9 or 1940-9, whichever is greater.

BIBLIOGRAPHY

BOOKS, MONOGRAPHS, AND PAMPHLETS

ALTMAN, OSCAR. *Savings, Investment and National Income*. Washington, Temporary National Economic Committee, 1941. Monograph no. 37.

ALVORD, E. C. "The Taxation of Undistributed Profits from the Business Point of View." *How Shall Business be Taxed?* New York, Tax Policy League, Inc., 1937.

—— "The Undistributed Profits Tax." *Proceedings of the National Tax Association*, 1937.

—— "Would Integration of Corporate and Individual Taxes Injure Business?" *Proceedings of the National Tax Association*, 1947.

American Institute of Accountants. *Accounting and Tax Problems in the Fifties*. Technical Papers from Sixty-second Annual Meeting, 1949. New York, 1950.

Association of British Chambers of Commerce and the Federation of British Industries. *Definition of Taxable Business Profits*. Joint Submission to the Tucker Committee, London, 1949.

Association of Certified and Corporate Accountants. *Memorandum*. London, 1949.

BARNES, GEORGE E. "Comments on Corporation Tax Programs." *Proceedings of the National Tax Association*, 1946.

BLAKEY, ROY G. "Evaluation of Postwar Tax Proposals Made by Various Groups and Individuals." *How Should Corporations be Taxed?* New York, Tax Institute, Inc., 1947.

BLAKEY, ROY G. and GLADYS C. *The Federal Income Tax*. New York, Longmans, Green & Co., 1940.

BLOUGH, ROY. "Flat versus Graduated Rates for Business Net Income Taxes." *How Shall Business be Taxed?* New York, Tax Policy League, Inc., 1937.

BOWEN, HOWARD R. *The Future of the Corporation Income Tax*. New York, Irving Trust Co., 1946.

—— "The Taxation of Small Business." *Proceedings of the National Tax Association*, 1946.

——— "Optional Partnership Treatment of Corporate Earnings." *How Should Corporations be Taxed?* New York, Tax Institute, Inc., 1947.

BROWN, H. G. *The Economics of Taxation.* New York, Henry Holt & Co., 1924.

BUCHANAN, N. S. *The Economics of Corporate Enterprise.* New York, Henry Holt & Co., 1940.

BUCK, A. E. *Financing Canadian Government.* Chicago, Public Administration Service, 1949.

BUEHLER, ALFRED G. "Critique of Present Methods of Business Taxation in the United States." *How Shall Business be Taxed?* New York, Tax Policy League, Inc., 1937.

——— "Some Comments on the Taxation of Small Business." *Proceedings of the National Tax Association,* 1946.

BURTON, PAUL W. *Cases and Materials on Taxation.* St. Paul, West Publishing Co., 1948. 2nd ed.

BUTTERS, J. KEITH. "Should the Profits of Small Corporations be Taxed Like Partnership Earnings?" *How Should Corporations be Taxed?* New York, Tax Institute, Inc., 1947.

——— "Would the Complete Integration of the Corporate and Personal Income Taxes Injure Small Business?" *Proceedings of the National Tax Association,* 1947.

BUTTERS, J. KEITH and LINTNER, JOHN. *Effect of Federal Taxes on Growing Enterprises.* Boston, Division of Research, Graduate School of Business Administration, Harvard University, 1945.

BUTTERS, J. KEITH, LINTNER, JOHN, and NILAND, POWELL. *Effects of Taxation Corporate Mergers.* Boston, Division of Research, Graduate School of Business Administration, Harvard University, 1951.

Canadian Tax Foundation. *Conference on the Income Tax Bill, Report of Proceedings.* Toronto, 1947.

——— *Memorandum of Recommendations on Bill 454, "An Act Respecting Income Taxes," Submitted to the Minister of Finance.* Toronto, April 1, 1948.

——— *The Income Tax Bill, a Review and Analysis.* Toronto, 1948.

——— "Corporate Profits and Dividends under the Income Tax Act." *Draft Report of the Third Tax Conference, held on December 5 and 6, 1949.* Toronto, 1950.

——— *Bill 296 to Amend the Income Tax Act, Memorandum Submitted to the Minister of Finance.* Toronto, May 29, 1951.

CANN, NORMAN D. "Requisites of Financial Statements to Meet Income Tax Regulations." *Second Annual Accounting Institute.* Georgia Society of Certified Public Accountants and University of Georgia, College of Business Administration, 1949.

CARTER, K. LEM. and STEWART, J. L. *Private Companies, Special Tax on Undistributed Income.* Toronto, C.C.H. (Canadian) Ltd., 1950.

C.C.H. (Canadian) Ltd. *Canadian Tax Reporter.* Toronto.

——— *The New Depreciation System.* Toronto, C.C.H. (Canadian) Ltd., August 1950.

COLM, GERHARD and LEAMANN, FRITZ. *Economic Consequences of Recent American Tax Policy. Social Research, Supplement.* New York Graduate Faculty of Political and Social Science, New School for Social Research. 1938.

Colonial Sugar Refining Company Ltd. *Capital Erosion and the Income Tax Assessment Act.* Sydney, Australia, October 26, 1950.

Committee for Economic Development. *A Postwar Federal Tax Plan for High Employment.* New York, 1944.

——— *Taxes and the Budget: A Program for Prosperity in a Free Economy.* New York, 1947.

——— *Economic Policy for Rearmament.* New York, 1950.

——— *Paying for Defense.* New York, November 16, 1950.

Committee on Postwar Tax Policy. *A Tax Program for a Solvent America,* 1945. Roswell Magill, Chairman. New York, 1945.

——— *A Tax Program for a Solvent America,* 1947. New York, 1947.

CONNOLLY, JOHN L. "Alternative Methods of Taxing Corporate Earnings at the Personal Level." *Proceedings of the National Tax Association,* 1948.

Controllers Institute of America. *Replacement Costs and Depreciation Policies.* New York, 1948.

Council of Retail Distributors. *Memorandum on the Taxation of Trading Stocks.* Submission to the Tucker Committee, London, 1949.

CURRY, O. J. "Utilization of Corporate Profits in Prosperity and Depression." *Michigan Business Studies,* vol. IX, no. 4. Ann Arbor, Bureau of Business Research, School of Business Administration, University of Michigan, 1941.

DALTON, HUGH. *Principles of Public Finance.* New York, Alfred A. Knopf, 1932.

DARRELL, NORRIS. "How Long Should the Accounting Period be for Corporate Income Tax Purposes?" *How Should Corporations be Taxed?* New York, Tax Institute, Inc., 1947.

DEAN, ARTHUR H. *An Inquiry into the Nature of Business Income under Present Price Levels.* New York, American Institute of Accountants, Study Group on Business Income, February 1949.

Dominion Association of Chartered Accountants. *Brief to Senate Committee.* Toronto, April 1946.

DOUGLAS, MONTEATH. *The Tax Treatment of Corporation Profits and Dividends in Canada.* Toronto, Canadian Tax Foundation, October 15, 1949. Mimeographed.

EDWARDS, HERBERT, and EDWARDS, ALAN M. *Profits Tax.* London, Gee and Co., Ltd., 1948. 2nd ed.

FORD, ROBERT S. *The Allocation of Corporate Income for the Purpose of State Taxation.* Special Report of the State Tax Commission, no. 6. Albany, New York State Tax Commission, 1933.

—— "Some Economic Aspects of the Present Corporate Income Tax." *Proceedings of the National Tax Association,* 1947.

FOULKE, ROY A. *A Study of the Theory of Corporate Net Profits.* New York, Dun and Bradstreet Inc., 1949.

GAA, CHARLES JOHN. *The Taxation of the Corporate Income.* Urbana, University of Illinois Press, 1944.

GAARE, HOWARD A. "Influence of Federal and State Income Taxation on Accounting Theory and Practice." *Technical Papers Presented at Mountain States Accounting Conference.* Denver, 1950.

GASTON, J. FRANK. *Effects of Depreciation Policy.* New York, National Industrial Conference Board Inc., 1950.

GILLIM, MARION HAMILTON. "Summary of Conflicting Views Concerning the Incidence of a General Income Tax." *The Incidence of Excess Profits Taxation.* New York, Columbia University Press, 1945.

GOODBAR, JOSEPH E., and BERGERON, LORENZO U. "Unrecognized Consequences of Income Tax." *A Creative Capitalism.* Boston, Boston University Press, 1948.

GOODE, RICHARD. "Alternative Approaches to the Integration of Corporate and Individual Income Taxes." *Proceedings of the National Tax Association,* 1947.

—— "The Postwar Corporation Tax Structure." *How Should Corporations be Taxed?* New York, Tax Institute, Inc., 1947.

—— *The Postwar Corporation Tax Structure.* Washington, U.S. Treasury Department, Division of Tax Research, 1948.

—— *The Corporation Income Tax.* New York, John Wiley & Sons, 1951.

GORDON, MOLYNEUX L. *A Digest of Income Tax Cases.* Toronto, Goodfellow Printing Company, Limited.

GRAELY, PAUL. "Impact of Economic Income, or Replacement Costs, on Public Utilities." *Replacement Costs and Depreciation Policies.* New York, Controllers Institute of America, 1948.

GRANT, EUGENE L., and NORTON, PAUL T., Jr. *Depreciation.* New York, Ronald Press, 1949.

GROVES, HAROLD M. "Equity and Expediency in Business Taxation." *How Shall Business be Taxed?* New York, Tax Policy League, Inc., 1937.

---- "Postwar Federal Taxation." *Proceedings of the National Tax Association,* 1944.

---- *Production, Jobs and Taxes.* New York, McGraw-Hill Book Co., 1944.

---- *Financing Government.* New York, Henry Holt & Co., 1945. 2nd ed.

---- *Postwar Taxation and Economic Progress.* New York, McGraw-Hill Book Co., 1946.

---- "Revision of the Corporation Income Tax." *Proceedings of the National Tax Association,* 1947.

GUEDALLA, PHILIP. *Mr. Churchill.* Toronto, Musson Book Co., 1942.

HAAS, GEORGE C. "The Taxation of Undistributed Profits from the Point of View of the Federal Tax Structure." *How Shall Business be Taxed?* New York, Tax Policy League, Inc., 1937.

HANNAN, J. P. *A Treatise on the Principles of Income Taxation.* Sydney, Law Book Co. of Australia Pty. Ltd., 1946.

HANSEN, ALVIN H. *Fiscal Policy and Business Cycles.* New York, W. W. Norton Inc., 1941.

HART, ALBERT G. *Defense without Inflation.* New York, Twentieth Century Fund, 1951.

HART, ALBERT G., and BROWN, E. CARY. *Financing Defense.* New York, Twentieth Century Fund, 1951.

HEARNE, W. L. "Depreciation, Depletion, and Research and Development Costs." *How Should Corporations be Taxed?* New York, Tax Institute, Inc., 1947.

---- "Does the Present Tax System Discourage Business Enterprise?" *How Should Corporations be Taxed?* New York, Tax Institute, Inc., 1947.

HENDERSON, JAMES M. *Introduction to Income Taxation.* Chicago, Callaghan and Company, 1943.

HICKS, J. R. *Value and Capital.* Oxford, Clarendon Press, 1939.

HOAGLAND, HENRY E. *Corporation Finance.* New York, McGraw-Hill Book Co., 1947. 3rd ed.

HOUSTON, G. SIDNEY. "Twin Cities Program for Postwar Taxation." *Proceedings of the National Tax Association,* 1944.

How Shall Business be Taxed? New York, Tax Policy League, Inc., 1937. (Articles listed under individual authors.)

How Should Corporations be Taxed? New York, Tax Institute, Inc., 1947. (Articles listed under individual authors).

HUNTER, M. H. "Shall We Tax Corporations or Business?" *Proceedings of the National Tax Association*, 1936.

HYMING, CLIFFORD J. *Taxation of Corporate Enterprise.* Washington, Temporary National Economic Committee, 1941. Monograph no. 9.

Institute of Chartered Accountants in England and Wales. *Memorandum for the Committee on Taxation of Trading Profits Appointed by the Chancellor of the Exchequer.* London, December, 1949.

Institute of Taxation. *Recommendations of the Council of the Institute of Taxation to the Committee on Taxation of Trading Profits.* London, 1949.

JACOBY, NEIL H. *Retail Sales Taxation.* Chicago, Commerce Clearing House Inc., 1938.

JAMES, GEORGE F. "United States Tax Legislation during and since World War II." *Studies in International Tax Law*, vol. V. The Hague, International Fiscal Association, 1947.

JAMES, GEORGE F., and DAYTON, FELIX. "Taxation of Business Profits." *International Fiscal Association Tax Congress*, 1948. Vol. 10. Rotterdam, 1948.

Joint Committee of Councils, Chartered Accountants of Scotland. *Representations to the Tucker Committee on Taxation of Trading Profits.* 1949.

JUDGE, GRANT E. "Tax Administration from the Point of View of the Corporation." *Proceedings of the National Tax Association*, 1940.

KAPLAN, A. D. H. *Small Business: Its Place and Problems.* Committee for Economic Development Research Study. New York, McGraw-Hill Book Co., Inc., 1948.

KEITH, E. GORDON. "New Data on Tax Exempt Organizations." *Proceedings of the National Tax Association*, 1945.

—— "The Corporation in the Tax System." *Proceedings of the National Tax Association*, 1946.

KENDRICK, M. SLADE. *The Undistributed Profits Tax.* Washington, The Brookings Institution, 1937.

KENT, ARTHUR H. "The Legal Machinery of the Present Corporate Income Tax System." *Proceedings of the National Tax Association*, 1947.

KEYNES, JOHN MAYNARD. *The General Theory of Employment, Interest and Money*. London, Macmillan and Co. Ltd., 1936.

KIMMEL, LEWIS H. *Postwar Tax Policy and Business Expansion*. Washington, The Brookings Institution, 1943.

---- *Depreciation Policy and Postwar Expansion*. Washington, The Brookings Institution, 1946.

LASSER, J. K. *Your Corporation Tax*. New York, Simon and Schuster, 1946.

Law Society of Upper Canada. *Special Lectures on Taxation*. Toronto, Richard DeBoo Limited, 1944.

LENT, GEORGE E. "Alternative Methods of Taxing Corporation Earnings at the Personal Level: The Withholding Approach." *Proceedings of the National Tax Association*, 1947.

---- *The Impact of the Undistributed Profits Tax, 1936–1937*. Studies in History, Economics and Public Law, no. 539. New York, Columbia University Press, 1948.

LINCOLN, E. E. *Applied Business Finance*. New York, McGraw-Hill Book Co., 1941. 5th ed.

LUTZ, H. L. *Guideposts to a Free Economy*. New York, McGraw-Hill Book Co., 1945.

MACKAY, R. DEW. *Definition of the Term Income: Address to the Taxation Section of the Canadian Bar Association*. Washington, D.C., September 20, 1950.

Machinery and Allied Products Institute. *Capital Goods Industries and the Federal Income Taxation*. Chicago, 1940.

MAGILL, ROSWELL F. *Taxable Income*. New York, Ronald Press, 1936. Rev. ed., 1945.

MAGILL, ROSWELL, PARKER, L. H. and KING, ELDON P. *A Summary of the British Tax System with Special Reference to Its Administration*. Washington, U.S. Government Printing Office, 1934.

MARSHALL, ALFRED. *Principles of Economics*. London, Macmillan and Co., Ltd., 1916. 7th ed.

MATTHEWS, M. BEVERLEY. *Capital Gains: Address to the Toronto Board of Trade Club*. October 2, 1950.

MAY, GEORGE O. *Financial Accounting*. New York, Macmillan Co., 1946.

---- *Business Income and Price Levels, an Accounting Study*. New York, American Institute of Accountants, Study Group on Business Income. July 1, 1949.

MERING, OTTO VON. *The Shifting and Incidence of Taxation*. Philadelphia, Blakiston Co., 1942.

MILLER, ROBERT N. "The Taxation of Intercorporate Dividends." *Proceedings of the National Tax Association*, 1938.

MOYERS, DONALD P. "Corporate Income Tax Compliance and Procedural Problems." *Proceedings of the National Tax Association*, 1948.

MUSGRAVE, R. A. "Should an Absolute Corporation Tax be Retained?" *Proceedings of the National Tax Association*, 1947.

National Association of Cost Accountants. *Year Book 1940: Proceedings of the Twenty-first International Conference.*

National Industrial Conference Board, Inc. *The Shifting and Effects of the Federal Corporation Income Tax.* New York, 1928.

—— *Effects of Taxes upon Corporate Policy.* New York, 1943.

—— *Wages, Prices, Profits.* New York, 1949.

National Tax Association. "Report of the Committee of the National Tax Association on Federal Taxation of Corporations." *Proceedings of the National Tax Association*, 1938; 1939.

—— *Preliminary Report of the Committee on the Federal Corporate Net Income Tax.* July 1949. Mimeographed.

—— *Final Report of the Committee on the Federal Corporate Net Income Tax.* August 1950. Mimeographed.

NELSON, G. N. "Taxation of Corporate Holding Companies." *Proceedings of the National Tax Association*, 1938.

—— "Taxation of Corporate Surplus." *Proceedings of the National Tax Association*, 1939.

NEWCOMER, MABEL. "European Taxation of Business." *How Shall Business be Taxed?* New York, Tax Policy League, Inc., 1937.

NEWPORT, CECIL A., and SHAW, OLIVER J. *Income Tax Law and Practice.* London, Sweet and Maxwell Ltd., 1949. 21st ed.

NEWTON, R. WAYNE. "Corporation Income Taxes as Applied to Coops." *Proceedings of the National Tax Association*, 1945.

New York State Society of Certified Public Accountants, Committee on Federal Taxation. *Recommendations for Modification of Internal Revenue Code, with Especial Reference to Income and Estate Taxes.* New York, 1947.

New York Stock Exchange. *Jobs and Taxes.* August 1949.

NORTON, PAUL T., Jr. "Present Federal Income Tax Practice Penalizes New and Small Businesses." *Proceedings of the National Tax Association*, 1949.

OLIVER, JOHN W. *Taxation—Management Problem. Reading Course in Executive Technique*, vol. 7. New York, Funk and Wagnalls Co., 1948.

PATON, W. A. *Accounting.* New York, Macmillan Co., 1924.

PAUL, RANDOLPH E. "The Taxation of Personal Holding Companies." *Proceedings of the National Tax Association*, 1938.

——— *Taxation for Prosperity*. New York, Bobbs-Merrill Co., 1947.

PERRY, J. HARVEY. *Taxation in Canada*. Toronto, University of Toronto Press, 1951.

PETRIE, J. R. *Some Economic Aspects of the Taxation of Corporate Income and Dividends: Address to 1949 Tax Conference of the Canadian Tax Foundation*. Montreal, December 5, 1949. Mimeographed.

——— *The Effect of New Taxes on Marketing*. Canadian Tax Foundation, 1951.

——— "Inflation." *Inflation and Price Control*. Toronto, Canadian Tax Foundation, 1951.

PLAXTON, H. A. W. *The Law Relating to Income Tax and Excess Profits Tax of the Dominion of Canada*. Toronto, Carswell Co. Ltd., 1947. 2nd ed.

POOLE, KENYON E. *Fiscal Policies and the American Economy*. New York, Prentice-Hall, 1951.

RAO, V. K. R. V. *Taxation of Income in India*. Calcutta, Longmans, Green & Co. Ltd., 1931.

RUML, BEARDSLEY. "Fiscal Policy and Taxation." *Proceedings of the National Tax Association*, 1944.

RUML, BEARDSLEY and SONNE, H. C. *Fiscal and Monetary Policy*. Washington, National Planning Association, 1944.

RUTTENBERG, S. H. "Does the Present Tax System Discourage Business Enterprise?" *How Should Corporations be Taxed?* New York, Tax Institute, Inc., 1947.

SCHREIBER, LOUIS. "The Place of the Corporate Income Tax in the Tax System." *Proceedings of the National Tax Association*, 1947.

SELIGMAN, E. R. A. *Shifting and Incidence of Taxation*. New York, Columbia University Press, 1921.

——— *The Income Tax*. New York, Macmillan Co., 1921.

——— "Income Taxes and the Price Level." *Proceedings of the Academy of Political Science*, vol. XI, 1924.

——— *Essays in Taxation*. New York, Macmillan Co., 1925. 10th ed.

SELIGMAN, EUSTACE. "A Postwar Program for the Taxation of Corporations and Their Shareholders." *Proceedings of the American Philosophical Society*, 1944.

SHERE, LOUIS. "The Fiscal Significance of the Corporation Income Tax." *Proceedings of the National Tax Association*, 1947.

SHOUP, CARL. "The Taxation of Undistributed Profits from the Theoretical Point of View." *How Shall Business be Taxed?* New York, Tax Policy League, Inc., 1937.

SHULTZ, WILLIAM J. *American Public Finance.* New York, Prentice-Hall Inc., 1942. 3rd ed.

SIMON, Rt. Hon. Viscount, ed. *Simon's Income Tax.* London, Butterworth and Co. Publishers Ltd., 1948.

SIMONS, HENRY C. *Personal Income Taxation.* Chicago, University of Chicago Press, 1938.

——— "Postwar Federal Tax Reform." *Proceedings of the National Tax Association,* 1943.

——— *Federal Tax Reform.* Chicago, University of Chicago Press, 1950.

SLICHTER, SUMNER H. "Business Profits." *Testimony before Joint Committee on the Economic Report of the President,* Washington, December, 1948. Mimeographed.

——— *The American Economy.* New York, Alfred A. Knopf, 1949.

SMITH, DAN THROOP and BUTTERS, J. KEITH. *Taxable and Business Income.* New York, National Bureau of Economic Research, Inc., 1949.

Society of Incorporated Accountants and Auditors. *Taxation of Trade Profits.* London, October 17, 1949. Mimeographed.

——— *Taxation Course at Ashridge.* London, June 1950.

SOMERS, HAROLD M. *Public Finance and National Income.* Philadelphia, Blakiston Co., 1949.

SONNE, H. C. "How Should Corporations be Taxed?" *How Should Corporations be Taxed?* New York, Tax Institute, Inc., 1947.

SPICER, E. E. and PELGER, E. C. *Income Tax.* London, H.F.L. (Publishers) Ltd., 1948. 18th ed.

SPORRER, M. J. "Some Effects of Federal Income and Excess Profits Taxes on Corporate Organization." *Proceedings of the National Tax Association,* 1944.

STAPLES, RONALD. "Computation of Taxable Profits." *International Fiscal Association Tax Congress,* 1948. Vol. 9. Rotterdam, 1948.

STIKEMAN, H. H. *Canada Tax Cases.* Toronto, Richard De Boo Limited.

——— "A Consideration of Corporation Taxation." *Proceedings of the Canadian Bar Association,* vol. 30. Toronto, 1947.

STIKEMAN, H. H. and HAMILTON, A. W., eds. *Canada Tax Manual.* Toronto, Richard De Boo Limited.

SWEENEY, H. W. *Stabilized Accounting.* New York, Harper & Bros., 1936.

SWORTZ, HAROLD T. "Administration of the Federal Corporation Income Tax." *Proceedings of the National Tax Association,* 1948.

TAITEL, MARTIN. *Profits, Production Activities and New Investment.* Monograph no. 12. Washington, Temporary National Economic Committee, 1941.

Tax Foundation, Inc. *War Taxes and Industry.* New York, August 4, 1942. Mimeographed.

Tax Institute, Inc. *Capital Gains Taxation.* New York, 1946.

---- *How Should Corporations be Taxed?* Symposium, 1946. New York, 1947.

Tax Policy League, *How Shall Business be Taxed?* Symposium, 1936. New York, 1937.

Taxation Institute of Australia. *Private Company Tax: Ascertainment of Distributable Income,* Circular no. 154. Sydney, 1949.

Temporary National Economic Committee. *Relative Efficiency of Large, Medium-Sized, and Small Business.* Monograph no. 13. Washington, 1941.

TERBORGH, GEORGE. *Depreciation Policy and the Postwar Price Level.* Chicago, Machinery and Allied Products Institute, April 1947.

---- *Dynamic Equipment Policy.* New York, McGraw-Hill Book Co., 1949.

TOWERS, GRAHAM. *Expectations and Events: Address to the Empire Club of Canada and the Canadian Club of Toronto.* November 9, 1950.

TULLY, ANDREW M. *The Tax Credit.* Special Report of the State Tax Commission, no. 15. Albany, New York State Tax Commission, 1948.

VICKREY, WILLIAM. *Agenda for Progressive Taxation.* New York, Ronald Press, 1947.

---- "The Effects of the Integration of Corporate and Individual Income Taxes on Business." *Proceedings of the National Tax Association,* 1947.

WALKER, MABEL L. Foreword in *How Shall Business be Taxed?* New York, Tax Policy League, Inc., 1937.

WILLIS, JOHN. *The Mitigation of the Tax Penalty on Fluctuating or Irregular Incomes.* Toronto, Canadian Tax Foundation, 1951.

WOLL, MATTHEW. "Should Corporations be Taxed as Such?" *How Should Corporations be Taxed?* New York, Tax Institute, Inc., 1947.

PERIODICALS

ADAMS, T. S. "Federal Taxes upon Income and Excess Profits." *American Economic Review, Supplement,* 1920.

---- "Immediate Future of the Excess Profits Tax." *Ibid.*

ADAMSON, A. V. "Private Company Taxation." *Chartered Accountant in Australia,* February 1949.

—— "Income Tax Payable by Companies and Shareholders." *Ibid.,* April 1950.

ALLEN, A. STUART. "Taxation and Corporate Capital." *Accountancy,* June 1950.

ALLEN, EDWARD L. "Alleged Deficiencies of the Corporate Income Tax." *Bulletin of the National Tax Association,* April 1945.

American Institute of Accountants. "Federal Income Tax Revisions: Institute's Recommendation Compared with Other Plans." *Journal of Accountancy,* February 1948.

ANDERSON, CLAY J. "Trends in Supply of Equity Capital." *Harvard Business Review,* September 1950.

ANDERSON, HAROLD C. "The Taxability of Dividends." *Taxes—The Tax Magazine,* February 1937.

ARMSTRONG, JOHN D. "Cooperatives and Income Tax Exemption." *Virginia Law Review,* April 1948.

ATLAS, MARTIN. "Average Income and Its Use in Taxation." *Accounting Review,* June 1938.

BAGLEY, WILLIAM C., Jr. "To Halt Price Rises: Curtailing Demand by Taxation Advocated as Inflation Curb." *New York Times* (Letters to the Editor), January 18, 1948.

BAILEY, GEORGE D. "Problems in Reporting Corporation Income." *Harvard Business Review,* September 1948.

—— "Concepts of Income." *Ibid.,* November 1948.

—— "Economic Restrictions on Earnings Determined under Present Accounting Conventions: Excerpts from Testimony before Subcommittee of Joint [Congressional] Committee on Economic Report." *Journal of Accountancy,* January 1949.

—— "Accelerated Depreciation: Criteria for Its Use." *Ibid.,* November 1949.

BALET, J. W. "Application of the LIFO Inventory Method to Income Tax Depreciation for Public Utilities." *National Tax Journal,* December 1948.

BALLANTINE, ARTHUR A. "Corporations and the Income Tax." *Harvard Business Review,* Spring 1944.

BEARD, CHARLES A. "Nine Categorical Denials." *Tax Outlook,* December 1947.

BECK, MORRIS. "British Anti-Inflationary Tax on Distributed Corporate Profits." *National Tax Journal,* September 1948.

—— "Capital Replacement Depreciation and Taxes." *Canadian Chartered Accountant,* September 1948.

——— "Ability to Shift the Corporate Income Tax." *National Tax Journal,* September 1950.

BECKHART, B. H. "Financial Implications of Rearmament." *Commercial and Financial Chronicle,* October 26, 1950.

BENJAMIN, HAROLD. "A Diminishing Depreciation Method Based on a Sine Curve Works with Any Scrap Value." *Journal of Accountancy,* April 1950.

BERLE, ADOLPH, A., Jr. "The Theory of Enterprise Entity." *Columbia Law Review,* April 1947.

BERRY, BERNARD M. "Appreciation of Fixed Assets." *Accountant,* February 21, 1948.

——— "Taxation of Trading Profits." *Ibid.,* January 28, 1950.

BINDER, B. H. "Income Taxation in the United Kingdom." *Canadian Chartered Accountant,* October 1949.

BING, RALPH A. "Price Controls and Higher Corporate Taxes—Double Squeeze on Profits." *Commercial and Financial Chronicle,* December 30, 1948.

BLACK, MARTIN L., Jr. "Some Accounting Aspects of Tax Exemption for Farmers' Cooperatives." *Accounting Review,* July 1948.

BLACKALL, FREDERICK S., Jr. "Should the Tax Laws Permit Speeding up Depreciation?" *Modern Industry,* March 15, 1947.

——— "Our Rusting Tools: How U.S. Tax Policy Discourages Industrial Expansion." *Tax Outlook,* November 1947.

BLACKETT, G. H. and LADIN, DAVID. "Disadvantages of Lifo for a Growing Retail Establishment." *Journal of Accountancy,* July 1949.

BLACKIE, WILLIAM. "What is Accounting Accounting for—Now?" *National Association of Cost Accountants Bulletin,* July 1, 1948.

BLAISDELL, DURWOOD A. "Depreciation Plan in Which Excess Replacement Cost Would be Charged to Year's Income." *Journal of Accountancy,* August 1949.

BLISS, CHARLES A. "The Reality of Inventory Profits." *Harvard Business Review,* September 1948.

BLOUGH, CARMAN G. "Recent Accounting Developments in the United States." *Canadian Chartered Accountant,* October 1947.

BLOUGH, ROY. "The Averaging of Income for Tax Purposes." *Taxes—The Tax Magazine,* October 1944.

——— "Some Aspects of Corporate Taxation." *Bulletin of the National Tax Association,* June 1946.

——— "An Anti-Inflation Program." *Commercial and Financial Chronicle,* October 5, 1950.

——— "Fiscal Policy as Inflationary Curb." *Ibid.,* November 9, 1950.

——— Fiscal Policy in a Defence Economy." *National Tax Journal,* December 1950.

BLUM, WALTER J. "The Decline and Fall of Capital Gains." *Taxes—The Tax Magazine,* September 1950.

BOCK, RUSSELL S. "Tax Problems of the Small Business." *Taxes—The Tax Magazine,* February 1947.

BOUGHNER, JACKSON L. "Income Tax Accounting and Business Operations." *Michigan Certified Public Accountant,* April 1950.

BOWEN, HOWARD R. "Taxation of the Net Income from Business." *Bulletin of the National Tax Association,* December 1945.

——— "The Incidence of the Corporation Income Tax." *American Economic Review,* March 1946.

BOWER, FRANK. "Taxation and Industrial Undertaking." *Accountant,* February 25, 1950.

BRADLEY, W. L. "Taxation of Cooperatives." *Harvard Business Review,* Autumn 1947.

——— "Classification for Tax Purposes of Reserves of Tax-Exempt Cooperatives." *Law and Contemporary Problems,* Summer 1948.

——— "What's Wrong with Tax Law?—From Viewpoint of Cooperatives?" *New York Certified Public Accountant,* January 1949.

BROAD, SAMUEL J. "The Impact of Rising Prices upon Accounting Procedures." *Journal of Accountancy,* July 1948.

——— "Recent Efforts to Increase Significance of Figure of Net Income." *Ibid.,* May 1950.

BROWN, E. CARY. "Pay-As-You-Go Corporate Taxes?" *American Economic Review,* September 1947.

——— "Tax Allowances for Depreciation Based on Changes in the Price Level." *National Tax Journal,* December 1948.

BROWN, E. C. and PATTERSON, GARDNER. "Accelerated Depreciation: A Neglected Chapter in War Taxation." *Quarterly Journal of Economics,* August 1943.

BROWNE, ROLLIN. "Adjustment of Tax Basis for Depreciation and Depletion: How Present Law Penalizes Taxpayers." *Journal of Accountancy,* March 1950.

BRUNDAGE, P. F. "Principles and Practice of Income Taxation in United States." *Canadian Chartered Accountant,* November 1949.

BUCK, WALTER M. S. "Theory of Straight Line Depreciation." *Appraisal Journal,* July 1948.

BUEHLER, A. G. "The Taxation of Business." *Bulletin of the National Tax Association,* December 1944.

——— "Taxation, No Check to Monopoly." Address before Tax Institute Symposium abstracted. *Commercial and Financial Chronicle,* December 12, 1946.

BURGESS, W. RANDOLPH. "Financing Defenses." *Commercial and Financial Chronicle,* November 9, 1950.

BURNET, ROBERT P. "Some Aspects of Finance Act." *Accountant's Magazine,* June 1949.

BUTTERS, J. KEITH. "Discriminating Effects of the Annual Computation of the Corporate Income Tax." *Quarterly Journal of Economics,* November 1939.

——— "Appraisal of the Postwar Tax Plans." *Harvard Business Review,* Winter 1944.

——— "Taxation and New Product Development." *Ibid.,* Summer 1945.

——— "Management Considerations on LIFO." *Ibid.,* May 1949.

Canada Tax Service B. Toronto, Richard De Boo Limited.

CARY, WILLIAM L. "Accumulations beyond Reasonable Needs of Business: Dilemma of Section 102(c)." *Harvard Law Review,* October 1947.

CHAMBERS, S. P. "Taxation and Supply of Capital for Industry in United Kingdom." *Lloyds Bank Review,* January 1949.

COLM, GERHARD. "Conflicting Theories of Corporate Income Taxation." *Law and Contemporary Problems,* Spring 1940.

——— "Fiscal Policy." *Tax Law Review,* October-November 1946.

COPELAND, M. A. "Suitable Accounting Conventions to Determine Business Income." *Journal of Accountancy,* February 1949.

COTTER, ARUNDEL. "Business Hunts 'Outs' on Replacement Costs." *Barron's,* November 22, 1948.

COWAN, ALVIN RANDALL. "Taxability of Corporate Distributions of Earnings and Profits." *Taxes—The Tax Magazine,* August 1946.

COWEN, K. H. "Federal Income Tax Aspects of Inventory Accounting." *National Association of Cost Accountants Bulletin,* December 1, 1948.

COYNE, JOHN M. "Capitalization of Corporate Surpluses—The New 15% Tax on Private Companies." *Canadian Chartered Accountant Tax Review,* January 1951.

CROWN, LEO W. "Inventory Pricing." *Taxes—The Tax Magazine,* April 1948.

DARRELL, NORRIS. "Recent Developments in Nontaxable Reorganizations and Stock Dividends." *Harvard Law Review,* June 1948.

DEVINE, JAMES W. "Taxing Corporations as Partnerships." *Taxes—The Tax Magazine,* June 1948.

DOHR, J. L. "The Next Step in Depreciation Accounting." *Journal of Accountancy,* February 1950.

Dominion Association of Chartered Accountants. "Tax Recommendations." *Canadian Chartered Accountant,* June 1946.

DONNELLY, A. S. "Accounting Problems in Taxation Returns." *Australian Accountant,* March 1949.

DORSEY, HAROLD B. "Elements Surrounding Burden of Double Taxation on Investment Market." *Exchange,* January 1948.

"Double Taxation upon Sale of Corporate Assets." *Yale Law Journal,* January 1947.

DOUGLAS, MONTEATH and PETRIE, J. R. "Taxation for Defence." *Financial Post,* December 9, 1950.

DOWNIE, A. DOUGLAS. "Investment Companies and Income Tax." *Canadian Chartered Accountant Tax Review,* October 1950.

DRUCKER, PETER F. "This War is Different." *Harper's Magazine,* November 1950.

DRYE, JOHN W., Jr. "Earned Surplus and Its Tax Problems for Stockholders." *Tax Law Review,* May 1949.

EATON, A. K. "Recent Developments in Corporate Taxation in Canada." *National Tax Journal,* March 1950.

ECCLES, MARRINER. "A Postwar Program for Small Business." *Taxes—The Tax Magazine,* August 1945.

"The Economics of Defence from a Tax Viewpoint." Canadian Tax Foundation, *Tax Bulletin,* January-February 1951.

—— "The Defense of the Dollar." *Fortune,* November 1950.

EDELMANN, CHESTER M. "Is Income Tax Accounting 'Good' Accounting Practice?" *Taxes—The Tax Magazine,* February 1946.

EDELSON, ROBERT I. "Accounting Methods—A Review of Some Fundamentals." *Taxes—The Tax Magazine,* March 1950.

EDWARDS, STANLEY E. "Problems Raised by the Undistributed Income Provisions of the Income Tax Act." *Canadian Chartered Accountant,* March 1951.

—— "Company Law Problems Arising under Part 1A of the Income Tax Act." *Canadian Bar Review,* November 1951.

EGERTON, R. P. "Replacement Accounting." *Canadian Chartered Accountant,* June 1949.

ELKIN, E. M. "Double Taxation of Dividends." *Bulletin of the National Tax Association,* February 1947.

ELLIS, A. C. "Cost Basis in Accounting Must be Used or We Upset Whole Business System." *Journal of Accountancy,* July 1950.

ELLIS, CECIL A. "The Financial Effects of Inventory Methods." *Canadian Chartered Accountant,* January 1948.

EMMANUEL, MICHEL G. "Earnings and Profits: Accounting Concept?" *Tax Law Review*, May 1949.

FERNALD, H. B. "Problems of Income Tax Administration." *Journal of Accountancy*, November 1945.

FITTS, E. GRANT. "Relation of Depreciation to Determination of Surplus and Earnings Available for Dividends." *Virginia Law Review*, September 1947.

FLYNN, W. H. "Notes on the New Depreciation Regulations." *Canadian Chartered Accountant Tax Review*, November 1950.

FOSTER, RALPH E. "Calculation of Corporation Taxes." *Canadian Chartered Accountant*, August 1946.

FOULKE, ROY A. "Expansion from Retained Earnings: Part 2." *Dun's Review*, December 1945.

FOURNIER, A. J. "Business Aspects of Carry-overs and Carry-backs." *Controller*, July 1946.

FREEMAN, E. STEWART. "Budgetary and Financial Policies for Industrial Corporations." *National Association of Cost Accountants Bulletin*, August 15, 1944.

FRIEDMAN, J. P. "Bureau Permits Use of LIFO by Retailers for Tax Purposes: Some of the Problems Involved." *Journal of Accountancy*, February 1948.

FROELICH, WALTER. "Role of Income Determination in Reinvestment and Investment." *American Economic Review*, March 1948.

GAVSIE, M. CHARLES. "Some Aspects of Income Taxation in Canada." *Canadian Chartered Accountant*, October 1949.

GELLER, MARTIN P. "Incidence of Federal Taxation upon Separate Entities." *New York Certified Public Accountant*, January 1948.

GEORGE, EDWIN B. "Some Economic Issues of Section 102." *Tax Review*, June 1947.

GILMOUR, A. W. "Diminishing Balance Depreciation under the Income Tax Act." *Canadian Chartered Accountant*, June 1950.

GLASSCO, J. G. "Trends in Post-War Tax Policy." *Canadian Chartered Accountant*, November 1947.

—— "The Treatment of Depreciation under the Income Tax Bill." *Ibid.*, December 1947.

—— "Depreciation Accounting." *Ibid.*, October 1948.

—— "Changes in Income Tax Law." *Ibid.*, February 1949.

GOLDBERG, LOUIS S. "A Plague on Both Their Houses: Accountant-Lawyer Differences over Tax Practice." *Journal of Accountancy*, September 1947.

GOODE, RICHARD. "The Corporate Income Tax and the Price Level." *American Economic Review*, March, 1945.

——— "The Incidence of the Corporation Income Tax: A Rejoinder." *Ibid.*, March 1946.

GORDON, D. M. "Administrative Tribunals and the Courts." *Law Quarterly Review*, 1933.

GORDON, MOLYNEUX L. "Taxation of Farmers." *Canadian Bar Review*, October 1949.

GRATTAN, C. HARTLEY. "Why Labor Wants Undistributed Profits Tax." *Barron's*, April 18, 1949.

GROVES, HAROLD M. "Personal versus Corporate Income Taxes." *American Economic Review*, May 1946.

——— "Personal versus Corporate Income Taxes." *Journal of Finance*, August 1946.

GUNN, J. A. L. "The Income Tax Assessment Act of 1970!" *Chartered Accountant in Australia*, November and December 1949.

GUTMAN, HARRY B. "Case for Incentive Taxation." *Controller*, September 1944.

HANES, JOHN W. "A Tax Policy for Enterprise." *Fortune*, June 1949.

HANNER, PER V. A. "Accounting and Taxation in Sweden in Relation to the Problem of Inflationary Profits." *Accounting Research*, January 1950.

HANSEN, H. E., and LUSARDI, F. R. "Depreciation under Review." *National Industrial Conference Board Business Review*, August 1947.

HARROD, ROY. "Taxation and Savings in Britain." *Taxes—The Tax Magazine*, May 1949.

HATFIELD, ROLLAND F. "Accounting and Income Tax Problems in Japan." *Minnesota Certified Public Accountant*, February 1950.

HEATON, JAMES S. "Income Tax—Basis of Assessment in Cases I and II—New Business." *Accountant's Magazine*, April 1948.

——— "Taxation of Dividends." *Ibid.*, May 1949.

——— "Income Tax and Nationalisation." *Ibid.*, June 1949.

HOLT, CHARLES C. "Averaging of Income for Tax Purposes: Equity and Fiscal Policy Considerations." *National Tax Journal*, December 1949.

HUDSON, PHILIP G. "Real Income and Income Tax." *Opinion and Comment*, November 18, 1947.

HUGHES, PERCY FREDERICK. "Profits Tax." *Certified Public Accountant*, February 1950.

Incorporated Accountants' Research Committee. "Reform of Taxation." *Accountancy*, December 1946.

"Inflation—The Problem." Canadian Bank of Commerce, *News Letter*, November 1950.

INNES, JAMES STEWART. "Aspects of Capital Cost Allowances." *Canadian Chartered Accountant Tax Review,* March 1951.

JACOBY, NEIL H. "Demand for Funds by American Business Enterprises: Retrospect and Prospect." *Journal of Finance,* October 1948, March 1949.

JEFFERSON, ROBERT W. "Effect of Taxation on Valuation of Inventories." *Illinois Certified Public Accountant,* December 1949.

——— "Income Tax Accounting." *Taxes—The Tax Magazine,* December 1949.

JOHNSON, PAUL F. "Inventory Pricing Problems." *Taxes—The Tax Magazine,* December 1949.

JOHNSTONE, J. C. "Taxes Leave Profits No Margin for Price Reductions." *Auditor,* July 1949.

Joint Committee of Councils of Chartered Accountants of Scotland, Taxation Committee. "Report." *Accountant's Magazine,* February 1947.

JONES, RALPH C. "Effects of Inflation on Capital and Profits: Record of Nine Steel Companies." *Journal of Accountancy,* January 1949.

KEEPING, GEORGE P. "Tax on Undistributed Income of Closely-Held Companies—Advantages and Disadvantages." *Canadian Chartered Accountant Tax Review,* September 1950.

KENT, ARTHUR H. "The Federal Revenue Act of 1936—Some Current Problems." *Taxes—The Tax Magazine,* April 1937.

——— "The Question of Taxing Capital Gains—The Case for Taxation." *Law and Contemporary Problems,* Spring 1940.

KEYSERLING, LEON H. "What Controls Do We Need?" *Commercial and Financial Chronicle,* October 26, 1950.

KING, C. L. "The Accounting Treatment of Certain Income Tax Items." *Canadian Chartered Accountant,* December 1947.

——— "Depreciation on Replacement Cost." *Ibid.,* August 1948.

KITRICK, S. "Depreciation Allowances in Great Britain." *Canadian Chartered Accountant Tax Review,* April 1949.

KLOOSTER, B. L. "Averaging Constructive Base Period Income." *Taxes —The Tax Magazine,* January 1947.

KOCH, ALBERT R., and STOCKWELL, ELEANOR J. "The Postwar Financial Position of Business." *Federal Reserve Bulletin,* December 1946.

KOHL, GERALD S. "Problem of Depreciation—1920 versus Today." *New York Certified Public Accountant,* September 1950.

KOHLER, C. H. "Taxation, Auditing and Ethics." *Canadian Chartered Accountant,* May 1949.

LACEY, K. "Profit Measurement and the Trade Cycle." *Canadian Chartered Accountant,* December 1948.

LANDMAN, J. H. "Comparative Tax Advantages of Corporations, Partnerships and Single Proprietorships." *Controller,* January 1948.

——— "Replacement Depreciation." *Dun's Review,* February 1949.

——— "The Old and New Depreciation Problem." *Taxes—The Tax Magazine,* October 1949.

——— "Depreciable Assets are Prepaid Expenses." *New York Certified Public Accountant,* September 1950.

LANG, JOHN J. "LIFO's 'Dollar Value' Inventory." *Taxes—The Tax Magazine,* May 1950.

LASSER, J. K. "Tax Accounting Incongruities." *Journal of Accountancy,* March 1947.

LASSER, J. K. and PELOUBET, MAURICE E. "Tax Accounting v. Commercial Accounting." *Tax Law Review,* March 1949.

——— "Tax Accounting v. Commercial Accounting." *Journal of Accountancy,* April 1949.

LELAND, SIMEON E. "Some Problems of Postwar Taxation." *Bulletin of the National Tax Association,* June 1945.

LEVIN, BENJAMIN B. "Carry-backs and Carry-overs in Business Planning." *Taxes—The Tax Magazine,* November 1949.

LEVINSON, SOL. "The Integration of Taxes on Income." *Taxes—The Tax Magazine,* May 1947.

LEVY, SAUL. "The Scope and Limitations of Accounting Practice in Federal Income Taxation." *Journal of Accountancy,* June 1950.

LITTERER, OSCAR F. "Corporation Income Tax and Production." *Bulletin of the National Tax Association,* April 1946.

LITTLE, LEO T. "Replacement Costs—An Economist's View." *Accounting Research,* November 1948.

——— "Direct Taxation and the Inflationary and Deflationary Effects of Fiscal Policy." *Ibid.,* July 1950.

MCCOLL, J. A. "To Incorporate or Not." *Canadian Chartered Accountant,* March 1950.

MACGILLIVRAY, C. K. "Taxation." *Canadian Chartered Accountant,* February 1948.

MCINTIRE, L. B. "Income Taxes and Capital Investment." *Accounting Review,* October 1945.

MCINTYRE, FRANCIS. "The Effect of the Undistributed Profits Tax upon the Distribution of the Corporate Earning—A Statistical Appraisal." *Econometrica,* July 1939.

MCMULLEN, S. Y. "Depreciation and High Costs: The Emerging Pattern." *Journal of Accountancy,* October 1949.

MACY, C. WARD. "The Corporation Net Income Tax and the Cost-Price Structure." *Bulletin of the National Tax Association*, May 1944.

——— "Incidence or Effects of the Corporation Income Tax." *American Economic Review*, December 1946.

MAGILL, ROSWELL. "Design for Our Federal Tax System." *Commercial and Financial Chronicle*, December 12, 1946.

——— "Four Urgently Needed Changes in Income Taxation." *Journal of Accountancy*, December 1949.

——— "Rearmament Poses Need for Sound Tax Program." *Tax Review*, October 1950.

MANNING, RAYMOND E. "Depreciation in the Tax Laws and Practice of the United States, Australia, Canada, Great Britain, New Zealand and South Africa." *National Tax Journal*, June 1948.

MASON, PERRY. "Depreciation and the Financing of Replacements." *Accounting Review*, December 1935.

MASS, BERNARD. "Who Pays Corporate Taxes?" *Conference Board Business Record*, February 1948.

MASSEL, MARK S. "Reappraisal of Depreciation and Obsolescence." *Harvard Business Review*, Autumn 1945.

MAVOR, JAMES. "The Taxation of Corporations in Ontario." *Journal of the Canadian Bankers' Association*, July 1900.

MAXWELL, C. R., Jr. "Averaging Fluctuating Income of the Individual for Income Tax Purposes." *Washington Law Review and State Bar Journal*, April 1945.

MAY, GEORGE O. "Should the LIFO Principle be Considered in Depreciation Accounting When Prices Vary Widely?" *Journal of Accountancy*, December 1947.

——— "Restudy of Concepts and Terminology of Business Income." *New York Certified Public Accountant*, January 1948.

MAYER, GERHARD J. "Declining Balance Depreciation." *Taxes—The Tax Magazine*, February 1947.

MILLS, LESLIE. "Problems of Differences between Financial Accounting Principles and Tax Accounting Concepts." *News Bulletin of Massachusetts Society of Certified Public Accountants*, May 1950.

MOFFET, H. S. "Capital Cost Allowance Problems." *Canadian Chartered Accountant Tax Review*, November 1950.

MOLLER, GEORGE. "Historic Costs—The Lesser Evil." *Canadian Chartered Accountant*, July 1949.

——— "The New Income Tax Regulations on Allowance of Capital Cost (Depreciation)." *Cost and Management*, January 1950.

MONACELLI, ALBERT H. "Canadian Taxes on Yankee Investments." *Taxes—The Tax Magazine,* April 1951.

MOON, R. W. "Undistributed Profits as Source of Company Finance." *Accounting Research,* January 1950.

MORTON, WALTER A. "Excess Profits Taxes versus Higher Regular Corporate Tax Rates." *National Tax Journal,* December 1950.

MUSGRAVE, R. A. "Three Plans for Post-war Taxation." *Federal Reserve Bulletin,* December 1944.

MYER, JOHN N. "Current Depreciation Mirage." *New York Certified Public Accountant,* January 1949.

---- "Depreciation and Recovery of Cost." *Ibid.,* May 1949.

---- "Depreciation and Maintenance of Capital." *Ibid.,* October 1949.

National Association of Cost Accountants. "Views on Tax Free Co-ops: Statement before House Committee on Ways and Means by Gus. C. Klippel." *Credit and Financial Management,* November 1947.

National City Bank of New York. *Monthly Letter on Economic Conditions,* November 1947; January 1949; July 1951.

NELSON, G. N. "The Taxation of Corporate Surplus." *Taxes—The Tax Magazine,* January 1937.

---- "The Question of Taxing Capital Gains—The Case against Taxation." *Law and Contemporary Problems,* Spring 1940.

NELSON, OSCAR S. "Taxing Obsolescence in Fixed Assets." *Accounting Review,* October 1945.

---- "Diminishing Depreciation Method Based on Geometric-Progression Formula." *Journal of Accountancy,* July 1950.

NELSON, ROBERT E. "The Dilemma of the Corporation in Tax Accounting for Dividends in Kind." *Journal of Accountancy,* January 1951.

NEWCOMB, JAMES F. "Way to Aid Small Business: Revised Tax Rate Would be Its Greatest Boon." *Credit and Financial Management,* October 1947.

NORRIS, HARRY. "Depreciation Allocations in Relation to Financial Capital, Real Capital and Productive Capacity." *Accounting Research,* July 1949.

NORTCLIFFE, E. B. "Revision of Balance Sheets in France." *Accountant,* June 25, 1949.

NORTON, PAUL T., Jr. "Declining Balance Depreciation Permitted by Internal Revenue is Not Realistic." *Journal of Accountancy,* July 1947.

OAKES, E. E. "The Incidence of the General Income Tax." *American Economic Review, Supplement,* March 1942.

O'CONOR, HERBERT R. "Problems of Replacement Cost and Tax Depreciation." *Public Utilities Fortnightly,* March 16, 1950.

O'NEILL, WALTER G. "Do Higher Corporate Taxes Deter Investment?" *Harvard Business Review,* Summer 1944.

PARKINSON, R. M. "The LIFO Method of Inventory Valuation." *Canadian Chartered Accountant,* May 1950.

PATON, W. A. "Depreciation and the Price Level." *Accounting Review,* April 1948.

——— "Measuring Profits under Inflation Conditions: A Serious Problem for Accountants." *Journal of Accountancy,* January 1950.

PEAIRS, C. A., Jr. "General Principles of Taxation: An Initial Survey." *Tax Law Review,* March 1951.

PELOUBET, MAURICE E. "Inventory Methods in the United States." *Canadian Chartered Accountant,* January 1948.

——— "Has LIFO Fallen?" *Journal of Accountancy,* April 1948.

——— "Are We Giving Away Our Capital without Knowing It? Discussion of Replacement Depreciation." *New York Certified Public Accountant,* June 1948.

——— "Analysis of the Effects of Taxation on Inventory Accounting and Policies." *Journal of Accountancy,* February 1950.

——— "Cost and Value Controversy." *New York Certified Public Accountant,* May 1950.

——— "Disclosure of Current Value of Lifo Inventories is Not Normally Useful: Figure Must be Estimate Based on Unreal Situation." *Journal of Accountancy,* June 1950.

PENTLAND, H. C. "The Royal Commission on Co-operatives." *Commerce Journal,* March 1947.

PERRY, J. HARVEY. "Development of the Canadian Corporation Income Tax." *Canadian Chartered Accountant,* January 1951.

PETRIE, J. R. "How Should Corporations be Taxed?" *Canadian Business,* January 1950.

——— "Some Aspects of Recent Corporation Income Tax Legislation in Canada." *Tax Policy,* September-October 1950.

——— "Small Business and Its Tax Problems." *Canadian Chartered Accountant,* December 1950.

——— "A Tough Budget?" *Canadian Business,* March 1951.

——— "What Kind of Taxes?" *Ibid.*

——— "Canada Tries Indirect Control of Inflation." *Tax Policy,* May–June 1951.

——— "Inflation and the Budget." *Canadian Business,* June 1951.

—— "Taxation in Relation to Defence Production and Inflation." *Industrial Canada,* July 1951.

—— "Paying for Government in Canada." *Public Affairs,* Autumn 1951.

——"Memorandum Respecting Part IA of the Income Tax Act Concerning Undistributed Income as Amended, 1951." Canadian Tax Foundation, *Tax Bulletin,* November-December 1951.

PIERCE, MELVILLE. "Inventory Valuation." *Canadian Chartered Accountant Tax Review,* March 1949.

—— "Business Profits and Income: Individuals." *Ibid.,* May 1949.

PINNOCK, LAWRENCE S. "Tax Aspects of Corporation versus Partnerships." *Utah C.P.A.,* September 1946.

PREST, A. R. "Replacement Cost Depreciation." *Accounting Research,* July 1950.

RAYMOND, F. I. "A Suggestion for the Double Taxation Problem." *Taxes—The Tax Magazine,* October 1946.

REIMER, CLARENCE F. "Major Differences between Net Income for Accounting Purposes and for Federal Income Taxes." *Accounting Review,* July 1948.

ROBERTSON, EDWARD H. "Effect of New Canadian Depreciation Law." *Journal of Accountancy,* March 1951.

ROTH, LOUIS. "Other Aspects of Capital Recovery Problem." *New York Certified Public Accountant,* March 1949.

ROWLAND, PETER M. B. "Taxation of Stock Exchange and Other Casual Transactions." *Accountant,* August 13, 1949.

RUBIN, ALVIN B. "Associations: Partnerships Taxable as Corporations." *Louisiana Law Review,* March 1948.

RUMBLE, WILFRED E. "Cooperatives and Income Taxes." *Law and Contemporary Problems,* Summer 1948.

RUML, BEARDSLEY. "Need We Tax away Prosperity?" *Nation's Business,* November 1946.

SANDERS, T. H. "Depreciation and 1949 Price Levels." *Harvard Business Review,* May 1949.

—— "Plant Depreciation and 1949 Price Levels." *Accounting Research,* July 1949.

SCHENK, WILLIAM E. "Should Cooperatives be Tax-Exempt?" *Opinion and Comment,* February 16, 1947.

SCHRAM, EMIL. "American Business and Risk Capital." *Vanderbilt Law Review,* June 1948.

SCULLY, V. W. T. "Administration of Income Tax." *Canadian Chartered Accountant,* April 1950.

SEGHERS, PAUL D. "Accelerated Depreciation and the Treasury's New Declining Balance Method of Computation." *Journal of Accountancy,* February 1947.

—— "Tax Accounting Compared with Recognized Accounting Principles." *National Tax Journal,* December 1948.

SEIDMAN, J. S. "What to Do about Section 102." *Taxes—The Tax Magazine,* July 1950.

—— "Comparison of Tax Advantages of Corporation v. Partnership or Sole Proprietorship." *Journal of Accountancy,* August 1950.

SELTZER, LAWRENCE H. "Evolution of the Special Legal Status of Capital Gains under the Income Tax." *National Tax Journal,* March 1950.

SHELTON, DAVID R. "Continuous Existence and End of Useful Life Concepts for Depreciation under Internal Revenue Code." *Virginia Law Review,* February 1948.

SHERE, LOUIS. "Federal Corporate Income Tax—Revenue and Reform." *National Tax Journal,* June 1949.

SHOUP, CARL. "Incidence of the Corporation Income Tax: Capital Structure and Turnover Rates." *National Tax Journal,* March 1948.

SILCOCK, T. H. "Accountants, Economists and the Valuation of Fixed Assets." *Economic Journal,* September 1949.

SIMONS, HENRY C. "Federal Tax Reform." *University of Chicago Law Review,* December 1946.

SINGER, ROBERT. "Double Taxation of Profits: A Comparison with the English Tax Laws." *Taxes—The Tax Magazine,* April 1948.

SLICHTER, SUMNER H. "Likely Characteristics of Our Defense Economy." *Commercial and Financial Chronicle,* August 31, 1950.

—— "Economic Problems of a Defense Economy." *Ibid.,* October 19, 1950.

—— "Some Current Economic Misconceptions." *Ibid.,* November 16, 1950.

—— "Business and Rearmament." *Atlantic Monthly,* November 1950.

SLITOR, R. E. "The Flexibility of Income Tax Yield under Averaging." *Journal of Political Economy,* June 1946.

SMITH, DAN THROOP. "Business Profits during Inflation." *Harvard Business Review,* March 1948.

SMITH, FURMAN. "Tax Effects of Corporate Distributions and Sales by Stockholders." *Tulane Law Review,* March 1948.

SOMERS, HAROLD M. "Economic Analysis of Capital Gains Tax." *National Tax Journal,* September 1948.

SONDERMAN, L. H. "Consumption of Fixed Assets." *Taxes—The Tax Magazine,* July 1946.

SOWARDS, HUGH L. "Should Co-ops Pay Federal Income Taxes?" *Tennessee Law Review,* June 1947.

SPILKY, ABRAHAM H. "Depreciation Based on Current Cost." *Taxes—The Tax Magazine,* March 1950.

SPRIGGS, M. G. "Background of Exceptional Depreciation Allowance." *Accountant, Tax Supplement,* September 27 and October 4, 1947.

STANLEY, W. F. "Straight-Line Depreciation at Average Rate May be Inaccurate in Growing Corporations." *Journal of Accountancy,* June 1949.

STEIN, EMANUEL. "Revision of the Federal Corporate Income Tax: A Proposal." *Tax Law Review,* January 1951.

STIKEMAN, H. HEWARD. "Taxation Law 1923-1947." *Canadian Bar Review,* January 1948.

STOY, JOHN M. "Accounting Theory and Taxable Income." *Taxes—The Tax Magazine,* May 1950.

STUDENSKI, PAUL. "Toward a Theory of Business Taxation." *Journal of Political Economy,* October 1940.

SUTTER, HARRY B. "Double Taxation of Dividends." *Trusts and Estates,* January 1948.

TANNENBAUM, JEROME. "Inventorying Raw Materials under LIFO." *Taxes—The Tax Magazine,* June 1947.

——— "The LIFO Method." *Ibid.*

TARLEAU, THOMAS N. "Tax Problems in the Valuation of Property." *Taxes—The Tax Magazine,* June 1947.

——— "Concept of Income for Federal Tax Purposes." *Tennessee Law Review,* February 1949.

"Tax Proposals to Aid Small Business." *Tax Policy,* December 1946.

"Taxation and Recovery." Round table. *Fortune,* May 1938.

"The Taxation of Private Companies in Australia." Canadian Tax Foundation, *Tax Bulletin,* March-April 1951.

Taxation Section of the Canadian Bar Association and the Legislation Committee of the Dominion Association of Chartered Accountants. "Recommendations on the Income Tax Act submitted to the Minister of Finance." *Canadian Chartered Accountant,* April 1950.

THOM, STUART. "About Your Taxes." *Financial Post,* November 4, 1950.

——— "Defining Taxable Income Held Not an Easy Matter." *Ibid.,* November 18, 1950.

TILLMAN, E. K. "Taxation and Corporate Entity: Case History." *Loyola Law Review,* June 1947.

"Trade or Business." *Taxation,* March, 1950.

TURNER, CLARENCE L. "Unreasonable Accumulation of Surplus." *Taxes—The Tax Magazine,* September 1948.

VICKREY, WILLIAM. "Averaging of Income for Income-Tax Purposes." *Journal of Political Economy,* June 1939.

——— "The Effect of Averaging on the Cyclical Sensitivity of the Yield of the Income Tax." *Ibid.,* September 1945.

VINEBERG, PHILIP F. "Taxable Income in Canada." *Canadian Chartered Accountant,* January 1947.

WADE, ALVIN C. "Accounting Methods for Income Tax Purposes." *Taxes—The Tax Magazine,* October 1948.

WATERS, L. L. "Taxation of Business Income and Its Consequences." *Your Business,* March 1947.

WATTLES, W. F. "The Development and Significance of the Depletion Allowance for Natural Resources." *Florida Law Journal,* February 1947.

WELLINGTON, C. OLIVER. "Accounting Income vs. Economic Income." *Canadian Chartered Accountant,* January 1949.

WELLS, ANITA. "Legislative History of Treatment of Capital Gains under Federal Income Tax, 1913–1948." *National Tax Journal,* March 1949.

WESTFALL, OTHEL D. "Integrating Federal Income Taxes on Corporations and Their Shareholders." *Taxes—The Tax Magazine,* March 1949.

WESTON, J. FRED. "Incidence and Effects of the Corporate Income Tax." *National Tax Journal,* December 1949.

WHEATLEY, E. H. "Commonwealth Income Tax Assessment Act, 1936–1947: Depreciation." *Chartered Accountant in Australia,* June 1948.

WHITELAW, A. W. "The Taxation of Private Companies." *Canadian Chartered Accountant Tax Review,* March 1951.

WHITWORTH, PETER E. "Profits Tax Peculiarities." *Accountant,* February 11, 1950.

WILCOX, E. B. "The Rise and Fall of LIFO." *Canadian Chartered Accountant,* April 1948.

WILCOX, E. B. and GREER, H. C. "The Case against Price-Level Adjustments in Income Determination." *Journal of Accountancy,* December 1950.

WILSON, KENNETH R. "Next Year's Taxes May Not be So Bad." *Financial Post,* November 18, 1950.

WOLKISER, ARTHUR M. "Risk Capital Shortage." *Trusts and Estates,* June 1948.

WOLKSTEIN, HARRY W. "Postwar Planning for Small Business." *Bulletin of the National Tax Association,* February 1946.

WOLMAN, LEO. "Our Present Prosperity—Is It Well Founded?" *Tax Review,* July 1950.

WUELLER, PAUL H. "Comparing Business Tax Burdens." *Bulletin of the National Tax Association,* June 1943.

WYNNE, WILLIAM H. "Taxation of Corporations in Canada." *Bulletin of the National Tax Association,* December 1941 and January 1942.

YEAGER, L. C. "How Taxes Dictate the Form of Business Ownership." *Robert Morris Associates Monthly Bulletin,* May 1946.

YOUNG, MICHAEL. "Is a Lower Income Tax the Answer to the Risk Capital Shortage?" *Saturday Night,* September 6, 1949.

YOUNG, R. T. "Profits Tax." *Accountant's Magazine,* March 1948.

ZOLLER, J. F. "Report of the Committee on Net Income Taxation as Applied to Business Corporations." *New York State Tax Bulletin,* May 1917.

GOVERNMENT DOCUMENTS

Australia

The Commissioner of Taxation. *Twenty-Fifth Report.* Canberra, 1944.

Royal Commission on Taxation, *Report.* Government Printer for the State of Victoria, 1921.

——— *Second Report,* Government Printer for the State of Victoria, June 29, 1922.

——— *Third Report,* Government Printer for the State of Victoria, August 4, 1922.

Royal Commission on Taxation. *First Report,* Canberra, 1932.

——— *Third Report,* Canberra, 1934.

Royal Commission on Taxation. *Proposed Form of Legislative Provisions Related to Income Tax,* Canberra, September 1935.

Canada

Commissioners, Combines Investigation Act. *Report, Canada and International Controls.* Ottawa, October 10, 1945.

Department of Agriculture. *Co-operation in Canada, 1949.* Ottawa, 1950.

Department of National Revenue. *Taxation Statistics 1950.* Ottawa, 1950.

Department of Reconstruction and Supply. *Encouragement to Industrial Expansion in Canada, Operation of Special Depreciation Provisions, November 10, 1944–March 31, 1949.* Ottawa, 1948.

Department of Trade and Commerce. *Investment and Inflation with Special Reference to the Immediate Post-War Period, Canada 1945–1948.* Ottawa, February 1949.

Dominion Bureau of Statistics. *National Accounts Income and Expenditure 1938–1947.* Ottawa, 1947.

—— *National Accounts Income and Expenditure 1947–1948 Revised.* Ottawa, 1949.

—— *Canada Year Book 1948–1949.* Ottawa, 1949.

—— *Inventory Accounting Methods of Canadian Manufacturers.* Ottawa, May 1949.

—— *Canada's International Investment Position, Selected Years 1926 to 1949.* Ottawa, 1950.

House of Commons. *Debates.* Budget Speeches: June 27, 1946; March 22, 1949; March 28, 1950; September 7, 1950.

House of Commons, Standing Committee on Banking and Commerce. *Minutes of Proceedings and Evidence.* No. 13. Ottawa, June 15, 1946.

Royal Commission on Co-operatives. *Report* (E. M. W. McDougall, Chairman). Ottawa, 1945.

Royal Commission on Prices. *Report* (C. A. Curtis, Chairman), vol. II. Ottawa, 1949.

Royal Commission on the Taxation of Annuities and Family Corporations. *Report* (W. C. Ives, Chairman). Ottawa, 1945.

Senate, Special Committee on the Income War Tax Act and the Excess Profits Tax Act. *Proceedings,* Nos. 1–6, 1945, and Nos. 1–13, 1946.

Great Britain

Committee Appointed to Enquire into the Present Position of Co-operative Societies in Relation to Income Tax. *Report.* Cmd. 4260. London, 1933.

Committee on National Debt and Taxation, *Report.* Cmd. 2800. London, 1927.

Income Tax Codification Committee. *Report,* vol. 1. Cmd. 5131. London, 1936.

Royal Commission on the Income Tax. *Report.* Cmd. 615. London, 1920.

Japan

Shoup Mission, General Headquarters Supreme Commander for the Allied Powers. *Report on Japanese Taxation.* Tokyo, September 1949.

New Zealand

Royal Commission Appointed to Inquire into the Subject of Land and Income Taxation in New Zealand. *Report.* Wellington, 1924.

United States

Congress, House. *Message from President of United States Transmitting Economic Report to Congress.* H. Doc. 36. 81st Cong., 1st Sess., Washington, 1949.

Congress, House, Committee on Ways and Means. "Corporation Tax Problems and General Revisions." *Revenue Revisions, 1947–48,* Part 2, Hearings. 80th Cong., 1st Sess., Washington, 1947.

——— "Tax Exempt Organizations—Co-operative Organizations." *Revenue Revisions, 1947–48,* Part 4. 80th Cong., 1st Sess., Washington, 1948.

Congress, Joint Committee on Economic Report. *Anti-inflation Program as Recommended in President's Message of November 17, 1947.* Hearings. 80th Cong., 1st Sess., Washington, 1948.

——— *Corporate Profits.* Hearings. 80th Cong., 2nd Sess., Washington, 1949.

Congress, Joint Committee on Economic Report, Subcommittee on Investment. *Volume and Stability of Private Investment.* 81st Cong., 2nd Sess., Washington, 1950.

Congress, Joint Committee on Economic Report, Subcommittee on Investment, Staff. *Factors Affecting Volume and Stability of Private Investment.* 81st Cong., 1st Sess., Washington, 1949.

Congress, Joint Committee on Economic Report, Subcommittee on Monetary, Credit, and Fiscal Policies. *Federal Expenditure and Revenue Policies.* Hearings. 81st Cong., 1st Sess., Washington, 1949.

——— *Monetary, Credit and Fiscal Policies: Collection of Statements Submitted by Government Officials, Bankers, Economists and Others.* 81st Cong., 2nd Sess., Washington, 1950.

——— *Report Pursuant to S. Com. Res. 26.* S. Doc. 129. 81st Cong., 2nd Sess., Washington, 1950.

Congress, Joint Committee on Economic Report, Subcommittee on Profits Hearings. *Profits.* Washington, 1949.

Congress, Joint Committee on Internal Revenue Taxation, Staff. *Analysis of Budget of Dominion of Canada for Fiscal Year Ending March 31, 1950.* Washington, 1949.

Congress, Senate, Committee on Finance. *Hearings on H.R. 8974.* 74th Cong., 1st Sess., Washington, 1935.

——— *Hearings on H.R. 8920.* 81st Cong., 2nd Sess., Washington, 1950.

Congress, Senate, Special Committee on Post-War Economic Policy and Planning. *Post-War Tax Plans for the Federal Government.* Senate Committee Print no. 7. 79th Cong., 1st Sess., Washington, 1945.

Congress, Senate. Special Committee to Study Problems of American Small Business. *Final Report: Small Business Finance and Taxation.* S. Rept. no. 46. 81st Cong., 1st Sess., Washington, 1949.

Council of Economic Advisers. *Third Annual Report to President,* Washington, 1948.

Department of Commerce. *International Transactions of the United States during the War, 1940–1945.* Washington, 1948.

Department of Commerce, Bureau of Foreign and Domestic Commerce. "Financing Corporate Capital Needs." *Survey of Current Business,* November 1948.

State Department. *Double Taxation: Taxes on Income.* Washington, 1946.

Temporary National Economic Committee. *Profits, Production Activities and New Investment.* Monograph no. 12. Washington, 1941.

——— *Savings, Investment and National Income.* Monograph no. 37. Washington, 1941.

——— *Taxation of Corporate Enterprise.* Monograph no. 9. Washington, 1941.

Treasury Department. *Business Loss Offsets.* Press Service no. S–505. Washington, 1947. Mimeographed.

——— "Business Loss Offsets." *Revenue Revisions, 1947–48.* Hearings, Part 5. 80th Cong., 1st Sess., Washington, 1948.

Treasury Department, Division of Tax Research. *Taxation of Small Business.* Washington, 1947. Mimeographed.

Union of South Africa

Social and Economic Planning Council. *Taxation and Fiscal Policy.* Report no. 7. Pretoria, 1945.

INDEX

Adams, T., cited 272n.
Agricultural organizations, 83
Alvord, E. C., 263n., 269n.
Anderson Logging Company v. *The King*, 36
Asset valuation, 27, 208–60; statement of the problem of, 208–13; concepts of income for purposes of, 213–18; inventory valuation, 218–32; fixed assets valuation, 232–55; obsolescence, 255–6; depletion, 256–9
Atlas, Martin, 197n.
Australia, Royal Commission on Taxation (1921), 191n., 195
Averaging: length of the averaging period, 191–3; simple average, 193–5; moving average, 195–7; progressive average, 197–8. *See also* Business losses

Badame v. *Minister of National Revenue*, 44
Bailey, George D., 213n., cited 214n., cited 238n.
Base stock method of inventory valuation, 222–3
Beckhart, B. H., 312n.
Benjamin, Harold, 235n.
Bennett, R. B., 52–3
Berry, Bernard M., 247n.
Beynon v. *Ogg*, 38
Blackie, William, 235n.
Blakey, Roy G., cited 111
Bliss, Charles A., cited 219n.
"Block system," 193–5
Blough, Roy, 105n., cited 109n., 145n., cited 147, 170n., 190n., 312n.
Boards of Trade, 83
Bowen, Howard R., cited 171–2, 173n., 177n., 178n., cited 288–9
British North America Act: allocation of taxing power, 8–9; tax exemptions under, 82
Broad, S. J., 235n., cited 248n.
Brown, E. C., 235n., cited 330n.
Brown v. *Minister of National Revenue*, 41, 43
Buchanan, N. S., 155n., 219n.
Budget speeches (Dominion): (1931), re double taxation, 52–3; (1946), re patronage dividends, 78; (1949), re loss carry-forward, 205, re 10% dividend credit, 300ff.; (1949, 1950), re undistributed profits, 64–5, 280; (1950), re capital gains, 45; (1951), re consolidated returns, 96, re inflation, 315
Buehler, A. G., cited 100, cited 108n., 173n.
Burgess, W. Randolph, 312n.
Business losses: statement of the problem of, 26–7, 185–90; offset by averaging devices, 190–200, by loss carry-over, 200–7, 255, 262
Business organization: effect of tax on form of, 26, 99–100, 171–3, 183. *See also* Partnership
Butters, J. Keith, 169n., 173n., 174n., cited 176n., cited 177n., 179n., cited 180, 187, 188, 205, 214n., 222n., cited 224n., 263n., cited 283n., cited 290, 291

California Copper Syndicate v. *Harris*, 36, 41
Campbell v. *Minister of National Revenue*, 45
Capital gains: as distinct from income, 33–50, 206; tax on, 13, 49–50, 267, 281–4
Carter, K. LeM., cited 70–1
Central Assets Ltd. v. *Minister of National Revenue*, 43–4
Chambers of Commerce, 83
Charitable organizations, 82–3
Charitable trusts, 83
Chrysler Corporation, 240n.
Churchill, Winston, 12n.
Colm, Gerhard, 270n.
Colwyn Committee, 135n., 141, 158n.

Commissioners of Inland Revenue v. *Stonehaven Recreation Ground Trustees,* 40
Common carriers, 99
Congress of Industrial Organizations (C.I.O.), 135
Connolly, John L., 263n., 284n.
Consolidated returns, 34n., 95–7
Consumption taxes, 10, 11, 120, 316
Co-operatives, 77–82
Co-operatives, Royal Commission on, 77–8, 79, 80
Copeland, M. A., 235n.
Corporate financing. *See* Saving and investment; Undistributed earnings
Corporation tax (Dominion): concept of, from 1917 to 1925, 50–2, from 1926 on, 52–3; and undistributed earnings, 53–77; and special corporations, 77–88; and ministerial discretion, 53, 88–95; rationale of, 23, 98–122; incidence of, 23–4, 123–43; economic effects of, 24–6, 144–84; capitalization of, 147; and the problem of business losses, 26–7, 185–207; as an instrument of fiscal policy, 6–7, 12, 111–16, 327–33. *See also* Asset valuation; Defence economy, taxation in; Double taxation; Income Tax Act; Integration; Rates; Revenue
Coyne, J. M., cited 69n.
Cragg v. *Minister of National Revenue,* 44–5
Credit unions, 84
Crown, Leo W., 224n.
Crown and municipal corporations, 82

Darrell, Norris, 189n., cited 201n., cited 203
Dean, Arthur H., 213n.
Deductions, under Income Tax Act, 137, 138
Defence economy, expenditures in, 12, 22, 309–11
Defence economy, taxation in, 9ff., 132; objectives of, 311–15; rates, 315–18; and deferred depreciation, 318–27. *See also* Excess Profits Tax
Depletion, capital cost, 256–8; flat rate, 258–9
Depreciation: the problem of, 233–5; straight-line basis of, 236–9; accelerated depreciation, 239–43, 254; replacement cost basis of, 243–7; revaluation, 247–8; diminishing balance, 248–53; through obsolescence, 255–6; deferred depreciation, 318–27
Dividend income: exclusion of from personal income tax base, 50, 285; comparative table of percentage of total personal income 1949 and 1950, 328. *See also* Double Taxation; Integration
Dividend policy: formulation of, 150–3, 286; volume of corporate saving, 153–5, 160; economic implications of, 155–8; effect of corporation tax on, 158–63. *See also* Saving and investment
Dividends credit: 10% credit on dividends, 68, 69, 95, 149, 171n., 262, 300ff.; dividends-paid credit, 290–4; dividends-received credit, 299–303
Dohr, J. L., 235n.
Double taxation, 27–30, 50–3; and regressivity, 24, 144–8. *See also* Integration and undistributed earnings
Douglas, Monteath, cited 311, 312n.
Drucker, Peter F., 312n.
Ducker v. *Rees,* 37

Eccles, Marriner S., 312n.
Economic effects of corporation tax: double taxation and regressivity, 144–8; on saving and investment, 148–66; on prices, 166–8; on corporate financing, 168–71; on form of business organization, 171–3; on small businesses and new enterprises, 173–80. *See also* Tax system
Edwards, Stanley E., cited 75
Elliott, C. Fraser, cited 88–9
Ellis, A. C., 235n.
Ellis, Cecil A., 224n.
Erichsen v. *Last,* 37
Excess profits tax, 13, 17, 107–9, 117, 142n., 154, 227n., 331–2. *See also* Defence economy, taxation in
Exchequer Court of Canada, 59, 61, 92
Executors of Massey v. *Minister of National Revenue,* 56
Exempt corporations, 82–8

Farming, 193–5
Fishing, 193–5
Fixed assets. *See* Asset valuation; Depreciation
Ford, R. S., cited 124n.
Foreign business corporations, 86
Foulke, Roy A., 210n., cited 214n.
Fraternal and benevolent societies, 83
Freeman, E. Stewart, cited 211n.

Gaston, J. Frank, 234n., 235n., 239n.
Gavsie, Charles, cited 225–6
Gilmour, A. W., cited 249n., cited 252n.
Glassco, J. G., cited 227n.
Gloucester Railway Carriage and Wagon Co. Ltd. v. *Commissioners of Inland Revenue,* 39
Goode, Richard B., 99n., cited 101, cited 102, cited 124, cited 131n., cited 134, 136n., cited 137, 142n., 145n., cited 146n., 147n., 163n., cited 169, 170n., 171n., 264n., cited 268, 284n., cited 296–7, 299n., cited 300, cited 304–5
Gordon, D. M., cited 89–90
Graely, Paul, 225n.
Groves, Harold M., cited 21n., 98n., 106n., cited 107, cited 108n., cited 109, 110, 112n., cited 125, 129n., cited 37n., cited 168n., cited 185, cited 187, cited 188, 190n., 194n., cited 201n., 203n., 204n., 205, cited 228, cited 233n., 235n., cited 241n., cited 243, 264n., 269n., cited 275, 277, 284n., cited 286, cited 288
Guedalla, Philip, 12n.

Hanes, John W., 262n.
Harris, Seymour, cited 156
Hart, A. G., cited 330n.
Hearne, W. L., 173n., cited 242
Hicks, J. R., 217n.
Hoagland, Henry E., 106n., 150n., cited 155n., 161n.
Holding company, 110
Housing corporations, 84
Hunter, M. H., cited 103
Hydro-Electric Power Commission of Ontario, 131n.

Incidence of corporation tax: as a short-run concept, 123–6; traditional theory of, 126–35; cost of production theory of, 135–41; diffusion theory of, 141–3
Income: as distinct from capital gains, 33–50; concepts of business income, 213–18. *See also* Dividend income
Income Tax Act (Dominion), 32, 35; re income versus capital, 37ff., 214–17; re prospectors' gains, 43, 48; re tax evasion through undistributed earnings, 59ff., 276–81; re special corporations, 78ff.; re ministerial discretion, 93–5; re deductions, 137, 138; re loss carry-over, 205, 207; re valuation of inventory, 226–8; re accelerated depreciation, 242; re diminishing balance method of depreciation, 248–53, 255–6; re deferred depreciation, 318ff. *See also* Corporation tax
Income War Tax Act (Dominion), 32, 33, 35, 50; income versus capital, 36ff.; re tax evasion, 53ff., 276; re special corporations, 77ff.; re ministerial discretion, 88–93; re valuation of inventory, 231; re depreciation, 249, 254
Incorporated Council of Law Reporting Case, 39–40
Insull Empire, the, 110
Integration: of corporation tax with personal income tax, 27–30, 50–1; total versus partial, 263–7; and undistributed earnings, 267–81; and capital gains, 281–4; alternative approaches to, 284–303
Intercorporate dividends, 54–5, 109–10, 206–7, 216n., 217
I.R.C. v. *Cock, Russel & Co. Ltd.,* 228
Inventory, valuation of, 218–32
Investment. *See* Saving and investment
Investment companies, 85–6, 276–7, 289
Ives Commission, 63–4, 277ff., 289n.

Jackson, R. H., cited 104n.
Jacoby, Neil, 134n.
Jones v. *Leeming,* 39

Keith, E. G., 123n.
Kent, Arthur H., 281n., cited 282n., cited 283
Keynes, J. M., 111ff., 217n.
Keyserling, Leon H., 312n.
Kimmel, Lewis H., 105n., 107, 234n., 235n., cited 236n.
Klooster, B. L., 190n.

Labour organizations, 83, 141–3, 182
Landman, J. H., cited 233, 235n., cited 236–7, 248n.
Lasser, J. K., 235n.
Leake, P. D., cited 135n.
Lent, George E., 264n., 269n., 273n., cited 274, 284n., 289

Licences, permits, and fees, 10, 11
Lifo (last-in-first-out), 223–6
Lincoln, E. E., 151n., 162n.
Lintner, John, 173n., 174n., 176n., 177ff.
Litterer, Oscar F., 126n., cited 129n., 136n.
Lockheed Aircraft Corporation, 283n.
Loss carry-over: carry-backs versus carry-forwards, 201–3, 207, 255; period of, 203–6; kind of loss to be carried over, 206–7. *See also* Business losses
Losses. *See* Business losses
Lutz, H. L., 204n.

McDonough v. *Minister of National Revenue,* 41–3
MacKay, R. deWolfe, cited 41
Macy, C. Ward, cited 124n., cited 131n.
Magill, Roswell, 299n., 312n.
Manning, Raymond E., 232n.
Martin v. *Lowry,* 38
Marshall, Alfred, cited 129
Mason, Perry, cited 236n.
Matthews, Beverley, cited 46n.
Mavor, James, 51
Maxwell, C. R., Jr., 190n., 198
May, George O., cited 236, 237n., 238n., 243n.
Mayer, Gerhard J., cited 252n.
Mering, Otto von, cited 124n.
Merritt Realty Co. v. *Brown,* 36–7
Ministerial discretion, 53; provisions of Income War Tax Act, 88–93; provisions of Income Tax Act, 93–5; Special Senate Committee on Taxation, 91ff.; re depreciation, 249. *See also* Tax Appeal Board; Trade and Commerce, Department of
Minot, James J., Jr., 178n.
Moller, George, 235n., cited 246n., cited 252n.
Monopoly profit, 107–9
Montreal Light Heat & Power Consolidated, 131n.
Morell, Admiral Ben, 239n.
Multiple taxation, 9, 110, 145
Mutual insurance corporations, 84

National Trust v. *Minister of National Revenue,* 56
Nelson, G. N., 281n., 284n.
Newcomer, Mabel, 105n.
Nicholson Ltd. v. *Minister of National Revenue,* 90–1
Non-profit corporations, 83
Non-resident-owned investment corporations, 87–8
Nortcliffe, E. B., 247n., 248n.

Oakes, E. E., cited 124n.
Obsolescence, 255–6
O'Meara, J. E., 81n.

Parkinson, R. M., 224n.
Partnership, 99, 140, 144, 171–3, 270; approach to taxing corporate income, 285–90. *See also* Undistributed earnings
Paton, W. A., 235n., cited 237n., 243n.
Patronage dividends, 77ff.
Patterson, Gardner, 235n.
Paul, R. E., 20n., 123n., 147n., 235n., 240n., cited 241–2
Pearn v. *Miller,* 38–9
Peloubet, Maurice E., 224n., 235n.
Pennsylvania Railroad Company, 161n.
Pentland, H. C., 81n.
Personal corporations, 84–5, 276ff., 289
Personal income tax, revenue from, 10, 11, 115, 119
Petrie, J. R., cited 311, 312n., 316n.
Pickford v. *Quirke,* 38
Pioneer Laundry Case, 90
Plaxton, H. A. W., 33n., cited 36
du Pont Company, 240n.
Prest, A. R., 234n., 235n., cited 244–5
Prices: theory of, 126ff.; effect of corporation tax on, 25–6, 166–8, 181–2. *See also* Incidence of corporation tax
Prices, Royal Commission on, 12–13, 219n.
Private companies, 63ff., 100, 279ff., 289–90
Production, 15–17; corporation tax as a cost of, 135–41. *See also* Incidence of corporation tax
Proprietorship. *See* Partnership
Public utilities, 99

Rates, 50–2; political and economic limits of, 12–13; from 1917 to 1952, 34; rate progression, 105, 177–8, 186n., 306–7; current rates, 316–17
Rationale of corporation tax: special benefits received, 99–102; ability to pay, 102–5; control of monopoly profit, 107–9; concentration of economic power, 109, 165; over-complication of corporate financial structure, 109–11; economic control and fiscal

policy, 111–16; fiscal yield, 116–20. *See also* Tax doctrines; Revenue
Real estate taxes, 10–11
Regressivity of corporation tax. *See* Double taxation
Repeal of corporation tax, 284–5
Revenue: objective of tax system, 15; table of sources of total revenue (1937–48), 10; comparative table of corporate income tax revenue, total income tax revenue, total federal tax revenue, and total revenue (1919–52), 114; federal tax receipts (1945–52), 115; yield of corporate income tax, 116–20; comparative table of corporation income taxes, total income taxes, and total tax revenue in Canada, the U.K., and the U.S. (1942–47), 118
Risk capital. *See* Saving and investment
Roosevelt, F. D., 274
Ruml, Beardsley, 98n., 100, 136n., cited 141n., 270n.
Rutledge v. *Commissioners of Inland Revenue*, 38
Ruttenberg, S. H., cited 173n.

Sanders, T. H., 235n.
Saving and investment, 24–5, 111ff., 181; of individuals, 148–50; of corporations, 150–66; relationship between personal and corporate saving, 153–4; effects of accelerated depreciation on, 240–1; forecast of private and public investment (1951), 326. *See also* Dividend policy
Schreiber, Louis, cited 103
Seligman, E. R. A., 124n.
Shere, Louis, cited 192n.
Shoup, Carl, cited 134n., cited 136n., 269n., cited 270n.
Silcock, T. H., 236n.
Simons, Henry C., cited 98n., 119, cited 170n., 194n., cited 224n., 281n.
Slichter, Sumner H., 152n., cited 158, 159n., 169, cited 171n., cited 211–12, 238n., 312n.
Small enterprises, 26, 30–1; definition of, 173–4; creation of, 174–5; expansion of, 175–80, 183–4, 196, 201–2; effect of dividends-paid credit plan on, 292; relief for, 305–8. *See also* Business losses, problem of; Depreciation, accelerated
Smith, Dan Throop, 214n., 222n., cited 224n.
Social security programme, 12, 14, 116
Sonne, H. C., 98n., 136n., cited 141n., cited 270n.
Special corporations: co-operatives, 77–82; crown and municipal corporations, 82; charitable organizations, 82; charitable trusts, 83; labour organizations, fraternal and benevolent societies, 83; agricultural organizations, boards of trade and chambers of commerce, 83; non-profit corporations, 83; mutual insurance corporations, 84; credit unions, 84; housing corporations, 84; personal corporations, 84–5; investment companies, 85–6; foreign business corporations, 86; superannuation trusts, 86; trusts under profit sharing plans, 86–7; non-resident-owned investment corporations, 87–8
Sprott, Mark F., 293n.
Stewart, J. L., 71n.
Studenski, Paul, 98n., 103–4
Succession duties, 10, 11, 120
Superannuation trusts, 86
Sweeney, H. W., 247n.

Tannenbaum, Jerome, 224n.
Tax agreements: World War II, 9; post-war, 9
Tax Appeal Board, 43, 44, 45, 48, 93, 94
Tax doctrines, 5–7, 10–11, 18, 20–2, 52, 98–122
Tax equity, 4, 7–8, 13–14, 17–19, 61, 145–8, 188, 192, 264–5, 302ff. *See also* Rationale
Tax system, 4–5; history of, 7–14; objectives of, 14–23, 262; economic effects of, 8, 13–14, 19; proposals for reform of, 261–3. *See also* Defence economy, taxation in; Integration
Terborgh, George, 236n., 244n., 246n.
Thom, Stuart, 44n., cited 46–9
Towers, Graham, 312n.
Trade and Commerce, Department of, 319ff.
Treasury Board, 58–61, 88
Tredwen, F. B., 135n.
Tremaine, Morris, 281n.
Trusts and profit sharing plans, 86–7
Tucker Committee (U.K.), 208n., 222–3, 229–31

Undistributed earnings, 53–76; on the discontinuance of a corporation, 54, 55, 57, 62; relief for past accruals of, 57, 63ff., 94, 279–81; tax-paid undistributed earnings versus tax-paid dividends, 75–7; and corporate financing, 25, 149, 152, 169, 170, 179–80, 183; and integration of corporate and personal income taxes, 269–81; inflationary effects of, 329–30. *See also* Dividend policy and saving; Investment

United Kingdom, income tax legislation in, 33, 40, 82, 205, 252, 253, 272, 294ff.; judicial interpretation of, 36ff.; Finance Act (1933), 81

United States, experience re undistributed earnings, 273–6

United States Steel Corporation, 239n.

Vickrey, William, cited 5, cited 104n., 190n., cited 191–2, 197, 264n.

Viner, Jacob, 125n.

Vorhees, Enders M., cited 135, cited 238n.

Wages, 25–6, 141–3, 182, 210, 328

Walker, Mabel L., cited 102n.

Walker v. *Minister of National Revenue*, 44

Westfall, Othel D., 269n.

Wilcox, E. B., 224n., cited 225

Wilson, Kenneth R., 312n.

Withholding tax, 294–9

Woll, Matthew, cited 159n.

Wright, R. S., cited 135n.

Young, Michael, 189n.

www.ingramcontent.com/pod-product-compliance
Lightning Source LLC
LaVergne TN
LVHW100250210926
848480LV00003B/881